EPICS, MYTHS AND LEGENDS
OF INDIA

BY THE SAME AUTHOR
Hindu Religion, Customs and Manners
Christians and Christianity in India and Pakistan
Kama Kalpa
The Story of the Cultural Empire of India
Incredible India
Kama Katha
Festivals and Holidays of India
Churches in India
Indian Women through the Ages

EPICS, MYTHS AND LEGENDS OF INDIA

A Comprehensive Survey of the Sacred Lore
of the Hindus, Buddhists and Jains

BY

P. THOMAS

D. B. TARAPOREVALA SONS & CO. PRIVATE LTD.

210 DR. D. NAOROJI ROAD, BOMBAY

IN PROFOUND GRATITUDE

TO

K. RAGHUPATHY IYER

Copyright © 1957 D. B. TARAPOREVALA SONS & CO. PRIVATE LTD.

This Edition 1989

This book can be exported from India only by the publishers, D. B. Taraporevala Sons & Co. Private Ltd. and this constitutes a condition of its initial sale and its subsequent sales. Infringement of this condition of sale will lead to civil and/or criminal legal action and prosecution.

PRINTED IN INDIA

Printed by Russi J. Taraporevala at Electrographic Industries, Division of D. B. Taraporevala Sons & Co. Private Ltd., Apte Industrial Estate, Worli, Bombay 400 018, and published by him for D. B. Taraporevala Sons & Co. Private Ltd., 210, Dr. Dadabhai Naoroji Road, Bombay 400 001.

AUTHOR'S ACKNOWLEDGMENTS

A list of the principal works I have consulted in writing this book will be found in the bibliography at the end of the book. Wherever I have quoted at length from any work, the book or the author has been particularly mentioned.

I have to acknowledge my indebtedness to Dr. R. J. Mehta, M.Sc., Ph.D., and Mr. P. V. Kane, M.A., LL.B., for giving me valuable suggestions; to the Director General of Archaeology, New Delhi, and the Curator, Prince of Wales Museum of Western India, Bombay, for allowing me to see the albums and various publications in their offices and select the illustrations. My deepest debt of gratitude is due to the late Mr. J. H. Taraporevala who originated the idea of the book and had helped me in many ways to write it..

I should also acknowledge the help I received from my sister Eliza in preparing the Index and Glossary of the book.

East Fort
Trichur-5

— P. THOMAS

NOTE TO THE ELEVENTH EDITION

Apart from additional illustrations, the Buddhist section has been considerably enlarged in this edition.

It is a matter of satisfaction for me to see that the interest in Indian lore the book has evoked, both in India and abroad, is on the increase, and my labours in the field have been fully appreciated by the scholar and general reader alike. The demand for a new edition of the book speaks for itself and makes further comments unnecessary.

P. THOMAS.

NOTE TO THE FIFTH EDITION

A Jain friend recently pointed out to me that no book on Indian myth and legend can be considered complete without an account of the mythology of the Jains. In appreciation of the force of his argument I have, in this edition, added a chapter on Jainism. Though Jainism has much in common with Hinduism it is still a separate religion with a lore of its own. Besides, it is one of the living religions of India and has, unlike Buddhism, considerable following in the land of its birth.

The inclusion of Jainism has naturally enlarged the scope of illustrations, and a number of plates have been added in this edition and the size of the book has considerably increased.

P. THOMAS.

PREFACE TO THE SECOND EDITION

When I sent the manuscript of the original edition of this work to the publishers, I had considerable misgivings about the popularity of the subject. But the sale of a fairly large edition of the book within a short time proves that the fundamental human craving for myths and legends cannot be adversely affected even by global wars, famines and mass massacres.

I had covered sufficient ground in the original edition which has saved me the trouble of making substantial changes in this one. Yet as nothing, myths not excluded, can ever remain static, I have made some alterations and additions which, I hope, would add to the attraction of the book. The story of Harischandra in Chapter XIII, is a notable addition made at the request of a Hindu friend who wishes "to dispel the notion some Europeans have that the Hindus are a lying lot". I must apologize for not having included this story in the original edition; for the story, though designed to drive home a moral, is singularly beautiful and is one of the most popular among the Hindus.

P. THOMAS.

CONTENTS

	INTRODUCTION	1
I.	COSMIC AND COSMOGONIC MYTHS	6
II.	THE HINDU PANTHEON — GODS	13
III.	THE HINDU PANTHEON — GODS (continued)	26
IV.	THE HINDU PANTHEON — GODDESSES	37
V.	SEMI-DIVINE BEINGS AND THE DEMI-GODS OF THE MAHABHARATA	45
VI.	ENEMIES OF THE GODS	57
VII.	DEATH AND SOUL-WANDERINGS	64
VIII.	LOVE AND SEX	72
IX.	THE SUN, MOON, EARTH AND PLANETS	79
X.	ANIMALS AND BIRDS	85
XI.	TREES, PLANTS AND FLOWERS	93
XII.	PRINCIPAL HINDU HOLIDAYS	96
XIII.	SOME POPULAR STORIES AND LEGENDS	101
XIV.	THE BUDDHA	113
XV.	JATAKA TALES	125
XVI.	JAINISM	131
	BIBLIOGRAPHY	142
	GLOSSARY AND INDEX	143

ILLUSTRATIONS

Between pages 12 and 13

I.	1	GANESHA
II.	2	NARAYANA
	3	MAHAPRALAYA
III.	4	KALKI
	5	VISHNU
IV.	6	BRAHMA
	7	GANESHA
V.	8	WORSHIP OF BRAHMA
	9	SHIVA AS TRINITY
	10	A HOLY MAN
	11	BRAHMA'S TEMPLE
VI.	12	HANUMAN
	13	MONKEYS BUILDING RAMA'S BRIDGE
VII.	14	HANUMAN ANNOUNCING SITA'S ACQUITTAL
	15	REUNION OF RAMA AND SITA
VIII.	16	HANUMAN BEFORE RAVANA
	17	PAVAN AND AGNI

Between pages 20 and 21

IX.	18	RAMA AND SITA RETURNING TO AYODHYA
	19	RAMA, SITA AND HANUMAN
X.	20	FISH INCARNATION
	21	BOAR INCARNATION
	22	NARASIMHA
	23	VAMANA
XI.	24	PERSECUTION OF PRAHLAD
	25	A VAISHNAVA
	26	CALL TO DEVOTIONAL DUTIES
XII.	27	HANUMAN INSULTING RAVANA
	28	BHIMA LIFTING HANUMAN'S TAIL
	29	LAKSHMANA WOUNDED
	30	HANUMAN WITH THE HILL GROWING MAGIC HERB
XIII.	31	HANUMAN KILLING AN ASURA
	32	HANUMAN KILLING AN ASURA
	33	HANUMAN PRESENTING THE RING TO SITA
	34	HANUMAN RECEIVING RAMA'S RING
XIV.	35	RAMA, HIS HALF BROTHERS, SITA AND HANUMAN
	36	SITA UNDER THE ASOKA TREE
	37	RAVANA WOOING SITA
XV.	38	THE TRIAL OF THE BOW
	39	BHARATA'S ARRIVAL IN CHITRAKUTA
XVI.	40	ANGADA AND THE MONKEY CHIEFS
	41	RAMA ENTHRONED

Between pages 28 and 29

XVII.	42	THE MONKEYS BESIEGE LANKA
	43	KUMBHAKARNA DEVOURING THE MONKEYS
XVIII.	44	KRISHNA
	45	VASUDEVA CARRYING KRISHNA
XIX.	46	VISHNU REPOSING ON ANANTA
	47	CHURNING OF THE MILK OCEAN
XX.	48	KRISHNA RIDING COMPOSITE HORSE OF GOPIS
	49	KRISHNA SUBDUING KALIYA
	50	KRISHNA WITH GOVARDHANA
	51	KRISHNA AND BALARAMA KILLING WRESTLERS
XXI.	52	KRISHNA AND THE GOPI'S
	53	RASALILA
XXII.	54	PARVATI EMBRACING THE LINGAM
	55	WORSHIP OF THE LINGAM
	56	KRISHNA PLAYING ON THE FLUTE
	57	RADHA AND KRISHNA
XXIII.	58	DEATH OF BALARAMA
XXIV.	59	KRISHNA PLAYING ON THE FLUTE
	60	VISHNU RIDING ON GARUDA
	61	BIRTH OF KRISHNA
	62	VISHNU WITH LAKSHMI AND PRITHVI

Between pages 36 and 37

XXV.	63	DEVAKI NURSING KRISHNA
	64	KRISHNA LIFTING GOVARDHANA
XXVI.	65	COWS LISTENING TO KRISHNA'S FLUTE
	66	KRISHNA WITH GOPIS' CLOTHES
	67	SURYA
	68	VARUNA
XXVII.	69	VISHNU AND LAKSHMI ON GARUDA
	70	BALARAMA
	71	KING OF THE NAGAS
	72	A HINDU ASTROLOGER
XXVIII.	73	A SHAIVA TEMPLE ATTENDANT
	74	MARRIAGE OF SHIVA AND PARVATI
	75	FAMILY OF SHIVA
	76	ASCETIC PRACTISING SELF TORTURE
XXIX.	77	SHIVA AND PARVATI ON MOUNT KAILAS
XXX.	78	SHIVA
	79	SHIVA DESTROYING AN ASURA
	80	SHIVA AND PARVATI
	81	NANDI
	82	PARVATI

XXXI.	83	GANESHA
	84	DANCING SHIVA
	85	SHIVA DANCING
XXXII.	86	SHIVA AND ARJUNA FIGHTING
	87	MAHISHASURAMARDINI
	88	SHIVA AS HUNTER
	89	SHIVA DESTROYING AN ASURA

Between pages 44 and 45

XXXIII.	90	KARTIKEYA
	91	LINGAM AND YONI
XXXIV.	92	ASCETICS OF SHIVA
XXXV.	93	KUMARA WITH HIS TWO WIVES
	94	PARVATI
	95	SURYA
XXXVI.	96	NARADA
	97	OFFERING OF POISON TO SHIVA
	98	FIVE FACED IMAGE OF GANESHA
	99	KARTIKEYA
XXXVII.	100	INDRA
	101	KHANDEHRAO AND CONSORT
	102	SARASVATI
	103	RAVANA
XXXVIII.	104	INDRA ON AIRAVATAM
	105	KUBERA
	106	AGNI
XXXIX.	107	SHIVA RIDING ON NANDI
	108	BRAHMA
	109	PARASURAMA
	110	KRISHNA DANCING ON KALIYA
	111	SURYA RIDING IN HIS CHARIOT
XL.	112	WORSHIP OF AGNI
	113	KUBERA
	114	A VAISHNAVA
	115	SOME VILLAGE IDOLS

Between pages 52 and 53

XLI.	116	DESTRUCTION OF MAHISHASURA
	117	A DOOR FRAME IN VINDHYA-VASINI TEMPLE
XLII.	118	SRI
	119	SCULPTURES OF KALI
	120	VISHNU AS MOHINI
	121	CHANDIKA
XLIII.	122	DURGA'S FIGHT WITH MAHISHASURA
	123	DURGA DESTROYING AN ASURA
	124	DURGA RIDING ON HER CHARGER
	125	PARVATI WORSHIPPING THE LINGAM
XLIV.	126	SHIVA-PARVATI
	127	SARASVATI
	128	LAKSHMI
XLV.	129	GANESHA, DURGA, KARTIKEYA
	130	INDRANI
	131	BHAVANI
XLVI.	132	ARDHANARI
	133	DEVI
	134	WORSHIP OF DURGA BY GODS
XLVII.	135	GANGA
	136	SARASVATI
	137	YAMUNA
XLVIII.	138	THE SAGE KAPILA
	139	PARVATI

Between pages 60 and 61

XLIX.	140	CHAMUNDI
	141	KAUMARI
	142	MAHESWARI
	143	VARAHI
L.	144	VAISHNAVI
	145	INDRANI
	146	BRAHMI
LI.	147	GUARDIANS OF THE UNIVERSE
LII.	148	A GAY RISHI
	149	DAKSHA AND WIFE
	150	GANDHARVA
	151	KINNARA ON LOTUS
LIII.	152	A STUDIOUS RISHI
	153	BRAHMA
LIV.	154	VYASA
	155	ARJUNA WINNING DRAUPADI
	156	DENUDATION OF DRAUPADI
	157	BHIMA CAUGHT BY THE ELEPHANT OF BHAGADATTA
LV.	158	DEATH OF BHISHMA
	159	FAMILY OF SHIVA
LVI.	160	APSARAS ALLURING SAGES

Between pages 68 and 69

LVII.	161	MANASA
	162	MOHINI DANCING
	163	DURGA KILLING MAHISHASURA
	164	A RAKSHASA
LVIII.	165	CREMATION
LIX.	166	TORTURES OF HELL
	167	YAMA
LX.	168	PLANETS AND SIGNS OF THE ZODIAC
LXI.	169	YAMUNA
	170	NAGA AND NAGINI
	171	WORSHIPPING THE SUN
	172	GIVING ALMS
LXII.	173	GARUDA AND HANUMAN
	174	CHANDRA
LXIII.	175	KALI
	176	HANUMAN
	177	KAMA
LXIV.	178	A SHAIVA MENDICANT
	179	GARUDA WITH A NAGINI
	180	GANESHA
	181	UMA

Between pages 76 and 77

LXV.	182	HANUMAN
	183	SANI
LXVI.	184	BANYAN TREE
LXVII.	185	TREE WORSHIP
	186	WORSHIPPING THE TULSI PLANT
	187	PRAYING PILGRIMS ON THE GANGES
	188	A DYING MAN BROUGHT TO THE GANGES
LXVIII.	189	BEGGARS' HARVEST ON DASARA DAY
	190	HOLI DANCERS
	191	THROWING COCOANUTS INTO THE SEA ON COCOANUT DAY

ILLUSTRATIONS

	192	CHOWPATI BEACH ON SHIVARATRI DAY
LXIX.	193	DASARA PROCESSION, MYSORE
	194	DASARA CELEBRATION, MYSORE
	195	LAKSHMI, GODDESS OF WEALTH
LXX.	196	DURGA PUJA
LXXI.	197	THE FEAST OF SERPENTS
LXXII.	198	HINDU MARRIAGE CEREMONY

Between pages 84 and 85

LXXIII.	199	CAR PROCESSION OF IDOLS
LXXIV.	200	BATHING CEREMONY OF JAGANNATH
LXXV.	201	DESCENT OF THE GANGES
LXXVI.	202	VITHOBA
	203	AN ATTENDANT OF JAGANNATH TEMPLE
	204	KRISHNA SUBDUING KALIYA
	205	REPEATING THE GAYATRI
LXXVII.	206	ANASUYA
	207	WORSHIP OF GANESHA
	208	DATTATREYA
	209	WORSHIP OF HANUMAN
LXXVIII.	210	KATHA
LXXIX.	211	ARDHANARI
	212	WORSHIP OF GANGA
	213	JAGANNATH
	214	ANNAPURNA DEVI
LXXX.	215	BUDDHA FROM TANJORE
	216	BUDDHA FROM MAYURBHANJ

Between pages 92 and 93

LXXXI.	217	QUEEN MAHAMAYA'S DREAM
	218	BIRTH AND SEVEN STEPS
	219	NATIVITY OF THE BUDDHA
LXXXII.	220	CASTING THE HOROSCOPE OF THE BUDDHA
	221	GAUTAMA APPROACHING THE BODHI TREE
	222	PRESENTATION OF THE CHILD TO THE SAGE
LXXXIII.	223	THE BODHI TREE
	224	SUBJUGATION OF THE ELEPHANT MALAGIRI
	225	SIDDHARTHA MEETING AN ASCETIC
	226	A BUDDHIST MONK
LXXXIV.	227	CONVERSION OF NANDA
	228	BODHISATVA IN TUSITA HEAVEN
	229	SUMEDHA MEETING DIPANKARA
	230	BODHISATVA UNDER MUSALIND'S PROTECTION
LXXXV.	231	ATTACK OF MARA
	232	MAHAKAPI JATAKA
	233	STATUE OF BODHISATVA
LXXXVI.	234	DIVISION OF RELICS
	235	DEVADATTA AND THE ASSASSINS
	236	FIRST SERMON
	237	SCENES DEPICTING CONVERSION OF NANDA
LXXXVII.	238	CHADANTA JATAKA
	239	MIRACLE AT SRIVASTI
	240	FEASTING BY MALLAS OF KUSHINAGRA
LXXXVIII.	241	THE SAGE BEHOLDING THE CHILD
	242	THE ELEPHANT CHADANTA
	243	BUDDHA AND RAHULA
	244	SIDDHARTHA ABOUT TO DEPART FROM HOME

Between pages 108 and 109

LXXXIX.	245	THE GREAT DECEASE
	246	SIDDHARTHA'S DRIVE THROUGH THE CITY
XC.	247	A BUDDHIST PILGRIM
	248	ADORATION OF THE STUPA
	249, 250	SCULPTURES OF THE BUDDHA
XCI.	251	ADORATION OF THE WHEEL OF THE LAW
	252	KUBERA AND HARITI
	253	THE BUDDHA TEACHING THE NAGAS
	254	WORSHIP OF THE ALMSBOWL OF THE BUDDHA
XCII.	255	WORSHIP OF THE RELICS OF THE BUDDHA
	256	ADORATION OF THE BUDDHA
	257	ENLIGHTENMENT
XCIII.	258	ASOKA AND QUEEN WORSHIPPING THE BODHI TREE
	259	A STUPA
XCIV.	260	THE GREAT RENUNCIATION
	261	THE BUDDHA'S COFFIN
	262	GAUTAMA MEETING HIS FUTURE WIFE
	263	MUSICAL ENTERTAINMENT IN THE PALACE
XCV.	264	JAIN SAINT GAUTAMESHWARA
	265	A JAIN GODDESS
	266	THE JAIN SCHOLAR HEMACHANDRA SURI
XCVI.	267	TRISALA IN HER PALACE
	268	TRISALA REJOICING AT THE MOVEMENT OF THE FOETUS
	269	PLUCKING OF THE HAIR
	270	CONSECRATION OF TRISALA

Between pages 124 and 125

XCVII.	271	A DIGAMBARA MONK IN PROCESSION
	272	A JAIN DEPUTATION
	273	SCENE FROM A JAIN TEMPLE
XCVIII.	274	SIDDHARTHA AND TRISALA
	275	NIRVANA OF PARSVANATH
	276	TRISALA RECOUNTING HER DREAM TO SIDDHARTHA
	277	BIRTH OF MAHAVIRA
XCIX.	278	TRISALA WITH ATTENDANTS
	279	MAHAVIRA
	280	A JAIN MARRIAGE PROCESSION
	281	A JAIN LAYMAN
	282	JAIN SCULPTURE AND ORNAMENT

INTRODUCTION

THE science of medicine, they say, grew out of black-magic. The horned witch-doctor was the forerunner of our physicians and surgeons. His cauldron of crabs, scorpions, vipers, hyena's teeth and noxious weeds was the first laboratory in the world; and out of it grew the science of chemistry and medicine. Similarly, art, religion and philosophy had a low origin in myths.

To a child, the stone over which it slips and falls, and the thorny bush on which it hurts its fingers appear to be beings with a malicious intent. It kicks the stone and frowns at the bush. We all remember our childhood days when clouds and rocks, plants and flowers could frighten or please us. We used to fondle, clothe and feed inanimate toys. Night had unknown terrors for us, and in spite of the assurances of our parents and nurses, we seldom ventured into the dark. Now, humanity in the lump can be conceived as an organism with a being, and the fears, hopes, despair and curiosity of the childhood days of mankind are embodied in myths and legends and have come down to us in traditions sacred and profane.

Man, being curious by nature, seeks causes of effects. To us moderns, science has been able to give satisfactory explanations for the immediate causes of phenomena, although the ultimate cause, to be sure, remains an enigma even to the most erudite. But to primitive man even the immediate causes of everyday occurrences were mysteries. Take, for example, the case of rainfall. While we at present know what causes rain, to primitive man rainfall was an enigma. He beheld the pleasant wonder of water falling from the sky upon the parched earth, causing vegetation to grow and clothe the earth in green. But where did the water come from? Air, obviously, could not support water. Nor could his primitive mind trace any connection between clouds and the ocean. His brain worked in the narrow sphere of his own limited experience and he came to the conclusion that there was a solid world above, capable of holding waters, and the lord of that world, well-disposed towards man, released the waters of the celestial lake for the benefit of humans. To worship him was the duty of grateful man. Thunder, lightning and storm proclaimed his prowess, and the rainbow, the sun, the moon and the star-studded heavens, the splendour of his abode.

We must remember that science is very young. As late as the fifteenth century when Columbus made known his intention to travel westward to reach the East and thus put to test the theory of a round earth, wise men thought him mad. Many kings and learned doctors refused to listen to him, and he had to go begging from one European capital to another for a ship and crew. So deep-rooted was the Christian belief in a static earth and a geographical heaven peopled by Cherubim and ruled by Jehovah, that when Copernicus (in the sixteenth century) proclaimed that the earth is mobile, he was persecuted by priests as a heretic!

Before Columbus the world was not correctly mapped. Even the Greeks, the most enlightened of ancient Europeans, knew little about the world and its peoples. They were acquainted with the races that inhabited countries bordering on the Eastern Mediterranean; of other peoples their knowledge was based on travellers' tales. Herodotus, known as the Father of History (fifth century B.C.), gives us, in his admirable history of the nations, a detailed account of all the peoples then known to Greeks; and if you read this book you will get an idea of how little the most learned knew in those days, how credulous the enlightened were. He says that ants dug out gold in India, and that Indians murdered and ate their infirm parents in order to save the trouble of supporting them! And it was the time when the Buddha's doctrines were gaining ground in this country! Herodotus had travelled through Asia Minor to Egypt and back to Greece, and was considered one of the most widely travelled Greeks of his age. Only gods and Titans could travel beyond the enchanted Pillars of Hercules (Gibraltar). Jason's voyage to Media (Persia) was recorded as a wonderful adventure. Ulysses lost his way in the Mediterranean and Homer wrote an epic about it.

Such a world was a fertile breeding place for myths. The most fantastic tales about distant countries and peoples were enthusiastically believed by the ancients. If some sailor or shipwrecked mariner returned to his homeland after a year's adventure in foreign lands and gave his countrymen exaggerated accounts of the people and places he saw, they were eager to exaggerate them still more and circulate weird tales about Cyclops with one eye and "men whose heads do grow beneath their shoulders." Even in our own days common folk are not above believing strange stories about foreigners. The idea of myth-making is real enough in war time when the lowest passions of man rise uppermost and enemies are depicted in the darkest colour. Readers are familiar with cartoons depicting enemy leaders as beasts, demons and incarnations of the devil. They are often spoken of as dragons or gorillas ravishing the fair maid "Liberty".

Enlightenment, all told, has not kept pace with scientific progress, and modern man retains most of the traits and tendencies of his primitive ancestor.

Where thought and reasoning are undeveloped, impulse is unrestrained and imagination wild. To the primitive man the whole nature was charged with weird possibilities; the air was filled with spirits, and demons lurked in caves and the hollow trunks of old trees. He fell down in terror before every grotesque shape. Thunder and lightning inspired awe and dread in him. Floods, droughts, earthquakes and other calamities were thought to be caused by malicious spirits who had either to be destroyed by benevolent deities or appeased by the sacrifice of victims. On the other hand, the spring breeze, flower-laden trees, seasonal rains, good harvests and other pleasant phenomena filled man with a sense of gratitude towards the benevolent spirits who were supposed to cause them.

As humanity grew, the collection of stories about spirits, good and bad, were enriched by legends of heroes who fought for the tribe and vanquished their enemies, and of sages who, by invention or legislation, advanced the cause of the tribe. These legends increased in number and variety and, in course of time, passed into mythology. Many of the gods and goddesses worshipped by man at present were once human beings who trod this humble earth.

Nor are all myths the result of ignorance, malice or hero-worship. Poetry too has enriched mythology. The ancients lived in intimate contact with nature and their life was not so artificial as ours. In those days, there were no cities, machines and mechanized means of transport. The habitations of ordinary people were not proof against wind and rain. They were literally sons of the soil. They had no sound system of irrigation, and agriculture was dependent upon the precarious rainfall or the vagaries of rivers. Their villages had no lights in the night, and the wolf, hyena, tiger and other beasts of the night and predatory tribes appeared under cover of darkness to devour and to loot. Before the invention of agriculture the plight of man was still worse and he wandered from place to place in search of pastures and game. Nor was that the beginning of the adventure of man upon this earth. There was a time when he lived in caves without knowing how to lay a fire or forge a weapon.

So, the ancients were Nature's children and their pliant minds reacted to the beauty of nature in a degree not possible for us to experience. "At the very dawn of history when man beheld the glorious orb of the day shedding an effulgent stream of light on all that exist, the night studded with myriads of beautiful stars, the crystal rills rumbling in the limitless forests, in the midst of wild scenery, when man beheld a storm spreading gloom all around, how a gentle breeze made all nature bloom, he very naturally became contemplative. Amazed and awe-struck at the sight of these phenomena of the natural world, he put to himself the question—what do these things reveal to me? What is the inworking light of all these? To the so-called uncivilized man living in that far-off age of faith, this panorama presented by the universe revealed the will of some unknown powers, unknown to him yet guiding him."

THE SCIENCE OF MYTHOLOGY

Myths, then, have a meaning. Just as strata of earth give an indication of the life of the earth and even of the progress of life through prehistoric times, myths are thought-fossils which teach us in allegories and symbols the story of cultures and civilisations that preceded ours, and the attempts of primitive man to solve various human problems. As reason and science advance, myths lose much of their religious and dogmatic character, but are not discarded entirely as futile. In fact they still find a prominent place in the emotional life of the community, in art, poetry and folklore. The cathedrals and palaces of Europe, and the murals, frescoes, paintings and sculptures in them are still a joy to the onlooker, be he Christian, pagan or atheist. The artists of Christendom have liberally borrowed from Greek and Egyptian mythology, and the Madonna, the Queen of Heaven, the main inspiration of renaissance art, is traced to the Egyptian Isis. Of the extent mythology has influenced art in India, every cave and temple and the idols and frescoes within, bear eloquent testimony.

Apart from its relation to art, mythology has a scientific aspect. By study of comparative mythology ethnologists have been able to elucidate many obscure points of racial migrations and fusions. The similarity between certain myths of different peoples inhabiting distant regions is striking. It is true that human nature is fundamentally the same, and similarity in expression of emotions and reaction to phenomena can be coincidental. But there are certain analogies which, by their very nature, point to something more than a coincidence. In the *Khandogya Upanishad*, for instance, there is the myth of the mundane egg: "The egg broke open. The two halves were one of silver, the other of gold. The silver one became this earth, the golden one the sky; the thick membrane (of the yolk) the mist with the clouds, the small veins, the rivers, the fluid, the sea; and what was born from it, the sun." Professor Max Muller observes that there is a Finnish myth of the creation exactly similar to this one, and maintains that such striking identity can scarcely be accidental.

Mythologists trace many Hindu, Greek and Scandinavian myths to a common origin. Philologists even establish etymological identity of many names of gods and goddesses. They surmise, with good reason, that the Hindus, Germans and Greeks had a common homeland whence their forefathers migrated in prehistoric times to different parts of the world, and that their common language and religion underwent many modifications by contact with new and alien environments. But even in these modified forms, there are striking analogies which establish a fundamental unity.

In function, the following Hindu and Greek (or Roman) deities are more or less identical:

Indra	...	Jupiter
Varuna	...	Neptunus
Balarama	...	Bacchus
Kartikeya	...	Mars
Surya	...	Sol
Chandra	...	Lunus
Viswakarma	...	Vulcan
Aswins	...	Castor and Pollux
Ganesha	...	Janus
Durga	...	Juno
Sarasvati	...	Minerva
Ushas	...	Aurora
Sri	...	Venus
Kama	...	Eros (Cupid)

Deities have different names and functions, and conclusions drawn from too great an emphasis on etymology or function can, no doubt, be misleading. But it cannot be denied that there is considerable evidence in support of the hypothesis of a common homeland for the people now known as Aryans. While the existence of "a common Aryan home" is generally accepted in theory, scholars have not yet been able to locate it. At one time controversy over this subject seemed to shake the foundations of the learned world. The dissertations of the controversialists were not always in the best interests of science, or particularly ethnology, but often took the form of racial arrogance and violent personal attacks. Practically every Aryan scholar claimed the "common homeland" for his own country and twisted and mutilated myths and proper nouns to fit in with his pet theory. Scholars who happened to be Semitic, on the other hand, took a malicious pleasure in ridiculing the whole thing as a figment of the imagination. As a result of this controversy, "it became possible to make out a more or less plausible case for any part of the world to be considered as the common homeland of the Aryans." When it came to this, Professor Max Muller, who was once an enthusiastic protagonist of the hypothesis, declared that the word "Aryan" had only a philological and not an ethnological significance. By "Aryan", he said he meant merely a group of languages allied to Sanskrit, and nothing more. The Arya Samajists, as we know, give an ethical interpretation to the word; according to them "Aryan" means "noble" and denotes no particular race. Thus, the "common Aryan home was dissolved into air, fire and water."

Be that as it may, the idea of a pure Aryan race still holds sway among many nations, particularly among Germans. Aryan myths indeed die hard.

Another analogy that interests students of comparative mythology is that of the Egyptian to the Indian mythological systems. Not only many myths, but even manners and usages are found common to ancient Egyptians and Indians. Like Indians, the Egyptians had a sort of caste system. Unlike the Hindu four, Egyptians had seven castes. Although rules of caste were not enforced as rigidly as in India, caste was the basis of the Egyptian social system. Egyptians worshipped the bull Apis, and Nandi, Shiva's bull, holds a unique position in Hindu animal mythology. Osiris is identified with the Hindu Iswara. "There is a striking resemblance between the legendary wars of the three principal gods in Egypt and India. As Osiris gave battle to Typhon, who was defeated at length, and even killed by Horus, so Brahma fought with Vishnu and gained an advantage over him, but was overpowered by Mahadeva, who cut off one of his five heads." In Egyptian cosmogony the sun-god Ra, we are told, shed tears of creative rays from which all beings sprang into existence; and in India we have the counterpart of the myth in Prajapati's creative tears from which all creatures are said to have come into being. The Egyptian Horus, like Brahma of the Hindu Triad, was born of a lotus. In the Chaos-Egg myth, Ra issues, like Brahma, from a golden egg.

There are numerous other points of contact between the two mythological systems. While common features in mythological conceptions among races considered Aryan can be explained by the hypothetical "common homeland," Indians and Egyptians are ethnologically so different that we can only attribute this affinity to cultural contact through some unidentified medium. Probably both Egypt and India met in Babylon; or else, the priests of one country went to the other to be enlightened. Any way, we cannot scoff, as Max Muller does, at the conclusion of a scholar who expressed that "Egyptian priests had come from the Nile to the Ganga and Yamuna to visit the Brahmins of India, as the Greeks visited them at a later time, rather to acquire than to impart knowledge."

Although each religion claims for itself exclusive divine origin, classical literature and the sacred books of different nations reveal to us strange and striking affinities in thoughts, customs and cults. The ruins of Babylon enriched many an alien pantheon. Many Greeks went to Egypt to learn sciences sacred and profane. Alexander's conquest opened up cultural contact between Greece and India. Before Alexander, the Persian king Darius had conquered Greece, and Cambyses Egypt. The Hebrews had learnt many things from Egypt and Babylon, though loth to acknowledge the source. Many of the present Christian mysteries and cults can be traced to the Mithraists, a sect that originated in Persia and became popular in Asia Minor and Mediterranean Europe. In ancient days religious fanaticism was not so blind as in medieval times, and all nations borrowed ideas and gods more freely than in later times. Hence the fluidity of myths and legends.

HINDU MYTHOLOGY

Hindu mythology is more than mythology. It is a living religion. Throughout India can be seen idols of gods and goddesses worshipped at present as was done hundreds of years ago. Most of them are true to type and could have easily stepped out of one of the Puranas.

Hinduism is essentially a religion of variety. While some of the thinkers reached the highest peak philosophy has ever dared to climb, the lower classes practised idolatry, animism and the perversions peculiar to some of the objectionable cults. The Bacchanalian orgies of Greece and Rome are things of the past. But in Indian villages during certain festivals, crowds with phallic emblems can be seen parading the streets, singing obscene songs. Kali may not, at present, claim human victims but is content with the meat and blood of goats and fowl; her form, however, is not changed. In temples dedicated to her, she is still seen in her characteristic dancing pose, wearing a garland of human skulls, her mouth dripping blood, ready to devour the worlds if her lust for blood is not sated. Ganesha, the elephant-god, and Hanuman, the ape-god, are also widely worshipped in India.

The "Revealed Wisdom" of the Hindus is called Srutis and consists of the four Vedas.* The rest of Hindu sacred literature is known as Smritis or tradition. The eighteen Puranas† and the two epics, *Mahabharata* and *Ramayana*. form the bulk of the Smritis. From the point of view of the mythologist, the Smritis are more important than the Srutis. In the former, Vedic myths have been elaborated and new myths added.

The study of the Vedas was the exclusive privilege of the Brahmins. For the common folk, the Smritis were considered good enough. They learnt stanzas of them by heart or listened to recitations by priests. Even now Katha (story-telling) is a regular institution and Brahmins, learned in sacred lore, can be seen reading passages from the Puranas or epics to enraptured audiences and explaining to them the meaning of myths and legends. While the lower classes are generally ignorant of the teachings of the Vedas and the philosophic schools, practically every Hindu is conversant with the tales of Rama and Sita, of the doings of Hanuman, of the adventures of the Mahabharata heroes and of the various activities of Krishna. In spite of the efforts of the Arya Samajists, the Hindu revivalists, to bring the Vedas to the masses, the religion of the vast majority of Hindus still remains Puranic, that is, mythological.

The myths in the Vedas are comparatively simple. The deities are magnified humans who cause rainfall, thunder, lightning and storms. Some of the hymns of the *Rig Veda* are poetically sublime and express the awakened soul's wonder on beholding the rosy dawn, the glorious sun rising above the hills, and the majesty and splendour of the heavens. The Vedic deities are resplendent, warlike beings who ride fleet horses, fight and vanquish the foes of their devotees or, exhilarated by the juice of the Soma, engage themselves in creative sport. Compared with the fantastic deities of the Puranas, they are almost human.

The reason for this simplicity of the Vedic myths is that, in the early Vedic times, Indo-Aryans were a semi-pastoral people who had just learnt the art of agriculture and were constantly on the move for new pastures. They had not yet settled down permanently, "and the wants and occupations of a vagrant life prevented them from falling into a great many superstitions which are the offspring of idleness. They were surrounded by hostile tribes and cattle-lifters against whom they had to put up a continuous fight. They had no use for lean and hungry philosophers who could wield neither sword nor club. They prayed

---

* The four Vedas are : *Rig Veda, Yajur Veda, Sama Veda* and *Atharva Veda*. Each Veda consists of two parts, *Samhita* (hymns) and Brahmanas (ritualistic precepts). The Upanishads are attached to the Brahmanas and contain mystical doctrines.

† The Puranas are of later origin than the epics, and deal mainly with the activities of celestials. The eighteen Puranas are divided into three groups, each consisting of six and connected with one of the members of the Hindu Trinity. Of all the Puranas. *Vishnu Purana* is the most comprehensive. A detailed account of Hindu sacred literature will be found in *Hindu Religion, Customs and Manners* (Taraporevela).

INTRODUCTION

for sturdy sons to ride fleet horses and confound the marauding Dasyus. Their gods too were of the same mettle. Rig Vedic Aryans did not delight in abstract principles thinner than air, but offered libations of Soma to Indra, the terrible wielder of the thunderbolt, who fought and scattered the enemies of Aryans."

In course of time, however, they subdued the neighbouring tribes, agriculture was developed, and settlements became more or less permanent; and those with a contemplative turn of mind found enough security and leisure to give rein to their fancies. Kingdoms were founded, schools of philosophy developed and people whom the lure of Maya troubled abandoned the pleasures and comforts of the world, and retired into forests to ponder over the mystery of life and death, other worlds and their inhabitants. Most of the Puranas are the works of these forest hermits. They saw visions, experienced the horrors of nightmares, and had moments of ecstasy and despair; and they confided their experiences to their disciples who carefully memorized and passed them down to posterity. Each Purana, though attributed to a single author, is in reality the work of different writers compiled at different times, and has a range of many centuries. The manner of weaving tales into tales, familiar to those who have read the *Arabian Nights*, made interpolation easy to practise.

Coherency is not one of the strong points of Hindu mythology. Most of the Vedic deities underwent a complete transformation in the Puranas and epics. Indra, the most important deity of the Vedic pantheon, degenerates, in the epics, into a second rate celestial profligate. In one myth, sun is male, in another female. Sun and moon are in one place mentioned as rivals, elsewhere as husband and wife. The dog is extolled as a deity in one place and, in another, mentioned as a vile creature. Sectarian quarrels have also corrupted the whole mythological system, each sect trying to establish the precedence and omnipotence of their own particular deity. Thus, while the Vaishnavas claim the descent of Ganga from the foot of Vishnu, the Shaivas attribute her origin to the head of Shiva. Shakti, the widely worshipped goddess of India, is variously described as the consort of Shiva or Vishnu, or identified with Maya, the energy of the Supreme Being, who, in union with her, produced all beings. And pantheism justifies everything.

Ever since the conquest of India by Aryans, there have been many irruptions of alien races into India. Religion, in those days, was not so well-organised and exclusive as it became in later times, and Indo-Aryans no less by necessity than by the synthetic character of their religion, absorbed many cultures alien to them, and these substantially enriched Hindu mythology. Every race that invaded and settled down in India found a place in the Hindu social system, and their gods, in the pantheon. The Nagas (snake-worshippers), the Gujaras, from whom Gujarat takes its name, Scythians, Parthians, Huns and several other peoples were conquerors of India whom Indo-Aryans conquered culturally.

Such cultural conquests are common enough in history. The Romans who conquered Greece were culturally conquered by the Greeks. The Mongols who subjugated Muslim countries were conquered by Islam. Islam itself stood in danger of being conquered by Hinduism. Akbar, the Hindus say, seriously thought of turning Hindu, but gave up the attempt on being ridiculed by Birbal, the court wit.

Be that as it may, the uncompromising attitude of Islam towards idolatry and its exclusive dogmatism prevented Islam from being absorbed by Hinduism. Hindu thought has, however, influenced Islam appreciably and some of its later developments (Sufism in particular) can be traced to this influence. If Hinduism has been able to influence so rigid a religion as Islam, its effect on the culture of earlier invaders of easy religious doctrines can very well be imagined.

Apart from conquerors, those whom the Indo-Aryans conquered also found a place in the Hindu fold. Dravidian and aboriginal influences are clearly traceable in the epics and the Puranas. Conquerors and the conquered, it is clear, cannot live together for long without being mutually affected.

Thus Hindu mythology developed out of a fusion of various cultures, and this is mainly responsible for the existence of many self-contradictory myths in it and for reducing it, as one writer puts it, to "a chaos of myths." But its very complexity makes Hindu mythology a fascinating subject for study.

As regards the mythology of the Buddhists and Jains, it draws its inspiration mainly from Hinduism. In its travels abroad, Buddhism of necessity borrowed many myths from alien lands, but I have made no efforts to include them in this book, as such an attempt will be outside its scope.

In conclusion, I may observe that in this book my main attempt has been confined to giving the reader a faithful representation of the mythological systems of the Hindus, Buddhists and Jains. Hence, while efforts have, of course, been made to elucidate obscure points, I have, as far as possible, refrained from making comments, complimentary or condemnatory.

Chapter 1
COSMIC AND COSMOGONIC MYTHS

EVER since man became capable of thought, the problem of the origin of the universe has been constantly troubling the thinking mind. Science and religion approach the subject from two different angles. The nebular and tidal hypotheses, the latest developments in cosmogonic science, instead of solving the problem, rather tend to widen the field of thought which is already vast enough. Scientists have also become doubtful of the validity of many of their nineteenth century conclusions. Sir James Jeans, for instance, observes (in his book *The Mysterious Universe*) that the religious conception of creation is not scientifically untenable. On the contrary, he says, it looks as though the universe was, like the spring of a watch, wound up by a master-hand, and is fast running itself out. Sir James admits that, in the light of modern scientific evidence on the subject, the conception of the universe as an automatic mechanism (a theory beloved of the nineteenth century physicists) has broken down, giving place to Berkley's conception of it as thought. Thus the theologian and the scientist seem to be nearer to each other now than ever before.

Readers are probably acquainted with the theory of creation enunciated by the Semitic group of religions. They say that Jehovah reduced primordial chaos to order, and brought the world into existence out of nothing. He created the earth and the living beings on it in six days, and appointed man lord of all creatures. On the seventh, he took rest. Although some modern Christians, anxious to reconcile the teachings of Genesis with Darwinism, interpret the six days to mean six ages which evolved man out of lower organisms through a process of natural selection, the orthodox accept the biblical account literally and pronounce all other theories of creation as heretical or irreligious.

In the sacred literature of the Hindus there are various accounts of how the universe originated. While most of them differ substantially from one another, because of the comprehensive synthesis of all Hindu conceptions they are all accepted as orthodox and no two are mutually exclusive.

HINDU COSMOGONY

The earliest Hindu account of the origin of the universe is given in the *Rig Veda*. In some hymns it is related that Indra "measured out" the heavens and earth, while in others Varuna is said to have done it. In a third account Agni, Maruts and Indra are mentioned as the three creators of the universe. In the Purusha Sukta hymn, again, it is said the gods performed a sacrifice with a giant and as a result the giant's body became the sky, his navel the air and his feet, the earth. "From his mind sprang the moon, from his eye the sun, from his mouth Indra and Agni, from his breath wind. The four castes also rose from him. His mouth became the Brahmana, his arms the Rajanya, his thighs the Vaisya and his feet the Sudra."

It was probably from this hymn that the later myth about the emanation of the four castes from Brahma, the first of the Hindu Triad, developed.

While most of the cosmogonic myths of the world attribute the work of creation to the Primal Male Deity who moulded creatures out of chaos or primordial matter, thus establishing a gulf between the creator and the created, one myth in the Upanishads describes man as literally the child of the Deity born of his consort. According to this account the Universal Soul took the shape of man. Beholding nothing but himself, "he said first *This I am*. Hence the name of I was produced. Therefore even now a man, when called, says first 'It is I,' and tells afterwards any other name that belongs to him. And because he, as the first of all of them, consumed by fire all the sins, therefore he is called Purusha.

"He was afraid; therefore man, when alone, is afraid. He then looked around and said: 'since nothing but myself exists, of whom should I be afraid?' Hence his fear departed; for whom should he fear, since fear arises from another?

"He did not feel delight. Therefore nobody when alone feels delight. He was desirous of a second. He was in the same state as husband and wife. He divided his self two-fold. Hence were husband and wife produced. Therefore was this only a half of himself as a split pea is of the whole. This void is thus completed by woman. He approached her. Hence were men born."

By far the most sublime Hindu conception of creation is found in one of the later hymns of the *Rig Veda*. The hymn has been rendered into English by Dr. Muir:

" Then there was neither Aught nor Nought, nor air nor sky beyond.
  What covered all? Where rested all? In watery gulf profound?
Nor death was then, nor deathlessness, nor change of night and day.
  That One breathed calmly, self-sustained; nought else beyond it lay.
Gloom hid in gloom existed first — one sea, eluding view.
  That One, a void in chaos wrapt, by inward fervour grew.
Within it first arose desire, the primal germ of mind.
  Which nothing with existence links, as sages searching find.
The kindling ray that shot across the dark and drear abyss.—
  Was it beneath? or high aloft? What bard can answer this?
There fecundating powers were found, and mighty forces strove.—
  A self-supporting mass beneath, and energy above.
Who knows, whoever told, from whence this vast creation rose?
  No gods had then been born, — who then can e'er the truth disclose?
Whence sprang this world, and whether framed by hand divine or no.—
  It's lord in heaven alone can tell, if even he can show."

Thus the poet begins as a theist and ends almost as an agnostic.

The conception of the origin of the universe given in some of the Puranas is comparatively primitive. In the *Bhagbata* there are many cosmogonic myths which are highly hair-splitting but not equally enlightening. In all these accounts, Narayana is said to be the Prime Lord who created everything by his will to create. In one place it is said, speech originated from his mouth, the Vedas from the humours of his body, nectar from his tongue, the firmament from his nose, the heaven and sun from the pupils of his eyes, places of pilgrimage from his ears, clouds and rain from his hair, flashes of lightning from his beard, rocks from his nails, mountains from his bones, etc., etc.

Narayana, the Primal Lord, is described as lying on a banyan leaf floating on primeval waters sucking his toe, the symbol of eternity. The myth appears self-contradictory as it attributes all creation to Narayana and yet leaves one in doubt as to his precedence over Nara, the primeval waters.

In the *Bhagbata* we are also given a description of the Mundane Egg. "Prakriti" (Nature) is said to be the mainstay of the three fundamental qualities, Satwa, Rajas and Tamas, which were originally in a passive state; but on their agitation by the "resistless destiny of creatures, the Prime Person presiding over Prakriti, and Kala (Time)," the principle of Mahatatwa, came into being. From this by a process too lengthy to be given in detail here, Tanmatras were produced. These, when combined with the Divine Power, generated the Golden Egg. "The Lord of the Universe reposed for over a thousand years on that egg devoid of any living creatures and lying on the surface of the ocean. While the Lord was so lying in self-communion, there issued from his navel a lotus with the shining brilliance of one thousand suns together. So large was the lotus that it could be the dwelling place of all the creatures. From this lotus sprang up Brahma, the self-created. Thereupon, being endowed with the powers of the Reverend One lying on the waters, Brahma created all beings and assigned to each of them name and form."

The work of creation was not, however, without difficulties. It seems Brahma himself was open to error and made mistakes. In his first attempt at creation he tumbled upon Ignorance which he cast away; and this became Night. Out of Night sprang forth the Beings of Darkness. Brahma having created nothing else at the time, the hungry beings of the void rushed towards Brahma himself to devour him. Thus assailed, Brahma cried out to his hungry sons: "Eat me not, I am your father." But some of the hungry ones cried: "Eat him even if he be our father." These became Yakshas; the others who cried: "Do not let him be saved," became Rakshasas.

Becoming wise, Brahma next created beings in whom the Satwa quality predominated and they became celestials. From his hip he created Asuras, from his feet the earth, from his smile fairies, etc., etc.

In another place in the *Bhagbata* we are told that Brahma, after certain initial failures, created four Munis (sages) namely, Sanaka, Sananda, Santana and Sanatkumara. But these sages were averse to the work of creation and betook themselves to austerities and the worship of Vasudeva, thus defeating the very purpose for which they were created. This filled Brahma with anger, and out of his wrath sprang forth the mighty Rudra who carried on the work of creation.

In his Code, Manu gives a different account of

creation. According to this authority, "He (the self-existent) having felt desire, and willing to create various living beings from his own body, first created the waters and threw into them a seed. That seed became a golden egg of lustre equal to the sun; in it he himself was born as Brahma, the parent of all the world. The waters are called Nara because they are sprung from Nara; and as they were his first sphere of motion he is therefore called Narayana. Produced from the imperceptible, eternal, existent and non-existent cause that male (purusha) is celebrated in the world as Brahma. After dwelling for a year in the egg, the glorious being by his own contemplation split in twain....Having divided his own body into two parts the lord (Brahma) became with the half a male and with the other half a female; and in her he created Viraj. Know thou that I (Manu) whom that male Viraj himself created am the creator of all this world."

Thus in this account, which is an amalgamation of many myths, Manu claims the credit of creation of the world to himself and incidentally establishes the priority of Narayana to Nara, an obscure point in many other myths.

In a different myth all creatures are said to have sprung up from the tears of Prajapati. Prajapati, who came into existence from non-existence, wept exclaiming, "for what purpose have I been born if (I have been born) from this which forms no support? The tears which fell into the water became the earth. That which he wiped away became the air. That which he wiped away upwards became the sky."

The myth illustrates the pessimistic view of life characteristic of Buddhism, Jainism and certain schools of Hinduism.

All that is best in Hindu cosmogonic conceptions is summarized by Sir William Jones in his hymn to Narayana. Sir William has beautifully caught the spirit of the ancient poets of India and the sublimity and representative character of the hymn will, it is hoped, excuse the length of the quotation.

" Spirit of Spirits, who though every part
Of space expanded, and of endless time,
Beyond the stretch of lab'ring thought sublime
Bad'st uproar into beauteous order start,
Before heaven was thou art :
Ere spheres beneath us roll'd, or spheres above,
Ere earth in firmamental ether hung,
Thou sat'st above; till, through thy mystic love,
Things unexisting to existence sprung,
And graceful descant sung.
What first impelled thee to exert thy might?
Goodness unlimited. What glorious light
Thy power directed? Wisdom without bound.
What proved it first? oh! guide my fancy right;
Oh! raise from cumbrous ground
My soul in rapture drowned,
That fearless it may soar on wings of fire :
For Thou, who only know'st, Thou only can'st inspire.
Wrapt in eternal solitary shade
Th' impenetrable gloom of light intense,
Impervious, inaccessible, immense,
Ere spirits were infused or forms displayed,
Brahm his own mind surveyed,
As mortal eyes (thus finite we compare
With infinite) in smoothest mirrors gaze;
Swift, at his look, a shape supremely fair
Leap'd into being with a boundless blaze,
That fifty suns might daze.
Primeval Maya was the Goddess named,
Who to her sire, with love divine inflame,
A casket gave with rich *ideas* filled,
From which this gorgeous universe he framed;
For, when the Almighty will'd
Unnumbered worlds to build
From Unity, diversified he sprang,
While gay creation laughed and procreant Nature rang.
First an all-potent, all-pervading sound
Bade flow the waters,—and the waters flow'd
Exulting in their measureless abode,
Diffusive, multitudinous, profound,
Above, beneath, around;
Then o'er the vast expanse primordial wind
Breathed gently, till a lucid bubble rose,
Which grew in perfect shape, an egg refined:
Created substance no such lustre shows,
Earth no such beauty knows.
Above the warring waves it danc'd elate,
Till from its bursting shell with lovely state
A form cerulean flutter'd o'er the deep,
Brightest of beings, greatest of the great :
Who, not as mortals steep,
Their eyes in dewy sleep,
But heavenly pensive on the lotus lay,
That blossom'd at his touch and shed a golden ray.
Hail, Primal blossom! hail empyreal gem.
Kamal or Padma, or whate'er high name
Delight thee, say, what four formed Godhead came,
With graceful stole and beamy diadem,
Forth from thy verdant stem?
Full gifted Brahma! Rapt in solemn thought
He stood, and round his eyes fire-darting threw;
But whilst his view-less origin he sought
One plane he saw of living waters blue,
Their spring nor saw nor knew.
Then in his parent stalk again retired,
With restless pain for ages he inquired,
What were his powers, by whom and why conferr'd :
With doubts perplex'd with keen impatience fired
He rose, and rising heard

COSMIC AND COSMOGONIC MYTHS

Th' unknown, all-knowing word
"Brahma! no more in vain research persist:
My veil thou canst not move:— go, bid all worlds exist."
Hail! self-existent, in celestial speech
Narayan; from thy wat'ry cradle named;
Or Venamala may I sing unblamed,
With flow'ry braids, that to thy sandals reach,
Whose beauties who can teach?
Or high Pitamber clad in yellow robes
Than sunbeams brighter, in meridian glow,
That weave their heav'n-spun light o'er circling globes?
Unwearied, lotus-ey'd, with dreadful bow
Dire Evil's constant foe!
Great Padma Natha, o'er thy cherish'd world,
The pointed *chakra* by thy fingers whirl'd
Fierce *Kytabh* shall destroy and *Methu* grim
To black despair and deep destruction hurl'd.
Such views my senses dim,
My eyes in darkness swim,
What eye can bear thy blaze, what utt'rance tell
Thy deeds with silver trump or manywreathed shell.
Omniscient spirit, whose all-ruling pow'r
Bids from each sense bright emanations beam,
Glows in the rainbow, sparkles in the stream,
Smiles in the bud and glistens in the flow'r
That crowns each vernal bow'r;
Sighs in the gale and warbles in the throat
Of every bird that hails the bloomy spring,
Or tells his love in many a liquid note,
While envious artists touch the rival string,
Till rocks and forests ring;
Breathes in rich fragrance from the sandal grove,
Or where the precious musk-deer playful rove,
In dulcet juice clust'ring fruit distils
And burns salubrious in the tasteful clove;
Soft banks and verd'rous hills
Thy present influence fills;
In air, floods, in caverns, woods and plains
Thy will inspirits all, thy sovereign Maya reigns.
Blue crystal vault and elemental fires,
That in the ethereal fluid blaze and breathe;
Thou tossing main, whose snaky branches wreathe
This pensive orb with intertwisted gyres;
Mountains, whose radiant spires
Presumptuous rear their summits to the skies,
And blend their emerald hue, with saphire light;
Smooth meads and lawn, that glow with varying dyes
Of dew-bespangled leaves and blossoms bright.
Hence! vanish from my sight,
Delusive pictures! unsubstantial shows!
My soul absorb'd one only Being knows,
Of all perceptions One abundant source,
Whence ev'ry object every moment flows;
Suns hence derive their force,
Hence planets learn their course:
But suns and fading worlds I view no more;
God only I perceive; *God* only I adore."

DURATION AND END OF THE UNIVERSE

The cosmic unit of time, according to Hindu mythical astronomy, is the Kalpa, or a day of Brahma the creator. Brahma creates in the morning, and at night the three divisions of worlds (Heavens, middle and nether regions) are reduced to chaos, every being that has not obtained liberation retaining its essence which takes form according to its Karma, when Brahma wakes up in the morning. Thus the eventful days and nights pass on, till Brahma reaches the hundredth year of his life when "not only the three worlds but all planes and all beings, Brahma himself, Devas, Rishis, Asuras, men, creatures and matter" are all resolved into Mahapralaya (the great cataclysm). After hundred years of chaos another Brahma is born.

The Kalpa or day of Brahma is equivalent to 4,320,000,000 earth-years and is divided into 1,000 Mahayugas (great ages) of equal length, each consisting of four Yugas or ages, namely, Krita, Threta, Dwapara and Kali.

In the Kritayuga (also called Satyuga) Dharma is said to be four-legged, that is, complete in its aspects; and the fourfold virtues of truthfulness, kindness, devotion and charity are constantly practised. The men of this age are described as "contented, kind, amiable, mild and possessed of self-control and forgiveness. They also observe the principle of equality and enjoy the bliss of a trained soul." In the *Mahabharata* Hanuman gives a graphic account of Kritayuga. "In that age," says Hanuman, "there were neither Gods, Danavas, Gandharvas, Yakshas, Rakshasas nor Pannagas; no buying and selling went on, no efforts were made by men; the fruit (of the earth) was obtained by their mere wishes. No disease or decline of the organs of sense arose through the influence of age; there was no malice, weeping, pride or deceit, no contention, no hatred, cruelty, fear, affliction, jealousy or envy. At that period the castes, alike in their functions, fulfilled their duties, were incessantly devoted to one Deity and used one Mantra, one rule and one rite. They had but one Veda."

The Kritayuga lasts for 1,728,000 years and the Deity during this period is said to be white.

In the Thretayuga, Dharma is three-legged, that is, virtue falls short by one-fourth. People become somewhat malicious and quarrelsome. Men of licentious temperament appear, but Brahmins conversant with the teachings of the Vedas far exceed their number. Although people become rather shrewd and act from motives, generally speaking, they are devoted to their duties and are punctual in the performance of religious ceremonies. The length of Thretayuga is 1,296,000 years, and in this age the Deity becomes red.

During the Dwaparayuga, Dharma becomes two-legged and is precariously supported. Falsehood, malice, discontent and dissensions greatly prevail. Devotion, kindness and forgiveness diminish by half. The Deity becomes yellow and the Veda fourfold. Some Brahmins study all the four Vedas, some three, others two and some none at all. The majority of Brahmins are, however, well-versed in the scriptures, and many noble Kshatriyas and Vaisyas follow their Dharma scrupulously. The Dwaparayuga lasts for 864,000 years.

The last is Kaliyuga, the present age of degeneration. Dharma in this age is one-legged and lies helplessly prostrate. "Only one-fourth of the whole amount of virtue remains as a residue; and even this small quantity disappears according as the causes of vices rapidly increase."

All the poets wax eloquent in describing the misery of the Kaliyuga. "In this age," says the author of *Bhagbata*, "most of the people are Sudras or slaves who are always subject to temptation; they are wicked, unkind, quarrelsome, unlucky and beggar-like. Deception, idleness, sloth, malice, dullness, distress, fear and poverty are foremost in men and darkness prevails upon them. They highly prize what is low and degraded. They are ever attended by misfortunes. They eat voraciously."

Men are led by their wives. Women become shameless, overbold and lascivious. They bear too many children. They eat much, talk much and their speech is disagreeable. Cities are filled with thieves and vicious men. Low and deceitful merchants conduct marketing. Kings become oppressive and draw out blood from their subjects. Householders neglect their duties and beg in the streets, and Brahmins degenerate to the level of Sudras. Droughts and floods devastate crops, and wars and famines depopulate the earth. In short, the condition of the world becomes so bad that wise men pray for the arrival of Kalki the destroyer.

The length of the Kaliyuga is 432,000 years and in this age the Deity becomes black.

It is interesting to note that we are said to be living in the sixth millennium of the Kaliyuga of the present Mahayuga. The current Kalpa is computed to be the first day of the fifty-first year of the life of our Brahma.

Thus the Hindu view of life is one of progressive degeneration. In this conception of a decaying universe, the mystics of all religious persuasions are strangely unanimous. Adherents of the Semitic group of religions believe in Eden, the earthly Paradise, whence Adam, the ancestor of man, was expelled for his misconduct and left to toil and die. There is an Egyptian myth which purports to say that man was immortal and happy in a by-gone age, but on hatching a conspiracy to usurp the throne of the Primal Father was caught red-handed and condemned to death.

According to Hesiod, the Greek poet, the mythical history of his country consists of five ages. "In the beginning the Olympians under Kronos created the race of the Men of Gold. In those days men lived like gods in unalloyed happiness. They did not toil with their hands for earth brought forth her fruits without their aid. They did not know the sorrows of old age, and death to them was like passing away in a calm sleep. After they had gone hence their spirits were appointed to dwell above the earth, guarding and helping the living.

"The gods next created the Men of Silver, but they could not be compared in virtue and happiness with the men of 'the older age of golden peace.' For many years they remained mere children and as soon as they came to the full strength and stature of manhood they refused to do homage to the gods and fell to slaying one another. After death they became the good spirits who live within the earth.

"The Men of Bronze followed springing from ash-trees and having hearts which were hard and jealous, so that with them 'lust and strife began to gnaw the world.' All the works of their hands were wrought in bronze. Through their own inventions they fell from their high estate and from the light they passed away to the dark realm of King Hades unhonoured and unremembered.

"Zeus then placed upon earth the race of the Heroes who fought at Thebes and Troy, and when they came to the end of life, the Olympian sent them to happy abodes at the very limits of the earth.

"After the Heroes came the Men of Iron—the race of these wild days. Our lot is labour and vexation of spirit by day and night, nor will this cease until the race ends, which will be when the order of nature has been reversed and human affection turned to hatred."

The fourth age, the age of Heroes, is considered to be an interpolation. Hesiod's scheme, it seems, had only four ages.

In its conception of the progress of life, mysticism is thus the antithesis of the doctrine of evolution.

The manner of destruction of the world at the end of the Kaliyuga is differently described in the Puranas. In one account it is related that Vishnu will appear as Kalki, "an armed warrior, mounted on a white horse, furnished with wings and adorned with jewels, waving over his head with one hand the sword of destruction and holding in the other a disc. The horse is represented as holding up the right fore-leg; and when he stamps on the earth with that, the tortoise supporting the serpent Shesha on whose hood the world rests, shall fall into the deep, and so rid himself of the load; and by that means all the wicked inhabitants of the world will be destroyed."

In the *Bhagbata* we are told that the "age of destruction is so horrible that during it the clouds never fall on the earth as drops of rain for one hundred years. The people then find no food to eat and being terribly oppressed by hunger they are compelled to eat one another. Being thus overpowered by what is wrought by time, the men gradually lead themselves to utter destruction."

Elsewhere the universal cataclysm is predicted in vivid details. "After a drought lasting for many years, seven blazing suns will appear in the firmament; they will drink up all the waters. Then wind-driven fire will sweep over the earth, consuming all things; penetrating to the nether world it will destroy what is there in a moment; it will burn up the universe. Afterwards many coloured and brilliant clouds will collect in the sky looking like herds of elephants decked with wreaths of lightning. Suddenly they will burst asunder, and rains will fall incessantly for twelve years until the whole world with its mountains and forests is covered with water. The clouds will vanish. Then the self-created lord, the first cause of everything, will absorb the winds and go to sleep. The universe will become one dread expanse of water."

* * * *

It may be mentioned that a day of Brahma is also divided into fourteen Manwantaras, over each of which presides a Manu or teacher who does not necessarily perish with the world at the end of a Mahayuga. In the *Mahabharata*, the sage Markandeya relates how our Manu was saved in the last Pralaya (cataclysm). The following is the story:

Manu, who was equal unto Brahma in glory, practised austerities for 10,000 years. One day while he was meditating on the Infinite, standing on one leg with uplifted hand by the bank of a stream, a fish rose from the water and asked for Manu's protection from the bigger fish that was chasing it. Manu took the fish from the stream and placed it in an earthen jar. The fish grew too big for the jar. Then Manu took it to a pond. The fish grew too big for the pond and begged to be taken to the Ganges. It was taken to the Ganges but it grew big for the Ganges too, and had to be taken to the ocean. In the ocean the fish smiled and revealed to Manu its identity as Brahma. It also predicted the approaching end of the world by a deluge, and asked Manu to build an ark and take in it, "the seven Rishis and all the different seeds enumerated by Brahmins of yore and preserve them carefully." Manu did as he was told, and when the deluge began, he set sail in his ship and fastened the cables of his ship to the horns of the fish.

"Along the ocean in that stately ship was borne
    the lord of men and through
Its dancing, tumbling billows, and its roaring
    waters; and the bark,
Tossed to and fro by violent winds, reeled on the
    surface of the deep,
Staggering and trembling like a drunken woman.
    Land was seen no more,
Nor far horizon, nor the space between; for every-
    where around
Spread the wild waste of waters, reeking atmos-
    phere, and boundless sky.
Now when all the world was deluged, nought
    appeared above the waves
But Manu and the seven sages, and the fish that
    drew the bark.
Unwearied, thus for years on years, the fish pro-
    pelled the ship across
The heaped-up waters, till at length it bore the
    vessel to the peak
Of Himavan."

Now the waters began to descend and Manu with them. In due time he reached the plains and took up the work of creation for the next Kritayuga.

The story has a parallel in the Hebrew myth of the deluge and Noah's Ark. Probably both have a common origin in the Babylonian legend of the Flood.

HINDU MYTHICAL GEOGRAPHY

From the meagre accounts in the Vedas, it is surmised that Vedic poets conceived the earth as "extended, broad and boundless, in shape like a wheel." There is no mention of oceans surrounding it. The most ancient cosmic conception is that "the earth and the sky alone constitute the universe. In this case the idea of the shape of the earth varies, for when it is united with the sky, it is compared to two great bowls turned toward each other, while, from another point of view, earth and sky are likened to the wheels at the ends of an axle."

Puranic myths, as usual, differ widely in their accounts of how the earth is supported and divided. In one place, the earth is said to be resting on the hood of the serpent Shesha, Shesha himself lying on a tortoise above primal waters. Elsewhere, four elephants are said to be supporting the earth. A third account tells us that four giants carry the earth on their shoulders, and earthquakes are caused by their changing shoulders when they get tired.

Some of the Puranas speak of seven mythical island continents of which the innermost is our world. This world is called Jambudwipa (island of the Jambu) because of the mythical Jambu tree that is said to be growing in one of its mountains. "The fruits of the tree are as large as elephants; and when they are ripe, they fall upon the mountain, and their juice forms the Jambu river, whose waters give health and life to those that drink of them."

In the centre of the world and supporting it is Mount Meru, 84,000 leagues in height. The holy land of Bharatavarsha from where alone is salvation possible, lies between the Himalayas and the salt sea

"On the summit of Meru is the city of Brahma extending 14,000 leagues, renowned in Heaven; around it are the cities of Indra and other regents of the spheres. About the city of Brahma flows the Ganges, encircling the city.

"In the foot-hills of Meru dwell the Gandharvas, Kinnaras and Siddhas; the Daityas, Asuras and Rakshasas in the valley."

Of all places, celestial and terrestrial, Bharatavarsha is said to be the best because it is a place of action whereas the others, blissful as they are, are regions of inertia.*

---

* Some Buddhist and Jain cosmic conceptions will be found in the respective chapters.

PLATE 1

GANESHA
(From Moor's *Hindu Pantheon*)

PLATE II

2

NARAYANA
(From Moor's *Hindu Pantheon*)

3

MAHAPRALAYA
(From Moor's *Hindu Pantheon*)

PLATE III

4
KALKI
(From Moor's *Hindu Pantheon*)

5 VISHNU   SHIVA   BRAHMA
(From Moor's *Hindu Pantheon*)

PLATE IV

6 BRAHMA, FROM CHIDAMBARAM
(Photo by E. S. Mahalingam)

FIVE-FACED GANESHA, FROM CHIDAMBARAM
(Photo by E. S. Mahalingam)

PLATE V

8 WORSHIP OF BRAHMA
(Prince of Wales Museum, Bombay)

9 SHIVA AS THE TRINITY
(Elephanta. From *Picturesque India* by Martin Hurlimann)

10 A HINDU HOLY MAN

11 BRAHMA'S TEMPLE, PUSHKAR
(From *Picturesque India* by Martin Hurlimann)

PLATE VI

12 HANUMAN
(From Moor's *Hindu Pantheon*)

13 MONKEYS BUILDING RAMA'S BRIDGE
(From Moor's *Hindu Pantheon*)

PLATE VII

14 HANUMAN ANNOUNCING SITA'S ACQUITTAL BY THE FIRE ORDEAL
(From Moor's *Hindu Pantheon*)

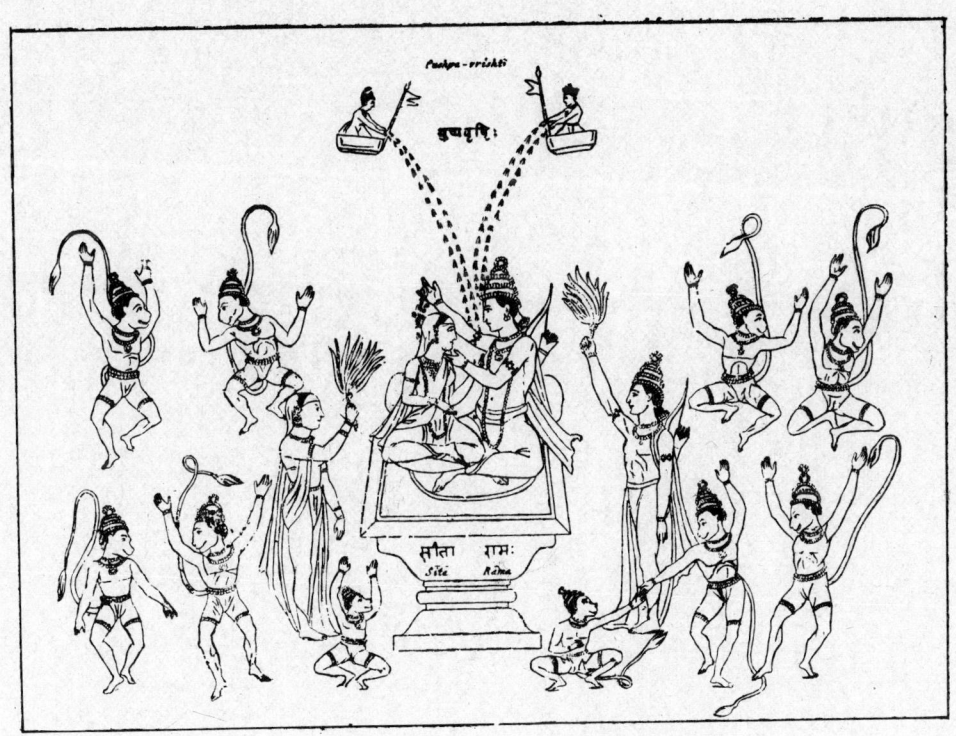

15 REUNION OF RAMA AND SITA AFTER THE FIRE ORDEAL
(From Moor's *Hindu Pantheon*)

PLATE VIII

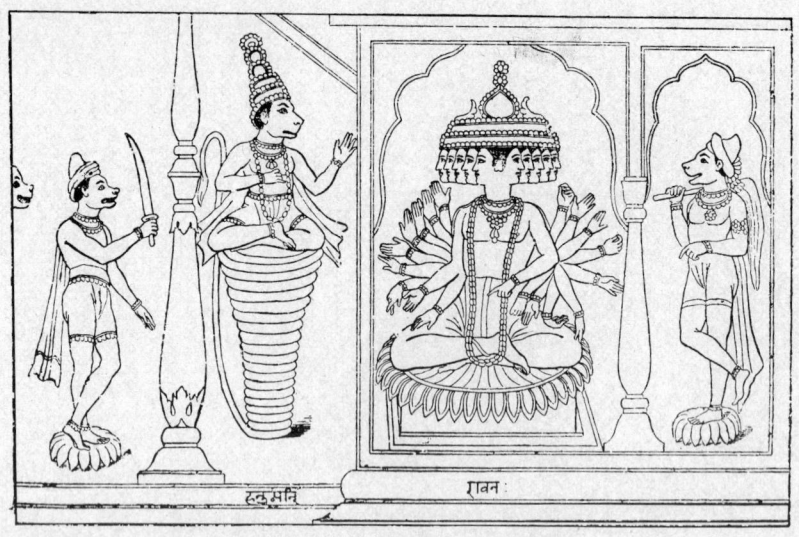

16   HANUMAN SITTING BEFORE RAVANA
(From Moor's *Hindu Pantheon*)

17   PAVAN THE WIND GOD   AGNI
     WITH HIS SON HANUMAN
(From Moor's *Hindu Pantheon*)

Chapter II
THE HINDU PANTHEON
GODS

STRICTLY speaking, the Hindus are monotheists. While the followers of the Semitic group of religions conceive God as male, the Hindus carry the idea higher and conceive the Deity as neuter. The Supreme Being, otherwise known as "Brahm", is without sex or attributes. But the Hindus hold that the Supreme Being can only be conceived in the abstract by the intellectually or spiritually gifted and the masses, for their worship, require deities with forms and attributes; and for their benefit certain aspects of the Supreme Being are personified into deities. Idolatry is also permitted because of the essentially pantheistic nature of Advaita, the predominating school of Hindu philosophy.

It must, however, be mentioned that the Brahmo Samaj (founded in the 19th century by Raja Ram Mohan Roy) and the Arya Samaj (also founded in the 19th century by Swami Dayanand) teach the exclusive worship of a personal Deity and prohibit idolatry. But the followers of these two persuasions are comparatively few and the vast majority of Hindus are Sanatanists (those who follow the ancient faith).

The number of deities in the Hindu pantheon are thirty-three crores and three. Practically every aspect of life has been deified and the pantheon enriched by animism, ancestor-worship and idle imagination. All forms of worship and all forms of thought are recognized as orthodox provided they formally accept the Vedas as revealed wisdom. Even the Sankhya, an atheistic school of Hindu philosophy, is considered orthodox because it admits the authority of the Vedas if only to interpret the text in its own way. Buddhism and Jainism are denounced as heretical as these repudiate the sanctions of the Vedas.

The Hindu pantheon has undergone many changes, and as it stands today is an evolved system (if it can be called a system) of deities. Gods who once occupied high positions lost their importance and were replaced by others; while the worship of some of them was totally discarded, others were given subordinate positions and remembered once or twice a year. Some gods fell with the defeat of their devotees in the battlefield and sectarian quarrels sealed the fate of many others.

Most of the ancient Hindu poets seem to have grasped the central fact of the mythical nature of the deities. While they mention the very name of the Supreme Being with the utmost reverence, their attitude towards minor deities and even towards the members of the Trinity is often irreverent and impious. Brahma, Vishnu and Shiva quail before the curses of pious mortals. These gods have their moments of passion, weakness, elation and sorrow. They weep over losses as humans do and, in a tight corner, are not above telling lies. In one place a god is depicted as a sage and philosopher and, in another, as a simpleton. Some gods have even committed crime and incest. But there is a moral attached to each tale of a god's misbehaviour.

In spite of all these weaknesses of the gods, the Hindus put great emphasis on the power aspect of the Deity. They vividly describe how a god or goddess destroyed a demon, and to throw the magnitude of the task into greater relief depict the demon as incredibly mighty. But the method by which his downfall was contrived leaves, at times, much to be desired even according to the ethical conceptions of humble humans. In rituals, architecture and art, special care is taken to overwhelm man by a sense of the immensity of the might of the godhead.

While the Greek ideal is beauty, and the Christian ideal love, the Hindu ideal of the Deity is Power. Even in rhythmic art (the dance of Shiva and Kali for instance) the idea of Power is overemphasised, the only exception being the dances of Krishna.

In Vedic times, the deities were few and simple. The Vedic pantheon consisted of 33 members who could be ultimately resolved into one. The rest of the deities were developments of the epic and Puranic times. In the Puranas "gods meet with gods, and being ultimately resolvable into one, as that one is approached, the clashing seems more and more frequent."

In describing the deities, the current Puranic order has been followed. All the Vedic deities are also mentioned in the Puranas, though given positions subordinate to the three great Puranic deities constituting the Triad.

THE HINDU TRIAD

The Hindu Triad consists of Brahma, Vishnu and Shiva, the creator, preserver and destroyer of the worlds respectively. The three major aspects of the Supreme Being are thus personified for the better understanding of the Deity, and it is emphasized that the Three is One. "In the obvious arrangement of the three grand powers of the Eternal One, creation and preservation precede destruction: this is the relative and philosophical rank of the Triad, but not always their theological or sectarian station. For as the Vaishnavas exalt Vishnu, so the Shaivas exalt Shiva to the place, and describe him with the power of the Deity or Brahm; as all things must at the end of time suffer destruction, so the personification of that power must be considered as ultimately paramount, although anterior to that inconceivable period, the preserving member of the Trinity may have apparent predominancy."*

Although Brahma, Vishnu and Shiva are said to be One, sectarians often try to establish the supremacy of Vishnu or Shiva, as the case may be, over the others. Brahma has few devotees at present, but from many accounts in the Vedas and the Puranas, it is clear that at one time he was widely worshipped and considered the foremost of the Triad.

A myth, obviously Shaivite in origin, gives the following account of the Trinity (Brahma is supposed to be relating the story to the gods and Rishis):

"In the Primal Night, when all beings and all worlds are resolved together in one equal and inseparable stillness, I beheld the great Narayana, soul of the universe, thousand-eyed, omniscient, Being and non-Being alike, reclining on the formless waters, supported by the thousand-headed serpent Infinite; and I, deluded by his glamour touched the Eternal Being with my hand and asked: 'Who art thou? Speak.' Then he of the lotus eyes looked upon me with drowsy glance, then rose and smiled and said: 'Welcome my child, thou shining grandsire.' But I took offence thereat and said: 'Dost thou O sinless god like a teacher to a pupil call me child, who am the cause of creation and destruction, framer of the myriad worlds, the source and soul of all? Tell me why dost thou speak foolish words to me?' Then Vishnu answered: 'Knowest thou not that I am Narayana, creator, preserver, and destroyer of the worlds, the Eternal Male, the undying source and centre of the universe? For thou wert born from my own imperishable body.'

"Now ensued an angry argument between us twain upon that formless sea. Then for the ending of our contention there appeared before us a glorious shining Lingam, a fiery pillar, like a hundred universe-consuming fires, without beginning, middle or end, incomparable, indescribable. The divine Vishnu bewildered by its thousand flames, said unto me, who was as much astonished as himself: 'Let us forthwith seek to know this fire's source. I will descend, do thou ascend with all thy power.' Then he became a boar, like a mountain of blue collyrium, a thousand leagues in width, with white sharp-pointed tusks, long-snouted, loud-grunting, short of foot, victorious, strong, incomparable—and plunged below. For a thousand years he sped thus downward, but found no base at all of the Lingam. Meanwhile I became a swan, white, fiery eyed, with wings on every side, swift as thought and as wind; and I went upward for a thousand years seeking to find the pillar's end, but found it not. Then I returned and met the great Vishnu, weary and astonished on his upward way.

"Then Shiva stood before us, and we whom his magic had guiled bowed unto him, while there arose about us on every hand the articulate sound of Aum, clear and lasting."

A Vaishnavite version of the same myth twists it towards the end to establish the supremacy of Vishnu. According to this version, Brahma falsely claimed to have reached the top of the Lingam while Vishnu admitted he could not find its base. On this, Shiva cut off one of Brahma's heads and acknowledged Vishnu as the greatest of the Triad for having spoken the truth.

BRAHMA†

In the *Yajur Veda*, the Supreme Being is introduced speaking thus: "From me Brahma was born; he is above all; he is Pitamaha, or the father of all men; he is Aja and Swayambhu or self-existing." Elsewhere he is described as "the first of the gods; framer of the universe; guardian of the world." "From him all things proceeded and in him pre-existed the universe; comprehending all material forms which he at once called into creation or arranged existence, as they are now seen, although perpetually changing their appearances by the operation of the reproductive power. As the oak exists in the acorn, as the fruit is in the seed, awaiting development and expansion, so all material forms existed in Brahma and their germs were at once produced by him."

In the Puranas different accounts of his origin are given. In one place he is described as having been born of the Supreme Being when the latter united with

---

* Edward Moor, *Hindu Pantheon*.

† Brahma is not be confused with Brahm, the impersonal Supreme Being without attributes; Brahma is a minor being in comparison, more or less magnified human being whose chief occupation is creation.

His energy, Maya. Elsewhere it is said he was hatched out of the Golden Egg that lay floating on primal waters. But the most widely accepted version is that he was born of a lotus that sprang up from Vishnu's navel, obviously a Vaishnavite myth.

Brahma has four heads. Originally he had five, of which one was cut off by Shiva. The *Matsya Purana* gives the following account of the origin of his heads:

"Brahma formed from his own immaculate substance a female who is celebrated under the names of Satarupa, Savitri, Sarasvati, Gayatri, and Brahmani. Beholding his daughter born from his own body Brahma became wounded with the arrows of love, and exclaimed, 'How surpassingly lovely she is!' Satarupa turned to the right side from his gaze; but as Brahma wished to look at her, a second head issued from his body. As she passed to the left, and behind him, to avoid his amorous glances, two other heads successively appeared. At length she sprang into the sky; and as Brahma was anxious to gaze after her there, a fifth head was immediately formed."

There are different versions of the incident that led to the loss of the fifth head of Brahma. In one account it is related that Shiva nipped it off with his nail when it began to babble about Brahma's superiority over Shiva. Elsewhere it is said that Shiva cut it off on its telling a lie, a myth already noticed. A third account is that Brahma was punished by Shiva in this manner for committing incest with his daughter in a drunken bout. A fourth version relates that Shiva cursed Brahma for asking an insolent boon by which Brahma wanted Shiva to be born as a son to him, and the power of this curse deprived Brahma of his fifth head.

In all these stories Shiva is said to have cut off the head, and hence it is surmised that the myths indicate the overthrow of the worshippers of Brahma by those of Shiva.

Brahma is depicted in art as a four-headed deity, red in colour. He is dressed in white raiment and rides upon a goose. Each of the four Vedas are said to have sprung from one of his heads. Hence he is considered the deity of wisdom, and intellectuals are particularly devoted to him.

The heaven of Brahma is described in the *Mahabharata* as "eight hundred miles by four hundred and forty miles high." Narada, the most gifted of all the sages, could not describe it in detail in two hundred years. Brahma's heaven is said to contain "in a superior degree all the excellence of other heavens; and that whatever existed on earth, from the smallest insect to the largest animal, was also to be found there."

At present there is no important temple exclusively dedicated to this deity except one at Pushkar in Ajmer. In certain temples dedicated to other gods, an idol of Brahma is also placed as a subsidiary deity and honoured. The work of creation is over, and probably the present-day Hindus think that man need not be over-grateful to the creator!

Brahma has many names of which the following are the most common: Prajapati (lord of creatures); Pitamaha (the great patriarch); Kamalasana (he who is seated on the lotus); Atmabhu (self-existent); Parameshti (the chief sacrificer); Hiranyagarbha (born of the Golden Egg); Savitripathi (husband of Savitri); and Adikavi (the first poet).

VISHNU

The Vaishnavas emphasize the principle of being (preservation) as the only reality. They maintain that nothing is destroyed. Destruction and creation are but changes of forms; the essence of things is indestructible. Hence the Deity in the character of preservation is supreme.

The *Bhagbata* observes: "Even I (Vishnu) was at first. Afterwards *I am that which is;* and he who must remain am I. Except the *First Cause,* whatever may appear in the mind, know that to be the mind's Maya or delusion, as light, as darkness. As the great elements are in various beings, yet not entering, (that is pervading, not destroying) thus am I in them, yet not in them."

In his personal character, Vishnu is the most lovable of all the deities. He is considerate and polite, full of forgiveness and tender thoughts towards his devotees. He is ever watchful of the welfare of gods and men, and in his dealings with their enemies is often more diplomatic than ruthless. The following myth aptly describes the genial disposition of the god: "Bhrigu (a sage) on being once asked in an assembly of the gods who of Brahma, Vishnu and Shiva was the greatest, undertook the task of ascertaining the point by a somewhat hazardous experiment. He first proceeded to Brahma, whom he purposely neglected to treat with his customary respect and decorum; which unusual proceeding drew upon him the indignation and lavish abuse of that deity. He then repaired to Shiva, to whom he behaved in a still more offensive manner; which roused in a much greater degree the anger of that impatient and vindictive personage. Bhrigu, however, on both these occasions by timely apologies, made his peace nad retired. He finally proceeded to the heaven of Vishnu whom he found asleep with Lakshmi sitting by him. Knowing the mild temper of the god, he judged that a mere appearance of disrespect would not, as in the two former cases, be sufficient to try it; he therefore approached the sleeping deity, and gave him a severe kick on the breast. On this Vishnu awoke; and instead of being indignant, he not only expressed his apprehensions and regret lest the sage should have hurt his foot, but benevolently proceeded to chafe it. Bhrigu, on witnessing this, exclaimed: 'This god is the mightiest, since he overpowers all by goodness and generosity.'"

Vishnu is represented in art as reposing on the coils of the serpent Shesha, his wife sitting at his feet. The stem of a lotus shoots up from his navel, and on the blossom sits Brahma. Vishnu has four hands in each of which he holds a Shank (conch shell), Chakra (a circular missile weapon), Gadha (mace), or Padma (lotus). His Vahan (charger) is Garuda, man-bird. The colour of the deity is black. His heaven is Vaikunta, made entirely of gold. "Its circumference is 80,000 miles. All its buildings are made of jewels. The pillars and ornaments of the building are of precious stones. The Celestial Ganges flows through it. In Vaikunta are also five pools containing blue, red and white lotuses. "On a seat glorious as the meridian sun, sitting on white lotuses is Vishnu and on his right side Lakshmi, who shines like a continued blaze of lightning, and from whose body the fragrance of the lotus extends 800 miles."

Vishnu has one thousand names but the scope of this book does not permit of mentioning them all. These names are strung together in verse and repeated by the pious as a sort of litany to obtain absolution from sins. The benefits that accrue from repeating these names are many. Even Yama, the Lord of Death, is said to have no power over a devotee of Vishnu. In the *Vishnu Purana* Yama tells one of his deputies: "I am lord of all men, Vaishnavas (worshippers of Vishnu) excepted. I was appointed by Brahma to restrain mankind and regulate the consequences of good and evil. But he who worships Hari (Vishnu) is independent of me. He who through his holy knowledge diligently adores the lotus foot of Hari is released from all the bonds of sin and you must avoid him as you would fire fed with oil." Again, "He who pleases Vishnu obtains all terrestrial enjoyments and a place in heaven and, what is best of all, final liberation. Whatever he wishes, and to whatever extent, whether much or little, he receives it when Achyuta (Vishnu) is content with him."

The Vaishnavas form the most powerful sect in India at present. They are distinguished, in South India particularly, by perpendicular marks on the forehead. Vishnu is worshipped by them as a single deity or jointly with his consort Lakshmi. He is also worshipped in one of his Avatars or incarnations.

* A Yojana is equivalent to about four miles.

THE AVATARS OF VISHNU

As the preserver of the universe, Vishnu had on many occasions left his celestial abode for other worlds and assumed various forms to destroy evil and establish the reign of righteousness. "Whenever the law fails and lawlessness uprises," says Krishna (an avatar of Vishnu) to Arjuna in the *Gita*, "O thou of Bharata race, then do I bring myself to bodied birth. To guard the righteous, to destroy evil-doers, to establish the law, I come into birth age after age."

The Avatars of Vishnu are numerous, but ten are considered the most important. They are: Matsya or fish; Kurma or tortoise; Varaha or boar; Narasimha or man-lion; Vamana or dwarf; Parasurama; Ramachandra; Krishna; Buddha; and Kalki. Of these the first five are said to have taken place in worlds other than ours; in the next four, Vishnu lived on earth as man; and the last is yet to come at the end of the world.

Balarama, the brother of Krishna, and Lakshman, the brother of Ramachandra, are also mentioned in some Puranas as Avatars of Vishnu. In fact the Hindus often exalt any distinguished personage as an Avatar, and many besides those already mentioned are also spoken of as Avatars. But we will confine ourselves to a description of the ten widely accepted Avatars.

1. MATSYA

This is merely a Vaishnavite version of the fish myth already noticed in the first chapter. While in the *Mahabharata*, Brahma is said to have appeared before Manu in the form of a fish, the Puranas assert it was Vishnu who did so and predicted the deluge and saved Manu from the universal cataclysm. The fish that propelled Manu's ship across the waters to the Himalayas is said (in the *Bhagbata*) to have been "of golden colour, having a horn, and a body extending over ten million Yojanas."*

2. KURMA

In this Avatar, Vishnu assumed the form of a tortoise to serve as a resting point for the mountain Mandara with which the gods and Asuras churned the milk-ocean for ambrosia. A full account of this operation will be found in Chapter VI.

In the *Satapatha Brahmana* there is the following account of Brahma having assumed the form of a tortoise: "Having assumed the form of a tortoise, Prajapati (Brahma) created offspring. That which he created he made. Hence men say: 'All creatures are the descendants of Kasyapa (meaning tortoise).' This tortoise is the same as Aditya."

This is probably the nucleus of the myth which

the Vaishnavas developed into an Avatar of Vishnu.

3. VARAHA

Vishnu is fabled to have once raised the earth from primal waters under which it lay submerged. For accomplishing this feat he had to take the form of a boar.

In this account, as in the previous two myths, an earlier Brahma myth is twisted and given a Vaishnavite character. In the *Taittareya Brahmana* we are told: "the universe was formerly water, fluid. With that water Prajapati practised arduous devotions (saying): 'How shall this universe be (developed).' He beheld a lotus leaf standing. He thought 'There is something on which this rests.' He as a boar—having assumed that form—plunged beneath towards it. He found the earth down below. Breaking off a portion of her he rose to the surface." Again, according to the *Satapatha Brahmana*, "formerly the earth was only the size of a span. A boar called Emusha raised her up."

The *Ramayana* converts this Brahma myth to an Avatar of Vishnu by the simple method of bracketing Brahma with Vishnu: "In the beginning all was water through which earth was formed. Thence arose Brahma, the self-existent, the imperishable Vishnu. He then becoming a boar, raised up this earth and created the whole world."

The *Vishnu Purana* gives the following exposition of the subject: "At the close of the last age, the divine Brahma endowed with the quality of goodness awoke from his night of sleep and beheld the universal void. He, the supreme Narayana, invested with the form of Brahma concluding that within the waters lay the earth and being desirous to raise it up, created another form for that purpose. And as in the preceding ages he had assumed the shape of a fish or a tortoise, so in this he took the form of a boar. Having adopted a form composed of the sacrifices of the Vedas for the preservation of the whole earth, the eternal, supreme, and universal soul plunged into the ocean."

According to the *Vayu Purana*, the form of a boar was chosen "because it is an animal delighting in water."

Another version of this myth is that a demon Hiranyaksha propitiated Brahma by penances and received a boon which exempted him from hurt by god, man or beast. But while enumerating all possible forms of beings from whom he claimed exemption, he omitted, through an oversight, to include the boar in the list. After receiving the boon Hiranyaksha began to persecute gods and men. In his arrogance he stole the Vedas while Brahma was asleep, and dragged the earth into his abode in the nether regions under the waters; and Vishnu, assuming the form of a boar, killed him with his tusks, regained the Vedas and caused the earth to float once again.

The boar is described in the *Vayu Purana* as "ten Yojanas in breadth, and a thousand Yojanas in height; his colour dark and his roar like thunder. His bulk was vast as a mountain; his tusks were white, sharp and fearful; fire flashed from his eyes like lightning; and he was radiant as the sun. His shoulders were round, fat and large; he strode along like a powerful lion; his haunches were fat, his loins slender and his body was smooth and beautiful."

4. NARASIMHA

Vishnu assumed the form of man-lion to kill Hiranyakasipu, the brother of Hiranyaksha, who had been slain by Varaha. Hiranyakasipu too, like his brother, propitiated Brahma and obtained a boon which gave him immunity from all conceivable forms of danger. He could not be killed by god, man or beast. He could die neither by day nor by night; neither inside nor outside his home. Thus protected, he proceeded to claim divine honours for himself and prohibited all forms of worship in his kingdom. But his own son Prahlad was an ardent devotee of Vishnu, and the lad was caught red-handed in the act of worshipping that deity. Hiranyakasipu advised his son to give up his devotional exercises but Prahlad refused. He was flogged and sent to a preceptor notorious for his atheistic doctrines. On his return from his teacher Prahlad was, however, found to be as ardent a devotee of Vishnu as ever. This enraged Hiranyakasipu beyond all measure and, "highly exasperated, he commanded serpents to fall upon his disobedient and insane son and bite him to death. The serpents did their worst, but Prahlad felt them not. The snakes cried out to the king, 'our fangs are broken, our jewelled crests are burst; there is fever in our hoods, and fear in our hearts; but the skin of the youth is still unscathed. Have recourse, O King of the Daityas, to some other expedient.'"

Other forms of torture followed. But, elephants "vast as mountains" could not hurt Prahlad. Nor could he be killed by being thrown down precipices. Attempts at drowning him in the ocean also failed. Steadfast in his meditation of Vishnu, Prahlad came out of all these ordeals unscathed. Baffled, Hiranyakasipu decided to win over his son by arguments.

One day, while Hiranyakasipu was sitting in his palace and speaking to his son on the fallacy of Vishnu-worship, the latter began to chant the praises of Vishnu. "Where is your Vishnu?" Asked Hiranyakasipu in a rage. "Everywhere," replied Prahlad. "Is he in this pillar?" Asked Hiranyakasipu again. "Certainly," said Prahlad. "Then I will kill him," said the demon-king and, getting up, kicked the pillar.

Out of the pillar sprang forth Narasimha, and he

tore Hiranyakasipu to pieces. It is said the incident took place in twilight (which is neither day nor night) on the doorway of Hiranyakasipu's palace (which is neither inside nor outside his home); and since man-lion is neither god, beast nor man, the provisions of Brahma's boon were respected to the letter.

5. VAMANA

Bali, a grandson of Prahlad, ruled his kingdom well and wisely but was ambitious. He decided to enlarge the frontiers of his kingdom and began to perform a great sacrifice. Indra, king of the gods, was troubled as it was evident that Bali's object was to acquire the celestial kingdom and drive away the gods from their abode. Indra consulted his preceptor Brahaspati who confirmed his fears and added that, as Bali's sacrifice had gone too far, nothing could be done to prevent his conquest of Indra just then, and the gods would be well advised to leave their kingdom. This was done.

Afterwards Vishnu was propitiated by the gods by penances and prayers and he took birth as the son of Brahaspati.* The child was a deformed dwarf. When he reached boyhood he went to Bali begging alms and Bali, famous for his generosity, told the dwarf he could have anything he wanted. The dwarf made Bali promise on oath that he would give him three paces of land. The pigmy then grew to inconceivable proportions and measured the three worlds in two paces. There was no more land for the third pace and Bali was accused of not having kept his promise and sent to the nether regions.

A legend tells us that Bali was much devoted to his subjects and begged Vishnu to permit him to visit his lost kingdom once a year, and that Vishnu agreed. Onam, the most important festival in Malabar, is annually celebrated for the reception of Bali, and during the ten days of this festival there is exceptional feasting and merry-making in the land so that the ancient king may feel at ease seeing his people happy.

Bali was probably a popular Dravidian king whom the Aryans overcame by strategy. Scholars even opine that he was king of Mahabalipuram or Mamallapuram (an ancient city, now in ruins, near Madras).

6. PARASURAMA

The story of this Avatar indicates a caste-conflict between Brahmins and Kshatriyas in which the former were victorious. Vishnu is said to have been born as a militant Brahmin to annihilate the Kshatriyas who had become arrogant and begun to oppress Brahmins.

Jamadagni, a **Brahmin hermit**, who lived in the woods had a faithful and virtuous wife who was the mother of his five sons. One day she went to the river to bathe and, as ill-luck would have it, saw in the river a handsome man sporting with a damsel. She looked at the amorous pair, took pleasure in unholy thoughts and even desired to enjoy the company of the handsome man. On her return to the hermitage her husband "beholding her fallen from her perfection and shorn of the lustre of her sanctity" reproached her and was exceedingly wroth.

All the sons of the hermit were, at that time, out in the woods gathering berries. They came home one by one and Jamadagni asked each of them to kill his mother. Four sons refused to become matricides. The angry sage cursed his disobedient sons and they became idiots. Lastly came Parasurama, the youngest, to whom Jamadagni said: "Kill thy mother who has sinned; and do it without repining." Rama promptly took his Parasu (axe; hence his name Parasurama) and cut off his mother's head. Jamadagni, greatly pleased with his son, asked him to demand of him any boons he wished. Rama begged for these boons: "The restoration of his mother to life with forgetfulness of having been slain and purification from all defilement; the return of his brothers to their natural condition; and for himself invincibility in single combat, and length of days." These were granted.

The incident that led to Parasurama's swearing undying vengeance on Kshatriyas is thus related in and *Ramayana*.

One day, Karthavirya (a Kshatriya king with one thousand arms) went out hunting and strayed into Jamadagni's hermitage. The sage's wife received him with deference and extended to him the hospitality of her hermitage. Walking about the compound, the king saw the hermit's wonderful cow Kamadhenu which yielded whatever was desired of her. He thought that a powerful king like himself should possess such a cow and not a hermit living in the forest, and hence drove her off. Neither Jamadagni nor any of his sons was in the hermitage at that time and the hermit's wife could do nothing to prevent this shameful violation of the rules of hospitality.

Shortly after, Rama returned and, on hearing what had happened, started in hot pursuit of Karthavirya. Rama overtook and killed him in battle and brought back the cow.

News of Karthavirya's death reached his sons and they marched on the hermitage of Jamadagni with a big army. They arrived at the sage's abode at a time when his sons were away, caught the unresisting old man, put him to death, and made good their escape. Parasurama was greatly enraged at this dastardly act

---

* In a different version he is said to have been born of the sage Kasyapa.

and took an oath that he would destroy the whole race of Kshatriyas.

It is said that in twenty-one campaigns he cleared the earth of Kshatriyas, and that all the so-called Kshatriyas who exist at present are sons of Brahmins born of Kshatriya ladies.

In the *Ramayana* there is an account of an encounter between Parasurama and Ramachandra in which the latter was victorious. Ramachandra, as will be noticed presently, was also an Avatar of Vishnu, and as the story of Vishnu overcoming Vishnu might appear absurd, the conflict was made to centre round two bows (of Vishnu and of Shiva) which were used in the combat. It is said Vishnu's bow came out victorious and Ramachandra's dynasty was saved from the wrath of Parasurama.

The legend is considered an interpolation which was put in the text to establish beyond doubt Ramachandra's claim for Avatarship, and is in conflict with the widely accepted belief of Parasurama's invincibility.

7. RAMACHANDRA

The Hindu epic *Ramayana* (a work of 24,000 Slokas or stanzas in length) chronicles in detail the story of Rama, called Ramachandra to distinguish him from Parasurama. The object of this Avatar was to kill the ten-headed demon Ravana, king of Lanka (Ceylon). Ravana by his austerities propitiated Brahma and Shiva who granted him certain boons by virtue of which he could not be killed by gods, Gandharvas or demons. Ravana was contemptuous of men and disdained to ask for immunity from them. After receiving the boons he started persecuting gods and men. The gods, greatly distressed, approached Brahma who observed that Ravana could only be killed by a god assuming human form; and Vishnu, as the preserver, agreed to be born as man. The other gods also promised to help him by either assuming various forms and descending to earth or by imparting their energy to men and animals.

At that time there reigned in Ayodhya (modern Oudh), a king named Dasaratha. He was a descendant of the illustrious solar dynasty of kings and ruled his kingdom justly and well. The king had three wives but no sons, and hence after many years of vain austerities, he at last performed the horse sacrifice, the utmost a king could do to please the gods; and as a result, he was blessed with four sons. Rama, the eldest (in whom Vishnu assumed human form), was born of Kausalya, Bharata of Kaikeyi, and Lakshman and Satrughna of Sumitra.

From the very childhood Rama and Lakshman became inseparable companions. The two boys gave promise of a great military career and, at a tender age, were taken by the sage Viswamitra to the forest abodes of hermits where they distinguished themselves by killing many wicked Rakshasas who harassed the poor hermits.

While the boys were wandering in the forests they heard that Janaka, king of Mithila, had a lovely daughter, Sita by name (she was an incarnation of Lakshmi, Vishnu's wife, and was born of no woman but of mother earth herself, and was picked up by Janaka from a paddy-field) who was to be given in marriage to any one who could bend a powerful bow Shiva had given Janaka. Viswamitra conducted the young princes to Janaka's court and Rama not only bent the great bow but broke it. He married Sita and with his bride proceeded to Ayodhya where they were enthusiastically received by Dasaratha and the citizens.

Seeing that he was growing old and Rama had come of age, Dasaratha decided to instal Rama on the throne. An auspicious day was fixed for the installation ceremony and a proclamation was issued to the effect. And in Ayodhya there was great rejoicing. Kausalya, mother of Rama, was the happiest lady in the Kingdom.

Now, Kaikeyi, the second wife of Dasaratha, had a maid-servant named Manthara, "crooked in mind and body." On the eve of Rama's installation on the throne, she approached Kaikeyi and addressed her thus: "O senseless woman, why art thou idle and content, when such misfortune is thine?" Kaikeyi was not aware of any misfortune impending or manifest and told her servant so. "O my lady," said Manthara, "a terrible destruction awaits thy bliss, so that I am sunk in fear immeasurable, and afflicted with heaviness and grief; burning like fire, have I sought thee hurriedly. Thou art verily a Queen on Earth, but though thy lord speaks blatantly he is crafty and crooked-hearted within and wills thee harm. It is Kausalya's welfare that he seeks, not thine, whatever sweet words he may have for thee. Bharata, thy son is discarded and Rama is set upon the throne. Indeed, my girl, thou hast nursed for thy husband a poisonous snake. Now quickly act and find a way to save Bharata, thyself and me."

The wicked hunchback worked up Kaikeyi to a pitch of jealousy, and the latter sought an audience with the king and begged of him a boon. The king, in a weak moment, swore he would do anything to please his beloved Kaikeyi; upon which she asked him to set Bharata on the throne and send Rama into exile to wander for fourteen years in the forests of Dandaka. "Thus, the king," says the poet, "was snared by Kaikeyi like a deer in a trap."

Unable to go back on his word, Dasaratha was overcome with grief and shut himself up in his private apartments. Kaikeyi herself acquainted Rama of what had happened and Rama readily agreed to go into exile. Rama broke the news to Sita and asked her to remain in Ayodhya and be a comfort to his parents, and described in vivid detail the horrors of forest life to which a tender lady like herself was not accustomed. But Sita answered: "O my Lord! A father, mother, son, brother or daughter-in-law indeed abide by the results of their actions; but a wife, O best of men, shares in her husband's fate. Therefore I have been ordered no less than thou, to exile in the forest. If thou goest there I shall go before thee, treading upon thorns and prickly grass. I shall be as happy there as in my father's house, thinking only of thy service. I shall not cause thee trouble but will live on roots and fruits. And there will be pools, with wild geese and other fowl and bright with full-blown lotus flowers, where we may bathe. There I shall be happy with thee even for a hundred or a thousand years."

Thus Sita decided to accompany Rama. So did Lakshman. And the three departed for the forests in the South amidst the lamentations of the citizens of Ayodhya. Fate thus decreed that the day of rejoicing be turned into a day of mourning.

Within a week of the departure of Rama, Dasaratha died of grief.

When these things were happening in Ayodhya, Bharata, son of Kaikeyi, was away in the city of Girivrija, the capital of his maternal uncle's kingdom. Messengers brought him news of Rama's departure and he hurried to Ayodhya where he learnt everything in detail. Bharata, enraged at the conduct of his mother, reproached her as the murderer of Dasaratha: "Like a burning coal born for the destruction of our race art thou, whom my father unwittingly embraced. Thou didst little know my love for Rama. Only for his sake it is, who calls thee mother, that I renounce thee not."

Bharata, trying to make amends for his mother's malicious conduct, went in search of Rama and found him wandering in the forests of Chitrakuta in the garments of a hermit. He acquainted him of their father's death and implored him to come back to Ayodhya. But Rama refused and told his brother that he was in honour bound to remain in exile for fourteen years. Persuasion and entreaties proving of no avail, Bharata returned to Ayodhya with a pair of Rama's sandals which he kept on the throne as a symbol of Rama, and ruled as his Viceroy.

Now, while the giantess Surpanakha, sister of Ravana, was going on one of her depredatory excursions in the forest of Dandaka she saw Rama and fell madly in love with him. The bold female expressed her love, but Rama gave a negative reply and added that she might try her luck with Lakshman who probably wanted a mate. She then approached Lakshman who too spurned her love. The angry giantess, imagining that Sita was the cause of her disappointment, tried to devour her, and Lakshman cut off her nose, ears and some accounts add, breasts. In this condition Surpanakha went to her younger brother Khara and he sent fourteen Rakshasas to slay Sita and the two men, and "bring their blood for Surpanakha to drink." But Rama killed all the Rakshasas. Then Khara himself with an army of fourteen thousand Rakshasas set out to chastise Rama. Rama destroyed the Rakshasa host and, in single combat, killed Khara himself.

Surpanakha now proceeded to Ravana and told him what had happened to Khara and herself and, finding that he was not impressed, added that Sita was exceedingly beautiful and was more fit to be his wife than Rama's, a point of view Ravana could very well appreciate. As he was well-informed of the power of his enemy, Ravana had recourse to strategy. He asked his uncle Maricha, a magician, to assume the form of a golden deer, gambol near the hut where Rama lived and raise desire in Sita to possess it. Ravana's plan was that Sita should send Rama and Lakshman away to capture the deer when he could carry off Sita without trouble.

The ruse succeeded, Sita expressed a desire to possess the beautiful deer and Rama started chasing it. Unable to capture the deer yet unwilling to let it go, Rama shot it with an arrow, and the wounded animal cried out in the voice of Rama: "O Sita, O Lakshman" as though Rama was in danger and sought their help. Sita asked Lakshman to proceed immediately to the scene of danger, and, on his departure, Ravana, who was hiding nearby, came out of the bush, caught Sita, placed her in his aerial car and drove off to Lanka. On his way, Jatayu, the king of vultures (supposed to be an Avatar of Garuda, Vishnu's Vahan), fought Ravana with his talons and beak but was fatally wounded. Sita blessed the bird and said he would live long enough to relate the event to Rama. She also cried out to the trees and plants of the forest and to the river Godavari to tell Rama that the demon Ravana stole his Sita.

Ravana took Sita to Lanka. There he wooed her with many sweet-words but Sita would have none of him and called him a cursed demon and a ravisher of chaste women. He could not have recourse to violence, for once before, when he had by force embraced another man's wife, he had been cursed that he would die the moment he did it again to any woman. So Ravana was content to woo and intimidate Sita by turns, and leave it to time to change her heart in his favour.

PLATE IX

18 RAMA AND SITA RETURNING TO AYODHYA IN RAVANA'S CAR PUSHPAKA
(Photo : K. A. L. Rao)

19 RAMA, SITA AND HANUMAN
(Photo : K. A. L. Rao)

PLATE X

20 FISH INCARNATION
(From Dacca.
Copyright : Archaeological Dept. of India)

21 BOAR INCARNATION
(From Khajuraho
Copyright : Archaeological Dept. of India)

22 NARASIMHA
(Bronze. Madras Museum)

23 VAMANA
(British Museum)

PLATE XI

24 PERSECUTION OF PRAHLAD
From Halebid. Copyright: Archaeological Department of India)

25 A VAISHNAVA BLOWING THE SACRED CONCH
(From a painting by Solvyns)

26 THE CALL TO DEVOTIONAL DUTIES
(From a painting by Solvyns)

PLATE XII

27　HANUMAN INSULTING RAVANA
(Photo : K. A. L. Rao)

28　BHIMA LIFTING HANUMAN'S TAIL

29　LAKSHMANA WOUNDED

30　HANUMAN BRINGING THE HILL WITH THE MAGIC HERB
(Photo : K. A. L. Rao)

PLATE XIII

31 HANUMAN KILLING AN
    ASURA
    (Photo : K. A. L. Rao)

32 HANUMAN KILLING AN
    ASURA
    (Photo : K. A. L. Rao)

33 HANUMAN PRESENTING
    RAMA'S RING TO SITA
    (Photo : K. A. I. Rao)

34 HANUMAN RECEIVING
    RAMA'S RING
    (Photo : K A. L. Rao)

PLATE XIV

35 SATRUGHNA   BHARATA   LAKSHMAN   RAMA   SITA   HANUMAN
(Ivory : From Trivandrum)

36 SITA UNDER THE ASOKA TREE
(From a stone plaque in a Bangalore
temple. Photo : K. A. L. Rao)

37 RAVANA WOOING SITA
(From a Rajput painting)

PLATE XV

39 BHARAT'S ARRIVAL AT CHITRAKUTA
(From *The Ramayana of Tulsidas*
Tr. by F. S. Growse)

38 THE TRIAL OF THE BOW
(From *The Ramayana of Tulsidas*
Tr. by F. S. Growse)

PLATE XVI

RAMA ENTHRONED
(From *The Ramayana of Tulsidas*
Tr. by F. S. Growse)

ANGADA AND THE MONKEY CHIEFS
(From *The Ramayana of Tulsidas*
Tr. by F. S. Growse)

When Rama and Lakshman returned to the hermitage after killing the magic deer and saw not Sita, they were greatly alarmed. They even suspected that Khara's demons had devoured her. They wandered over hills and valleys looking for Sita and came across Jatayu lying in a pool of blood. The bird told them all that had taken place and, on the termination of the tale, died. Rama was much grieved by the death of this noble bird and cremated its dead body as though it were one of his near relatives.

Now plans were made to regain Sita. Rama and Lakshman entered into an alliance with the monkey-king Sugriva who, in return for Rama's help in regaining his kingdom from his half brother Bali who had usurped his throne and exiled him, promised to support Rama in his campaign against Ravana. Rama killed Bali and restored the throne to Sugriva. Thereafter, Sugriva raised a huge army of monkeys and bears and with them Rama and Lakshman marched towards Lanka. The army reached the Southern Sea, and Rama, finding no way of fording the strait, decided to construct a bridge. In the meantime, in his search for Sita, Hanuman, a monkey chief had found her in Lanka and informed her of the coming deliverance. Hanuman had jumped over to Lanka from the mainland and, unperceived by guards, entered Ravana's pleasure-garden where he saw Sita sitting sad and lonely under an Asoka tree. Rakshasa women stood guard over her. Eluding the vigilance of the guards, Hanuman climbed the Asoka tree, and at an opportune moment began to chant the praises of Rama lest Sita should take fright on seeing him. On hearing the sweet name of her lord, Sita looked up and saw Hanuman who by many gestures made her understand that he was a friend. He came down and bowed to Sita and told her how Rama sorrowed in her absence and how he had made up his mind to avenge her wrongs. He also gave her the signet ring which he had received from Rama, and on touching it, Sita was overcome with joy as though she had felt the hand of Rama himself.

After delivering his message to Sita, Hanuman sported himself in the royal park destroying the king's favourite plants and flowers. The Rakshasas caught him, tied his hands and feet and took him to Ravana. Before Ravana, Hanuman contrived to sit on a higher level than he, by coiling his long tail and making a seat of it. Ravana would have killed the insolent monkey but for the fact that Hanuman described himself as an envoy whose life, by the rules of diplomacy, was sacred. He, however, asked his attendants to set fire to the monkey's tail. Clothes dipped in oil were wound round Hanuman's long tail and set fire to. But the monkey escaped with his burning tail and, jumping from one building to another, set the whole of Lanka ablaze. After this, he jumped back to the mainland and acquainted Rama with all that he had done in Lanka.

The bridge across the strait was built and the army of Rama crossed over to Lanka. Vibhishana, Ravana's brother, was won over by Rama, and he divulged many secrets about Ravana's powers and the defences of Lanka.

The Rakshasas came out of the city and fierce battles were fought with varying fortune. Twice were Rama and Lakshman wounded by the indomitable Indrajit, Ravana's son, who had conquered Indra himself and Kumbhakarna (Pot-Ear), Ravana's huge brother, caught the monkeys by the hundreds and devoured them. Rama and Lakshman were restored to health by a magic herb Hanuman brought from the Himalayas within an incredibly short time. In spite of terrible losses the monkey host pressed hard upon the Rakshasas who were destroyed in large numbers. Indrajit, Kumbhakarna and other Rakshasa generals were slain. At last Ravana himself came out and met Rama in single combat. It was a terrible encounter. The earth trembled and the gods from above gazed on. "Each like a flaming lion fought the other; head after head of the Ten-necked one did Rama cut away with his deadly arrows, but new heads ever rose in place of those cut off, and Ravana's death seemed nowise nearer than before. The arrows that had slain Maricha, Khara and Bali could not take the king of Lanka's life away. Then Rama took up the Brahma weapon given to him by Agastya: the Wind lay in its wings, the Sun and Fire in its heads, in its mass the weight of Meru and Mandara. Blessing that shaft with Vedic Mantras, Rama set it on his mighty bow and loosed it, and it sped to its appointed place and cleft the breast of Ravana, and bathed in blood, returned and entered Rama's quiver."

On Ravana's death there was great rejoicing in heaven and the gods showered celestial flowers on Rama.

Ravana slain, Vibhishana brought Sita to Rama in a gaily decorated car. But to the amazement of all, Rama was cold to her; in fact, he refused to accept her. For, said he:

"Ravana bore thee through the sky
And fixed on thine his evil eye;
About thy waist his arms he threw,
Close to his breast his captive drew;
And kept thee, vassal of his power,
An inmate of his ladies' bower."

Sita was deeply humiliated by these cruel words of Rama and, to prove her innocence or perish in the attempt, decided to undergo the fire-ordeal. At her request Lakshman prepared the pyre and Sita jumped into it. The sky itself proclaimed her innocence and Agni, the god of fire, conducted her to Rama and asked him to accept her. Rama took her hand and observed that even before the ordeal he was convinced of her purity but wanted to prove it to others.

The term of exile was now over, and Rama, Sita and Lakshman together with many monkey generals and their wives proceeded to Ayodhya. They entered the city in great pomp and Rama was crowned king. And then ensued a reign of prosperity unprecedented in history or even mythology.

"Ten thousand years Ayodhya, best
With Rama's rule, had peace and rest,
No widow mourned her murdered mate,
No house was ever desolate,
The happy land no murrain knew,
The flocks and herds increased and grew,
The earth her kindly fruits supplied,
No harvest failed, no children died.
Unknown were want, disease, and crime,
So calm, so happy was the time."

But once again trouble started. A washerman in the kingdom beat his wife suspected of adultery, and drove home the point by observing that he was not a fool like Rama to believe that a wife who had been kept for years by another man was pure. The story reached the ears of Rama and to save Sita and himself from slander he sent her away to a hermitage. She was pregnant at the time and in the hermitage Sita gave birth to twins. The children, on their reaching boyhood, were sent to Rama. On seeing the lovely boys, recollections of the dear old days overpowered Rama and he called back Sita to his court. Gladly did Sita come to her lord. But she was again asked to prove her innocence in an assembled court. Even Sita could not bear this and she called upon mother-earth, who gave her birth, to receive her back. The earth opened and received her daughter in her bosom.

"After this Rama grew tired of life, and Time came to inform him that his work was done. Hearing this, the good king proceeded to the banks of the sacred stream and forsaking his body ascended to his home in heaven."

Thus ends the story of Rama and Sita, unrivalled for pathos in the whole realm of epic literature.

It may be mentioned, that the *Ramayana* marks a definite stage in the development of Hindu society. While in the Vedic times women were comparatively free socially and economically, the ideal woman of the *Ramayana* has no life apart from her husband's.

8. KRISHNA

In Krishna we have the most popular of all the Avatars. Although the main object of the Avatar was to kill Kansa, a demon born of a woman, Krishna is mostly remembered by his devotees for his various other activities. He was brought up among a pastoral people and, as a child, was the pet of the milkmaids. As a boy he tended flocks and played with the sons of cowherds in the fields and pastures of Vrindavan. As a youth he was the beloved of the village damsels with whom he sang and danced in the Arcadian fields of Ambadi. In middle age he distinguished himself as a ruler, diplomat and soldier. He was a faithful friend and a wise counsellor. He served as envoy for the Pandavas in their negotiations with the Kauravas. In the Mahabharata battle he drove Arjuna's chariot. And it was he who sang the *Bhagvadgita* (the song celestial), which contains the cream of Hindu philosophy.

Ugrasena, king of Muthra, had a beautiful wife and a demon became enamoured of her. One day, he assumed the form of Ugrasena and had conjugal relations with her; and of this union was born Kansa. Even as a child Kansa was cruel and, coming of age, he fought with his father, imprisoned him and usurped the throne. His oppression became intolerable and the ever-patient earth herself revolted. She assumed the form of a cow and went to the gods for redress of her wrongs. The gods conducted her to Brahma who conducted them to Shiva, who, in turn conducted them to Vishnu. Vishnu promised to deliver the earth of her burden of Kansa and decided to assume human form to destroy him.

Kansa had a sister named Devaki and on the occasion of her marriage with Vasudeva, a noble in the kingdom, a strange thing happened. Kansa himself was driving the bridal car when a voice thundered from the sky: "Fool! The eighth child of the damsel you are now driving shall take your life." Kansa was alarmed and was about to slay Devaki when Vasudeva interceded on her behalf and implored him to spare the lady, and added that he would give over her children to Kansa as soon as they were born. Kansa spared the lady but put her and her husband under guard.

Six children were born to Devaki and Kansa destroyed the little innocents one after another. Devaki conceived for the seventh time. The embryo was Lakshman who, from his celestial abode, descended to the earth to keep Rama company in his incarnation as Krishna, and had to be saved. So Vishnu by his divine power transferred the embryo from the womb of Devaki to that of Rohini, another wife of Vasudeva, and a report of miscarriage was sent to Kansa. Rohini gave birth to the child and he was called Balarama.

Devaki conceived for the eighth time. The embryo grew and Kansa strengthened the guard that watched Devaki. On the eve of the night the child was to be born, the Lord appeared to Vasudeva and told him:

"Tonight will Devaki deliver her son. Take him hence to Yasoda, wife of Nanda, the herdsman. She too will give birth to a child. Placing your child by her side bring hers to Devaki."

At midnight Krishna was born. The guards were fast asleep and the door of the prison stood wide open. Vasudeva took the child and fled towards Nanda's home and the great serpent Shesha went before him as a guide. The Yamuna was in floods but on Vasudeva's approach the waters receded. He forded the river, reached Nanda's house, gained Yasoda's apartments without anyone (not even Yasoda) seeing him, and exchanging the babes returned safely to his prison.

The guards now woke up and hearing the cry of the new-born babe sent word to Kansa who rushed to Devaki's bed-chamber and seized the child. But while raising it to dash it on a stone, the babe escaped into the sky and exclaimed: "Fool! I am Yoganidra, the great illusion. The child that is destined to kill you is born; he is alive and well."

Kansa took fright and shut himself up in his palace. Fearing no more harm from Vasudeva and Devaki he, however, set them free.

Vasudeva took his son Balarama also to Nanda and asked him to bring him up with Krishna. Lest Kansa should try to harm the children, he asked Nanda to leave Muthra and repair to Gokula where there were plenty of pastures and water for the cattle. And Nanda with the children went to Gokula and lived there among his kinsmen, all cowherds.

Kansa finding no way of distinguishing the child destined to kill him, ordered a general massacre of children. His agent Putana, a female fiend, on sucking whose breast children died instantly, offered Krishna breast. Krishna took it and sucked so hard that Putana died on the spot.

Now it appeared fairly certain to Kansa that Krishna was the child destined to destroy him, and a demon was sent to kill him. Krishna was wandering alone in the woods when the demon appeared; and he caught the demon by the leg and dashed his head against a rock. Another demon assuming the form of a huge raven caught Krishna in his beak; but the boy grew hot and the raven released its hold. Thereupon Krishna stamped its nether beak with his foot and turned the other inside out with his hands, and thus destroyed it. Yet another demon came as a huge serpent and swallowed Krishna, but the latter grew to such proportions inside the reptile's stomach that its belly burst open and the serpent died.

Nor were Krishna's activities confined to combating the powers of evil sent against him by Kansa. He was full of childish tricks and played many practical jokes on the milkmaids. He stole butter and milk, and when questioned, accused someone else. He organized children's raids into the orchards of cowherds who were full of complaints against him. Once, while the village girls were bathing in a stream, he stole their clothes, hid himself in a tree and made them come to him naked. He used to delight the girls by playing on his flute, and dancing.

Krishna also cleared the countryside of many demons that haunted it. The serpent Kaliya that lived in the river Kalindi skirting the pastures of Gokula was a menace to the herdsmen and cattle, and Krishna made him depart from the river. One day in a buoyant mood he took the mountain Govardhana and held it as an umbrella over Gokula to save the village from excessive rain caused by Indra.

Reports of the prowess of Krishna reached Kansa and he devised a grand plan for killing the boy. He sent Akrura, one of the few virtuous men in the kingdom, to Gokula with a polite invitation to Balarama and Krishna to go over to Muthra and witness some athletic sports he was organising. Akrura delivered the message but acquainted the boys of the evil designs of Kansa and asked them not to accept the invitation. But Krishna allayed his apprehensions and accepted the invitation. The two boys then proceeded to Muthra in the midst of the lamentations of the Gopis (milkmaids).

On their way a demon named Kesin in the pay of Kansa assumed the form of a horse and attacked the boys. But Krishna fearlessly approached the horse and thrusting his hand into its mouth, caused the animal to swell and burst. Balarama and Krishna then proceeded towards the great city. They were clad in poor clothes and desired to put on better ones before entering the city. On the outskirts of Muthra they met Kansa's washerman who refused to lend them clothes. Krishna killed the washerman and the two boys put on the clothes of Kansa; thus dressed in finery, they entered Muthra.

The lists were prepared and the day for sports was fixed. Two fierce wrestlers were told off by Kansa to kill Balarama and Krishna by fair means or foul, and as an additional precaution an elephant was kept in readiness to trample the boys to death if the wrestlers failed in their attempt. But Krishna slew not only the wrestlers and the elephant, but vanquishing Kansa's guards slew the demon-king too.

Krishna then released Ugrasena, Kansa's father, and installed him king of Muthra. Thereafter, Balarama and Krishna took up their abode in Muthra with their parents Vasudeva and Devaki.

After some years, Muthra was attacked by two demon-kings, friends of Kansa, and unable to defend the city, Krishna and the people deserted Muthra and built Dwaraka, an impregnable fortress that "could be defended by women." From here Krishna fought his enemies and regained Muthra.

As the virtual ruler of Dwaraka, Krishna fought and killed many evil kings, of whom Shishupala is particularly worthy of note, and will receive our attention later. These kings had ravished many women and kept them imprisoned in their palaces, and Krishna, to save them the fate of growing into old maids, married them himself. They were sixteen thousand in number. In addition to these, Krishna married eight other ladies of whom Rukmini, the daughter of Bhishmaka, king of Vidarbha, is considered the incarnation of Lakshmi.

Krishna was the friend and counsellor of the Pandava princes and in the conflict between them and the Kauravas helped them with his advice as he was prevented by a vow from taking active part in the combat. He served as the charioteer of Arjuna and on many occasions it was Krishna's excellent horsemanship that saved that hero from death. In fact, he was considered the "man behind the scene" who directed the military operations for the Pandavas, and Gandhari, the mother of Kauravas, filled with grief at the loss of her beloved sons, cursed Krishna and predicted that he and the whole Yadu race of whom he was a member would perish even as the Kauravas did.

A legend relates how this event took place. Some Yadava boys desiring to play a practical joke on the sage Narada dressed up Samba, a son of Krishna, as a pregnant woman, took him to the holy man and asked: "What child will this woman give birth to?"

"To an iron rod," said the angry sage, "and it will be the cause of the destruction of your race."

The boys took the words of Narada as a joke but Samba began to show actual signs of pregnancy. In due time he delivered an iron rod and king Ugrasena ordered it to be ground to powder and thrown into the sea. The rod was practically ground to powder but a small portion could not be broken and this, together with the dust, was thrown into the sea. The iron dust was washed ashore and grew into rushes. The unbroken piece was swallowed by a fish which was caught by a fisherman. The fisherman sold the piece of iron found in the belly of the fish to a hunter named Jara and the latter made it into an arrow point.

Krishna was now informed by the gods of the impending destruction of the race. Trying to save his people Krishna advised them to leave Dwaraka and migrate to a place called Prabhasa. The citizens started for Prabhasa but on their way halted by the seashore and indulged in liquor and merry-making. A quarrel broke out between two drunkards which soon spread to the whole camp. Krishna and Balarama tried to make peace but could not succeed. The fight became violent and the combatants seized for arms the rushes that grew out of the iron dust, and the whole race of Yadus, except Balarama and Krishna, perished on the fatal day. The two brothers then proceeded to a forest nearby, and while they were sitting on a rock, a serpent crawled out of the mouth of Balarama—the serpent Shesha of whom he was, according to some accounts, the incarnation—leaving the lifeless body on the rock. The lone Krishna now sat on the riverbank meditating on the sadness of life, and the hunter Jara, who was wandering in the forest in search of game, mistook him for a deer and shot him with the fatal arrow made of the cursed rod. And Krishna, the last but by no means the least of the Yadavas, died.

9. THE BUDDHA

Myths connected with the Buddha will be noticed in Part II. It may, however, be mentioned here how the Buddha who taught doctrines considered heretical by orthodox Hindus came to be honoured as an Avatar of Vishnu. "The Brahmanical writers," observes Rev. Wilkins,* "were far too shrewd to admit that one who exerted such immense influence and won so many disciples could be other than an incarnation of the deity; but as his teaching was opposed to their own, they cleverly say that it was to mislead the enemies of the gods that he promulgated his doctrine, that they, becoming weak and wicked through error, might be led once again to seek the help and blessing of those whom they had previously neglected."

"At the commencement of the Kaliyuga," says the *Bhagbata*, "will Vishnu become incarnate in Kikata, under the name of Buddha, the son of Jina, for the purpose of deluding the enemies of the gods."

In the *Skanda Purana* the doctrines he taught are thus summarized: "Vishnu as the Buddha taught that the universe was without a creator; it is false therefore to assert that there is one universal and supreme spirit, for Brahma, Vishnu and Shiva and the rest are names of mere corporeal beings like ourselves. Death is a peaceful sleep, why fear it? .... He also taught that pleasure is the only heaven and pain the only hell, and liberation from ignorance the only beatitude. Sacrifices are acts of folly." Lakshmi is also mentioned as having assumed the form of a woman and taught the female disciples "to place all happiness in sexual pleasures; as the body must decay let us, before it becomes dust, enjoy the pleasure it gives."

While it it true that the Buddha repudiated the sanctions of caste, preached the futility of sacrifices and passed the Deity by, he was, as will be seen later, anything but a hedonist.

* *Hindu Mythology*.

10. KALKI

As noticed elsewhere (page 10), according to a Hindu legend the end of the world will be brought about by Vishnu in his Avatar as Kalki. In the *Vishnu Purana* the need for destroying the world and building it anew is thus vividly described: "The kings of the earth will be of churlish spirit, violent temper and ever addicted to falsehood and wickedness. They will inflict death on women, children, and cows; they will seize the property of subjects, be of limited power, and will, for the most part, rapidly rise and fall; their lives will be short, their desires insatiable, and they will display but little piety. The people of various countries intermingling with them will follow their example; and barbarians being powerful in the patronage of princes, whilst purer tribes are neglected, the people will perish. Wealth and piety will decrease day by day until the world shall be wholly depraved. Property alone will confer rank, wealth will be the only source of devotion, passion will be the sole bond of union between the sexes, falsehood will be the only means of success in litigation, and women will be the objects merely of sensual gratification. Earth will be venerated only for its mineral treasures (i.e. no spot will be particularly sacred); the Brahmanical thread will constitute a Brahmin; external types will be the only distinctions of the several orders of life, dishonesty will be the universal means of subsistence, weakness will be the cause of dependence, menace and presumption will be the subterfuge for learning, liberality will be devotion, and simple ablution will be purification. Mutual assent will be marriage, fine clothes will be dignity, and water afar off will be esteemed a holy spring. The people unable to bear the heavy burden imposed upon them by their avaricious sovereigns will take refuge among the valleys and be glad to feed upon wild honey, herbs, roots, fruits, flowers and leaves; their only covering will be the bark of trees, and they will be exposed to cold and wind, and sun and rain. No man's life will exceed three-and-twenty years. Thus in the Kali Age shall decay flourish, until the human race approaches annihilation."

In some measure, it may be mentioned, the description is representative of the present age; but the age in which the author of the *Vishnu Purana* lived was probably no better.

Chapter III

THE HINDU PANTHEON
GODS (Continued)

SHIVA

SHIVA (auspicious) may not strike the reader as an appropriate name for the god of destruction. But as destruction is considered a necessary prelude to creation, the Shaivas hold that the god of destruction is also the god of creation. The essence of existence is dynamic; what is indicated by destruction is the ever-occurring change in the universe. Nothing lasts; everything is in a state of flux, being destroyed and rebuilt. What we consider continuity of existence is in reality constant, gradual and unperceived change. We are not what we were ten years ago; why, a second ago we were different. All things are subject to the ravages of Time and nothing in this universe is permanent. Hence the Shaivas consider destruction as the only real aspect of the Deity.

Although at present the worshippers of Shiva are as powerful as the Vaishanavas, if not more, the name of Shiva is not found in the Vedas. The Shaivas, however, maintain that in Vedic times he was known as Rudra and thus manage to obtain the sanction of the Vedas for the worship of Shiva. He was in all probability a non-Aryan god adopted by Indo-Aryans. Some scholars are of opinion that he belongs to the Indus Valley civilisation.

In the Vedas the following account of Rudra's origin is given: "The lord of beings was a householder and Usha (the Dawn) was his wife. A boy was born (to them) in a year. The boy wept. Prajapati said to him, 'Boy, why dost thou weep since thou hast been born after toil and austerity?' The boy said, 'My evil has not been taken away, and a name has not been given to me. Give me a name.' Prajapati said, 'Thou art Rudra' ... He was Rudra because he wept (from *Rud* to weep)."

Many hymns of the *Rig Veda* are addressed to Rudra. "What can we utter to Rudra," runs one, "the intelligent, the strong, the most bountiful, which shall be most pleasant to his heart, so that Aditi may bring Rudra's healing to our cattle and men and kine, and children? We seek from Rudra, the lord of songs, the lord of sacrifices, who possesses healing remedies, his auspicious favour; from him who is brilliant as the sun, who shines like gold, who is the best and most beautiful of the gods."

In the Puranas, while Rudra is used as a synonym of Shiva, he is also spoken of as a son of Brahma. One myth relates that Brahma by severe austerities propitiated Shiva who was requested to be born of Brahma. Shiva, having already given the promise of granting any boon Brahma desired, agreed, and added a curse by which Brahma lost his fifth head.

The Puranic account of the origin of Shiva is given elsewhere and need not be repeated here.

The habits and appearance of Shiva are somewhat peculiar. He is represented in art as an ascetic clad in tiger skin. He is white in complexion but his neck is black. His matted locks are tied in the coils of a serpent which holds its hood raised over his head. Another reptile adorns his neck and a third one serves as the sacred thread. To enhance his looks Shiva wears a digit of the moon on his head. He has a third eye on the forehead.

Unlike his compeers Brahma and Vishnu, Shiva has no celestial palaces to dwell in. Although he repairs to Mount Kailas to practise austerities where he dwells under a tree, he is more or less a homeless wanderer. The scriptures often speak of him as a wandering mendicant haunting cremation grounds and lonely places accompanied by "ghosts, goblins, witches, imps, sprites and evil spirits." In these expeditions he carries a skull in one hand and a begging bowl in the other. In his martial character he is depicted as holding a trident. Shiva is said to be much attached to the city of Benares.

The *Vishnu Purana* says he was condemned to a wanderer's life on account of the sin he committed in cutting off Brahma's head. The legend relates that Brahma and Shiva were born simultaneously of the Supreme Being and began to fight for supremacy. In the combat Shiva caught one of Brahma's heads by its hair with one hand, and cut it off with the other. But the hand that held Brahma's head was paralysed and it could not drop the head which hung heavily from his hand. While Shiva stood thus weakened, Brahma created a fierce demon and let him loose on Shiva, who, unable to resist, fled and took asylum in Benares.

In this city he was absolved of the sin committed in killing a Brahmin (Brahma is considered the father of Brahmins) and the head of Brahma was severed from his hand. He was, however, condemned, as penance, to live as a wanderer and beg in the streets of heaven for a living.

A myth explains how Shiva came to possess a black neck. In the churning of the milk ocean (Ch. VI) the serpent that was used as the churning rope vomited poison and Shiva, to prevent its dropping into the ocean and poisoning ambrosia, drank it himself; but before it could reach his stomach and scorch it, Parvati (his wife), choked him and the poison got stuck, giving the neck a black hue.

Shiva is also fabled to have received the Ganges in his locks when she descended to the earth from her celestial course, a full account of which will be given later.

The Puranas describe a violent feud between Shiva and Daksha (a son of Brahma) that culminated in the ruin of the latter. Daksha had a lovely daughter, Sati by name, and when she came of age he sent an invitation to all the gods requesting them to come for her Swayamvara (marriage by choice) so that she could wed a god of her choice. He did not, however, invite Shiva as he considered a person of his appearance and habits not a proper match for his daughter. But Sati was an ardent devotee of Shiva and had taken a vow not to marry anyone else. And so, when on the wedding day, Sati entered the hall where the gods were assembled and could not find Shiva, she was sorely disappointed, and imploring Shiva to become manifest and receive the wedding garland, she threw it upwards. Shiva, it is said, appeared there and received the garland. Thus baffled, Daksha gave his daughter in marriage to Shiva with as good a grace as he could command under the circumstances.

This was the beginning of the feud. The next assemblage of the gods took place in Brahma's palace. On Daksha entering, all the gods except Brahma and Shiva rose to receive him. Brahma as the father of Daksha was not expected to rise, but Shiva ought to have risen when his father-in-law appeared. Daksha made his obeisance to Brahma and looking at Shiva obliquely with his eyes addressed the assembly thus: "Hear me, ye Rishis and gods, while I, neither from ignorance nor passion, describe what is the practice of virtuous persons . . . But this shameless being (pointing to Shiva) detracts from the reputation of the guardians of the world—he by whom, stubborn as he is, the course pursued by the good is transgressed. He assumed the position of my disciple, inasmuch as like a virtuous person, in the presence of Brahmins and of fire he took the hand of my daughter who resembled Savitri. This monkey-eyed fellow, after having taken the hand of my fawn-eyed daughter, has not even by word of mouth shown suitable respect to me, whom he ought to have risen and saluted. Reluctantly I gave my daughter to this impure abolisher of rites and demolisher of barriers, like the word of the Veda to a Sudra. He roams about in dreadful cemeteries attended by hosts of ghosts and spirits, like a mad man, naked with dishevelled hair, wearing a garland of dead men's skulls and ornaments of human bones, pretending to be Shiva (auspicious), but in reality Ashiva (inauspicious), insane, beloved by the insane, lord of ghosts, beings whose nature is essentially darkness. To this wicked-hearted lord of the infuriate whose purity has perished, I have, alas! given my virtuous daughter at the instigation of Brahma."

Not content with this vituperation Daksha started cursing and said: "Let this Bhava (a name of Shiva), lowest of gods, never at his worship of the gods receive any portion along with the gods Indra, Upendra (Vishnu) and others." Daksha then left the assembly and went home.

Daksha sat nursing his grievance, and when he performed a great sacrifice invited all the gods except his enemy. But, while Sati was sitting on Kailas she saw throngs of gods passing by the road, and, on enquiry came to know that they were going to attend Daksha's sacrifice. Greatly mortified by the slight, she went to Shiva and asked him why he was not invited. He gave an evasive reply and tried to pacify her by sweet words, but Sati was inconsolable and went to her father's house uninvited.

On reaching Daksha's house Sati asked her father why her husband was not invited to the sacrifice. Daksha fondly took his daughter on his knee and said: 'Listen, my darling, while I explain the reason why thy husband has not been invited. It is because he is the bearer of a human skull, a delighter in cemeteries, accompanied by ghosts and goblins, naked or merely clothed with a tiger's or elephant's skin, covered with ashes, wearing a necklace of human skulls, ornamented with serpents, always wandering about as a mendicant, sometimes dancing and sometimes singing and neglecting all divine ordinances. Such evil practices, my darling, render thy husband the shame of the three worlds and unworthy to be admitted to a sacrifice where Brahma, Vishnu and all the immortals and divine sages are present?" Sati, however, was not to be cajoled and loudly asserted her husband's superiority over the other gods. A lengthy argument followed and Sati, to vindicate her husband's honour, jumped into the sacrificial fire and burnt herself to death.

Shiva, on hearing of his beloved's death, was infuriated and immediately proceeded to Daksha's house.

He produced several demons from his hair and these speedily put an end to the sacrifice. A violent conflict ensued in which Shiva assumed the form called Vira Bhadra and cut off Daksha's head and put his adversaries to flight. Thereafter he took the charred body of Sati and addressed it thus: "Arise, arise, O my beloved Sati! I am Shankara, thy lord; look therefore on me who have approached thee! With thee I am mighty: the framer of all things and the giver of every bliss; but without thee, my energy, I am like a corpse powerless and incapable of action: how then, my beloved, canst thou forsake me? With smiles and glances of thine eyes, say something sweet as Amrita, and with the rain of thy words sprinkle my heart, which is scorched with grief. Formerly, when thou didst see me from a distance, thou wouldst greet me with the fondest accents; why then to-day art thou angry, and wilt not speak to me, thus sadly lamenting? O lord of my soul, arise! O mother of the universe, arise! Dost thou not see me here weeping? O beauteous one! thou canst not have expired. Then, O my faithful spouse! why dost thou not honour me as usual? And why dost thou thus, disobedient to my voice, infringe thy marriage vow?"

Shiva, having spoken thus, kissed the body of Sati again and again, pressed it to his bosom and in a fit of madness began to dance. He danced round the world seven times with the body of his spouse, and the violence of his grief and rhythm began to tell upon the world and its creatures. Vishnu, not knowing what Shiva's mad dance would lead to, cut the body of Sati into fifty pieces and these fell to the earth. The weight of the body now gone from his hand, Shiva came to himself. He was then supplicated by the gods and was pacified. He even repented of his action in killing Daksha and agreed to restore him to life. But in the confusion that interrupted the sacrifice the severed head of Daksha was lost, and in its place he was given a goat's head and restored to life.

Sati was reborn as Uma, the daughter of the Himalayas (hence her other name Parvati, meaning, born of a mountain); but by that time Shiva had become averse to sexual pleasures and Uma had to practise austerities for several years before she could marry him.

The following is the Puranic account of the origin of the third eye of Shiva. One day, while he was sitting on Mount Kailas, Parvati stole from behind and in a playful mood closed his eyes with her hand. The result was catastrophic. The three worlds were plunged in darkness, and devoid of heat and light life began to perish. But a third eye immediately issued forth from Shiva's brow and saved the universe.

Shiva is the god of rhythm and in Hindu mysticism his dance represents the ever-present motion in the universe. In joy and in sorrow he dances. He dances over the dead body of the Asura he kills, the symbolic dance of the ultimate triumph of good over evil. There is a legend of how he danced the mystic dance seeing which the gods and the serpent Shesha were dazed:

"Once upon a time there lived in the forest of Taragam ten thousand heretical hermits who taught anti-Shaivite doctrines. Shiva decided to teach them the truth. He bade Vishnu accompany him in the form of a beautiful woman and the two entered the wild forest, Shiva disguised as a wandering Yogi, Vishnu as his wife. Immediately all the Rishis' wives were seized with violent longing for the Yogi; the Rishis themselves were equally infatuated with the seeming Yogi's wife. Soon the whole hermitage was in an uproar; but presently the hermits began to suspect that things were not quite what they seemed; they gathered together and pronounced quite ineffectual curses on the visitors. Then they prepared a sacrificial fire, and evoked from it a terrible tiger which rushed upon Shiva to devour him. He only smiled and gently picking it up he peeled off its skin with his little finger and wrapt it about himself like a silk shawl. Then the Rishis produced a horrible serpent; but Shiva hung it round his neck for a garland. Then there appeared a malignant black dwarf with a great club; but Shiva pressed his foot upon its back and began to dance, with his foot still pressing down the goblin. The weary hermits overcome with their own efforts, and now by the splendour and swiftness of the dance and the vision of the opening heavens, the gods having assembled to behold the dancer, threw themselves down before the glorious god and became his devotees."*

It is said the serpent Shesha was so enamoured of the dance that he left Vishnu and practised austerities for several years to behold the vision again.

Shiva too like Vishnu has a thousand names of which one of the most popular is Mahadeva (great God). He is known by this name because in strength he is supposed to be greater than all the gods put together. The *Mahabharata* gives an account of how he became so powerful. The Asuras received a boon from Brahma by which they came in possession of three castles which could only be destroyed by the deity who was able to overthrow them by a single arrow. The Asuras then waged war on the gods and no god was mighty enough to send the arrow that could demolish the castles. Indra, the king of the gods, consulted Shiva who said that by transferring half his strength to them the gods would be able to overcome

---

* *Myths of the Hindus and Buddhists*, by Sr. Niveditta **and Dr. A. Coomaraswamy.**

PLATE XVII

43 KUMBHAKARAN DEVOURING THE MONKEYS
(Form *The Ramayana of Tulsidas*
Tr. by F. S. Growse)

42 THE MONKEYS BESIEGE LANKA
(Form *The Ramayana of Tulsidas*
Tr. by F. S. Growse)

PLATE XVIII

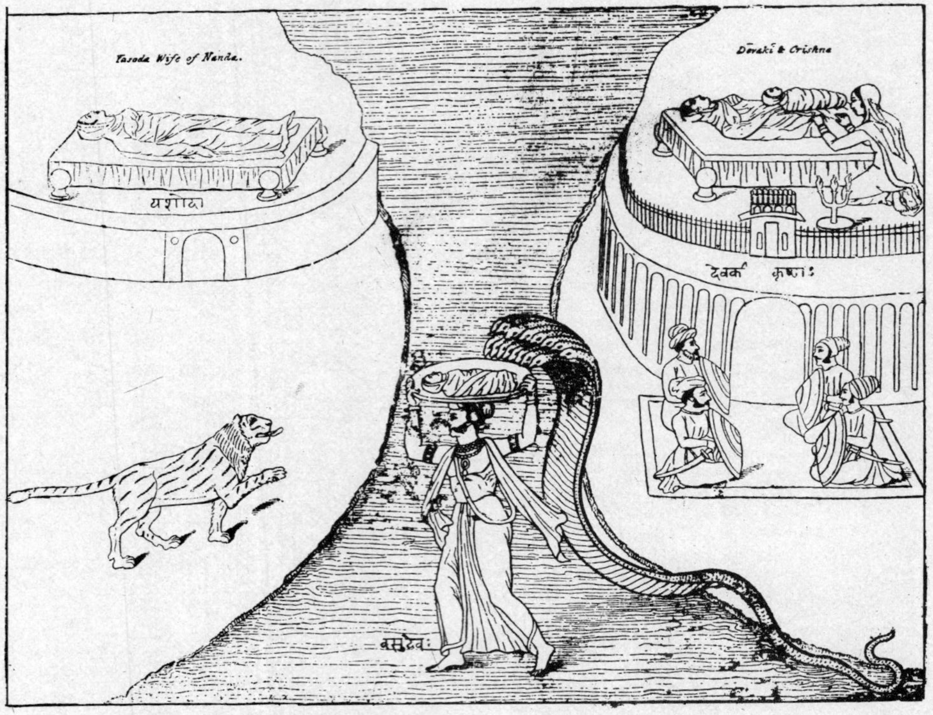

45 VASUDEVA CARRYING KRISHNA TO YASODA
(From Moor's *Hindu Pantheon*)

44 KRISHNA
(From Moor's *Hindu Pantheon*)

PLATE XIX

46   **VISHNU REPOSING ON ANANTA**
(From **Moor's** *Hindu Pantheon*)

47   **CHURNING OF THE MILK OCEAN**
(From **Moor's** *Hindu Pantheon*)

PLATE XX

48 KRISHNA RIDING A COMPOSITE HORSE OF GOPIS
(From *Pictures of Indian Myths & Legends*)

49 KRISHNA SUBDUING KALIYA
(From Halebid. Copyright : Archaeological Dept. of India.)

50 KRISHNA WITH THE MOUNTAIN GOVAR-DHANA
(From Halebid. Copyright : Archaeological Dept. of India)

51 KRISHNA AND BALARAMA KILLING THE WRESTLERS
(Copyright : Archaeological Dept. of India)

PLATE XXI

52 **KRISHNA AND THE GOPIS**
(From Moor's *Hindu Pantheon*)

53 **RASALILA**
(From Moor's *Hindu Pantheon*)

PLATE XXII

54 PARVATI EMBRACING THE LINGAM
(From *Elements of Hindu Iconography* by Gopinatha Rao)

55 WORSHIP OF THE LINGAM
(From a painting by Mrs. Belnos)

56 KRISHNA PLAYING ON THE FLUTE
From Somnathpur. (Copyright: Archaeological Dept. of India)

57 RADHA AND KRISHNA
(Copyright: Archaeological Dept. of India)

PLATE XXIII

DEATH OF BALARAMA
(From *Pictures of Indian Myths & Legends*)

PLATE XXIV

59 KRISHNA PLAYING ON HIS FLUTE
(From South India)

60 VISHNU RIDING ON GARUDA
(From Ajmer. Copyright: Archaeological Dept. of India)

62 VISHNU WITH LAKSHMI & PRITHVI
(Madras Museum)

61 BIRTH OF KRISHNA
(Copyright: Archaeological Dept. of India)

their enemies. But all the gods together could not sustain half Shiva's strength and hence they transferred half of their combined strength to Shiva, who now destroyed the Asuras and retained the gods' strength to himself.

Shiva had on occasions assumed human form. The *Mahabharata* says that he once appeared before Arjuna as a hunter in the manner described below.

When the Pandava princes were wandering in the forests, Yudhishtira, knowing that the quarrel between them and the Kauravas would inevitably lead to war, asked his brother Arjuna to propitiate Shiva by penances and obtain from him a boon of invincibility. Arjuna repaired to the forests of the Himalayas and there practised austerities for many months, living on nothing but air. He raised so much energy by the severity of his penances that the worlds stood in danger of being burnt away. And Shiva decided to appear before his devotee and grant him the desired boon.

One day while Arjuna was in the act of worshipping the Lingam of Mahadeva, a boar rushed at him. He seized his bow and arrows and shot the boar. Arjuna's shaft had scarcely struck the boar when another dart shot by an unknown person killed the beast. Presently a hunter appeared and began to revile Arjuna for having interfered with his sport. Arjuna, on the other hand, thought himself the aggrieved party and a quarrel broke out between the two; they decided to settle it by an appeal to arms. First they fought with bows and arrows and Arjuna, renowned archer as he was, could not get the better of the hunter. Then they wrestled. In the midst of the combat Arjuna suddenly remembered that in his martial zeal he had forgotten to complete his worship, and taking the garland of flowers intended for worship, threw it on the Lingam of Shiva. But the garland fell on the neck of the hunter who was now metamorphosed into Shiva. Arjuna fell down before the god and adored him, and Shiva, pleased with the devotion and physical strength of Arjuna, granted him the desired boon and sent him back to his brother.

Shiva is most widely worshipped in the form of the Lingam (phallus) and this cult will be dealt with in detail in Chapter VIII. The god is often worshipped together with his consort, sons and his Vahan Nandi (bull) but seldom alone.

The Shaivas (worshippers of Shiva) are distinguished especially in South India by the caste-mark of three horizontal lines on the forehead. While the vast majority of Shaivas worship the deity quietly and decently, it must be mentioned that there is a lower order of mendicants, charlatans and mad men who practise various forms of self-torture and infest river banks and streets in India and prey upon pilgrims and women. Some of them sit motionless for days and nights together and others lie down on beds of spikes. They never wash their bodies but smear them with ashes and dirt. Some devotees cut deep wounds in their flesh and others hang down from the branches of trees head downwards. Perpetual motion is the passion of some and they literally walk themselves to death. Disguised as the mendicants of Shiva there are also a large number of common rogues who cheat, rob and intimidate the credulous.

Western travellers are often attracted by these devotees of Shiva and propagandists use them to give India a bad name and misrepresent Hindus to their countrymen.

GANESHA

Next to Vishnu, Shiva and their consorts, Ganesha is the most widely worshipped deity in India. He is represented as having an elephant's head on a human trunk. His Vahan is the rat. Ganesha is the god of prudence and sagacity, and as the remover of obstacles is invoked by all Hindus at the beginning of every undertaking. "If a Hindu builds a house an image of Ganesha is previously propitiated, and set up on or near the spot; if he writes a book Ganesha is saluted at its commencement, as he is also at the top of a letter; beginning a journey, Ganesha is implored to protect him, and for the accommodation of travellers his image is occasionally seen on the roadside, especially where two roads cross . . . It is common to see a figure of the god of prudence in or over banker's and other shops; and upon the whole, there is perhaps no deity in the Hindu pantheon so often seen and addressed."

Although Ganesha is considered to be the eldest son of Shiva and Parvati, the Puranas attribute his origin to one or the other of the couple but not to both. It may be mentioned here that Shiva and Parvati together could not have progeny. The gods fearing that children born of such union would be too terrible to live with requested Shiva not to beget any children. Shiva consented, but Parvati, coming to know of it, was enraged, declared that the wives of other gods also must remain barren like herself and cursed them accordingly. So none of the goddesses could bear children. The so-called sons and daughters of the gods are mind-born children or those produced in some mysterious way unknown to mortals.

According to an account in the *Matsya Purana*, Parvati produced Ganesha to cure her husband of his habit of surprising her while she was in the bath-tub. One day, she "took the oil and ointments used at the bath, and together with other impurities that came from her body formed them into the figure of a man to which she gave life by sprinkling it with the water of the Ganges." She then kept him as the door-keeper of her bathing apartments. Presently Shiva came, and seeing Ganesha was considerably surprised. He, however, tried to force an entry and a quarrel broke out between the two in which Shiva cut off Ganesha's head. When Parvati came out and saw that her son was killed, she gave herself up to lamentations, and to conciliate her, Shiva ordered the first head to be found of any living being to be brought to him. This happened to be an elephant's, and Shiva clapped it on the trunk of Ganesha and gave him life.

In another account of the origin of Ganesha we are told that Parvati worshipped Vishnu for a son and Vishnu himself took the form of a babe and became her son. On hearing of the birth of the child the gods came to congratulate Parvati, and while all the gods looked at the wonderful babe, Sani (the planet Saturn) fixed his gaze on the ground. Parvati asked him why he did not look at her child, and Sani told her that he was under the curse of his wife who, in a moment of jealousy, had declared that whomsoever he gazed on should instantly perish. The proud mother, however, thought that her child was immune from all danger and in her elation, said that Sani could very well look at her child. Sani looked, and the head of the child severed from its body and flew to Vaikunta, the heaven of Vishnu, where it united itself to its original substance. Parvati cursed Sani and the unfortunate celestial became lame. She then began to wail, and to console her Vishnu mounted Garuda and set out in search of a head. He found an elephant sleeping by a river bank and cutting off its head brought it to Parvati who clapped it to Ganesha's trunk, and Brahma gave him life.

The elephant, it must be mentioned, is considered an animal of great prudence and sagacity, and Ganesha's head is probably symbolic of these characteristics of the god.

In the *Varaha Purana* Shiva alone is said to have produced Ganesha. "The immortal and holy sages observing that no difficulty occurred in accomplishing good or evil deeds which they and others commenced, consulted together respecting the means by which obstacles might be opposed to the commission of bad actions, and repaired to Shiva for counsel to whom they said: 'O Mahadeva! God of gods, three-eyed bearer of the trident, it is thou alone who canst create a being capable of opposing obstacles to the commission of improper acts.' Hearing these words Shiva looked at Parvati, and whilst thinking how he could effect the wishes of the gods, from the splendour of his countenance there sprang up into existence a youth shedding radiance around, endowed with the qualities of Shiva, and evidently another Rudra, and captivating by his beauty the female inhabitants of heaven.

"Uma (Parvati) seeing his beauty was excited with jealousy, and in her anger pronounced this curse: 'Thou shall not offend my sight with the form of a beautiful youth; therefore assume an elephant's head and a large belly, and thus shall all thy beauties vanish.' Shiva then addressed his son saying: 'Thy name shall be Ganesha, and the son of Shiva; thou shalt be chief of the Vinayakas and the Ganas; success and disappointment shall spring from thee; and great shall be thine influence among the gods, and in sacrifices and all affairs. Therefore shalt thou be worshipped and invoked the first on all occasions; the object and prayers of him who omits to do so shall fail.' "*

In the *Skanda Purana* yet another account of the origin of Ganesha is given. "During the twilight that intervened between Dwapara and Kali Yugas, women, barbarians and Sudras and other workers of sin" obtained entrance to heaven by visiting the shrine of Somnath, and heaven became overcrowded and hells were without inhabitants. In this predicament Indra and other gods appealed to Shiva for help who asked them to address their complaints to Parvati. Parvati was propitiated and she rubbed her body and "produced a wondrous being with four arms and an elephant's head" who created obstacles to men going to heaven by diverting their longing for pilgrimages (particularly to Somnath) to desire for the acquisition of wealth.

The story was probably invented by some clever priest of Somnath to attract pilgrims to the shrine!

Ganesha has only one tusk; the other was knocked off by Parasurama. This gentleman one day visited Mount Kailas, the abode of Shiva. At the gate he was met by Ganesha who told him that his father was asleep and could not see visitors. Parasurama, however, was in a hurry, wanted immediate audience and asked Ganesha to go and wake up Shiva. Ganesha was of opinion that Parasurama was not a visitor of such great importance that he could distrub his father's sleep, and said so. The two started an argument which led to blows. Ganesha caught Parasurama in his trunk and threw him violently to the ground. Parasurama picked himself up and threw his axe on Ganesha which knocked off one of his tusks.

Now Parvati came on the scene and was about to curse Parasurama when the gods interceded on his behalf, and Brahma promised her that, though deprived of one of his tusks, her son should be worshipped by the other gods.

Ganesha is considered very skilled in sacred sci-

* W. J. Wilking, *Hindu Mythology*.

ences, and is a good scribe besides. It is said that Vyasa dictated the *Mahabharata* to him and he took it down. Before agreeing to be the scribe of Vyasa, Ganesha, however, told the poet that he had no time to waste but should be kept fully engaged. Vyasa, on the other hand, stipulated that the scribe should take down the dictation intelligently. And it is said that while Ganesha pondered over the meaning of the stanza he wrote, Vyasa composed the next one; thus the whole work was written.

It is also related that Ganesha won his wives Siddhi and Buddhi by his learning and logical talents. Both Ganesha and his younger brother Kartikeya fell in love with the ladies and it was agreed between them that they should run a race round the world and the winner obtain the ladies as the prize. Ganesha sat at home, and when Kartikeya returned from his weary travels, proved to him, by quoting extensively from sacred literature relating to geography, that he (Ganesha) had done the world tour and returned much earlier; and then he married the ladies. The fraud was discovered later when nothing could be done.

Ganesha is blessed with a good appetite and is said to be pleased with offerings of piles of edible stuff, particularly fruits.

KARTIKEYA

Kartikeya is the god of war and the generalissimo of the celestial armies. Shiva who used to lead the celestial hosts gave up his military career and took to the practice of austerities, and the gods, without a general, were defeated by the Asuras and driven out of their Kingdom. Indra became a wanderer in the forests, and one day while he was meditating on how to regain his kingdom he heard a cry of a damsel in distress. He proceeded to the spot wherefrom the voice came, and there saw the demon Kesin trying to do violence on a beautiful girl. On seeing Indra, Kesin fled and the girl, whose name was Devasena (army of the gods), asked Indra to find a husband for her. Indra took her to Brahma and requested him to provide a martial husband for her who should also lead the celestial hosts. Brahma agreed and decided that Agni should have a son by the waters of the Ganges.

At that time, the seven great Rishis were performing a sacrifice, and while Agni (the god of fire) issued forth from the sacrificial fire, he saw the wives of the Rishis and fell in love with all of them. But as they were married, respectable women, Agni kept his desire to himself and repaired to a forest to cool his passion. There, Swaha, daughter of Daksha, saw him and fell in love with him, but he loved her not. Swaha, by her divine power, knew that Agni was in love with the wives of the Rishis and disguising herself as the wife of one of the Rishis approached Agni. The virtuous god hesitated for some time but temptation proving too strong he yielded at last. Swaha departed but came again in the guise of another Rishi's wife. Thus she managed to visit him six times and get six "germs" of Agni. These were deposited in a golden reservoir "which being worshipped by the Rishis generated a son; Kumara or Kartikeya was born with six heads, a double number of ears, twelve eyes, arms and feet, one neck and one belly." When he came of age he married Devasena and regained the celestial kingdom from the Asuras.

The *Shiva Purana* gives a different account of Kartikeya's birth. In this work it is said an Asura named Taraka by severe austerities forced Brahma to grant him a boon by which he could only be killed by a son of Shiva. This was the time when Shiva was living without a spouse, Sati having destroyed herself in Daksha's sacrificial fire. Taraka was well aware of Shiva's ascetic leanings and was over-confident that the god would not marry again. So, after receiving the boon from Brahma "he became so arrogant that Indra was forced to yield to him the white-headed horse Uchchaisravas; Kubera gave up his thousand sea-horses; the Rishis were compelled to resign the cow Kamadhenu that yielded everything that could be wished; the sun in dread gave no heat and the moon in terror remained always full; the wind blew as Taraka dictated."

So the tyrannical Asura had to be destroyed and for this purpose it was necessary to make Shiva marry. Sati was reborn as Uma, the daughter of the Himalayas, and began to practise devotions to propitiate Shiva and marry him. But this god sat immersed in meditation and was insensible to the supplications of the devotee. Indra, becoming desperate, asked Kama, the god of love, to proceed to Kailas and by his art raise sexual desire in Shiva. Kama reluctantly undertook the mission as it was pretty certain that anyone who disturbed the Great God in his meditation would not get away with it. He, however, proceeded with his wife Rati (passion) and friend Vasantam (spring) to Kailas, where he saw the Great God seated on a tiger skin with his eyes closed, hands resting on the thighs, lost in meditation, calm and majestic as an ocean without a ripple on its surface. Wind itself dared not disturb the god, and the leaves of the trees remained still. There was perfect silence and quiet all around and the courage of the god of love failed him. At that moment Uma came in the neighbourhood and, while gathering flowers, she showed an excellent profile to Mahadeva, and Kama, emboldened by her beauty, shot his arrow laden with love. The shaft struck Mahadeva and he woke up from his Samadhi (meditation) "like a sea suddenly troubled by a storm." He looked for the cause of the disturbance of his Samadhi and saw the god of love slinking away with his bow and arrows. Shiva in his wrath opened his third eye and burnt Kama to ashes.

The shaft of Kama had no other effect than that of disturbing Shiva, and Uma had to practise severe austerities for years before she was marrried to him. Even after the marriage the couple had no progeny, and the gods in their distress sent Agni to Mahadeva as their spokesman. Agni reached Kailas at an opportune moment when Shiva had just left his wife. Assuming the shape of a dove he managed to get a "germ" of Mahadeva and with it proceeded to Indra. But unable to support "the germ" he dropped it in the Ganges "on the banks of which river arose a boy, beautiful as the moon and bright as the sun, who was called Agnibhuva, Skanda and Kartikeya."

"It happened that six daughters (the Pleiads) of as many Rajahs, coming to bathe, saw the boy and each called him her son, and offering the breast, the child assumed to himself six mouths and received nurture from each; whence he is called Shashtimatriya (having six mothers). But in fact, the child had no mother for he came from his father alone."

In course of time a conflict ensued between Kartikeya and Taraka in which the demon was slain.

Kartikeya is widely worshipped, particularly in South India, where he is better known as Subrahmanya. In Maharashtra, Kartikeya is usually considered a misogynist and a bachelor (hence his name Kumara), and women are not allowed to worship at his shrines; in fact the unlucky woman who visits Kartikeya's shrine is feared to lose her husband and suffer widowhood in seven successive rebirths. In other regions, he is not, however, considered celibate and is even worshipped with his consorts; as already noticed he is said to have married Devasena and wooed Siddhi and Buddhi. Some accounts even make him the husband of several wives. Kartikeya's Vahan is the peacock.

INDRA

In Vedic times Indra was the most important deity of the pantheon. More hymns are addressed to him in the *Rig Veda* than to any other single deity. The following extracts from an invocation in the *Rig Veda* will give the reader a fair idea of the position he occupied in the Vedic Pantheon:

"Thou hast grasped in thine arms the iron thunderbolt; thou hast placed the sun in the sky to be viewed (dwelling) on further side of this atmospheric world, deriving thy power from thyself, daring in spirit; thou for our advantage, hast made the earth the counterpart of thy energy; encompassing the waters and the sky thou reachest up to heaven. Thou art the counterpart of the earth, the lord of the lofty sky, with its exalted heroes. Thou hast filled the whole atmosphere with thy greatness. Truly there is none other like unto thee, whose vastness neither heaven and earth have equalled, nor the rivers of the atmosphere have attained its limit, nor when, in his exhilaration, he fought against the appropriator of the rain; thou alone hast made everything else in due succession.

"I declare the mighty deeds of this mighty one. At the Trikadruka festival Indra drank of the Soma, and in its exhilaration he slew Ahi. He propped up the vast sky in empty space; he hath filled the two worlds and the atmosphere; he hath upheld the earth, and stretched it out. Indra has done these things in the exhilaration of the Soma. He hath meted out with his measure the eastern regions like a house; with his thunderbolt he has opened up the sources of the rivers.

"Let us worship, with reverence, the mighty Indra, the powerful, the exalted, the undecaying, the youthful. The beloved worlds (heaven and earth) have not measured nor do they (now) measure the greatness of this adorable being. Many are the excellent works which Indra has done; not all the gods are able to frustrate the counsels of him, who established the earth, and this sky, and wonder-working, produced the sun and the dawn. O innoxious god, thy greatness has been veritable since that time, when as soon as thou wast born, thou didst drink the Soma. Neither the heavens nor the days, nor the months, nor the season can resist the energy of thee (who art) mighty."

In the Vedas, Indra is often spoken of as the god of rain and lightning and his weapon as the thunderbolt with which he slew the demon of drought and caused the clouds to release their waters.

In the Puranas Indra is given a place subordinate to that of the members of the Trinity and their consorts and sons, but as the king of the celestials he occupies a unique position in the pantheon. Indra, in the Puranas, is not the name of a deity but a title for the king of the gods. The life of one Indra is said to be a hundred divine years (one divine year is equivalent to three hundred and sixty earth years) after which period a god or even a meritorious mortal is raised to the throne. The surest way for anyone to become Indra is to perform one hundred sacrifices on the completion of which the reigning Indra has to abdicate. The Puranas relate that some mortals tried to perform these sacrifices and Indra frustrated their attempts by stealing the victims of the sacrifices. By austerities also mortals can attain to the position of Indra, and it is said that whenever mortals practise austerities the reigning Indra sends the voluptuous dancers of his court to distract them.

Indra, though king of the gods, is not invincible. We have already seen that Bali conquered Indra by sacrifices and drove out the celestials from their kingdom. In the *Ramayana* it is related that Indrajit, Ravana's son, overcame Indra in battle and took him prisoner to Lanka where he served Ravana as a menial.

Indra is the regent of the east. He rides on the white elephant Airavata and possesses the wonderful horse Uchchaisravas both of which rose out of the milk ocean when it was churned for ambrosia. His weapon Vajra (lightning) is deadly, but the rainbow is also considered the visible symbol of a mighty bow he possesses. The name of the reigning Indra is Purandara and he has one thousand eyes. The author of the *Ramayana* (who, by the way, seems to take a peculiar pleasure in narrating the many tales of Indra's weaknesses) relates how he came to possess so many eyes.

Gautama, Indra's Guru (teacher), had a young and pretty wife named Ahalya, and Indra fell in love with her. One day while the sage was out, Indra stole into his house and addressed Ahalya in terms of passionate love. The lady was willing. But before any harm could be done Gautama came home and seeing the two together, cursed Indra who became covered with a thousand marks of disgrace. Indra repented and implored his Guru to forgive him and the good sage changed the thousand marks of disgrace into as many eyes.

This leniency, however, was lost upon Indra. The persevering deity waited for another opportunity and, one occurring, he again sneaked into his Guru's house. Once again Gautama came and saw the two together, but this time too late; the mischief had been done. The angry sage cursed Ahalya and she became a stone. He turned Indra into a eunuch. The gods, however, interceded and Indra, after the performance of a small sacrifice, was restored to manhood. Gautama also declared that Ahalya would regain her lost state when Vishnu should become incarnate as Ramachandra. It is said in the *Ramayana* that Rama, while wandering in the forests of Dandaka, touched Ahalya with his feet and restored her to her former state.

The heaven of Indra is called Amaravati where he holds court with his wife Indrani. All delights and pleasures are found there. Pious mortals go to the heaven of Indra to enjoy the reward of their good actions. The aim of life is liberation; but those who have not done sufficient good deeds to merit it are sent to Indra's heaven, from where, after some time, they are again sent to this earth to be reborn according to their Karma.

AGNI

Agni is the god of fire. If we are to judge the importance of a Vedic deity by the number of hymns addressed to him, he was, in Vedic times, second in importance only to Indra. In the Puranas he occupies a subordinate position, but because of the inherent importance of fire in all Hindu ceremonials and its utility in daily life, Agni to this day is held in great veneration by all classes of Hindus. Agni is also identified with Rudra, Shiva, and Surya (the sun).

"Agni is a lord, protector, king of men. He is the lord of the house, dwelling in every abode. He is guest in every home; he despises no man, he lives in every family. He is therefore considered as a mediator between gods and men, and as a witness of their actions; hence to the present day he is worshipped, and his blessing sought on all solemn occasions, as at marriage, death, etc. In these old hymns Agni is spoken of as dwelling in the two pieces of wood, which being rubbed together produce fire; and it is noticed as a remarkable thing that a living being should spring out of dry (dead) wood. Strange to say, says the poet, the child as soon as he is born begins with unnatural voracity to consume his parents. Wonderful is his growth seeing that he is born of a mother who cannot nourish him; but he is nourished by the oblations of clarified butter which are poured into his mouth and which he consumes."

It is difficult to get a coherent account of the parentage of Agni although in several places his parents are mentioned. In one place he is spoken of as the son of Brahma, elsewhere as the offspring of Dyaus (Heaven) and Prithvi (Earth). According to a third account he is the son of Kasyapa and Aditi, while a fourth one tells us that he is the son of Angiras, king of the Pitris (fathers of mankind).

The reason why Agni consumes everything yet remains pure is given in the *Mahabharata*. The sage Bhrigu, it is said, once carried away a woman betrothed to an Asura, and this person in his search for his beloved went to Agni and asked him where she was, as Agni, in his nature of fire, had access to all places. Agni with his characteristic truthfulness told him where she was and the Asura brought back his beloved. Bhrigu came to know of Agni's part in the affair and cursed him to eat everything pure and impure. Agni remonstrated with him and said that in speaking the truth he only did what was becoming of a god and that the whole attitude of Bhrigu in the affair was anything but proper. Bhrigu was convinced and added a blessing to the curse; accordingly, though Agni was to eat everything, he could still remain pure. Hence even impure things when consumed by fire become pure.

Dr. Muir in the following verses explains the nature and function of the deity:

Great Agni, though thine essence be but one,

Thy forms are three; as fire thou blazest here,
As lightning flashest in the atmosphere,
In heaven thou flamest as the golden sun.

It was in heaven thou hadst thy primal birth;
By art of sage skilled in sacred lore
Thou wast drawn down to human earths of yore,
And thou abidest a denizen of earth.

Sprung from the mystic pair, by priestly hands
In wedlock joined, forth flashes Agni bright;
But oh! ye heavens and earth, I tell you right,
The unnatural child devours the parent brands.

But Agni is a god; we must not deem
That he can err or dare to comprehend
His acts which far our reason's grasp transcend;
He best can judge what deeds a god beseem.

And yet this orphaned god himself survives:
Although his hapless mother soon expires,
And cannot nurse the babe as babe requires,
Great Agni, wondrous infant, grows and thrives.

Smoke-bannered Agni, god with crackling voice.
And flaming hair, when thou dost pierce the gloom
At early dawn, and all the world illume,
Both heaven and earth and gods and men rejoice.

In every home thou art a welcome guest,
The household tutelary lord, a son,
A father, mother, brother all in one,
A friend by whom thy faithful friends are blest.

A swift-winged messenger, thou callest down
From heaven to crowd our hearts the race divine
To taste our food, our hymns to hear benign,
And all our fondest aspiration crown.

Thou, Agni, art our priest: divinely wise,
In holy science versed, thy skill detects
The faults that mar our rites, mistakes corrects,
And all our acts completes and sanctifies.

Thou art the cord that stretches to the skies,
The bridge that spans the chasm, profound and vast,
Dividing earth from heaven o'er which at last,
The good shall safely pass to Paradise.

Thou levellest all thou touchest; forests vast
Thou shear'st, like beards which barber's razor shaves.
Thy wind-driven flames roar loud as ocean's waves,
And all thy track is black when thou hast past.

But though great, Agni not dost always wear
That direful form; thou rather lov'st to shine
Upon our hearths, with milder flame benign,
And cheer the home where thou art nursed with care.

Though I no cow possess and have no store
Of butter, nor an axe fresh wood to cleave,
Thou gracious god with my poor gift receive
These few dry sticks I bring — I have no more.

Preserve us lord: thy faithful servants save
From all the ills by which our bliss is marred;
Tower like an iron wall our homes to guard,
And all the boons bestow our hearts can crave.

And when away our brief existence wanes,
When at length we our earthly homes must quit,
And our freed souls to worlds unknown shall flit,
Do thou gently with our cold remains.

And then thy gracious form assuming guide
Our unborn part across the dark abyss
Aloft to realms serene of light and bliss
Where righteous men among the gods abide."

In art Agni is represented as a red man with three flaming heads, as many legs and seven arms, wearing a garland of fruits. He rides on a ram.

VARUNA

In Vedic times Varuna occupied an important position in the pantheon and was particularly worshipped for his omniscience. The following hymn describes the character of the deity:

The mighty Lord on high, our deeds, as if at hand espies;
The gods know all men do, though men would fain their deeds disguise.
Whoever stands, whoever moves or steals from place to place,
Or hides him in his secret cell,—the gods his movements trace.
Wherever two together plot, and deem they are alone,
King Varuna is there, a third and all their schemes are known.

This earth is his, to him belong those vast and
  boundless skies;
Both seas within him rest, and yet in that small
  pool he lies.
Whoever far beyond the sky should think his
  way to wing,
He could not there elude the grasp of Varuna
  the king.
His spies descending from the skies glide all
  this world around,
Their thousand eyes all-scanning sweep to earth's
  remotest bound.
Whatever exists in heaven and earth, whate'r
  beyond the skies,
Before the eyes of Varuna, the King, unfolded
  lies.
The ceaseless winkings all he counts of every
  mortal's eyes:
He wields this universal frame, as gamester
  throws his dice.
Those knotted nooses which thou fling'st O god,
  the bad to snare,
All liars let them overtake, but all the truthful
  spare.

Later, Varuna was deprived of his omniscient powers and in the Puranas he appears as the god of the oceans. He is said to be in possession of innumerable horses. He also fell from the high moral plane he occupied in the Vedas. It is said that both Varuna and Surya (sun) fell in love with the dancer Urvasi and jointly produced on her Agastya who, in spite of this licentious heredity, became celebrated for his ascetic virtues.

Varuna's Vahan is a monster fish called Makara. It has the head of a deer, legs of an antelope and the body and tail of a fish. Varuna is not worshipped now but is propitiated before voyages. Fishermen also invoke him before venturing out into the sea. All Hindus, however, when they happen to behold the sea fold their hands and mutter prayers to Varuna.

Varuna is the regent of the west.

YAMA

Yama occupies in Hindu mythology the position Pluto does in Greek mythology. He is the god of death and holds charge of the several hells mentioned in the Puranas. In this destructive capacity he is said to be a deputy of Shiva. He rides on a buffalo, attended by two dogs each with four eyes. The dogs assist him in dragging unwilling souls into hell.

Yama has a clerk named Chitragupta who keeps record of the good and bad actions of mortals. When a person dies he is conducted to Yama who calls upon Chitragupta to read out the account of his deeds.

This is read out and a balance struck; and if the balance happens to go against him he is taken to hell where, under the supervision of Yama, he is tortured.

In the Vedas, Yama is said to be the first mortal who died and went to heaven of which he became the monarch. Nowhere in these books is he said to be the king of the nether regions. But then in Vedic times the conception of hell had not fully developed.

In the *Bhavishya Purana* there is an account of Yama's marriage with a mortal woman. He fell in love with Vijaya, the pretty daughter of a Brahmin, married her and took her to Yamapuri, his abode. Here he told her not to enter the southern regions of his spacious palace. For some time Vijaya remained obedient, but afterwards curiosity overpowered her and "thinking that Yama must have another wife" there she entered the forbidden region, and there saw hell and souls in torment; and among the tormented souls was her mother. She also met Yama there and implored him to release her mother. Yama told her that the release could only be obtained by some of her relatives performing a sacrifice. The sacrifice was performed and Yama's mother-in-law was released.

Yama is the regent of the south and hence this direction is considered inauspicious by the Hindus. Death is euphemistically referred to as "going south."

For other myths connected with Yama, refer to Chapter VII.

KUBERA

Kubera is the god of wealth. But he is better known for his acquisitive tendencies than for generosity, and hence Hindus desirous of obtaining wealth do not worship him. He does not seem to care for praises or oblations but is content with his own prosperity and splendour. His city Alaka is considered to be the wealthiest in the celestial regions.

It is said in the Puranas that he was once in possession of Lanka, also the richest city on earth. He came to possess it in the following manner: "Brahma had a mental son named Pulastya, who again had a mental son named Vaisravana (Kubera). The latter deserted his father and went to his grandfather Brahma who, as a reward, made him immortal and appointed him the god of riches with Lanka for his capital and the car Pushpaka for his vehicle."

But he could not retain Lanka for long. This city had been expressly built for the Rakshasas by Viswakarma, and its citizens had deserted it for fear of Vishnu, and it was the city thus deserted that Kubera occupied. Sumala, a Rakshasa, determined to regain Lanka and drive off Kubera, sent his daughter to woo Kubera's father. She managed to marry him and had four sons by him of whom Ravana was the eldest.

Ravana performed austerities and received a boon of invincibility from Shiva. After this he drove off his half-brother Kubera from Lanka and seized his car Pushpaka. This was the car in which Ravana carried off Sita. It is related in the *Ramayana* that sometime after the conquest of Lanka, Rama restored the car to its original owner.

Kubera is the regent of the north. Thus Kubera completes the list of the regents of the cardinal points. There are also regents for the other four points of the heavens, but they are differently mentioned. It is, however, popularly believed that Agni rules the south-east; Nirrita (a Vedic deity of minor importance), south-west; Vayu (the god of wind), north-west; and Isani (a form of Shiva), north-east. Brahma guards the Zenith and the serpent Shesha, the Nadir.

THE MARUTS

Maruts are storm deities who had great importance in Vedic times. In one hymn of the *Rig Veda* they are said to be one hundred and eighty in number, in another twenty-seven. The Puranas speak of them as forty-nine.

In the *Ramayana* it is related that Diti, mother of the Asuras, sorrowed on the death of her sons at the hands of the celestials, and asked her husband Kasyapa for a boon by which she could beget a child who should destroy Indra, king of the gods. Kasyapa granted the boon and Diti conceived. But Indra, coming to know of it, stole to her apartments and "treated her in a very indelicate and barbarous manner, dividing with his tremendous weapon, Vajra, the foetus, with which she was quick, into forty-nine pieces; which at the request of the afflicted Diti, were transformed by Indra into the Maruts or winds."

The leader of the Maruts or rather the essence of the different aspects of wind is called Marut, Vayu or Pavan, who is often mentioned in the Puranas as the god of physical strength.

ASWINS

These Vedic deities are twins, the personification, according to some accounts, of Night and Day. They are not, however, inimical to each other but are very intimate, and in Surya (the daughter of the Sun) have a common wife. They won her in a chariot race in which they defeated the other gods.

In the Puranas Aswins are spoken of as the physicians of the celestials.

TWASHTR

He is the celestial architect, the Vulcan of the Hindus. He is generally commissioned by the gods to build their palaces and lay out their gardens. At times he also works for the enemies of the gods.

In some hymns of the Vedas he is spoken of as the creator of the universe. In the Puranas he is known as Viswakarma and is little more than a skilled artisan.

PUSHAN

The Aryans, while they were nomads, worshipped Pushan, the god of travellers, who protected them from highwaymen and prevented their cattle from straying; many hymns in the Vedas are addressed to him. But when they settled down, they forgot Pushan, and one rarely comes across his name in the Puranas. He was, however, present at Daksha's sacrifice and fought on the side of Daksha; Shiva knocked off his teeth and whenever the Puranas mention Pushan's name he is described as a toothless old god struggling for speech.

The above account of the gods is not complete. Many minor gods and some important ones like Surya (sun), Soma (moon), Kama, Hanuman, etc., remain to be mentioned. These will receive our attention in proper places; in the next chapter we will give some thought to the goddesses.

PLATE XXV

63 DEVAKI NURSING KRISHNA
(From Moor's *Hindu Pantheon*)

64 KRISHNA LIFTING GOVARDHANA
(From Moor's *Hindu Pantheon*)

PLATE XXVI

65 COWS LISTENING TO KRISHNA'S FLUTE
(Ivory: From Trivandrum)

66 KRISHNA WITH THE GOPI'S CLOTHES
(Wood Carving, Madras Museum)

67 SURYA
(From Santal Parganas)

68 VARUNA
(Prince of Wales Museum, Bombay)

PLATE XXVII

69 VISHNU AND LAKSHMI RIDING ON GARUDA
(From Ajmer. Copyright : Archaeological Dept. of India)

70 A SEATED IMAGE OF BALARAMA
(From Khajuraho. Copyright : Archaeological Dept. of India)

71 KING OF THE NAGAS
(From Griffith's *Paintings in Ajanta Caves*)

72 A HINDU ASTROLOGER CALCULATING AN ECLIPSE
(From a painting by Solvyns)

PLATE XXVIII

73 A SHAIVA TEMPLE ATTENDANT
(From a painting by Solvyns)

74 MARRIAGE OF SHIVA AND PARVATI
(From Ellora)

75 THE FAMILY OF SHIVA
(Ivory : From Trivandrum)

76 AN ASCETIC PRACTISING SELF-TORTURE
(From a painting by Solvyns)

PLATE XXIX

SHIVA AND PARVATI ON MOUNT KAILAS
(From Moor's *Hindu Pantheon*)

PLATE XXX

78
SHIVA
(From Colombo)

79 SHIVA DESTROYING AN ASURA
(From Belur Copyright: Archaeological Dept. of India)

80 SHIVA AND PARVATI
(From Khajuraho.
Copyright: Archaeological Dept. of India)

81 NANDI
(From South India)

PLATE XXXI — DANCING DEITIES

82 PARVATI
(Kuruvatti Temple. Photo: India Office Library)

83 GANESHA
(From Mayurbhanj)

84 SHIVA
(Madras Museum)

85 SHIVA
(Madras Museum)

PLATE XXXII

86 SHIVA AND ARJUNA FIGHTING
(Halebid. Copyright : Archaeological Dept. of India)

87 MAHISHASURAMARDINI
From Chidambaram
(Photo by E. S. Mahalingam)

88 SHIVA (AS HUNTER) & WIFE
(Sculpture from South India)

89 SHIVA DESTROYING ASURA
From Art Gallery, Tanjore.
(Photo by E. S. Mahalingam)

Chapter IV
THE HINDU PANTHEON
GODDESSES

WHILE to the layman the male appears the more energetic of the sexes, to the mystic the female stands for the active principle, particularly when ruthless action is indicated. In Greek mythology the Furies, Scylla and Charybdis, are well-known for their destructive propensities. Pallas among the Greeks and Isis among the Egyptians are noted for their active virtues. The Hindus personify the energy of a god and speak of it as his wife (Shakti). While, according to higher conceptions, the Shakti of a god is not separate from himself, for the better understanding of the active aspect of the deity she is brought within the compass of human perceptive capacity and endowed with an entity of her own.

It may be mentioned that mother cults and myths, fairly universal among mankind, are of very ancient origin and most of them can be traced to the matriarchal phase of social development when women held a better position in society than men.

THE CONSORT OF SHIVA

In the consort of Shiva we have a representation of woman in her various aspects. In the preceding chapter we have noticed her in her character of Sati, the virtuous woman and devoted wife, who, to vindicate her husband's honour, immolated herself in fire. In the medieval times many a devoted Hindu widow, as is well known, immolated herself in the funeral pyre of her husband.

Sati was reborn as Uma (Parvati), daughter of Himavan (the Himalayas) and Mena. She was exceedingly beautiful and was over-confident of the affection of her husband who had so madly mourned her death. Hence she gave herself up to singing and dancing, spent her time in decorating her person with flowers and ornaments, and hoped Shiva would come to woo her in due time. But in this she was disappointed. The Great God sat on Mount Kailas immersed in meditation. He had lost all desire for the company of women and had taken delight in asceticism. When Uma saw that her beauty could not attract Shiva she hoped to win his favour by devotion, and began to worship his image assiduously. In this too she failed; Shiva sat insensible to all the supplications of the devotee. She then gave up the world, became contemptuous of physical beauty and began to practise severe penances and starve her body. She lived on air, remained in ice-cold water for days and nights together, and did many other things besides. One day, while she was standing on one leg with uplifted arm, a Brahmin of short stature appeared before her and asked her why she was thus torturing her lovely body. Uma told him that she was in love with Shiva and wanted to marry him. The Brahmin laughed and asked her if she knew that Shiva was an ugly, homeless mendicant of dirty habits, a haunter of cemeteries and an ill-tempered old god besides. Uma said she knew all this and more, and defended the greatness of Shiva. But she was no match for the Brahmin who described Shiva's habits so horribly that Uma could not bear to hear such blasphemy any longer: and she closed her ears with her hands and shouted at the Brahmin. On this the Brahmin stood before her as Shiva, smiling. Uma fell down and worshipped him. He took her by the hand, told her that it was no longer necessary for her to practise austerities and sent her back to her father; Shiva went to Himavan and married Uma in accordance with the prescribed rites.

Uma lived with her husband on Kailas. She is often described in the Puranas as an ideal housewife cheering Shiva with her delightful company and sweet conversation. But there were also domestic quarrels between them. One day, for instance, while Shiva was reading and explaining to his wife some abstruse philosophic point, Uma felt sleepy. When the Great God asked for her approval of his interpretation of the text, he happened to look at her and saw her nodding. He rebuked her for being inattentive. But Uma maintained she was really attentive and had closed her eyes to contemplate the meaning of his words the better, upon which Shiva asked her to repeat the last words he uttered. Poor Parvati could not, and was thus caught red-handed. The angry god cursed his wife to become a fisherwoman. Immediately Parvati fell from Kailas to the earth as a fishermaid.

Shiva, determined to forget so indifferent a wife, assumed his characteristic Yogic pose and began to practise concentration. But he found it difficult to mediate, and his thoughts wandered after Parvati. He made some more attempts at concentration but failed. At last the thought of Parvati became tormenting to him and he decided to regain his lost wife. He asked his servant Nandi to become a shark and break the nets of the fishermen among whom Parvati lived.

Parvati who fell on the seashore as a fishermaid was picked up by the chief of fishers and brought up as his daughter. She was exceedingly beautiful and, when she came of age, all the young fishermen of the village wished to marry her. The depredations of Nandi, in the meantime, had become quite intolerable and the worried chief declared that his daughter would be given in marriage to the person who would catch the shark. Shiva was only waiting for this opportunity. He assumed the form of a fisherman and easily enough caught the shark. And then he married Parvati, and with her went back to Kailas.

There were also other causes of dispute between Shiva and Parvati as it very often happened that Shiva wanted to curse a person whom his wife wanted to bless. On the other hand, the felicity of their domestic life is eulogized at great length in many of the Puranas. All told, the married life of Shiva and Parvati is a faithful representation of the average human family. Parvati is a fond mother, a prudent though somewhat assertive wife, and, like all women, wise and childish at once.

Now we come to the terror aspect of woman personified as Shiva's consort. In this character she is known by various names of which the most popular is Durga. Although in essence she is said to be the energy of Shiva, the Puranas observe that the Durga form of her was produced "from the radiant flames that issued from the mouths of Brahma, Vishnu and Shiva as well as from the mouths of other principal deities," for the destruction of Mahisha (buffalo-demon), an Asura who had conquered the celestial kingdom and driven out the gods from there. It is said she appeared before the gods as "a female of celestial beauty with ten arms into which the gods delivered their weapons, the emblem of their powers." On this occasion she received "from Vishnu the discus; from Shiva, the trident; from Varuna, the conch or shell; from Agni, a flaming dart; from Vayu, a bow; from Surya, a quiver and arrow; from Yama, an iron rod; from Brahma, a lead-roll; from Indra, a thunderbolt; from Kubera, a club; from Viswakarma, a battle-axe; from Samudra, precious stones and offensive weapons; from the milky ocean, a necklace of pearls; from Mount Himalayas, a lion for a charger; and from Ananta, a wreathed circlet of snakes."

Armed with these terrible weapons she proceeded to Vindhya mountains. Here Mahisha happened to see her and tried to capture her. But Durga, at the end of a fierce combat, during which the demon transformed himself into various shapes, pierced him with a spear and killed him.

A story is also told of how she killed Sumbha and Nisumbha, two Asura brothers. These demons performed austerities for 11,000 years and received a boon from Shiva by the power of which they could be slain by no god. After receiving the boon, they declared war on the gods, who in their distress went to Brahma, Vishnu and Mahadeva for protection. Mahadeva advised them to address their complaint to his consort as no god could kill the demons but a goddess could. So Durga was propitiated by a religious ceremony and she agreed to destroy the demons.

Durga then assumed the shape of a woman of celestial beauty and proceeded to the Himalayas where Chunda and Munda, two spies of Sumbha and Nisumbha, saw her. They sent word to their masters of the presence of the lovely lady in the forest, and added that she would be a desirable addition to their women's apartments. On hearing this Sumbha sent a messenger to Durga with a polite invitation to her to visit him and be his wife. Durga told the envoy that she had taken a vow to marry only the person who could defeat her in single combat and added that Sumbha might try his luck. The messenger returned to Sumbha but he paid no heed to the message of Durga and sent his general Dhumralochana to seize Durga and bring her to him. Dhumralochana set out with a huge army but Durga set up a dreadful roar which destroyed practically the whole army and the general. The news reaching Sumbha and Nisumbha, they sent Chunda and Munda to capture the goddess. Durga first devoured the armies of these in easy mouthfuls of thirty to hundred demons, and, after thus destroying the whole army, she caught Chunda by the hair and cut off his head. Seeing this Munda advanced, and was also slain in a similar manner.

Now, Sumbha and Nisumbha themselves proceeded to the Himalayas with an army consisting of legions of demons. Durga produced several goddesses from her locks and a terrible combat between the demons and goddesses took place. The armies of the demons were destroyed by the goddesses, when Sumbha engaged Durga in single combat. Sumbha was slain after a fierce fight; then Nisumbha advanced, but he too was killed. After this, the goddesses celebrated the victory by feasting on the carnage.

It is said she received her name Durga on account of her having killed an Asura named Durga. This demon "conquered the three worlds and dethroned Indra, Vayu, Chandra, Yama, Varuna, Agni, Kubera, Isani, Rudra and Surya." The wives of the Rishis were compelled to celebrate his praises. He sent all the gods from their heavens to live in forests, and at his nod they came and worshipped him. He abolished all religious ceremonies; the Brahmins, through fear of him forsook the reading of the Veda; the rivers changed their courses; fire lost its energy; and the terrified stars retired from sight. He assumed the forms of the clouds and gave rain whenever he pleased; the earth through fear gave an abundant increase, and the trees yielded flowers and fruits out of season. The gods in their distress approached Shiva who conducted them to his wife. Parvati undertook to destroy the demon and created Kalaratree (the dark night) whom she sent to kill him. Kalaratree engaged the Asuras in battle, but after some initial successes was defeated and put to flight. Then Parvati herself came out of Mount Kailas, and a celebrated contest took place. Durga's army consisted of 100,000,000 chariots, 120,000,000,000 elephants. 10,000,000 swift-footed horses and innumerable soldiers. "As soon as the giant drew near, Parvati assumed one thousand arms, and called to her assistance different kinds of beings. The troops of the giant poured their arrows on Parvati, thick as the drops of rain in a storm; they tore up the trees, mountains, etc., and hurled them at the goddess, who, however, threw a weapon which carried away many of the arms of the giant; then he, in return, hurled a flaming dart on the goddess; she turned it aside. He discharged another; but this also she resisted by a hundred arrows. He next let fly an arrow at Parvati's breast; but this too she repelled as well as two other instruments, a club and a spike. At last Parvati seized Durga and set her left foot on his breast; but he disengaged himself and renewed the fight. The beings (9,000,000) whom Parvati caused to issue from her body then destroyed all the soldiers of the giant. In return Durga caused a dreadful shower of hail to descend, the effect of which Parvati counteracted by an instrument called Shoshunu. He next breaking off a piece of a mountain threw it at Parvati who cut it into seven pieces by her arrows. The giant now assumed the shape of an elephant as large as a mountain and approached the goddess; but she tied his legs and, with her nails, which were like scimitars, tore him to pieces. He then arose in the form of a buffalo, and with his horns cast stones, trees and mountains at the goddess, tearing up the trees by the breath of his nostrils. The goddess next pierced him with her trident when he reeled to and fro and renouncing the form of a buffalo assumed his original body as a giant with a thousand arms and weapons in each. Going up to Parvati, the goddess seized him by his thousand arms and carried him into the air, whence she threw him down with dreadful force. Perceiving, however, that this had no effect she pierced him in the breast with an arrow, when the blood issued in streams from his mouth and he expired"*

Durga is represented in art as a woman of gentle countenance with ten arms in each of which she holds a weapon. With one foot she presses on the body of Mahisha and the other rests on her Vahan, the lion, which is depicted as lacerating the body of Mahisha. She wears a crown on her head and her clothes are magnificently jewelled.

The most formidable aspect of the consort of Shiva is Kali who, it is said, destroyed Kal, Time, itself. Kali is widely worshipped in India as the goddess of terror and the lower classes are particularly devoted to her. Most of the devil dances, dark rites and obscene ceremonials practised in India can be traced to her. She is the goddess of epidemics and cataclysms. She is evidently of non-Aryan origin, a relic of aboriginal savagery incorporated in Hinduism as the personification of destruction.

Kali is propitiated by sacrifices of animals and birds. At one time men were also offered to her as victims. In the *Kalika Purana* Shiva tells his sons: "The flesh of the antelope and the rhinoceros give my beloved; and she is pleased for five hundred years. By a human sacrifice, attended by the forms laid down, Devi is pleased one thousand years; and by a sacrifice of three men, one hundred thousand years. By human flesh Kamakshi, Chandika, and Bairavi who assume my shape, are pleased one thousand years. An oblation of blood, which has been rendered pure by holy texts, is equal to ambrosia; the head and flesh also afford much delight to the goddess Chandika."

The proper method of ritual killing of the victim is thus described:

"Let the sacrificer repeat the word Kali twice, then the words Devi, Rajeswari; then *Lawah Dandayai, Namah!* which words may be rendered–Hail, Kali! Kali! hail Devi! goddess of thunder; hail! iron-sceptred goddess!—let him then take the axe in his hand and again invoke the same by the Kalaratriya text as follows: Let the sacrificer say *Hrang! Hring!* Kali Kali! O horrid toothed goddess! eat, cut, destroy all the malignant—cut with this axe; bind, bind; seize seize; drink blood; *Spheng, Spheng;* secure, secure; salutation to Kali—Thus ends the Kalaratriya Mantra."

Bhavani, whom the Thugs used to invoke before starting on their depredatory expeditions, was a form of Kali. Kali is also worshipped in different forms by thieves and many criminal tribes in India.

Kali's insatiable thirst for blood was occasioned by the circumstance of her having killed an Asura named Raktavira whose blood she drank. This Asura had received a boon from Brahma by the power of which

C. Coleman, Mythology of Hindus.

every drop of his blood that fell on the ground became capable of creating innumerable Asuras like himself. Kali in her fight with him held him aloft, pierced him with a spear and drank every drop of blood that gushed from his wound and thus managed to kill him.

Kali is represented in art as a black, half-naked woman of terrible aspect, with claws and tusks, wearing a garland of skulls, her tongue hanging out and mouth dripping blood.

The reason why Kali is painted black is because of her supposed mastery over Time. Shiva as the god of destruction is identical with the all-devouring Time and his distinguishing colour is white. In contrast to him Kali represents the dark abysmal void which is above time, space and causation.

The consort of Shiva is known by many names of which the most familiar are Sati, Parvati, Uma, Devi, Durga, Kali, Bhavani, Anna Purna Devi and Chinna Mustaka. As Parvati and Uma she is generally worshipped together with her consort and sons, but in the more active aspects she is worshipped alone. As the Shaivas worship the Great God in the form of the Lingam, the Shaktas worship his consort as Yoni (the mark of the female); the combined form of Lingam and Yoni representing sexual union, is also worshipped. The Shaktas elevate her to the position of the Primal Mother from whom "everything proceeds, who pervades everything and is conterminous with the Supreme Being himself, who is without beginning or end and is vaster than the universe." As the Supreme Being she is also spoken of as having been worshipped by Brahma, Vishnu and Shiva.

Like Shiva, Kali too is a deity of rhythm. Once, it is said, in her joy of conquest she started dancing and lost herself in the rhythm of the dance. She became mad with the joy of the dance; the worlds stood in danger of collapsing under her feet, and Shiva laid himself before her. She stepped over the body of Shiva when she came to herself.

LAKSHMI

Lakshmi is the consort of Vishnu and is the goddess of wealth and material prosperity. She is fabled to have risen, together with many other precious things, from the milk-ocean when it was churned for ambrosia, and as such is the Hindu counterpart of the Greek goddess of beauty, Venus Aphrodite. Lakshmi, because of her surpassing loveliness is also called Padmam (the lotus). When she appeared on the surface of the sea her resplendent beauty captivated all the gods, and Shiva asked for her hand. But he had already seized the moon that had sprung up from the sea and hence Vishnu pressed his claim for Lakshmi. The goddess herself preferred Vishnu, and Shiva, in despair, it is said, drank poison, which, however, was prevented by the good offices of Parvati, from reaching his bowels.*

The rise of Lakshmi from the sea is thus described:

"Her eyes oft darted o'er the liquid way.
With golden light emblaz'd the darkling main;
And those firm breasts, whence all our comforts well,
Rose with enchanting swell;
Her loose hair with the bounding billows played,
And caught in charming toils each pearly shell
That idling, through the surgy forest stray'd;
When ocean suffered a portentous change,
Toss'd with convulsion strange;
For lofty Madar from his base was torn,
With streams, rocks, woods—by gods and demons whirled.
While round his craggy sides the mad spray curled —
Huge mountain! by the passive tortoise borne.
Then sole, but not forlorn,
Shipp'd in a flower, that balmy sweets exhal'd,
Over dulcet waves of cream Pad-mala sail'd
So name the goddess, from her lotus blue.
Or Kamala, if more auspicious deem'd;
With many petaled wings the blossom flew,
And from the mount a flutt'ring sea-bird seem'd,
Till on the shore it stopp'd—the heav'n-lov'd shore,
Bright with unvalu'd store
Of gems marine, by mirthful Indra wore;
But she, (what brighter gem had shone before?)
No bride for old Maricha's frolic son,
On azure Hari fix'd her prosp'ring eyes.
Love bade the bridegroom rise;
Straight ov'r the deep, then dimpling smooth he rush'd
And tow'rd the unmeasur'd snake—stupendous bed!
The world's great mother, nor reluctant led;
All nature glow'd when'er she smil'd or blush'd;
The king of serpents hush'd
His thousand heads, where diamond mirrors blazed,
That multiply'd her image as he gazed."

Some Puranas speak of Lakshmi as a daughter of the sage Bhrigu. On account of a Rishi's curse on Indra, the celestials had to leave their kingdom and Lakshmi took asylum in the milk-ocean which, when the memorable churning took place, gave her up to the gods again. The *Markandeya Purana* gives yet another account of the origin of Lakshmi and the con-

---
* For a different version of the myth explaining why Shiva drank poison see Chapter VI.

sorts of Brahma and Shiva. According to this account, Maya, the Primal Mother (the creative principle in its feminine aspect) "assumed three transcendent forms in accordance with her three Gunas or qualities, and each of them produced a pair of divinities: Brahma and Lakshmi, Mahesha and Sarasvati, Vishnu and Kali. After whose intermarriage, Brahma and Sarasvati formed the mundane egg which Mahesha and Kali divided into halves; and Vishnu together with Lakshmi preserved it from destruction."

Unlike her sister-in-law Durga, Lakshmi is renowned for virtues we consider feminine. She is ever devoted to her husband and is represented in pictures as sitting on the serpent Shesha massaging the feet of her lord. When Vishnu descended to the earth in his various incarnations, Lakshmi accompanied him. In the Ramachandra Avatar Lakshmi incarnated herself as Sita. As Rukmini she became the principal wife of Krishna. In other Avatars too she assumed appropriate forms and kept her husband company during his sojourn in worlds other than Vaikunta.

In spite of this devotion and constancy, Lakshmi, in her character of the goddess of wealth, is spoken of as fickle. The idea was, no doubt, inspired by the ever turning wheels of fortune.

While Sita is widely accepted as an Avatar of Lakshmi, a myth, obviously Shaivite in origin, speaks of her as an incarnation of Durga. After the conquest of Lanka, Rama, one day, spoke to Sita of the terrible combat that took place between himself and the ten-headed Ravana, and he somewhat emphasized his own prowess; upon which Sita smiled and told him that there was another Ravana with 1,000 heads, and asked Rama how he would like to meet him. Rama enquired about the kingdom of this Ravana and collecting a vast army of monkeys and men marched on his capital. But the 1,000-headed monster ate all his monkeys and men and put Rama himself to flight who came to Ayodhya and related the sad story to Sita. Sita then assumed her character of Durga and fought and killed the demon.

The following passage in the *Vishnu Purana* tells us the benefits that accrue from worshipping Lakshmi:

"From thy (Lakshmi's) propitious gaze men obtain wives, children, dwellings, friends, harvests and wealth. Health, strength, power, victory, happiness are easy of attainment to those upon whom thou smilest. Thou art the mother of all beings, as the god of god, Hari is their father; and this world, whether animate or inanimate is pervaded by thee and Vishnu." In another passage in the same Purana, Vishnu and Lakshmi are thus eulogized: "Sri, the bride of Vishnu, the mother of the world, is eternal, imperishable; in like manner as he is all-pervading, so also is she omnipresent. Vishnu is meaning, she is speech. Hari is polity, she is prudence. Vishnu is understanding, she is intellect. He is righteousness, she is devotion. He is the creator, she is creation. Sri is the earth, Hari the support of it. The deity is content, the eternal Lakshmi is resignation. He is desire, she is wish. Sri is the heavens, Vishnu, who is one with all things, is the wide extended space. The lord of Sri is the moon, she is his unfailing light. She is called the moving principle of the world, he is the wind which bloweth everywhere. The wielder of the mace is resistance, the power to oppose is Sri. Lakshmi is the light and Hari who is the Lord of all, the lamp. She, the mother of the world, is the creeping vine and Vishnu the tree round which she clings. She is the night, the god who is armed with the mace and the discus is the day. He, the bestower of blessing, is the bridegroom, the lotus-throned goddess is the bride. The god is one with all male—the goddess one with all female rivers. The lotus-eyed deity is the standard, the goddess seated on a lotus the banner. Lakshmi is cupidity, Narayana, the master of the world is covetousness; he who knows what righteousness is, Govinda, is love, and Lakshmi, his gentle spouse, is pleasure. But why thus diffusely enumerate their presence? It is enough to say in a word that of gods, animals and men, Hari is all that is called male, Lakshmi is all that is termed female. There is nothing else than they."

Lakshmi is generally worshipped together with her consort. When she is worshipped alone her devotees exalt her to the position of the energy of the Supreme Being. Lakshmi is represented as sitting at the feet of Vishnu in his repose on the snake Ananta, or as flying with him on his Vahan Garuda. Alone, she is pictured as standing on a lotus, her symbol.

SARASVATI

Sarasvati is the consort of Brahma, the creator, and hence is considered the goddess of all creative sciences. She is the patroness of music and poetry. One of her names is Vach meaning word. It is said she invented the Sanskrit language and the Devanagari script. The origin of the intricate science of Indian music is also traced to Sarasvati.

As Vach, she is one of the few goddesses mentioned in the Vedas. In a hymn of the *Rig Veda* Vach describes herself thus: "I range with the Rudras, with the Vasus, with the Adityas, and with the Viswadevas. I uphold both the sun and the ocean (Mitra and Varuna), the firmament (Indra) and fire, and both the Aswins. I support the moon (Soma) and the sun (entitled Twashtri, Pushan or Bhaga). I grant wealth to the honest votary who performs sacrifices, offers oblations, and satisfies (the deities). Me, who am the queen, the conferrer of wealth, the possessor of knowledge, and the first of such as merit worship the gods render universally, present everywhere, and pervader of all beings. He who eats food through me, as he who sees or who breathes, or who hears through me, yet knows me not is lost; hear then the faith which I pronounce. Even I declare this self who is worshipped by gods and men; I make strong whom I choose; I make him Brahma holy and wise; for Rudra I bend the bow, to slay the demon, foe of Brahma; for the people I make war on their foes; and I pervade heaven and earth. I bore the father on the head of this (universal mind) and my origin is in the midst of the ocean; and therefore do I pervade all beings, and touch this heaven with my form. Originating all beings I pass like the breeze; I am above this heaven, beyond this earth; and what is the great one that am I."

Although in the Vedas she is thus described, at present Sarasvati occupies a very subordinate position in the pantheon. Few images of Sarasvati are made, although one comes across many pictures of her in which she is depicted as a beautiful woman riding on a swan or peacock, with a Vina in her hand. Once a year scholars, students and musicians worship her, and books and musical instruments are placed for a day in front of an image or picture of Sarasvati; no reading or playing of music is done on this day. This holiday is known as Sarasvati Pooja and Hindu schoolboys look forward to it with great eagerness as a day of complete rest.

The Puranas, as usual, differ in their accounts of the origin of Sarasvati. As we have already seen some accounts relate that Brahma produced Sarasvati and married her. In one passage we come across the following story of the origin of Sarasvati, Lakshmi and Durga: Brahma, one day, visited Vishnu to consult him on some important matter and they, by their divine power, summoned Shiva to Vaikunta. While the three gods thus sat deliberating, from their combined energy there sprang forth a refulgent feminine form illuminating the whole firmament. Each of the gods wanted to possess her and she divided herself into three, Sarasvati, Lakshmi and Durga.

Although Gayatri is considered a synonym for Sarasvati, one myth speaks of her as the second wife of Brahma. In a sacrifice Brahma performed, he, as a married god, had to do certain rites together with his wife but Sarasvati was found absent. A messenger was sent to call her and she told him that she was busy in her toilet and Brahma could very well wait for some time. The messenger conveyed Sarasvati's message to Brahma, and the god in his wrath asked some of the assembled gods to find another wife for him. They brought to him Gayatri, the daughter of a sage, and Brahma married her and performed the rite. On the belated arrival of Sarasvati there was a terrible row. Gayatri, however, pacified her by her eloquence and agreed to occupy a position subordinate to her. In certain accounts Gayatri is said to be the only wife of Brahma, and Sarasvati of Ganesha.

* * * *

In addition to these principal goddesses, there are other goddesses of minor importance. They are either the wives of Devas (such as Indrani, wife of Indra, Yami, wife of Yama, etc.) who are not worshipped, or those worshipped by a limited number of people and have but local importance (such as Shitala in Bengal, Mariammen in the South, etc.).

Seven goddesses, some of whom already mentioned, constitute a minor pantheon called Sapta Matrikas or Seven Divine Mothers. They are (1) Brahmi, wife of Brahma, (2) Maheswari, wife of Maheswara (Shiva), (3) Vaishnavi, wife of Vishnu, (4) Kaumari, wife of Kumara (Kartikeya), (5) Indrani, wife of Indra, (6) Varahi, wife of Varaha, and (7) Chamundi, a form of Durga. Some accounts mention Divine Mothers as eight and include Narasimhi.

Manasa is a widely worshipped goddess of Bengal and the story of her feud with Chand Sadagar and his ultimate subjection throws an interesting sidelight on how the Aryans were forced to admit into the pantheon non-Aryan deities to whom they were once inimical. Manasa is worshipped in Bengal as the goddess of snakes, and, as such, is evidently of non-Aryan origin, probably a deity of the Nagas, the snake-worshippers. In a Puranic account of her life it is related that she was born of Shiva by a mortal woman. The following is the story of Manasa and Chand Sadagar.

Once upon a time there lived in Champaka Nagar a very wealthy merchant named Chand Sadagar. He was a devout worshipper of Shiva and was contemptuous of Manasa Devi and her devotees. He lived in the suburbs of the city in a palatial house surrounded by a spacious well laid out garden in which grew many kinds of beautiful flowers. To teach the proud merchant a lesson, Manasa let loose some of the snakes under her charge into the garden and they, by breathing poison, reduced the garden to a wilderness. But Chand by his devotion to Shiva had acquired magic powers by which he converted the wilderness to a garden again. Manasa then assumed the shape of a maiden, in beauty surpassing the moon and the lotus. Chand fell madly in love with her and asked for her hand. She promised to become his wife but wanted him before marriage, to transfer his magic powers to her. The infatuated merchant did so, when Manasa assumed her proper shape and asked Chand to worship her. The merchant's love was now turned into hatred and he stoutly refused. Manasa then destroyed his garden again but it had no effect on Chand who decided to carry on the feud at all costs.

Next, Manasa Devi sent serpents to his house and these bit his six sons to death. While Chand was sorrowing for his dead sons Manasa appeared before him and asked him to be a devotee of her. The obstinate merchant again refused.

Chand then set out on a voyage, and, while he was returning home with his ships laden with wealth, Manasa sent a gale into the sea which sank all his ships. Chand was about to be drowned when the goddess appeared before him and promised to save him if he would only worship her. But Chand preferred death. Manasa, however, wanted to convert and not to kill him, and hence saved his life, and he reached the shore. From the seashore Chand proceeded to the city where he was hospitably received by the citizens. But he came to know that Manasa was the tutelary deity of the city and he ran away from the place. On his way he begged for food and got some cooked rice. He placed the rice on the bank of a stream and descended to the water to wash his hands when a rat came out of a hole and ate all the rice. Chand then drank some water, ate some plantain-skins he picked up on the road, and applied to a farmer for a situation as a farm hand. He was employed, but Manasa turned his head; he worked stupidly and was turned out. Again he began to drift along and the hardships he suffered were many. But his hatred of Manasa increased with his miseries. At last, after undergoing innumerable troubles he reached his native city of Champaka Nagar where he resumed charge of his business.

In due time a son was born to Chand and he was named Lakshmindra. When Lakshmindra came of age he was betrothed to Behula, daughter of Saha. Behula's "face was like the open lotus, her hair fell to her ankles and the tips of it ended in the fairest curls; she had the eyes of a deer, and the voice of a nightingale, and she could dance better than any dancing girl in the whole city of Champaka Nagar."

But to the dismay of Chand, astrologers predicted the death of Lakshmindra by snake-bite on his nuptial bed. Chand knew his mortal enemy had planned his son's death and decided to frustrate her plans. He engaged a renowned architect to build a steel-house for his son, proof against attack by god, man, beast or worm. But Manasa appeared before the architect whom she intimidated by threats, and he, as desired by her, left a slit in one of the walls and closed it with a thin layer of metal.

After the marriage ceremony the couple were conducted to their nuptial chamber and, after seeing that no reptiles lurked in the chamber, the steel-door was closed. The marriage ceremony had been long and tiresome and Lakshmindra got into his bed and slept. Behula sat by her lord admiring the beauty of his face when, through the slit in the wall, a small snake crept into the room and grew into a big one. Behula offered the snake some milk and while it was drinking milk she slipped a noose round its neck and tied it to a post. Two other snakes came in, both of which suffered the fate of their predecessor. At last, tired by her long vigil, Behula fell asleep, and a snake crept into the room and bit Lakshmindra. Behula got up in time to see the snake crawling out through the slit after performing its cruel mission.

In the morning, when the door of the nuptial chamber was opened, Chand saw the dead body of his beloved son, and Behula wailing over it. The corpse was taken out, decked with flowers, was placed on a raft and allowed to drift down the river in the hope that some clever physician might see it and bring it back to life. (When a person dies of snake-bite it is believed life lingers in the body for a long time.) The faithful Behula would not leave the dead body of Lakshmindra and she, against the persuasions of all her relatives, sat on the raft by the side of her lord and floated down the river with him. The raft passed by the house of Behula's father, and her five brothers called out to her to leave the raft and go over to them. But she told them that a wife's place is with her lord and floated down the river leaving her brothers to tears and sorrow.

The raft floated down past villages and towns and the corpse began to decay; but Behula left it not. Days passed into weeks and weeks into months. At last, at the end of the sixth month the raft touched ground where Behula saw a woman washing her clothes. A little mischievous boy was playing about her, interfering with her work. The woman caught the boy, strangled him to death and went on with her work. After finishing the work she sprinkled some water over the dead body of the boy and lo! he came back to life! Behula saw the miracle and requested the washerwoman to restore her husband to life. The washerwoman (who was sent by Manasa for the purpose) conducted her to Manasa who promised to bring Lakshmindra to life provided she, Behula, would convert her father-in-law. Behula agreed and Lakshmindra was restored to life.

Lakshmindra and Behula now set out on their way home. They reached Champaka Nagar but stopped at the river-bank and sent for the mother of Lakshmindra. The old lady came and was overcome with joy on seeing her son, and asked them to accompany her. But Behula said they would enter the house only if Chand became a devotee of Manasa. Chand was informed accordingly. The prospect of meeting his long-lost son at last overcame the obstinacy of the man whom no terror could intimidate, and he promised to worship the goddess. It is said he worshipped her on the eleventh day of the waning moon of the same month. Chand, however, offered her flowers with his left hand, his face turned away from the image; but for all that Manasa was appeased, and from that day no one dared to oppose the worship of Manasa Devi.

PLATE XXXIII

90 KARTIKEYA
From Chidambaram
(Photo by E. S. Mahalingam)

91 LINGAM AND YONI
(Copyright: Archaeological Department of India)

PLATE XXXIV

ASCETICS OF SHIVA PRACTISING PENANCES
(From a painting by Solvyns)

PLATE XXXV

93 KUMARA WITH HIS TWO WIVES
From Chidambaram
(Photo by E. S. Mahalingam)

94 PARVATI
(From Colombo)

95 SURYA
From Art Gallery, Tanjore
(Photo by E. S. Mahalingam)

PLATE XXXVI

96 NARADA
(From Chidambaram. Copyright :
Archaelogical Dept. of India)

97 OFFERING OF POISON TO SHIVA
(Copyrigh: : Archaeological Department of India)

98 A FIVE-FACED IMAGE OF GANESHA
(From Bhuvaneswar. British Museum)

99 KARTIKEYA
(Copyright . Archaeological Dept. of India)

PLATE XXXVII

100 INDRA
(From Moor's *Hindu Pantheon*)

101 KHANDEHRAO AND CONSORT
(From Moor's *Hindu Pantheon*)

102 SARASVATI
(From Moor's *Hindu Pantheon*)

103 RAVANA
(From Seely's *Wonders of Ellora*)

PLATE XXXVIII

104 INDRA RIDING ON HIS ELEPHANT
AIRAVATAM
(From Somnathpur, Copyright:
Archaeological Dept. of India)

105 KUBERA
(After Cunningham, *The Stupa of Barhut*)

106 AGNI
(From Chidambaram, South India)

PLATE XXIX

107 SHIVA RIDING ON NANDI
(From Moor's *Hindu Pantheon*)

108 BRAHMA
(From Seely's *Wonders of Ellora*)

109 PARASURAMA
(From Moor's *Hindu Pantheon*)

110
KRISHNA DANCING ON KALIYA
(From Moor's *Hindu Pantheon*)

111 SURYA RIDING IN HIS CHARIOT
(From Moor's *Hindu Pantheon*)

PLATE XL

112 WORSHIP OF AGNI
(From a painting by Mrs. Belnos)

113 KUBERA HOLDING A MONEY BAG
Copyright : Archaeological Dept. of India)

114 A VAISHNAVA
(From a painting by Solvyns)

115 SOME VILLAGE IDOLS OF SOUTH INDIA
(From *Picturesque India* by Martin Hurimann)

Chapter V

SEMI-DIVINE BEINGS AND THE DEMI-GODS OF THE MAHABHARAT

THERE are, in Hindu mythology, beings who occupy an intermediary position between men and gods. Some of them are sainted mortals, some are beings (neither gods nor men) created as such by Brahma and others, incomprehensible creatures who are spoken of in some accounts as subordinate to the gods and in others as their parents. We must bear in mind that according to Hindu conceptions all beings from the highest god to the lowest insect are parts of a whole that is Brahm and can identify themselves with their essence in liberation; and as such it is inevitable that there should be considerable amount of confusion in the accounts of the innumberable celestials mentioned in the Puranas and the epics. To this must be added the fact that the names of these celestials are woven into a maze of astronomic, astral and ethical symbolism.

In the Institutes of Manu we are told that Brahma divided his own substance and "became half male and half female, or nature active and passive; and from that female he produced Viraj." Viraj by austerities produced the first Manu named Swayambhuva who was entrusted with the work of creation. Swayambhuva produced ten beings called Prajapatis, lords of creatures. These Prajapatis are named (1) Marichi; (2) Atri; (3) Angiras; (4) Pulastya; (5) Pulaha; (6) Kritu' (7) Prachetas or Daksha; (8) Vasishta; (9) Bhrigu and (10) Narada. They are said to represent Morality, Deceit, Charity, Patience, Pride, Piety, Ingenuity, Emulation, Humility and Reason, respectively.

These ten Prajapatis "produced deities and the mansions of deities, benevolent genii and fierce giants; blood-thirsty savages; heavenly quiristers; nymphs and demons; huge serpents and snakes of small size; birds of mighty wing; and separate companies of Pitris or progenitors of mankind."

The Prajapatis first created seven Manus or world teachers. As noted in the first chapter, the Kalpa or day of Brahma is divided into fourteen Manwantaras over each of which presides a Manu. We are living in the seventh Manwantara of the present Kalpa and the name of our Manu is Satyavrata. The Manus who preceded him were Swayambhuva (different from the first Manu son of Viraj), Swarochisha, Uttami, Tamasa, Raivata and Chakshusha. The Code of Manu was first promulgated by Swayambhuva, son of Viraj, and revealed to each of the seven minor Manus at the beginning of a Manwantara.

The ten Prajapatis also created seven Rishis celebrated in the scriptures as Saptarshis. They are Kasyapa, Atri, Vasishta, Viswamitra, Gautama, Jamadagni and Bhardwaja. Astronomically these seven Rishis constitute the constellation of the Great Bear. The wives of six of them shine as the Pleiads.

Some of the Prajapatis are also spoken of as Rishis. The meaning of the word Rishi is "sage" and the word is often indifferently used in Sanskrit texts. It may also be noted that Atri and Vasishta are mentioned both among the Prajapatis and the Saptarshis.

PRAJAPATIS

The Prajapatis are fathers of beings and not gods. They are not saviours of souls and hence are not worshipped. They are more noted for their prolific nature than for divine virtues. Although Manu claims for himself the credit of having created them, in some other accounts they are mentioned as having been directly produced by Brahma himself and as such are called the sons of Brahma.

1. Marichi is, according to some accounts, the father of Surya (Sun) and the progenitor of the solar dynasty of kings of whom Ramachandra was the greatest.

2. Atri is the progenitor of the lunar dynasty of kings to which the Pandavas and Kauravas belonged.

3. Angiras is seldom mentioned in the Puranas and occupies an unimportant position among the Prajapatis.

4. Pulastya is the father of Kubera, the god of wealth, who was born of his first wife. He married an Asura lady also, of whom was born Ravana, the king of Lanka.

5. Pulasha is a minor Prajapati seldom noticed.

6. Kritu is another minor Prajapati seldom noticed.

7. Prachetas or Daksha. We have already had occasion to speak of this son of Brahma in his character as the father of Sati and the enemy of Shiva. His goat's head is symbolic of his foolish pride. He had sixty daughters, thirteen of whom were married to Kasyapa, twenty-seven to Chandra (moon) and one to Shiva. It is not known what became of the others.

8. Vasishta is better known as a Rishi than as a Prajapati. It is said Agni related the *Agni Purana* to Vasishta for instructing him in the twofold knowledge of Brahma. Vasishta taught it to Vyasa who is reputed to be the author of the Purana in its present form.

9. Bhrigu. We have already seen elsewhere how this sage in an assemblage of the gods undertook to ascertain who of the members of the Trinity was the greatest. His peccadillo with an Asura lady which led to his cursing Agni has also been related. In the scuffle that took place in Daksha's palace, Bhrigu fought on the side of his brother and Shiva pulled out his beard.

Bhrigu is considered to be deeply versed in religious science. Varuna taught him the science and at the end of the course of his studies Bhrigu meditated on Brahm and recognized food to be Brahm: "for all beings are indeed produced from food; when born they live by food; toward food they tend; and they pass into food."

Not satisfied with this realisation of the Supreme Being, Bhrigu again meditated and discovered breath to be Brahm: "for all beings are indeed produced from breath; when born they live by breath; toward breath they tend; they pass into breath."

Bhrigu, however, did not consider this to be a true realisation of Brahm and again meditated and discovered intellect to be Brahm: "for all beings are produced by intellect; towards intellect they tend; and they pass into intellect."

Bhrigu thought he did not yet realize Brahm truly. So he again meditated deeply and knew Ananda (felicity) to be Brahm: "for all beings are indeed produced from pleasure; when born they live by joy; they tend towards happiness; they pass into felicity."

"Such is the science which was attained by Bhrigu, taught by Varuna and founded on the Supreme Ethereal Spirit; he who knows this rests on the same support; is endowed with (abundant) food, and becomes a blazing fire which consumes food; great is he by progeny, by cattle, and by holy perfections; great by propitious celebrity."

10. Narada is the most interesting of the Prajapatis and is more often spoken of as a Rishi. He is the favourite son of Sarasvati and, as such, is a talented musician and is depicted in art, like his mother, holding a Vina in his hand. He is also fond of fun and frivolity and is never so happy as when witnessing a good fight. When there are no quarrels among gods, men or Asuras, Narada feels somewhat depressed and carries tales so as to engender ill-feelings among people. He is a well-travelled sage and keeps himself in touch with everything that happens in the three worlds. No secret is unknown to him. No one's house is closed to him. Although he is an ally of the gods he is popular among the enemies of the gods too. He visits them often and in their midst poses as a hater of the vanities of the gods and describes himself as a lone outcaste in the celestial region, and goes back to the gods with all the information he wants. He is often employed by the gods as a messenger.

Narada is a gifted speaker, a good humorist and a great conversationalist. No party of gods is complete without him. He is popular among the ladies too. When there are no major quarrels abroad, he repairs to the ladies' apartments of some god, excites the jealousy of his wife with some tale of her husband's activities and thus engenders domestic quarrels and enjoys the fun.

Narada was a great friend of Krishna (the Avatar of Vishnu) and the two used to make jokes at each other's expense. One day Narada boasted in the presence of Krishna of his musical talents and Krishna asked him to play one of his best tunes. Narada did so when Krishna took a log of wood and gave it to a bear; the bear produced better melody from the log than Narada did from his celestial Vina.

On another occasion Narada told Krishna that 16,008 wives were too many even for a god and asked him if he could spare one of his wives as he (Narada) was a bachelor and longed for the company of the fair sex. Krishna readily agreed and told Narada he could take the lady whom he found without her husband. The sage immediately proceeded to the women's apartments and entered the room of the principal wife of Krishna. There he found Krishna enjoying her company. He then proceeded to the next room where he found Krishna again with another wife. The poor sage went to all the 16,008 rooms but found Krishna in every one of them and came away baffled.

SAPTARSHIS

The seven stars of the constellation of the Great Bear are spoken of by the Hindus as Saptarshis (seven Rishis) and the six Pleiads as their wives. To reconcile the difficulty of six women being considered the wives of seven men, the following explanation is given. The seven Rishis and their seven wives formerly lived together in the North Pole. Agni happened to see the ladies and fell in love with them. But he knew they were virtuous women and hence wandered about the world to cool his passion when he was seen by Swaha, daughter of Daksha, who fell in love with him. She came to know of his passion for the Rishis' wives and transforming herself into the form of the wife of every Rishi, except of Vasishta, had relations with him six times. This amour was witnessed by some wandering celestials who circulated slanderous rumours about the ladies and the Rishis drove them away from their original abode to the position of the Pleiads. Arundhati, wife of Vasishta, was not suspected and was allowed to remain with her husband. She is the small star seen near the constellation of the Great Bear.

The Pleiads, we have already noticed, nursed Kartikeya, the god of war, and in that myth they are mentioned as the daughters of six Rajahs. The story has a parallel in Greek mythology according to which Bacchus, the god of wine, was nursed by the Pleiads whom when he came to power, he translated to the heavens. The Greek account says the Pleiads were originally seven, but due to a quarrel one of the sisters left for the North Pole, and she is the Arundhati of the Hindus.

Most of the legends connected with the Rishis are found in the *Ramayana*. They lived in the great forests practising austerities and were the friends or family priests of Dasaratha and Rama. They enjoyed great occult powers and travelled through the three worlds at will. In the Tretayuga in which Rama lived, good men were like gods and the celestials held converse with mortals, and hence the apparent confusion of mortals with celestials. The Rishis and some of the legends connected with them are as follows:

1. Kasyapa. This sage is noted for his prolific nature. Many Devas (celestials) were born of him by his wife Aditi, of whom the twelve Adityas (suns) are the most prominent. He is the father of most of the Asuras too who were born of his wife Diti and hence called Daityas. Garuda, the Vahan of Vishnu, was born of his third wife Vinata. Most of the lunar mansions are, in some accounts, spoken of as the daughters of Kasyapa.

According to certain authorities Kasyapa is a Prajapati. As the progenitor of a prolific family, this title is, in fact, better suited to him.

2. Atri. Already noticed as a Prajapati. His wife in the Pleiads is Anasuya, celebrated for loyalty to her husband.

3. Vasishta. He was the family priest of Dasaratha, father of Ramachandra.

Astrologers watch the movements of Vasishta and Arundhati carefully as their influences are variously modified by their relative positions. Marriages that occur when the two are in auspicious conjunction "are sure to be happy and the couple would live together for a hundred years."

4. Viswamitra. This sage is an interesting personage in Hindu mythology. He was originally a Kshatriya but by austerities became a Brahmin; this is the only case related in Hindu scriptures of a Kshatriya ever having become a Brahmin by merit. The story is thus narrated:

One day Viswamitra went out on a hunting expedition and happened to stray into the hermitage of Vasishta. This Rishi showed him great hospitality and treated him and his retinue to a repast the like of which Viswamitra, king as he was, could not afford to give a guest of his. He wondered how a hermit could come in possession of so much wealth, and, on enquiry, came to know that Vasishta was the owner of the cow Kamadhenu, which was capable of complying with every request of its owner. The king now desired to possess the wonderful cow and offered the hermit a fabulous sum of money as its price. Vasishta refused; upon which the king offered him half his kingdom as the price of the cow. Vasishta again rejected the offer. The king now became angry and decided to drive away the cow by force. Vasishta resented this and the two fought. The hermit by his occult powers created many deadly weapons and put the king to flight. The baffled king now brooded on the impotence of royalty before priestly might and decided to become a Brahmin. He gave up his kingdom, repaired to the forest and began to propitiate Brahma by penances. He stood on one leg gazing at the sun for a thousand years and Brahma appeared before the devotee. But on Viswamitra's telling him what he wanted, Brahma told his devotee that he was asking for the impossible, and disappeared. But Viswamitra could not be put off like that, and he again began to practise austerities of an unheard of nature. Brahma could not sit in his heaven and again made himself manifest. But he told Viswamitra that it was well-nigh impossible for Brahma himself to make a Brahmin of a Kshatriya and gave him a weapon called Brahmastra. Armed with this weapon Viswamitra went to Vasishta and challenged him. The two fought. The Brahmastra was, however, overcome by a more powerful weapon used by Vasishta, and Viswamitra again repaired to the forests to practise austerities. This time he could not be satisfied with anything short of Brahminhood and equality of power with Vasishta, and so Brahma was forced to grant them to him.

It is said that all the worlds recognize Viswamitra as a Brahmin, but not so Vasishta. Although in public assemblies this sage politely addresses Viswamitra as a Brahmin, in private he holds the opinion that even Brahma cannot change the caste of a man, and is contemptuous of the Brahminical pretensions of Viswamitra.

Viswamitra is also mentioned in the Vedas as the seer to whom was revealed the celebrated Mantra "Gayatri", a repetition of which is considered of great merit by the Hindus. The following is the Gayatri:.

"This new and excellent praise of thee, O splendid playful sun Pushan, is offered by us to thee. Be gratified by this my speech: approach this craving mind, as a fond man seeks a woman. May that sun (Pushan) who contemplates, and looks into, all worlds be our protector."

"Let us meditate on the adorable light of the divine ruler (Savitri). May it guide our intellects. Desirous of food, we solicit the gift of the splendid sun (Savitri) who should be studiously worshipped. Venerable men guided by the understanding, salute this divine sun (Savitri) with oblations and praise."

5. Gautama. He is reputed to be the Guru (teacher) of Indra and we have already noticed the peccadillos of the king of the gods with Gautama's wife Ahalya. On one occasion the six Rishis plotted against Gautama and his wife, and persuaded Ganesha to appear before Gautama in the form of a cow and provoke him. Gautama was provoked, he struck the cow with a blade of grass and the cow died. This had the desired effect and Gautama fell into the snare of his brothers.

6. Jamadagni. He was the father of Parasurama and the husband of Renuka. He was killed by the sons of Karthavirya and this made Parasurama swear undying vengeance on all Kshatriyas. (Also see page 18).

7. Bharadwaja. This Rishi had his hermitage in the forests of Dandaka and is mentioned in the *Ramayana* as a great friend and well-wisher of Rama. During the exile of this prince he often visited the hermitage of Bharadwaja. After Rama's conquest of Lanka, Bharadwaja bestowed a boon on the prince by which all the trees from Bharadwaja's hermitage to Ayodhya stood in bloom.

Drona, the celebrated archer who taught the Pandava and Kaurava princes the art of war was the son of Bharadwaja produced in a mysterious manner.

All the Rishis including the Saptarshis are divided into four classes: i.e. "Rajarshi, (royal sage), Maharshi (great sage), Brahmarshi (sacred sage), and Devarshi (divine sage); of these the first is esteemed the lowest and the last highest." This classification is not, however, rigid and a Rishi mentioned as Maharshi in one place is at times described as a Devarshi, Brahmarshi or Rajarshi in another.

In addtion to the Saptarshis there are many other Rishis mentioned in the Hindu scriptures (such as Vyasa, the celebrated author of the *Mahabharata*, Durvasa, a portion of Shiva himself, Agastya, Suka and others). In fact any sage is referred to by the Hindus as a Rishi and in modern times the appellation is used to denote any distinguished poet, philosopher or saint.

Vasus. Among the earliest creations of Brahma are eight Vasus (personifications of natural phenomena) forming a Gana or group of gods. The Vasus are spoken of as solar deities and their names are Ahar (day), Dhruva (the pole-star), Soma (the moon), Dhanu (fire as heat), Anila (wind), Anala (fire as light), Pratyush (daybreak) and Pralihasa (twilight). There are nine of these Ganas, and Ganesha as his name indicates, is the leader of these groups.

Rudras. In the Vedas the Rudras are mentioned as storm deities, companions of Indra. The functions and nature of the Puranic Rudras are incomprehensible. According to the *Vishnu Purana*, Rudra sprang up, half-male, half-female, from the frown of Brahma. "'Separate yourself,' Brahma said to him; obedient to which command Rudra became twofold, disjoining his male and female natures. His male being he again divided into eleven persons of whom some were agreeable, some hideous, some fierce, some mild; and he multiplied his female nature manifold, of complexions black and white."

Pitris or Manes. The Code of Manu says: "from Rishis came Pitris or patriarchs; from the Pitris both Devas and Danavas; from the Devas, this whole world of animals and vegetables in due order." The Pitris are said to be "free from wrath; intent on purity; ever exempt from sexual passions; endued with exalted qualities; they are primeval deities who have laid arms aside." Many ceremonials are performed in honour of the Pitris and they are worshipped in all funeral rites, particularly in the Shraddha, the anniversary of departed ones. "The time most sacred to the manes or Pitris is the dark half of each month; and the day of conjunction is the fittest day."

Siddhas are beings enjoying great occult powers. They are "of subdued senses, continent and pure, undesirous of progeny and therefore victorious over death. They take no part in the procreation of living beings and detect the unreality of properties of elementary matter. They are eighty thousand in number."

Gandharvas are celestial minstrels. The Gandharva is half-man, half-bird.

Kinnaras are the male dancers of the celestial kingdom. In shape they are akin to the Gandharvas.

Apsaras are the dancing girls of Indra's court. They rose from the milk-ocean when it was churned and are of "resplendent and celestial form." But they did not undergo purification and hence no god could wed them. So they became women of easy virtue and dwelt among the Gandharvas. The Apsaras are six hundred million in number; some of the most important among them are Urvasi, Menaka, Rambha and Tilottama. The Apsaras occupy in Hindu mythology the position of the fairies of Western mythology.

The Gandharvas, Kinnaras and Apsaras do not live in heaven but inhabit the valleys of the mythical mountains. They are a law unto themselves in matters moral. They are, more or less, social outcastes and represent the actors, dancers and singers of this world of whom the Code of Manu speaks with supreme contempt.

THE MAHABHARATA

Most of the heroes mentioned in the *Mahabharata*, the great Indian epic of about 100,000 slokas or stanzas in length, are demi-gods. They are either incarnations of gods, or their sons born of mortal women. These demi-gods are best studied with the main story as the background, and hence the story is narrated below at some length. Moreover, no work on Hindu mythology can be complete without an account of the epic battle which symbolizes the ultimate triumph of good over evil. The *Mahabharata* also contains most of the legends and traditions of the race and is known and honoured as the fifth Veda.

While the Dwaparayuga was drawing towards a close, there ruled in Hastinapur (Delhi) a king of the Somavansa (lunar dynasty) whose name was Shantanu. One day he went out hunting and saw by a mountain stream a lady who was beautiful as a nymph. The king fell in love with her and asked for her hand. She agreed to become his queen but made him promise that he would not express resentment at any of her actions.

Shantanu and Ganga (this was the lady's name) lived happily together and a son was born to them. Ganga took the babe in her arms, proceeded to the Ganges and drowned the child in the river. Shantanu saw this unnatural behaviour of the mother and was grieved, but because of the promise he had made to her he said nothing and kept his peace. Ganga gave birth to six more sons and all of them were drowned in the river. When at last, an eighth child was born to her and she decided to drown that child too, Shantanu objected. Ganga then assumed the form of a goddess and said to Shantanu: "Know me to be the incarnation of the Celestial Ganges, the mother of the eight Vasus who were cursed by a Rishi to become mortals. I have liberated seven of my children, the eighth is with you. Take care of him, he will be great and invincible in battle. But you have broken the pledged word and I cannot remain with you any longer." Saying this she flew upwards and disappeared among the clouds.

Shantanu named the child Bhishma and brought him up with great care. The child grew into magnificent manhood and gave promise of a great military career.

Some years passed and Shantanu again went out hunting. He saw beside a village ferry, Satyavati, the beautiful daughter of the king of the fishers, and fell in love with her. But her father would only consent to the marriage if Shantanu promised that Satyavati's son would be made heir to the throne. This the king would not do, for he loved Bhishma dearly and would not deprive his great son of his birthright for the satisfaction of his own love. So he returned to Hastinapur with a heavy heart.

Bhishma happened to notice his father's dejection and, on enquiring of the king's men, came to know the cause of it. The young prince immediately proceeded to the chief of the fishers and told him that he had renounced his right to the throne and Satyavati might be married to Shantanu. But the chieftain did not want any claimant to the throne to appear afterwards and asked Bhishma to remain celibate. Bhishma agreed and took an oath accordingly. After this, Satyavati was entrusted to Bhishma who drove her in his chariot to Hastinapur and presented her to his father. Shantanu was overcome by the nobility of sentiments evinced by his son and blessed him to become invincible.

Shantanu on his death, left a son named Vichitravirya who died soon after his marriage. His wives Ambika and Ambalika then had, according to the sanctions of Niyoga,* relations with the sage Vyasa who was practising austerities in the forest. This sage had matted locks, a beard that reached to his ankles and a stinking body, and appeared loathsome to the young queens. So, when Vyasa embraced Ambika this lady closed her eyes and consequently her child, Dhritarashtra, was born blind; Ambalika turned pale and hence her son Pandu was born pale. Dhritarashtra,

---

* An ancient usage by which a man could raise issue to his impotent or deceased friend or brother by his wife. It will be noticed that the Jews had a similar custom.

because of his blindness, could not become King and hence Pandu, when he came of age, was installed on the throne.

Pandu married Kunti and Madri, but unfortunately could not have conjugal relations with them as he had fallen under the curse of a Rishi. But Kunti before marriage had received a boon by which she could worship any of five gods of the pantheon and beget a son by each. To test the efficacy of the boon she had already worshipped Surya (the sun) and obtained a son named Karna whom she had to cast off as, at that time, she was unmarried. Kunti told Pandu of the boon and with his permission she worshipped Dharmaraja (Yama), Vayu (the god of wind) and Indra in turn and was blessed with three sons, Dharmaputra (Yudhishtira), Bhima and Arjuna. She could obtain one more son but she generously transferred this power to Madri, the second wife of Pandu, who worshipped the twin Aswins, and gave birth to the twins Nakula and Sahadeva.

After the birth of his sons Pandu went out with his wives for a pleasure trip into the forests where, animated by the charm of the forest scenery and maddened by love, he forgot the curse, approached Madri and on touching her, fell down dead. Madri immolated herself on the funeral pyre of her husband.

After Pandu's death Dhritarashtra acted as regent for his sons with Bhishma as the counsellor. The blind king had one hundred sons (called the Kauravas) of whom Duryodhana was the eldest and Dussasana the second. The Pandavas (the sons of Pandu) and the Kauravas were brought up together; the former were more energetic, and in games often beat the latter. And Duryodhana from his very childhood became jealous of his cousins and tried to destroy them by fair means or foul.

When the boys came of age for instruction in the use of weapons, it became necessary to find a competent teacher for them; and one was found more or less by chance. One day while the boys were playing at ball in a field, the ball rolled away and fell into a well. They stood wondering what to do, when they saw a thin dark Brahmin sitting under a tree nearby, and appealed to him for help. The Brahmin took a ring from his finger and threw that too into the well. "Princes," said he to them, "if you promise me my dinner I shall draw the ball for you by means of blades of grass and then my ring with an arrow." The princes promised him not only a dinner but riches for life; upon which he shot a blade of grass into the well, shot others behind it till a chain of them was formed with which he drew up the ball. Then he shot an arrow into the well which returned to his hand with the ring. The children did not know how to reward so great a man, and said so. "Go to your grandsire Bhishma," said the Brahmin, "and tell him what you have seen; he will reward me."

The eager boys went to Bhishma and related to him all that had happened. The great Vasu smiled. He knew that the Brahmin was the renowned archer Drona, son of Bharadwaja, who had come to Hastinapur on a purpose. He sent for Drona and, without asking any questions, appointed him instructor of the princes.

Drona taught the princes the use of various weapons and the boy Arjuna distinguished himself in archery. He singled out this prince and gave him special training in the use of bow and arrow. Arjuna too had a natural talent for marksmanship and he even practised at night. One dark night Drona happened to hear the twang of the bow, and he proceeded to the spot whence the noise came and saw Arjuna practising. He embraced his disciple and said: "Arjuna, thou shalt be great in battle."

On the completion of the education of the princes, in accordance with the custom of the time, a day was fixed for the princes to make a public display of their skills in the use of weapons. Lists were prepared, criers went out proclaiming the date and time of the tournament, and all arrangements were made to accommodate guests and the public.

At the appointed time, Dhritarashtra the king, together with his wife Gandhari, appeared in the Royal Gallery. Bhishma, guests and priests, nobles and ministers then took their seats. The citizens and common people thronged to the public galleries. And amidst the sounding of trumpets and drums, Drona, dressed in white entered the lists with his son Aswathaman, followed by the princes. The princes, on a signal from Drona, dispersed in various directions and shot arrows on the targets previously fixed for the purpose. The aim of every archer was sure and no arrow missed its mark. The sky was clouded with the shafts the princes shot in all directions. After archery a display in horsemanship was given. "The princes leapt on the backs of spirited horses, and vaulting and careering, turning this way and that, went on shooting at the marks." After this, there was a chariot race and the delighted spectators cheered the victors.

Now came the time for single combat. Duryodhana and Bhima entered the arena with their clubs. The two princes fought with equal skill and the enthusiastic spectators took sides, one party cheering Duryodhana and the other Bhima. The feelings among the public and the combatants ran high and Drona, to avoid a serious fight, stopped the contest and separated the combatants. Then Drona silenced the music for a moment and introduced Arjuna to the spectators as the most skilful of his pupils. The young prince acknowledged his teacher's compliment with becoming humility and gave a wonderful display of his skill in archery. "Such were the power and lightness of Arjuna that it seemed as if with one weapon he created fire, with another water, with a third mountains and as if with a fourth all these were made to disappear. Now he appeared tall and again short. Now he appeared fighting with sword or mace, standing on the pole or yoke of his chariot; then in a flash he would be seen on the car itself and in yet another instant he was fighting on the field. And with his arrows he hit all kinds of marks. Now as if by a single shot, he let fly arrows into the mouth of a revolving iron boar. Again he discharged twenty-one arrows into the hollow of a cow's horn swaying to and fro from the rope on which it hung. Thus he showed his skill in the use of the bow and mace, walking about the lists in circles."

Just as the cheering of the crowd was at its highest, an unknown person of noble bearing entered the lists, and there was the sudden silence of expectation. The unknown soldier was Karna, son of Surya, the first-born of Kunti, whom she had cast away. He had been picked up by a charioteer and brought up as his own son. Karna had learnt the use of weapons at the feet of Parasurama to whom he had gone disguised as a Brahmin, as Rama was well-known for his anti-Kshatriya activities. Karna had learnt everything from Rama when the fraud was discovered. Rama in his anger cursed Karna. According to this curse Karna was to be successful in all battles except the last in which the wrong use of a weapon was to lead to his death.

Karna was "tall and well-built, of magnificent bearing, capable of slaying a lion." He wore a shining armour and declared in a loud voice that he could perform all the feats Arjuna had done and challenged him to single combat. Arjuna felt insulted and cried out that Karna would meet his death at his hands. "Speak thou in arrows, prince," said Karna, "as becoming a soldier." The challenge was accepted. Kunti, who recognised her first born, fainted in the Royal Gallery where she was sitting.

Now one difficulty arose for Karna to engage Arjuna in combat. Princes could fight only princes and Karna could show no royal lineage. He was the son of a charioteer. Duryodhana, who was bursting with jealousy on seeing the honours paid to Arjuna, now came forward. He declared that if Arjuna would only fight with a prince, his father, Dhritarashtra, would make Karna king of Anga. To the old king his son's word was law, and he asked the chief priest to step forward and crown Karna king of Anga then and there. The priest did as he was told and Karna was declared king of Anga. Karna and Duryodhana then embraced each other and the former swore that from that day onward he would be the constant friend and companion of Duryodhana.

At that moment a shrivelled old man entered the lists and advanced towards Karna. It was his foster father the charioteer, who came to congratulate his son on his having become a king. Karna publicly acknowledged him as his father and embraced the old man. And then Bhima cried: "Here indeed is a hero! Methinks the whip is the proper weapon to fight with the son of a charioteer." Karna looked towards the sun whom he knew by intuition as his father. His lips trembled to make answer, but before he spoke Duryodhana answered Bhima. "The lineage of heroes," said he, "is ever unknown. They found their own kingdoms and dynasties. What does it matter where a brave man comes from? Even if Karna were of low birth, my friendship has ennobled him. Let him who dares measure swords with Karna."

Now there arose an uproar in the crowd of spectators and the sun went down. The tournament was declared closed and the two bowmen parted without a combat.

DRONA'S REVENGE

Drona had not come to Hastinapur merely to make a living. He had a deep motive in undertaking the instruction of the princes. His special care in training Arjuna was also in accordance with this motive. With the assistance of the princes he wished, in short, to wreak vengeance on Drupada, the Panchala king, who had once humiliated him. The following is the story of their enmity.

Drupada and Drona were educated under the same teacher and, when they lived under the roof of their teacher, were great friends. One day Drona told Drupada of his poverty, and the young prince promised that he would, on becoming king, give Drona wealth and honours. On the completion of their education, the two boys went to their respective parents and practically forgot each other.

Drona was the son of the poor hermit Bharadwaja and found it difficult to make both ends meet. But he put up with his poverty till a son, Aswathaman, was born to him, when, moved by the needs of the child, he left the hermitage to seek his fortune. First he went to his old friend Drupada who was now a king, spoke to him of the good old days of their boyhood, reminded him that he had even promised to make him king of half the kingdom of Panchala and hinted that he, Drona, was in need of his help. Drupada, on the other hand, wondered at the presumption of the Brahmin who, on the strength of foolish promises made in childhood, claimed friendship with the mighty king of the Panchalas, and turned him out.

All the thoughts of Drona were now turned to revenge. He forgot his poverty and applied himself to the study of the science of war, practised the use of various weapons and in course of time became proficient in the art. But alone, he could not punish Drupada and hence he decided to form some powerful alliances; and he hoped to find an ally in the princes of Hastinapur.

According to the usages of the ancient Hindus, students had to give the teacher's fee at the termination of the course of instruction. The fee was paid either in coin or by services whichever the teacher desired. When the education of the princes was over, they asked Drona to name his fee. "Bring ye," said he to the princes, "the king of the Panchalas in chains to me." And he looked hopefully at Arjuna with eyes of affection.

The princes set out with an army and invaded the kingdom of Panchala. Drupada met them in battle but Arjuna by his skill in archery and by stratagem managed to break the ranks of the enemy and capture the king, whom he brought in chains to Drona.

Drona saw Drupada and smiled. He asked the king whether he would now care to cultivate his friendship. Drupada felt deeply humiliated and remained silent. "Whether you desire it or not, Drupada," said Drona, "I wish to be your friend. And lest you should feel lowered by my friendship, I like to be your equal and shall have half your kingdom." Saying this he released Drupada and sent him back to the other half of his kingdom.

It was now Drupada's turn to live for revenge. His mind was filled with wrath against the spiteful Brahmin, and with admiration for the skill of Arjuna. He practised austerities, performed sacrifices and propitiated Brahma who appeared before him and asked him what he wanted. Panchala prayed for a son who would kill Drona and a daughter who would wed Arjuna. The boon was granted; a son, whom he named Dhrishtadyumna, and a daughter were born of Drupada.

THE CONFLAGRATION AT BENARES

Yudhishtira came of age and it became incumbent on Dhritarashtra to give up office and crown him king. But Duryodhana, son of Dhritarashtra, was an ambitious man and desired the kingdom for himself. He prevailed upon his weak-minded father to plan the destruction of the Pandavas. The blind king was much attached to his son, and the desire to see him crowned king overcame his sense of justice, and a plot was hatched to destroy all the Pandavas.

The date of the annual festival held in honour of Shiva in Benares was approaching, and courtiers told off for the purpose began to praise to the Pandavas the beauty of the city of Benares and the splendour of the festival. The five princes very naturally expressed a desire to attend the festival and this was exactly what Dhritarashtra and his evil son wanted. They caused a house to be constructed for the stay of the Pandavas in Benares, and the architect was secretly instructed to fill the walls with inflammable materials. The unsuspecting Pandavas and their mother proceeded to Benares and stayed in the house built for them. But on the eve of the night on which Duryodhana had decided to set fire to the house, a messenger from Hastinapur came to the Pandavas. The plot had been discovered by Vidura, a relative and well-wisher of the Pandavas who lived in Dhritarashtra's court, and it was he who sent the messenger to the Pandavas to inform them of the nature of the house they were living in, and of the intention of Duryodhana to set fire to it that very night.

Purochana, the accomplice of Duryodhana who was charged with the task of setting fire to the house, came to the house as a wayfarer and was allowed to sleep in the verandah. Presently came a group of travellers, an old woman and her five sons, and the princes allowed them too to sleep in the house. The Pandavas kept awake for a long time and Purochana, tired by the vigil, fell asleep. Then the Pandavas set fire to the house and escaped with their mother into the forests on the other bank of the Ganges, unperceived by any of the citizens. In the morning, people saw the charred bodies of five men and a woman, and took them for those of the Pandavas and their mother. All the citizens lamented the death of the noble princes and their aged mother. The jealousy between the Pandavas and the Kauravas was well-known and foul play was suspected; but no one dared to accuse the king. In Hastinapur, Duryodhana put his own interpretation on the death of Purochana. The man, he thought, had drunk and, after setting fire to the house, slept in the verandah. The Kauravas, however, mourned the death of their kinsmen in due form, and rendered the dead bodies royal honours.*

The Pandavas, in the meantime, disguised themselves as mendicant Brahmins, and after meeting with many adventures in the forest, came to the township of Ekachakra where they stayed. Here they came to know that Draupadi, daughter of the king of the Panchalas, was to be given in marriage to the winner in a test of skill in archery. They together with some

---

* The misfortune to the travellers is justified by a legend which purpports to say that they were incarnations of certain detities who could only get liberation in this manner.

PLATE XLI

117 A DOOR FRAME IN VINDHYAVASINI (DURGA) TEMPLE
(Copyright: Archaeological Department of India)

116 DESTRUCTION OF MASHISHASURA
(From Mayurbhanj)

PLATE XLII

118
SRI
(From Java)

119 SCULPTURES OF KALI
(From Ellora)

120
VISHNU AS MOHINI
(From Madura)

121 CHANDIKA
(From Raj-Shahi)

PLATE XLV

129 GANESH   DURGA   KARTIKEYA
(From *Mythology of the Hindus* Charles Coleman)

130 INDRANI
(From Seely's *Wonders of Ellora*)

131 BHAVANI
(From *Mythology of the Hindus* by Charles Coleman)

PLATE XLVI

132
ARDHANARI
(From Moor's *Hindu Pantheon*)

133 DEVI
(From Moor's *Hindu Pantheon*)

134 DURGA BEING WORSHIPPED BY THE GODS
(From Moor's *Hindu Pantheon*)

PLATE XLVII

YAMUNA
(Khajuraho. Copyright : Archaeological Department of India)

SARASVATI
(British Museum)

135 GANGA
(Khajuraho. Copyright : Archaeological Department of India)

PLATE XLVIII

138 THE SAGE KAPILA
(Anuradhapura)

139 PARVATI
(*Indian Art at Delhi* Sir George Watt)

Brahmins of Ekachakra, proceeded to the capital of the Panchala King.

THE MARRIAGE OF DRAUPADI

Drupada heard the report of the death of the Pandavas and was much grieved, for he had, as already mentioned, intended to give his daughter in marriage to Arjuna. Now that he believed that Arjuna was no more, he decided to find a husband for his daughter as skilled in archery as Arjuna himself. So he caused a mighty bow to be made with which the successful suitor for Draupadi's hand had to shoot five arrows in succession through a ring suspended at a great height.

Many were the kings and knights who assembled in Panchala's court to win the beautiful Draupadi. Karna and Duryodhana were there. When all the royal guests had taken their appointed places, Dhrishtadyumna entered the platform with his sister and declared in a voice rich as thunder: "Oh, ye monarchs that are assembled here to-day, behold the bow and the yonder ring! He who can shoot five arrows through that ring—having birth, beauty and strength of person—shall obtain today my sister as his bride." Then he introduced each of the assembled kings by name and lineage to his sister. One by one the kings stepped forward, strung the bow and shot arrows at the mark; but none could shoot even a single arrow through the ring. Duryodhana failed; various other kings renowned for their skill in archery also failed. And then came the turn of Karna, the king of Anga. The great bowman stepped forward and his bearing left none in doubt as to the result. The Pandavas who were sitting among the Brahmins thought that the princess was lost. Karna took the bow strung it with ease and grace, took aim and was about to shoot when Draupadi rose from her seat and cried out: "Let him not shoot! I will not wed the son of a charioteer." Karna smiled a bitter smile, glanced at the sun, threw the bow down and returned to his seat.

Some more kings tried their luck but all failed. When no other suitor of royal blood was left, a person with matted locks, dressed in deer-skin rug, rose from among the Brahmins and stepped into the arena. There was a murmur of resentment among the princes, but the Brahmins cheered him. The general opinion, however, was that the sight of the beautiful Draupadi had deranged the man. But his bearing was impressive and no one stopped him. He stepped round the bow in the act of worshipping it, took and strung it and shot five arrows in quick succession through the ring. The Brahmins cheered him loudly. A Brahmin had beaten all the Kshatriyas at their own game!

Drupada declared that the young Brahmin had won his daughter, and Draupadi acknowledged him as her lord. But the princes felt insulted. They rose up in arms against the Brahmins and Drupada, and a severe conflict ensued in which the Pandavas and the Panchalas vanquished their enemies and put them to flight. The bridegroom then disclosed his identity to Drupada and the king was overcome with joy at finding that the young Brahmin was none other than Arjuna. The Pandavas did not stay in Drupada's court for long but took leave of the Panchala king and returned to their mother who was in Ekachakra. Arjuna was the first to reach her. "Today," said he to Kunti, "I have received in alms something precious." "Good," said Kunti, "but share it as usual with all your brothers." And thus Draupadi came to be the wife of all the Pandavas.

In the scuffle that occurred in Drupada's court Karna and Duryodhana recognised Arjuna and Bhima. They reported the discovery to Dhritarashtra who convened a council of ministers and took counsel. Duryodhana wanted to dispose of the Pandavas by foul methods. Karna was a soldier and he voted for a straight and open fight. Bhisma and Drona advised Dhritarashtra and his son to refrain from their evil activities and recognize the Pandavas' right to the kingdom. After much discussion and argument, the opinion of these elders prevailed and it was decided to divide the kingdom equally and give one-half to the Pandavas. An envoy was accordingly despatched to Yudhishtira, and this prince accepted the offer and returned to Hastinapur with his brothers, mother and Draupadi.

THE GAME OF DICE

The Pandavas, after receiving their portion of the kingdom, built a city which they called Indraprastha and a palace in it, the beauty of which even the gods envied. The palace was built by the renowned architect Mayasura and its flooring and ceiling were of such marvellous workmanship that a visitor could not distinguish crystal floors from water. Duryodhana was invited to see the palace and, while being taken around, he mistook water for a crystal floor and fell into a pleasure bath. Draupadi, who happened to see him, clapped her hands and laughed in pleasant raillery. But Duryodhana felt humiliated and swore in his heart that he would avenge this insult. He went back and plotted the ruin of the Pandavas and of Panchali (Draupadi).

Yudhishtira had a weakness for gambling, and Sakuni, the maternal uncle of Duryodhana, was noted for sharp practice in the game. Duryodhana sent out a challenge to Yudhishtira to play at dice with him. In those days deciding the fate of kingdoms by the throw of dice was a recognized form of contest between kings, and Yudhishtira could not in honour refuse to accept the challenge. Besides, he too loved gambling. So he went to Hastinapur and gambled with Sakuni whom Duryodhana had appointed on his behalf. In the game Yudhishtira began to lose. Whenever Yudhishtira lost a stake, Duryodhana laughed aloud and taunted him. This exasperated Yudhishtira and a madness seized him. He gambled away villages, towns, cities and finally the whole kingdom. Jewels, personal belongings, houses, chariots, horses and elephants were also lost, and he was left with nothing to offer as a stake. Yudhishtira then offered himself and his brothers as a stake, and lost. The mad king finally offered Draupadi and lost her also.

This was Duryodhana's hour of revenge. Draupadi had insulted him in Indraprastha; he would now insult her in the presence of the assembled guests. He sent for her and, when she came, asked his ribald brother Dussasana to strip her naked before the assembly! Dussasana caught her by the hair and clothes and dragged her. The whole assemblage of men sat still as though paralysed by the immensity of the outrage. Draupadi cried aloud to the gods to descend to the earth and save her. In a moment, her weakness was turned into hatred and rage. She looked like the goddess Durga herself. She tore her hair and cried: "I will not tie this hair till it is anointed with the blood of Duryodhana and Dussasana." At that moment Dhritarashtra heard the howl of a jackal in the distance. An ass brayed. The fate of the Kauravas was sealed. A nameless terror seized the old king and he cried out in spite of himself: "Draupadi, my sons have sinned. Ask any boon you desire so that I may expiate their sins." "Grant me my freedom and the freedom of my husbands," she said. "Granted," said the old man, and Dussasana immediately left Draupadi.

Duryodhana now felt troubled. What he had gained in gambling was lost through the folly of the old king. The free Pandavas could become a potent source of danger. So he challenged Yudhishtira again; "a last throw of dice," he declared, "and the chances are equal for you and me. If you lose, you and your people should live as exiles in the forest for twelve years and pass the thirteenth in some city unrecognized by any. If you are recognized in the thirteenth year, you have to pass another twelve years in the forests as forfeit. If I lose, I will do the same."

"Agreed," said Yudhishtira, and the fatal dice were thrown. Yudhishtira lost.

The Pandavas with Kunti and Panchali retired into the forest. During their wanderings in the woods, they had many adventures with men, demons and beasts. They knew that their quarrel with the cousins would inevitably lead to war and hence took care to form alliances with some kings. They propitiated gods by penances and received from them many powerful weapons. The dishevelled hair of Draupadi was also a perpetual reminder of the need for revenge, and the princes kept themselves in training for the coming struggle. In their forest dwellings they were visited by many of their friends of whom Krishna (the Avatar of Vishnu) was one. He was their cousin on the maternal side and was particularly fond of Arjuna to whom he gave his sister Subhadra in marriage.

At last the thirteen years' exile was over, and Bhima and Arjuna counselled Yudhishtira to send word to Duryodhana to return their share of the kingdom or prepare for war. Yudhishtira was a pacifist and did not like to precipitate a war with his kinsmen. Krishna too advised the desirability of an amicable settlement and offered to go himself to the court of Dhritarashtra and plead for the cause of the Pandavas. All accepted the advice of Krishna, and he went to Hastinapur as the envoy of the Pandavas.

Duryodhana in the meantime had not been idle. During his cousins' exile he had made vast military preparations and entered into alliances with many powerful kings. So when Krishna came with his peace offer, Duryodhana very naturally took it as a sign of the weakness of the Pandavas and treated the envoy with contempt. Krishna first asked for Indraprastha and half the kingdom. When this was refused, he asked for five provinces so that each of the Pandavas could rule as the chieftain of a province; this was also refused. Krishna then begged in succession for five towns, five villages and, at last for five houses. The entreaties of Krishna only exasperated Duryodhana who declared that he would not give the Pandavas as much land as a pin-point and in his arrogance asked his men to seize Krishna and whip him. Krishna fought the Kauravas and made good his escape.

The envoy went back to Yudhishtira and reported the failure of his mission. Now no course was left open but to declare war. Accordingly war was declared and all the allies of the Pandavas were informed.

On the declaration of war, Kunti was troubled by strange fears. Karna was her first born and a formidable enemy of her other sons. In the coming struggle either he or her other sons would be killed; that was plain. Hence she decided to disclose his identity to Karna and dissuade him from fighting on the side of Kauravas. One morning, while Karna was walking by the bank of a stream, Kunti accosted him. Karna saluted the royal matron and asked her what she wanted of him. Trembling, she told him the story of his birth and asked him not to fight on the side of the Kauravas. The son of Surya smiled. "Mother," said he, "you have come too late. I owe my position, fame and riches to Duryodhana and I cannot in honour desert him now even for the sake of my aged mother. The call of duty must be answered first. But this much I tell you, mother, I will engage only Arjuna in battle; with the rest of your sons, I have no quarrel. So, in any case you will have five sons, either with or without me. For the rest, well, Heaven alone knows. Now I have to go, mother, God be with you."

Kunti went back to the Pandavas wondering what a strange son Surya had bestowed upon her.

The field chosen for the battle was the plain of Kurukshetra near Delhi. The forces of the Pandavas were put under the command of Dhrishtadyumna, son of Drupada, who marshalled the multitude of elephants, chariots, horses and foot-soldiers in the form of a crescent. The Kaurava forces were marshalled in opposition by Bhishma in the form of a bird on its wing.

All the elders, namely, Bhishma, Drona and others, fought on the side of Duryodhana. They knew well that the cause of the Kauravas was not just, but they were attached to the court of Dhritarashtra and were duty bound to obey the orders of the king. They did all they could to prevent a war; but the old king, dominated by his overpowering son, had decided to wage war, and as soldiers they had to fight for their king. The whole theme of this epic emphasizes in fact, the need for subordinating one's personal sentiments to the exigencies of duty.

When Arjuna saw, arrayed against him in battle, the friends of his boyhood days, Drona his teacher, Bhishma his grandsire and many others whom he loved, the stout heart of the bowman sank, not because of fear but because of the cruel fate that placed him in the position of the potential destroyer of those beloved to him. He threw down his bow, and sat down wondering of what profit was a kingdom to him if it was to be won at such a cost.

Then Krishna, the charioteer of Arjuna, took him by the hand and infused courage into him by revealing the *Gita* (the song celestial) to him. In the *Gita* are emphasized the greatness of duty, the imperishability of the soul and the illusion that is destruction. No man is destroyed. The essence of being is indestructible and the perishable outward body is changeable as clothes. The soldier who kills without malice, without the desire of gain, without personal sentiment clouding his sense of duty, is the highest type of man. Nay, for a soldier to shirk his duty of killing on the battlefield is a sin. "Hence, Arjuna," says he, "stand up, take the bow and fight."

Arjuna's despondency was now overcome and the soldier in him rose again. All was ready for the battle. The signal for action was given, and the fateful struggle began.

The whole day they fought and in the night both sides took rest. Day after day went by, the two sides fighting with all their might. The havoc the arrows of Bhishma worked in the Pandava ranks began to sway the tides of battle. Bhishma was the incarnation of a god and a life-long celibate, and in the three worlds there was not his equal in chariot fight. Whoever came in front of the great warrior met with instant death. Nine days he fought, and it became clear to every one that as long as Bhishma lived there was no hope of victory for the Pandavas. Hence the Pandavas took counsel among themselves. Yudhishtira now remembered that Bhishma had, on the eve of the battle, expressed his sympathy for the Pandava cause, and asked him to consult him if he ever stood in need of his advice. He would now go to Bhishma, and ask him how he could be vanquished in battle!

Accordingly, on the night of the ninth day the Pandavas went into the Kaurava camp (the rules of ancient chivalry permitted such commerce at night; in the Trojan war, it will be remembered, the Greeks and the Trojans often feasted together at night) and sought an audience with Bhishma. The great warrior received his grandchildren affectionately and asked them what they wanted. Yudhishtira reminded him of his promise and asked him how he could be vanquished. Bhishma smiled. He knew his time had come. "Yudhishtira," he said, "you have done well to come to me. I alone know the secret of my weakness. I am invincible by god, man or beast; yet, I will not fight a woman or a eunuch. You know the rest. But beware," he added, "I would not suffer myself to be killed by anyone except Arjuna or Krishna." He blessed his grandchildren and sent them back. Krishna could not fight because of a vow he had taken; so it became the sad duty of Arjuna to shoot the fatal shaft that was to kill his grandsire.

On the tenth day of the combat, while the battle was raging, there appeared before the car of Bhishma Shikhandin, a eunuch, who challenged him. Bhishma laughed. "Shikhandin!" he exclaimed, and stood still. And Arjuna shot an arrow which mortally wounded Bhishma who fell down on the ground. He was taken by the Pandavas to their camp where, after predicting victory to the Pandavas and instructing Yudhishtira in the art of good government, he gave up the ghost, and ascended to his celestial abode.

Drona took the place of the fallen hero. Five days did this general fight. He too was invincible in a straight fight, and as long as he lived no one could defeat the Kauravas. But Drona had a weak spot. He was greatly attached to his son Ashwathaman, and it was the thought of safety of his son that made him fight with irresistible energy. Moreover, there was a prediction to the effect that as long as Drona lived Ashwathaman would be safe.

On the fifteenth day of the struggle, when the battle was raging and Drona was fighting with the might of a god, a rumour went forth that Aswathaman was dead. Drona was dismayed, but so great was his faith in the prediction that he would not believe the rumour, and went on fighting. He could not, however, see his son who was fighting far away from him in the field. "Aswathaman is dead," cried Bhima in his thunderous voice. So did Arjuna and many other Pandava generals. "Liars," retorted Drona, "I can believe none of you. If Yudhishtira tells me, I will believe him, because he is incapable of telling a lie and his testimony can never be false." At that moment Bhima shot an arrow, killed an elephant named Ashwathaman, and Yudhishtira saw it. Presently Yudhishtira came in hearing range of Drona. "Yudhishtira," shouted the fond father, "is my son Aswathaman alive?" "Aswathaman," replied Yudhishtira, "is dead; I mean," he added in an inaudible tone, "Aswathaman the elephant."

Drona's energy left him and he dropped his bow. Dhrishtadyumna, son of Drupada, who was waiting for the opportunity, immediately killed the redoubtable hero who had humiliated his father.

After the death of the two great generals, Duryodhana became apprehensive of victory. But Karna, his bosom friend and the mortal enemy of Arjuna, was still alive. He was now appointed the generalissimo of the Kaurava forces, and the son of Surya fought with extraordinary skill and courage. One by one all the Pandavas except Arjuna came within range of his bow but he disdained to kill them because of the vow he had made to his mother. Karna did not meet Arjuna on the first day of his generalship, as Arjuna was fighting in another sector. But the next day the two heroes met and closed in for mortal combat. Arrows after arrows were shot and the whole army stopped fighting to watch the terrible combat the like of which they had never beheld. Arrows like snakes, arrows like hooded cobras, arrows like birds, whistling arrows, arrows like flames filled the sky and each shaft was cut by a countershaft shot by the opponent. At last, to end the combat, Karna took the mortal arrow given him by Indra, and shot it. But alas! it was the wrong weapon. Karna forgot that a serpent whom Arjuna had once harmed, had entered into it and the arrow when Karna shot it, assumed more speed than the archer gave it. Krishna, the ever-vigilant charioteer of Arjuna, put extra weight into the car and pressed it down, and the shaft that was aimed at the throat of Arjuna sped away with his diadem. The dismayed Karna wondered what had gone wrong. Then the curse of Parasurama came to his mind. The end was nigh. Earth itself now gaped and began to swallow the wheels of Karna's car, and his charioteer cried helplessly. The son of Surya made a supreme effort to fight Fate itself; he jumped from the car and began to disengage its wheels. Arjuna advanced with his bow. "In the name of honour," cried Karna, "do not shoot. All the laws of chivalry lay down that one in a chariot should not shoot an enemy standing on the ground."

"Where were honour and the laws of chivalry when my wife was insulted?" asked Arjuna in derision, and he shot the arrow he had worshipped all along for the destruction of Karna. Karna was cut in twain, and died on the spot. "When Karna fell, the rivers stood still, the Sun set in pallor, the mountains with their forests began to tremble and all creatures were in pain; but evil things and the wanderers of the night were filled with joy."

After the fall of Karna, Duryodhana fought a forlorn battle and was killed by Bhima in single combat. It is said that at the end of the battle not a single one of the active combatants who fought on the side of the Kauravas remained alive. Evil was destroyed in its entirety.

Chapter VI

ENEMIES OF THE GODS

ACCORDING to Hindu ethical conceptions there is neither perfect good nor absolute evil. Good and evil are comparative terms; without evil there can be no good, and no evil without good. Hence in Hinduism there is no parallel to Jesus, the perfect man and God, or Lucifer the Devil. Rama, the hero of the *Ramayana*, the nearest approach to the idea of perfection, was by no means without faults; he killed Bali, the half-brother of Sugriva, hiding himself behind a tree, an act blamable by all the laws of chivalry; he discarded his innocent wife in order to placate public opinion. Yudhishtira, the hero of the *Mahabharata*, was a gambler; when victory in the Mahabharata battle depended on his telling a lie, Yudhishtira, though reluctantly, did tell a lie and for this sin he was taken up to the gates of hell.

On the other hand, Ravana and Duryodhana, the villains of the epics, were not without virtues. Ravana was a good ruler and a devoted son, and his ten heads were symbolic of his vast knowledge, proficiency in the six Shastras (sciences) and the four Vedas. Duryodhana was a faithful friend, dutiful son and able statesman. The besetting sin of Ravana was foolish pride together with a love for other people's wives, and that of Duryodhana, love for power. Apart from these vices, both of them can be favourably compared to many of the heroes of the epics.

The gods too are imperfect. In the quarrel for precedence among the members of the Trinity, Brahma, as we have seen, unhesitatingly spoke an untruth for which he lost his fifth head. Vishnu often had recourse to treachery in overcoming his foes. Shiva's wrathful nature led him to commit Brahmanicide, the most heinous crime a mortal or god could commit.

No being, then, whether god or man, is perfectly good. The Supreme Being is not exactly a being, but is without attributes and as regards That One, there is no point in saying IT is good; because IT is above good and evil. The conception of good and evil arises out of the inherent incapacity of the mortal mind to perceive realities; the perception of ordinary mortals is relative, and hence the illusion of ethical notions. While, for all practical purposes in human relations, the Hindus do recognize the need for a distinction between good and evil and emphasize its importance in the scriptures, they hold that ultimate reality is ONE and good and evil have no place in IT.

Another interesting point that strikes the student of Hindu mythology is the close relationship the Hindu mystics trace between good and evil. Both Daityas (Asuras born of Diti) and Adityas (celestials born of Aditi) are the sons of the sage Kasyapa; thus, good and evil are half-brothers. The Pandavas and the Kauravas, personifications of good and evil respectively, were cousins. Shishupala, the bitterest enemy of Vishnu, was, as we shall see presently, an incarnation of one of his most ardent devotees.

The above are the higher ethical conceptions embodied in some of the myths, related in the scriptures, of gods and their enemies; for the rest, most of the fables narrated about their conflicts can be classed in the category of the stories told of Jack, the Giant Killer.

The enemies of the gods have many names, such as Rakshasas, Daityas, Danavas, Yakshas, Asuras, etc. Of these, "Asura" is the most commonly used word in Hindu sacred literature, and the most incomprehensible. "Sura" means god and "A-sura" indicates a non-god. "Sura" also means one who drinks spirituous liquors and then "A-sura" means one who abstains from drinking. The ancient Aryans, it must be remembered, drank hard, and Asuras were probably non-Aryans who did not know the art of distilling. In one myth it is related that when the goddess of wine appeared on the milk-ocean with a bowl of Sura (liquor) the gods partook of it and their enemies did not, from which circumstance the latter came to be called Asuras. A yet another interpretation is that "Asura" is the Hindu name for Assyrian. The Aryans before their migration into India were possibly inimical to the Assyrians and had occasion to fight with them.

In some accounts the word is used in a racial sense to denote non-Aryan races of barbarous habits; in others it is used with an ethical import to indicate evil persons. We have seen that the Asura Kansa was the uncle of the god Krishna. Prahlada was the son of the Asura Hiranyakasipu, but is revered in the three worlds as a great soul. One of the hymns of the *Rig Veda* is addressed to an Asura; in this capacity he is then as good as a god!

In "their earliest conception the Rakshasas seem to be those unknown creatures of darkness to which the superstition of all ages and races has attributed the evils that attend this life, and a malignant desire to injure mankind. In the Epic period they seem to be personifications of the aborigines of India, presented under the terrible aspect of vampires flying through the air sucking blood, &c., in order to heighten the triumphs of the Aryan heroes who subdued them. In this character they play a very prominent part in the *Ramayana*, the beautiful epic of Valmiki. Here they are led by Ravana, the king of Lanka, which is supposed to be the island of Ceylon and its capital and they are subdued by Dasarathi Rama, the hero of the poem. In the Puranic period they are infernal giants, the children of the Rishi Pulastya, and enemies of the gods. They are then divided into three classes; (1) The slaves of Kubera, the god of wealth, and guardians of his treasures; (2) malevolent imps, whose chief delight is to disturb the pious in their devotions; and (3) giants of enormous proportions, inhabiting the nether regions and hostile to the gods."*

The Asuras and their conflicts with gods have also astronomic and astrologic meanings and many of the myths indicate the motions of the heavenly bodies and their crossing one another's sphere of influence.

Of the numerous Asuras mentioned in Hindu scriptures, three pairs were the most celebrated. They were incarnations of Jaya and Vijaya, two warders of Vishnu's palace who offended some Rishis and fell under their curse. They were given the choice of undergoing six births on earth or other worlds as devotees of Vishnu or three as his enemies, and they chose the latter as leading to the speedier return to Vishnu. During their Asura births they remained ignorant of their celestial origin. They were first born as Hiranyaksha and Hiranyakasipu, then as Ravana and Kumbhakarna and lastly as Kansa and Shishupala. In the first two they were brothers, and in the last relatives. How Hiranyaksha, Hiranyakasipu and Kansa were killed by Vishnu in his Avatars has been narrated in the second chapter. The destruction of Ravana has also been related, but this celebrated Asura is worthy of further notice.

RAVANA

Wild tales of Ravana's strength are told. In the *Ramayana* it is said: "Where Ravana remains, the sun loses his force; the winds cease to blow; the fire ceases to burn; the rolling ocean seeing him stills its waves." The mighty giant "had ten faces, twenty arms, copper coloured eyes, a huge chest, and white teeth like the young moon. His form was as a thick cloud or the god of death with gaping mouth. He had all the marks of royalty; but his body bore the impress of wounds inflicted by all the divine arms in his warfare with the gods. It was scarred by the thunderbolt of Indra, by the tusks of Indra's elephant Airavata, and by the discus of Vishnu. His strength was so great that he could agitate the seas, and split the tops of mountains. He was a breaker of all laws and a ravisher of other men's wives. He once penetrated into Bhogavati (the serpent capital of Patala), conquered the great serpent Vasuki, and carried off the beloved wife of Takshaka. He defeated his half-brother Kubera (the god of wealth) and carried off his self-moving chariot called Pushpaka. He devastated the divine groves of Chitraratha, and the gardens of the gods. Tall as a mountain-peak he stopped with his arms the sun and the moon in their course, and prevented their rising."

The army of Ravana consisted of numerous legions of demons, each legion 14,000 strong. These demons had frightful shapes: "some were prodigiously fat, others exclusively thin; some dwarfish, others enormously tall and humpbacked; some had only one eye, others only one ear; some enormous paunches and flaccid, pendent breasts, others long projecting teeth, and crooked thighs; some could assume any forms at will, others were beautiful and of great splendour."

Ravana conquered the celestial kingdom with this ill-assorted army and brought all the gods in chains to Lanka and made them serve him. "Indra made garlands of flowers to adorn his person. Agni was his cook. Surya (sun) supplied light by day and Chandra (moon) by night. Varuna purveyed water for the palace and Kubera furnished cash. The deities constituting the nine planets arranged themselves into a ladder by which (they serving as steps) Ravana ascended his throne. Brahma (the great gods were also there) was a herald proclaiming the giant's titles which were numerous. Vishnu instructed the dancing girls and selected the fairest for the royal bed. Shiva held the office of royal barber and trimmed Ravana's beard. Ganesha had the care of the cows, goats, and herd. Vayu swept the house. Yama washed the linen."

In a fable it is related how Ravana obtained the Atmalingam (the real Lingam), Uma and a boon of immortality from Shiva and lost all the three through his folly.

It happened that Ravana's mother was a devotee of Shiva and was in the habit of worshipping a Lingam. One day Indra stole the Lingam and the pious lady started fasting. Ravana went to his mother and told her not to fast and that he would bring her the Atma-

---
* E. Moor, *The Hindu Pantheon.*

lingam itself from the person of Shiva. He pacified his mother and started for Kailas. Reaching the abode of Shiva, Ravana betook himself to the practice of austerities. He stood on his head in the midst of five fires for ten thousand years. At the end of every thousand years he cut off one of his heads and threw it into the fire. Nine heads of Ravana were thus chopped off. While he was about to cut his last throat Shiva appeared before him and asked him to name his boons. Ravana asked for three boons: Immortality, the possession of the Atmalingam and marriage to a woman as beautiful as Uma, the wife of Shiva, whom Ravana happened to see in the course of his austerities. Shiva gave him the Atmalingam and granted him the boon of immortality with a stipulation that he should not in any way harm Shiva. As for the wife, Shiva said that in the three worlds there was not a woman to equal Uma in beauty; thereupon Ravana asked for Uma herself. Mahadeva showed some reluctance to part with his wife but Ravana threatened to perform austerities more severe than those from which he had just emerged. Thus intimidated, the Great God surrendered his wife.

As soon as Ravana received the boons, Narada appeared before him and persuaded him to believe that Shiva had no power to grant a boon of immortality and the deity, in granting such a boon had, in fact, fooled the king of Lanka. Ravana was carried away by Narada's eloquence and in his anger tore off mount Kailas where Shiva was meditating and threw it away. This was against Shiva's stipulation, and the boon of immortality became ineffective.

Ravana then took Uma, placed her on his shoulders, and with the Atmalingam in his hand, proceeded towards Lanka. All the gods were now alarmed. Uma herself cried out to Vishnu to save her from Ravana. The god of preservation then took the form of an old Brahmin and appeared before Ravana. He saluted the Asura king respectfully and asked him from where he had got the old hag on his shoulders. "You blind old fool of a Brahmin," said Ravana, "can't you see she is no old hag but Uma, wife of Shiva, the most beautiful lady in the three worlds?" "Emperor of Lanka," said the Brahmin, "it ill becomes so just a ruler as yourself to revile an old Brahmin without cause. If you do not believe my words, please look at the lady yourself and then say whether she is a hag or not." Uma took the hint and immediately transformed herself into an old hag; and when Ravana looked at her he was surprised to see that the old Brahmin had spoken the truth. He dropped the old woman there and then, and proceeded southwards with the Atmalingam.

Ravana had not gone far when he wished to answer the call of nature. The Lingam could not be placed on the ground as Shiva had told him that if once the Lingam were to touch ground, it would remain there. So he looked for somebody to hold it for him and found a cowboy tending his flock. Ravana beckoned to him, and when he came gave him the Lingam to hold and warned him not to place it on the ground. The cowboy (he was Ganesha who had assumed this form) told Ravana that he would hold the Lingam for one hour and no more. Ravana agreed and retired to a bush nearby but he took more than one hour to return. So Ganesha dropped the Lingam on the ground and disappeared. When Ravana came back, he saw the Lingam sinking into the ground and caught hold of it. But the Lingam transformed itself into a cow and began to sink again and left only its ears above ground.

There is a place on the west coast of India called Gokarnam (cow's ear) and a temple there, dedicated to the Atmalingam. Thousands of devotees from the four corners of India visit the temple for the annual festival.

KUMBHAKARNA (POT-EAR)

This brother of Ravana was so named because his ears were like earthen pots. Kumbhakarna was eighty-four leagues in height and his body was as vast as a mountain. His breath was like whirlwind and his speeh like thunder. No palace in Lanka could accommodate him and hence he chose as his abode a spacious mountain cave.

Like his brother Ravana, Kumbhakarna also aspired for immortality and performed austerities to propitiate Brahma. It should be noticed that in every case a boon of immortality was granted to an Asura, there were certain conditions attached to it and the gods managed to find some loophole in the wording of the boon and made it ineffective. So Kumbhakarna wanted a boon of unconditional immortality and told Brahma so, when this deity appeared before him. Brahma refused to grant such a boon and disappeared. This happened several times. At last the heat produced by the severity of Kumbhakarna's penances became unbearable and the three worlds stood in danger of being burnt away. In this predicament Brahma asked his wife Sarasvati to enter into the tongue of Kumbhakarna and give it a twist when he next begged for the boon. As soon as Sarasvati took her place in Kumbhakarna's mouth, Brahma appeared before him and asked him what he wanted. Kumbhakarna asked for "eternal life," but the twisted tongue stuttered "eternal sleep." "Granted," said Brahma, and the ambitious giant was condemned to eternal sleep. He pleaded for mercy and Brahma allowed him to wake up occasionally.

While the battle for Lanka was raging, Ravana found it difficult to stem the tide of invasion and sent hosts of Rakshasas to wake up Kumbhakarna who was then sleeping for nine months. The demons proceeded to Kumbhakarna's cave and found him slumbering, "drunk with sleep, vast as hell, his rank breath sweeping all before him, smelling of blood and fat." Before waking up the eternal slumberer, the Rakshasas prepared for him a dish of Pilau in which hundreds of buffaloes and deer were cooked with vast quantities of rice. The food was piled up as high as Mount Meru and then the demons started hurling rocks and trees at Kumbhakarna so as to wake him up. But the breath of Pot-ear blew off these missiles. The exasperated demons then started hacking him with axes but Pot-ear slept the harder. Then they drove thousands of elephants over his vast body and this had the desired effect. Pot-ear at last yawned and woke up, and seeing food fell heartily to it. But he was dissatisfied with the fare and bitterly complained against his stingy brother for keeping him on a starvation diet. More animals were then massacred and cooked. Pot-ear was now half-fed; for the rest he was told that there were chances of getting an excellent feed on the battle-field as a good number of monkeys and bears had crossed over to Lanka. The prospect of getting such a feed drove off his sleep completely and he was now thoroughly roused. And with a roar that shook the three worlds Kumbhakarna ran to the scene of action.

The very sight of Kumbhakarna frightened the monkeys. The giant caught the monkeys and bears in hundreds and began to devour them in easy mouthfuls. No missile could produce any effect on his hide. The monkeys fled in terror and even Hanuman, the most courageous of them, stood at a safe distance. Lakshman tried to arrest his march but could not succeed. At last Rama himself engaged him in action. After a severe contest Rama cut off one of Kumbhakarna's arms which in its fall destroyed many monkeys. "Then with a sacred shaft Rama cut away the other arm and with two keen-edged discs he cut away the demon's legs and with a shaft of Indra he struck away his head; and he fell like a great hill and crashed down into the sea and the gods and heroes rejoiced."

SHISHUPALA

Shishupala was the king of Chedi and a contemporary of Krishna. As soon as he was born he brayed like an ass. The infant had three eyes and four arms, and astrologers predicted that he would lose his third eye and extra arms at the sight of the man who was destined to kill him later. The mother of Shishupala visited many of her friends and relatives with the child, but no one deprived it of its extra eye and arms.

One day, however, Krishna visited Chedi and as he took the child in his lap, the third eye of Shishupala disappeared together with the extra arms. The mother of the child then approached Krishna and made him promise to grant her a request. Krishna asked her to name her boon and she said: "Promise me that if my son Shishupala offends you, you will forgive him." "Yes," replied Krishna, "if he offends me one hundred times, a hundred times will I forgive him."

Shishupala grew up and became a powerful king. Rukmini, daughter of the king of Vidarbha, was betrothed to him but the lady loved Krishna and asked him to carry her away to Dwaraka. Krishna accordingly proceeded to Vidarbha with his brother Balarama and a select party of soldiers, and carried away Rukmini on the day of her wedding. (Marriage by capture was a recognized form for Kshatriyas in ancient days.) This and many other incidents led to bitter enmity between Krishna and Shishupala, and although the latter offended Krishna many times, he forgave him because of the promise he had made to the queen of Chedi. Krishna forgave him one hundred times. Shishupala insulted him yet another time under the following circumstances and was killed by him.

After the Pandavas had received half the kingdom from Dhritarashtra, Yudhishtira was crowned king of Indraprastha, and for the coronation ceremony many neighbouring kings and chieftains were invited. For a particular ceremony one of the assembled dignitaries had to be named the chief guest, and Yudhishtira, on the advice of Bhishma, gave the place of honour to Krishna. Shishupala immediately got up and asked Yudhishtira on what grounds Krishna was chosen for the honour. Krishna was not a king, he said, nor the wisest, ablest or bravest among the assembled guests. If the honour were to go by age, Vasudeva, Krishna's father was there and he ought to have been preferred to his son; if, by learning, Drona, the teacher of the Pandavas ought to have been chosen; if treaty-alliances were of importance, Drupada, father-in-law of the Pandavas was the proper person to be honoured; if reverence were the criterion for the choice, Bhishma, the grandsire of the Pandavas, ought to have been preferred to Krishna. "Then on what grounds, Yudhishtira," asked Shishupala, "did you choose this common fellow of deceitful nature, notorious for his low birth among cowherds? I consider your choice as an insult to me and all the assembled guests."

Many of the kings could very well appreciate the force of Shishupala's argument, and they blamed Yudhishtira for his thoughtlessness. Then it was given out that Bhishma had suggested Krishna's name, and the grandsire publicly acknowledged his responsibility in the matter and rebuked Shishupala for unnecessarily creating factions. Shishupala's wrath was

PLATE XLIX
DIVINE MOTHERS

140 CHAMUNDI

141 KAUMARI

142 MAHESWARI

143 VARAHI

Pudukkottai Museum
(Photos : F. S. Mahalingam)

PLATE L
DIVINE MOTHERS

144 VAISHNAVI

145 INDRANI
Pudukkottai Museum
(Photos : E. S. Mahalingam)

146 BRAHMI

PLATE LI

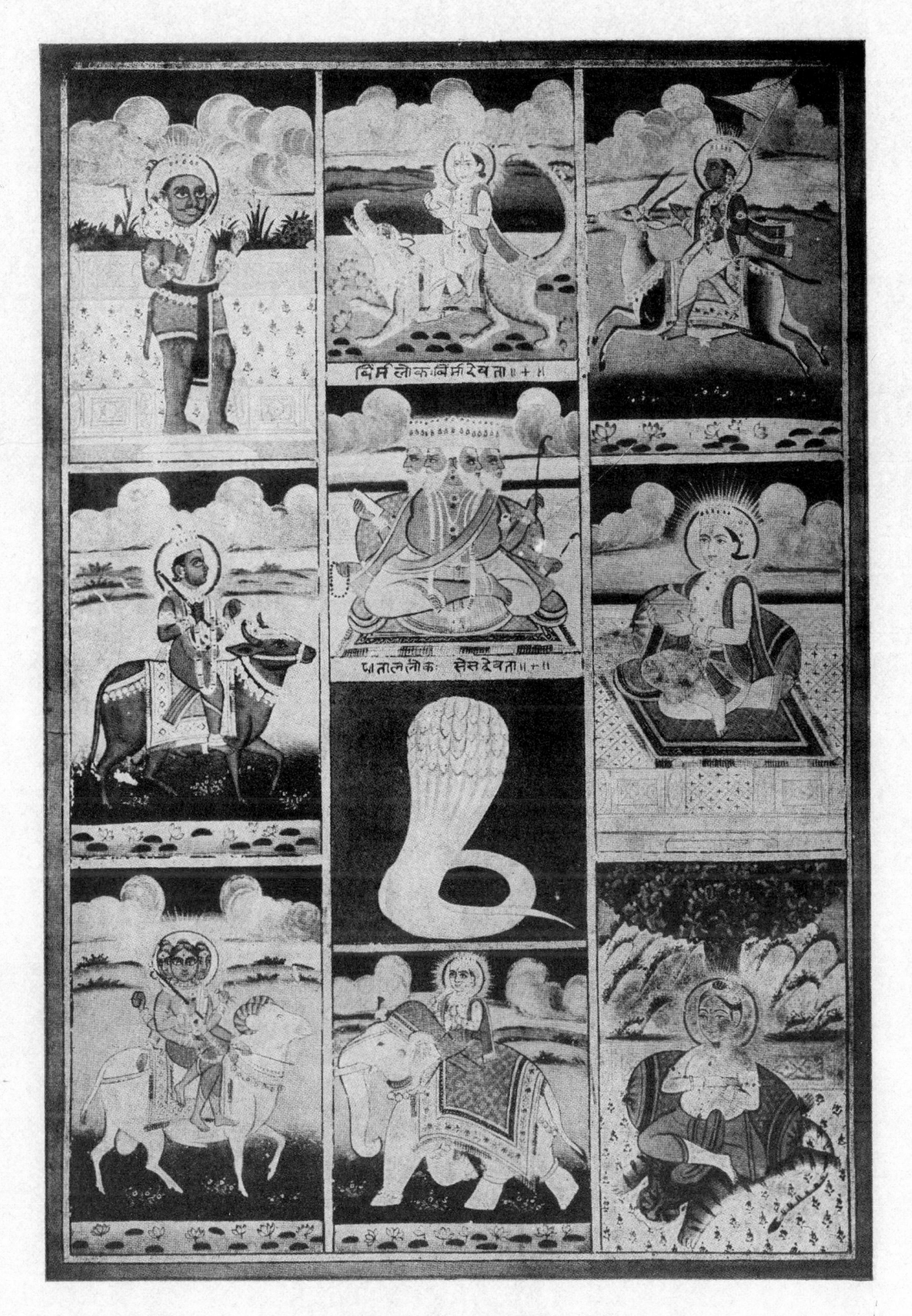

147 GUARDIANS OF THE UNIVERSE
Column 1. Top to bottom: Nirrita, Yama, Agni.
2. Top to bottom: Varuna, Brahma, Ananta, Indra.
3. Top to bottom: Vayu, Kubera, Isani.
(From *Pictures of Indian Myths & Legends*)

PLATE LII

148 A GAY RISHI
(From Coomarswamy's *Viswakarma*)

149 DAKSHA AND WIFE
(From Bellary)

150 A GANDHARVA
(Ajanta. From Grunwedel's *Buddhist Art in India*)

151 A KINNARA ON A LOTUS
(From Anuradhapura)

PLATE LIII

152 A STUDIOUS RISHI OR SAGE
(From *Arts and Crafts of India and Ceylon,* Coomaraswamy)

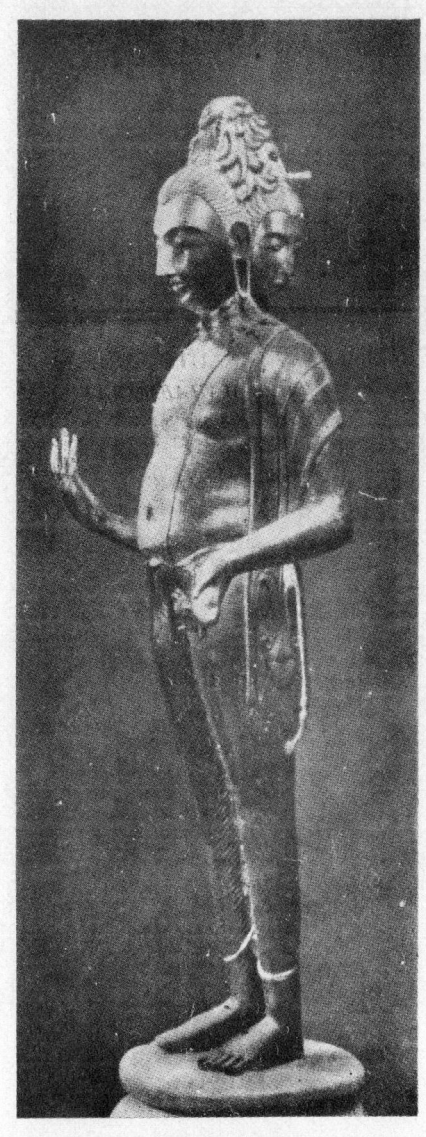

153 BRAHMA
(From *Art of India and Pakistan* Sir Leigh Ashton)

PLATE LIV

154 VYASA, AUTHOR OF
     THE MAHABHARAT

155 ARJUNA WINNING DRAUPADI
(From Halebid. Copyright: Archaeological Dept. of India)

156 DENUDATION OF DRAUPADI

157 BHIMA BEING CAUGHT BY THE ELEPHANT OF
     BHAGADATTA, AN ENEMY GENERAL, IN THE
     MAHABHARATA BATTLE
(Belur. Copyright: Archaeological Dept. of India)

PLATE LV

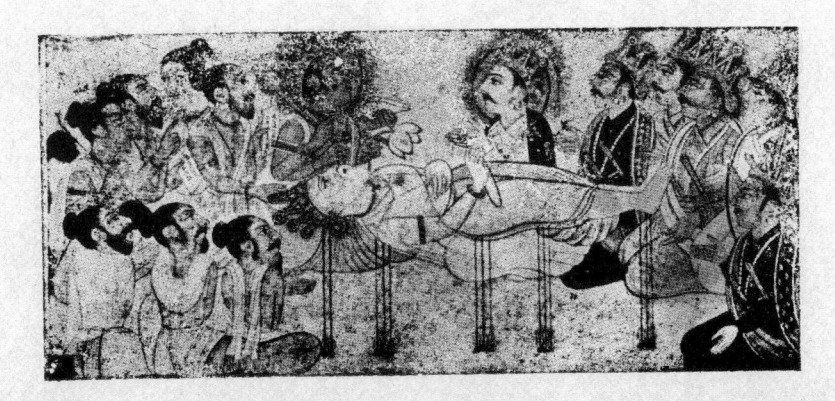

158 DEATH OF BHISHMA
(Rajput Painting, Coomaraswamy Collection)

159 FAMILY OF SHIVA
(Bijapur Silver. From *Indian Art at Delhi*, Sir George Watt)

PLATE LVI

APSARAS ALLURING AUSTERE SAGES FROM THEIR DEVOTIONS
(From Khajuraho. Copyright: Archaeological Dept. of India)

now turned against Bhishma and he called the venerable old man a fool, a hypocrite and a reprobate. "While you pretend to remain celibate," said Shishupala, "you corrupt other men's wives. Is it not known in the three worlds that you captured the daughters of the king of Kasi from their father's home on the day of marriage and took them by force to Hastinapur? We are not fools to believe your explanation that the ladies were intended for your half-brother Vichitravirya. Vichitravirya died childless; then how did Ambika and Ambalika give birth to Dhritarashtra and Pandu? You are unmarried because you are incapable of being faithful to the marriage-bed. Verily you are a fit companion for Krishna, the notorious seducer of the Gopis."

Shishupala went on in this strain and the coronation ceremony was on the point of being interrupted by a factional fight. Then Krishna, no more able to bear the outrageous language of Shishupala, threw his weapon, the discus, on him which cut him into two.

Of Shishupala it is said, he hated Vishnu (Krishna) more than any other of his (Vishnu's) enemies did. He plotted Krishna's ruin even in his sleep. But as his thoughts were always concentrated on Vishnu, albeit in spite, he went to heaven immediately after his death.

With Kansa and Shishupala the cycle of births to which the warders Jaya and Vijaya were condemned, was completed.

KALA YAVANA

We have noticed in the second chapter that Krishna and his people had to desert their ancestral city, Mathura, and migrate to Dwaraka, a fortress they built in the sea for the purpose. Mathura was deserted because of the invasion of Kala Yavana. Jarasandha, king of Magadha, had already laid siege to the city when Kala Yavana appeared at its gates with an army of three crores of Mlechchas (barbarians). The two invaders joined their forces and Krishna fought seventeen battles against them at the end of which he was defeated and made to desert the city.

After the migration to Dwaraka, Krishna collected an army of Yadavas (his own picked fighters) and engaged Kala Yavana in action. Krishna lost the battle and fled for life, pursued by his powerful foe. He was chased into the mountains and took refuge in the cave where Muchukunda was sleeping.

This Muchukunda was the indomitable son of king Mandhata of the Ikshvaku race and had fought many battles for the gods when they had no general. On the birth of Kartikeya, Indra asked Muchukunda to take rest, and granted him a boon by which he could remain asleep till the descent of Vishnu to earth in his Avatar as Krishna. Indra also declared that the disturber of Muchukunda's sleep would suffer instant death as penalty. After receiving the boon Muchukunda repaired to a mountain cave and fell asleep.

Krishna now entered the cave and covered the sleeping Muchukunda with his own yellow robe and hid himself in a corner. Kala Yavana entered the cave, mistook Muchukunda for Krishna and gave him a severe kick. Muchukunda got up and Kala Yavana fell down dead.

The origin of Kala Yavana is obscure. He was probably a foreign invader, as his name Yavana indicates. The *Bhagbata* says that he was sent by the sage Narada to aid the king of Magadha. Whatever his origin, Kala Yavana has at present a number of devotees in India who worship him as a Deva (god) and call Krishna "an impious wretch, a merciless tyrant, and implacable and most rancorous enemy."

BHIMA AND BAKA

While the Pandavas were living in Ekachakra (Page 52), one day Kunti saw their host, his wife and son beating their breasts and wailing. The good lady asked them why they were thus sorrowing and was told by the host that either himself or his son was to be sent the next day as a meal for a cannibal Asura named Baka. This demon lived in the forest and because of his unrestrained slaughter of the men, women and children of Ekachakra, the people of the town had implored him not to indulge in wanton destruction, and agreed to send him daily for breakfast a man with a cartload of cooked rice and vegetables. Each house of the town had to send a man by turn, and now had come the turn of the house in which the Pandavas lived.

The old Brahmin first offered to go himself. "I am an old man nearing death," said he to his son, "and it does not matter whether I die tomorrow or a few days later. But you are young, my son, and have a life to live."

But the young man would not permit his aged parent to be eaten alive by a cannibal, and as persuasions proved of no avail, it was decided to send the son to Baka. Kunti now told the Brahmin lady that she had five sons and it was only fair that she should send one of them to Baka in preference to the only son of her hostess. The good people would not allow their guests to suffer on account of them but Kunti told them that her son Bhima was a match for any Asura and had, in fact, killed many Asuras stronger than Baka. She assured them that her son would kill Baka and rid the town of his tyranny once for all. So Bhima was sent with the cart of food to Baka.

Bhima drove the cart into the forest with a light heart but before reaching Baka felt hungry. This son of Kunti was famous for his gluttony and is often referred to in the *Mahabharata* as Vrikodara (one with a wolfish hunger). Bhima unyoked the oxen, spread the meal before him and fell heartily to it.

In the meantime Baka felt hungry and wondered why his breakfast was not coming. Determined to teach the people of Ekachakra a lesson, he started towards that town. On the way he saw Bhima at his breakfast, and from the cart and the nature of the fare surmised that the meal had actually been meant for him. Baka, however, waited for Bhima to finish eating because he could then eat Bhima himself and save the trouble of eating Bhima and the meal separately.

When Bhima finished eating his meal, Baka rushed towards him with his mouth open like a cave. But Bhima took his club and knocked off the cannibal's teeth. The giant then uprooted a tree, and the two began to fight. The people of Ekachakra heard the roar of Baka and the clash of weapons, and came to see the combat. After a severe combat Bhima killed the demon with his club and won the everlasting gratitude of the people of Ekachakra.

THE STORY OF KACHA AND DEVAYANI

There was a time when the gods did not know the art of bringing dead people back to life. Ushanas (also called Shukra), the preceptor of the Asuras, knew the art, and so the Asuras who were killed in battle by the gods were brought back to life by Ushanas and came again to fight with the gods. The gods took counsel among themselves and sent Kacha, son of their priest Brahaspati, to Ushanas so that he might learn the art from the preceptor of the Asuras.

Kacha went to Ushanas and revealed his identity to him with a frankness that pleased him and he accepted Kacha as his disciple. Kacha was a devoted and diligent pupil and his teacher became very fond of him. Ushanas had a lovely daughter named Devayani and the young Kacha served her as though her commands were those of the Guru himself. The conduct and bearing of Kacha were lovable and the young lady became much attached to him; and she missed him very much when he went out into the forest to tend his teacher's flocks.

Now the Asuras came to know of Kacha's purpose in becoming the disciple of their preceptor, and decided to destroy him. So one day when Kacha was tending his master's flocks the Asuras fell upon him and killed him, cut his body into pieces and gave it to the wolves and jackals of the forest. When night came, the cows returned to the pen without Kacha. And Devayani said to her father: "The sun has set, the evening fire is lit and the cattle have returned to the pen; but Kacha is not come. O father, I will not live without Kacha."

Ushanas meditated, and by the power of his meditation came to know that Kacha had been killed by the Asuras and his body given to the jackals and wolves of the forest. He called out to Kacha to come to life, and Kacha came to life by tearing the bowels of the jackals and wolves and returned to his teacher.

Next day, Kacha went to the forest, and while he was picking flowers for Devayani, the Asuras fell upon him and killed him. They ground his body to powder and dissolved it in the seven seas. But when evening came and Kacha returned not, Devayani told her father that her lover was missing, and Ushanas called out to Kacha and brought him back to life.

For a third time the Asuras waylaid Kacha and killed him. This time they burnt his body, dissolved the ashes in wine and gave it to Ushanas to drink, and the unsuspecting sage drank the wine. When evening came and Kacha returned not, Devayani was grieved and told her father that she could not live without Kacha. Ushanas meditated, and by the power of his meditation came to know that Kacha was in his own stomach. Now he could not call Kacha back to life without killing himself. In this predicament Ushanas asked his daughter to choose between her father and lover. Devayani wanted both, and wept beating her breast and tearing her hair.

Kacha now spoke gently from the stomach of his teacher: "My teacher, I have served you for a thousand years now, and I have not disobeyed you in thought, word or deed all these years. Treat me as your own son and teach me now the art of bringing dead people back to life, so that I may come out of your body and then restore you back to life."

Ushanas admitted that this was the only way out of the difficulty and imparted to him the great secret. After that he asked Kacha to come out of his body and Kacha came out tearing the bowels of his teacher. Once he was out, he brought his teacher back to life.

Now the time came for Kacha to return to the gods and he went to Devayani to take farewell of her. But Devayani would not let him depart. She loved him as her own life, could not think of living without him and said so. "It is only meet," said she, "that we should now be married according to the prescribed rites." But Kacha could not think of marriage with her. He was devoted to her because she was his teacher's daughter. "Thou art as a mother or sister unto me," said he to Devayani. But she loved him to distraction and would not be pacified by anything short of marriage with Kacha; and when Kacha ultimately refused, her love turned to hatred. "Kacha," said she, "you owe everything to me. When you were slain by the Asuras it was I who persuaded my father to bring you back to life. It was because of me that you learnt the art of bringing dead people back to life, for I told my father that I could not live without you. And since you spurn my love, I now curse you, and the knowledge you have gained from my father shall be ineffective when used by you."

Kacha replied: "Your entreaties did not make me deviate from the path of virtue, and your threats cannot now intimidate me. Although through the power of your curse the knowledge of the charm of life has been rendered ineffective when used by me, I can yet impart the knowledge to others in whom it will be fruitful. My conduct in the whole affair has been honourable and I go back to my father with a clear conscience."

Kacha went back to the gods and was welcomed by them as the saviour of the race, and Indra bestowed many boons upon him.

The story probably has its origin in matriarchal times when women proposed and husbands lived in the houses of their wives. The idea stressed again is the importance of duty. Kacha, even at the risk of being thought callous and unchivalrous, breaks off with Devayani. She, on the other hand, tries to keep Kacha among her own people and on her failure to achieve the purpose makes an attempt to deprive him of his power to harm her own race. In the conflict, however, the man comes out triumphant.

It may be added here that time healed the wound, and Devayani married a king named Jajati.

THE CHURNING OF THE MILK-OCEAN

The sage Durvasa, a portion of Shiva himself, one day, attended an assembly of monarchs on earth and received from them a garland of flowers as a present. On his way back to the celestial regions the sage meditated on the relative merits of the various gods and came to the conclusion that Indra was the proper person to receive the garland from him. Accordingly, he took the garland to the king of the gods and presented it to him. Indra received the garland with a great show of humility, thanked the sage for the distinguished favour and as soon as Durvasa departed gave it to one of his state elephants to play with. The elephant had not destroyed the garland out of recognition when Durvasa, as ill-luck would have it, returned to tell Indra something, and found the elephant playing with the garland. The angry sage immediately cursed Indra and all the gods under him to lose their energy and become as feeble as mortals. After pronouncing the curse he went back without even entering Indra's palace.

Now Bali, king of the Asuras, declared war on the gods and marched on Amaravati with a huge army. The emaciated gods were no match for the Asuras and defeat appeared certain. So they proceeded to Shiva and narrated to him the story of their misfortune. Shiva was powerless against the curse of Durvasa and he conducted them to Brahma who, in his turn, conducted the troop to Vaikunta, where Vishnu was sleeping on the serpent Ananta. They eulogized Vishnu, singing his thousand names, and the god of preservation, hearing the melody of their voices woke up and asked the gods what they wanted. They told him the tale of their woe; upon which Vishnu meditated and said that a dose of ambrosia, the cream of the milk-ocean, alone could restore them to their former state.

No ordinary churning-stick could agitate the milk-ocean sufficiently and the mountain Mandara had to be torn off and used as a churning stick. The gods alone could not lift the mountain nor twirl it in the ocean, and hence Vishnu asked Indra to declare a truce with the Asuras on their own condition, promise them an equal share in the ambrosia and thus obtain their labour for the churning of the ocean. Indra asked Vishnu whether it would be prudent to give the Asuras a share in the ambrosia as by feeding on it, the Asuras would become stronger than the gods; upon which Vishnu told him to leave that to him.

A truce was accordingly declared and the gods and the Asuras uprooted Mandara and placed it in the milk-ocean. Vast quantities of potent herbs were dropped into the ocean to flavour ambrosia. The gods then caught Vasuki, the huge serpent that lived in the nether regions and twisted him round the mountain as a churning rope. Vishnu asked the gods to man the head-end of the rope, but the Asuras suspected foul play and asserted their right to that side. So the gods took the tail-end, with the result that the hot breath that emanated from the mouth of Vasuki weakened the Asuras while the gods were invigorated by the cool breezes that blew from the ocean.

As the churning progressed, the mountain began to sink into the muddy bottom of the sea and could not be twirled round. Vishnu now took the shape of a huge tortoise (Kurma Avatar) dived into the ocean and supported the mountain on his back. After this, things went merrily on.

On the surface of the ocean began to appear one by one what are called the Chaturdasa Ratnam (fourteen precious things). These were the moon (which Shiva took), the Parijata tree, the elephant Airavatam (both of which Indra claimed), the cow Surabhi or Kamadhenu (which was given to the seven Rishis) Varuni, the goddess of Vine with a bowl of wine called Sura (which the gods drank), the Apsaras (who went to live with the Gandharvas), the white horse Uchchaisravas (which was given to Bali from whom it was taken by Indra after the defeat of Bali in the battle that followed the drinking of ambrosia), the goddess Lakshmi, a conchshell, a mace, a jewel called Kaustubha (all of which Vishnu took) and Dhanwantari (the author of the Ayurveda system of medicine) with the bowl of ambrosia.*

As soon as Dhanwantari appeared with the bowl of ambrosia, the gods and the Asuras left the churning rope and madly rushed towards the physician. In the scuffle, the Asuras succeeded in seizing the bowl, and they made away with it. But a quarrel broke out among the Asuras themselves on the question as to who should be served first. Then appeared in their midst a damsel of celestial beauty, with her face like a lotus in bloom, heaving breasts, waist like an island, and her person adorned with necklaces, bangles and anklets. She stepped merrily into the midst of the Asuras, her anklets jingling, and smiled sweetly on them. The Asuras now forgot all about ambrosia and stood wondering at the beauty of Mohini (such was the name of this form of Vishnu). Mohini threw her glances at the bowl of ambrosia, and a gallant Asura suggested that she should decide how to share ambrosia, and all the Asuras cheered him. Mohini smiled and asked them whether it would be prudent to leave such a momentous decision to a woman. "Wise men have said," said Mohini with a mischievous smile, "that women are unreliable." All the Asuras laughed heartily and were now convinced without any doubt that she could be trusted, and swore that they would abide by her decision unconditionally. Mohini then remarked that the gods and Asuras had toiled equally hard in raising ambrosia and should get an equal share. and made them sit in two rows. She took the bowl and served the row of gods first. After the last god had been served Mohini disappeared with the bowl!

A terrible uproar ensued on her departure and the gods and the Asuras fought a fierce battle. But the gods who were strengthened by the draughts of ambrosia they had drunk, easily defeated the Asuras and put them to flight.

One of the Asuras had disguised himself as a god and sat in the row of the gods. He had just quaffed a mouthful of ambrosia when Surya (sun) and Chandra (moon) who were sitting on either side of him detected the fraud and pointed him out to Vishnu. This deity immediately cut him into two with his weapon, but by virtue of the nectar he had drunk, both the portions of the demon remained animate and Brahma translated them into the heavens as planets. The upper portion is called Rahu and the other Ketu. It is said that Rahu is even now the mortal enemy of the sun and moon and that eclipses are caused by his trying to devour them.

It may be added that Shiva became enamoured of the Mohini form of Vishnu and hence he went to Vaikunta and requested his compeer to assume that shape again. Vishnu obliged him but Shiva chased Mohini with the intention of doing violence on her; on this, Vishnu assumed his male form but the infatuated Shiva caught him, embraced him and became one with him.

The churning of the milk ocean is narrated in almost all the Puranas with slight modifications. Scholars interpret the myth in many ways. Some observe that it signifies an astronomic phenomenon and others that it indicates a prehistoric battle. There is as yet no satisfactory interpretation of this important myth.

* * * *

Christian and Muslim readers who are not familiar with the trend of Hindu religious thought might wonder why the gods found so much difficulty in overcoming their foes and why the great gods granted inconvenient boons to their adversaries. The answer is that unlike the Christian or Muslim God, Hindu gods are not omnipotent. Although in invocations gods are often addressed as omnipotent and their strength is over-emphasized, according to orthodox conceptions, the powers of the gods are limited. They are creatures and are subject to laws. The law embodied in the Veda is binding on Brahma, Vishnu and Shiva, and all the other gods. If an Asura or a man performs austerities according to the prescribed rules, the god has to grant the desired boon. If he does not, he will be punished by the law. Only the Supreme Being is above the law, and as regards That One, it is beside the point to ask if IT is inimical to the Asura; the Asura is not separate from IT; in fact, the Asuras and the gods find their fundamental oneness in IT.

---

* Of the appearance of poison during the churning, there are two versions; one is that poison floated on the surface of the ocean together with the Chaturdasa Ratnam, and the other that, under the strain of the pull, Vasuki vomited it.

Chapter VII

DEATH AND SOUL WANDERINGS

THE mystery of death has been the most inspiring source of religious and metaphysical speculation. In fact religion can be broadly defined as man's challenge to death. Something in man tells him that he is eternal and that death is a delusion or, more properly speaking, a revolution in existence as compared with the evolutionary process we call life. The belief that death does not put an end to existence is fairly universal among mankind, though, to be sure, conceptions of after-life vary from gross superstitions to beliefs which are almost scientific. Dreams and psychic phenomena also confirm man's faith in an after-life and an invisible world where spirits move and hold communion with the sub-conscious mind.

Among the followers of the great organised religions of the world, the after-life is differently understood by the masses and the intellectuals. Take, for instance, Christianity. The Christian theologians conceive the next world as a realm of values above time and space where individuality survives death in a way incomprehensible to the intellect but perceivable by the spiritually gifted. But to make this conception intelligible to the common people, the realm of values is ruthlessly spatialized and hence we get the popular Christian belief in a geographical heaven, a kingdom where the good enjoy everlasting bliss, and a hell where the wicked are tormented by devils.

The same distinction between higher and lower conceptions regarding death and after-life is met with in Hinduism too. According to Advaita (the predominating school of Hindu philosophy) death is an illusion. "Aham Brahmam Asmi" (I myself am Brahm) or "Tat Twam Asi" (You are That One), says the Advaitin. But all people, the Hindus hold, cannot realize this identity of the individual with Reality. Moreover, the Hindus are quite alive to the mischief such a philosophy of life is capable of making among the generality of mankind, and hence for the benefit of the common people a more practical form of religion is preached. And in this religion, the need for laws of ethics is stressed and warning of punishments after death for evil-doers and promise of rewards for good people are held out.

In the Vedic times religious speculation had only just begun, and we find no traces in the *Rig Veda* of a belief in the transmigration of souls. The Aryans, who performed the prescribed sacrifices properly and kept the laws, went, after death, to the heaven of Indra. The Vedic heaven is a place of joy, "where wishes and desires are, where the region of the sun is, where food and delights are found." "There the noise of flutes and song resounds and Soma, Ghee and honey flow." The souls of the pious are conducted to heaven by the god Pushan. The people who enjoy the bliss of heaven are those who perform sacrifices and reward the priests; "for sacrifices and sacrificial fee are indissolubly connected." Heroes who risk their lives in battle also go to heaven.

In the *Rig Veda* there are but vague references to hell. It is hinted that the wicked after death are cast into regions of darkness. In the *Atharva Veda*, however, we come across clear references to hells and torture-chambers.

The only verse in the *Rig Veda* which can be said to embody the doctrine of metempsychosis is the following one which is found in a hymn addressed to the departing soul.

"The sun receive thine eye, the wind thy spirit;
   go as thy merit is, to earth or heaven.
Go, if it be thy lot, unto the water;
   go make thine house in plants with all thy members."

The verse, however, does not necessarily point to the doctrine of metempsychosis but is more or less indicative of the dissolution of the body into its elements. The general trend of thought in the *Rig Veda* suggests a belief in Paradise as a place of reward and annihilation as punishment.

Yama, according to Rig Vedic conceptions, is in charge of heaven and not of hell. References indicate that he was the first man who died and went to heaven. Yami is said to be his wife in some accounts, and sister in others.

In the *Atharva Veda* and the Brahmanas attached to the Vedas, we find clear definitions of hell. The

Naraka Loka of the *Atharva Veda* is "the abode of female goblins and sorceresses, the place of blind or black darkness." In the *Satapatha Brahmana* hell is referred to as a place where "men cut up men and men eat men." The *Kausitaka Brahmana* says that "the animals man eats in this world will devour him in the next."

The doctrine of metempsychosis is emphasized in the Upanishads, the codes and all later works. The conception is tinged with animism which was prevalent among the aborigines whom the Aryans conquered, and probably also among the foreign invaders who later fought successful wars with the Aryan settlers. When the doctrine of metempsychosis gained ground, the older Vedic beliefs were not, however, entirely discarded. What happened was a compromise, and souls that did not attain liberation were sent for a period to heaven or hell, and then again made to undergo births "into a good or bad form as a Brahmin, warrior or householder, or as a dog, pig or Chandala." The *Kausitaka Upanishad,* however, "sends all souls to the moon and then allows some to go by the path of the gods to Brahma; while the others who have been proved wanting return to earth in such form as befits their merit, either as a worm, or fly, or bird, or lion, or boar, or tiger, or serpent, or man, or something else." The codes and the Puranas accept this dual system of punishment or rewards as the most authoritative.

While the general belief is that as soon as a man is conducted to Yama, Chitragupta, who registers all actions of men and women, reads out a full account of his deeds and strikes a balance which decides whether the man deserves punishment or reward, there is a school of thought which holds the view that a balance is not struck but rewards and punishments run on parallel lines; that is, after a man is tortured for his bad actions he is taken to heaven where he is allowed to enjoy the fruit of his good deeds.

HELLS

The number of hells are in some accounts said to be seven, each one set apart for torturing a particular kind of sinner. The *Bhagbata*, however, names twenty-eight hells and describes most of them in detail.

The hell called Tamisra is a region of darkness where robbers and adulterers are tortured by Yama's servants.

Selfish persons and egotists go to Andhatamisra, the hell of greater darkness.

Those who wantonly hurt creatures are put into the hell called Raurava where Ruru ("an animal more cruel than serpents") tears them to pieces without killing them.

Cruel men are cast into Kumbhipaka and boiled in oil.

Kalasutra is the hell reserved for Brahminicides. Its bottom is a burning furnace and ceiling a frying pan. The sinner has to endure agonies in this hell "for as many years as there are hairs on the body of the beasts."

Heretics are tortured in Asipatravana where the servants of Yama tear their bodies with the sharp edges of the branches of the palmyra palm (the branch of this palm has two saw-like edges).

Kings who oppress their subjects are crushed between two rollers in the hell called Sukramukha.

Those who kill mosquitoes, bugs and other blood-sucking insects are cast into Andhakupa where the main torture is sleeplessness.

Inhospitable people and selfish householders are transformed into worms and thrown into the hell called Krimibhojana, full of worms, where they eat one another.

For the sin of simony, souls are torn to pieces by red hot pincers in the hell called Taptasurmi.

Those who marry outside their caste are made to embrace red-hot human forms in the hell called Vajrakantaka.

Sexual perverts are cast into a sea of burning filth and made to undergo various kinds of perverted tortures.

The person who gives false evidence is taken by the emissaries of Yama to the top of a mountain and hurled into Avichimat. They take him again to the mountain-top and throw him down into the pit, how many times, it is not mentioned.

Misers are taken to the hell called Suchimukha where steel wires with sharp projections are woven round their bodies like cocoons.

Kings and ministers who sow dissension among religious teachers are, after death, thrown into Vaitarani. "The Vaitarani river is like an entrenchment going round all the infernal regions, In this river, fed on by aquatic animals, they (the souls in torment) do not die; but remembering their disastrous acts, they are cast into that stream, which is full of excreta, urine, pus, blood, hairs, nails, bones, fat, flesh and marrow and the sinners are boiled there."

"There are hundreds and thousands of hells in the abode of Yama," says the *Bhagbata*. These hells are situated in the nether regions "underground to the south above water." Yama is in charge of all of them. As god of death he has two functions. To judge souls (in which capacity he is known as Dharmaraja) and to mete out punishments.

HOW TO DEFEAT YAMA

Some of the Puranas speak of devotion as the

surest means of obtaining salvation. Even a mechanical recital of the names of Vishnu or Shiva is considered of great merit. A story is told of Ajamila, a sinful Brahmin, who was saved from the clutches of Yama's emissaries by his merely uttering "Narayana", a name of Vishnu.

Ajamila lived in open sin with a Sudra harlot and broke all the laws sacred to his caste. He never read the Vedas and never performed a sacrifice. Persuaded by the harlot he deserted his aged parents and supported the woman and himself by ill-gotten wealth. The harlot bore him ten sons and Ajamila was very fond of the youngest whose name was Narayana.

Now the time came for the sinner to die and even while he was gasping Ajamila was thinking of his youngest son. When the emissaries of Yama approached, he called out to his son, "Narayana, Narayana." Now Vishnu heard a man in distress calling out his name and immediately despatched his deputies to help him. They arrived at the house of Ajamila and seeing the grisly servants of Yama with ropes and chains in their hands, asked them what they wanted. Yama's emissaries told Vishnu's deputies that Ajamila had broken all the laws of God and man and that the time had come for the sinner's soul to be taken to hell for torment; upon which they were told that Ajamila had expiated for all his sins by uttering the name of Vishnu on his death-bed. Yama's servants were not quite convinced and there followed a long argument between the two parties, at the end of which it was agreed that the matter should be referred to Yama himself. Accordingly the emissaries of Yama went back to their master and reported the matter to him. Yama said that the deputies of Vishnu were right and that he, Yama, had no power over one who uttered the name of Vishnu on his death-bed.

Ajamila who happened to hear the conversation between the deputies of Yama and Vishnu, recovered from his illness on the departure of Yama's emissaries. He repented of his sins, gave up the pleasures of the world and retired into a forest where he lived the life of a hermit and obtained liberation.

A recital of the names of Shiva is no less meritorious. A robber was taken, after death, to Dharmaraja, and Chitragupta, the record-keeper of Yama's office, read out an account of all his deeds. It was a long list of heinous crimes and not a single good deed could be found in his favour. Chitragupta, however, revealed the fact that the robber, while plying his nefarious trade used to unwittingly invoke Shiva as "Hara" (a name of Shiva) while crying out "Ahara" (bring the booty) and "Prahara" (strike). On hearing this, Yama said he had not only atoned for all his misdeeds by the invocation but had acquired much merit, and judged him to be reborn as a king.

A fly in a temple of Shiva was reborn as the sage Pulaha, a son of Brahma.

Kubera, the god of wealth, was a robber in a former life. One night while he was robbing a temple of Shiva, the wick with which he was looking for booty went out and he had to light it ten times; by the merit of which act, he was reborn as the god of wealth!

The story of Markandeya is still more wonderful. Markandeya was an ardent devotee of Shiva and used to worship in Benares a Lingam of Shiva day and night. In the Book of Destiny, maintained in Yama's office, his life was recorded as sixteen years. At the end of this period the servants of Yama came to Benares to take away the devotee to Yamapuri. Markandeya saw the evil messengers and clung to the Lingam of Shiva. They did not dare to touch the Lingam and hence went back to Yama and reported the failure of their mission; upon which Yama came in person and, as he found it difficult to disentangle Markandeya from the Lingam, bound the devotee and the Lingam together with a rope. Shiva immediately appeared on the spot, kicked the god of death to death, and indulged in one of his wild dances.

By the death of Yama and the consequent immortality of all beings, the world was plunged into misery and, at the request of the gods, Yama was brought back to life.

CREMATION AND SHRADDHAS

There is as yet no agreement among scholars as to how the custom of cremating people originated. It is widely held that burial preceded cremation, and, that there was a time when mankind did not even know the art of burial and dead bodies were just thrown to wild animals. To this day there are communities who dispose of the dead in a similar manner. Dr. Rajendralal Mitra, in his interesting book *Indo-Aryans* opines that dogs were first tamed and trained for the purpose of eating corpses and points to many customs which establish a curious connection between death and the dog. Some communities in India and elsewhere show the dead body to a dog before taking it for final disposal. Among the Hindus there is a belief that the dog is capable of seeing the emissaries of Yama, and hence the howl of a dog is considered inauspicious in a sick man's house. Yama himself is attended by two dogs called Sarameyas.

In the *Rig Veda* there are traces of Aryans having once been a burying people. It seems even wives, horses and attendants were buried alive with a man to keep him company during his journey to the other world. By the time the Aryans settled down permanently in India, the custom was given up. Usages symbolic of the pre-Vedic rite persisted, and a wife was taken upto the grave of her husband and conducted back to her house. A sword or ornament was buried with the dead body. The ancient custom was, however, revived in the middle ages, when widows were burnt alive with their husbands. Sati was partially stopped by Akbar and totally prohibited by William Bentinck.

It is not known from what source the Indo-Aryans learnt the art of cremation. Although, under the influence of Christianity and Islam, in Europe and the major part of Asia people bury their dead, there was a time when cremation was the most common form of disposing of the dead body in these continents. Burial among Christians and Muslims is connected with a belief in resurrection and cremation among the Hindus is symbolic of the dissolution of the body into the elements or liberation.

The following are the injunctions laid down for the performance of the cremation ceremony among the Hindus:

"A dying man, when no hopes of his surviving remains, should be laid on a bed of Kusa (*Poa cynosuroides*) grass in the open air, his head sprinkled with water from the Ganges, and smeared with clay brought from the same river. A Shaligrama (a peculiarly shaped sacred stone) should be placed near him, holy strains from the Vedas should be chanted aloud, and leaves of holy basil scattered over his head.

"When he expires, the corpse must be washed, perfumed, and decked with wreaths of flowers, and carried by the nearest relations to some spot in the forest, or near water; the funeral pile is lighted from the consecrated fire maintained by the deceased; the nearest relation applies the flaming brand to the pile, hung round with flowers and the attendant priests recite the appropriate invocations: 'Fire! thou wast lighted by him; may he therefore be reproduced from thee, that he may attain the regions of celestial bliss. May this offering be auspicious.' All who follow the corpse walk round the pile, but may not view the fire; they then proceed to the river and, after bathing, present oblations of water from the joined palms of their hands to the manes of the deceased, saying, 'May this oblation reach thee.' Elegiac verses, such as the following, are then recited— '(1) Foolish is he who seeks for permanence in the human state; insolid, like the stem of the plantain tree; transient, like the foam of the sea. (2) When a body formed of five elements, to receive the reward of deeds done in its own former person, reverts to its five original principles, what room is there for regret? (3) The earth is perishable; the ocean, the gods themselves, pass away. How should not the bubble, mortal man, meet destruction?

(4) All that is low must finally perish; all that is elevated must ultimately fall; all compounded bodies must end in dissolution; and life be concluded with death."

Death on the banks of the Ganges or in the waters of the river is considered good for the departing soul.

The Hindus believe that the dead and the living stand in an intimate relationship and the actions of the one can influence the destiny of the other. Departed ancestors can cause prosperity to their progeny living on earth by performances of austerities or devotions. Similarly the tortures of souls in hell can be mitigated by the pious acts of mortals expressly dedicated for the purpose. We have already seen in a previous chapter that the mother-in-law of Yama was saved from hell by the performance of a sacrifice by a relative who was living on earth. In the code of Manu the necessity for performance of Shraddhas (ceremonies for the deceased) is emphasized. "Let the housekeeper," says Manu, "who knows his duty perform each day a Shraddha with boiled rice and the like or with water or with milk, roots and fruits; for thus he obtains favour from departed progenitors." The main item of the Shraddha is the feeding of Brahmins and giving them presents. Clothes and food given to Brahmins on this occasion are believed to reach the departed souls. If the Shraddha is performed for a woman, presents are given to a Brahmin woman.*

The goddess of funeral obsequies is Swadha. She lives among the manes and carries to them the offerings of mortals.

ARJUNA'S JOURNEY IN SEARCH OF A DEAD CHILD

While Krishna was the virtual ruler of Dwaraka there came, one day, to the gates of his palace a Brahmin with a dead child in his arms. He cried out that in a kingdom where Brahmin children died, a king had no right to rule. He had nine children, he said, all of whom had died in infancy. He started cursing Krishna and called him an impious and impotent ruler. Arjuna, who was sitting in the palace with Krishna heard the imprecations of the Brahmin and went down to the gate and tried to console him. He promised the Brahmin that he would make it his personal care to see that his next child would not perish. The Brahmin was sceptical and wanted to know who he was who could promise to do a thing which Krishna and Balarama could not. Arjuna told him that he was the third son of Kunti, the redoubtable bowman famed for his marksmanship in the three worlds, the proud possessor of the celestial bow Gandiva. And as an assurance to the Brahmin he swore that if he could not protect his

---

* Detailed descriptions of Shraddhas will be found in the author's work *Hindu Religion, Customs and Manners*.

PLATE LVII

161 MANASA
(Copyright : Archaeological Dept. of India)

162 MOHINI DANCING
(From Belur Copyright :
Archaeological Department of India)

163 DURGA KILLING MAHISHASURA
(From Belur. Copyright :
Archaeological Dept. of India)

164 A RAKSHASA
(From Java)

PLATE LVIII

CREMATION
(From a painting by Solvyns)

PLATE LIX

167 YAMA (From Chidambaram, S. India)

166 TORTURES OF HELL (From a painting in the Jaipur Manuscript of the *Razmnamah*)

PLATE LX

168 PLANETS AND SIGNS OF THE ZODIAC

PLANETS :—(1) Surya (2) Brahaspati. (3) Ketu. (4) Rahu. (5) Budha. (6) Mangala. (7) Chandra. (8) Sani. (9) Sukra.
SIGNS OF THE ZODIAC :—I. Mesha. II. Vrishabha. III. Mithun. IV. Kirk. V. Sinha. VI. Kanya. VII. Tula. VIII. Vrischika. IX. Dhanu. X. Makara. XI. Kumbha. XII. Meena.

(From Moor's *Hindu Pantheon*)

PLATE LXI

169 YAMUNA, PERSONIFICATION
OF THE RIVER JUMNA
(Copyright : Archaeological Dept. of India)

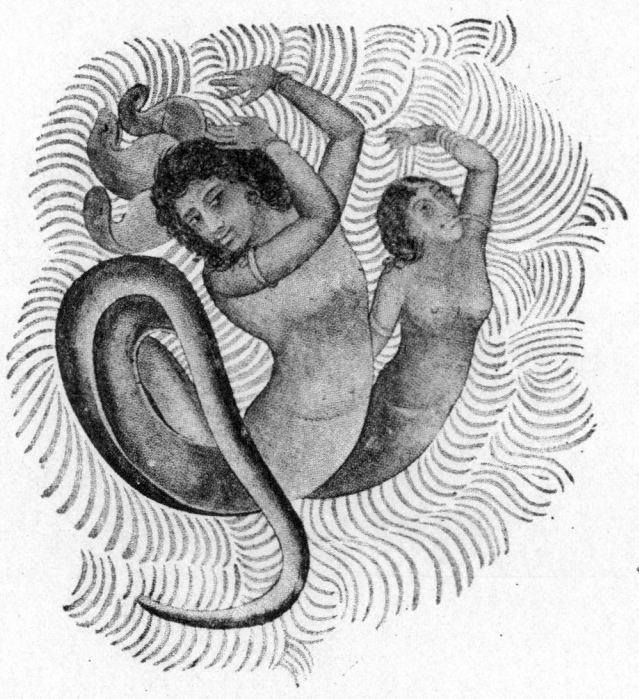

170   NAGA AND NAGINI
(From Griffiths' *Paintings in Ajanta Caves*)

171   WORSHIPPING THE SUN
(From a painting by Mrs. Belnos)

172 A HINDU LADY GIVING ALMS TO
A RELIGIOUS-MENDICANT

PLATE LXII

173 GARUDA AND HANUMAN
(From Moor's *Hindu Pantheon*)

174 CHANDRA
(From Moor's *Hindu Pantheon*)

PLATE LXIII

175 KALI
(From *Mythology of the Hindus* by Charles Coleman)

176 HANUMAN

177 KAMA
(From *Mythology of the Hindus* by Charles Coleman)

PLATE LXIV

178 A MENDICANT WITH THE SHIVA TRIDENT
(From *Picturesque India* by Martin Hurlimann)

179 GARUDA WITH A NAGINI
(From Sanghao. Indian Museum, Calcutta)

180 GANESHA
(From Mayurbhanj)

181 UMA
(From South India)

next child he would burn himself to death. The Brahmin thanked him and went home.

The Brahmin's wife conceived for the tenth time, and for her confinement Arjuna constructed an impregnable chamber of arrows through whch neither god nor man could enter. And when the day for delivery came he stood guard over the apartment. But alas! a few minutes after the birth of the child, it disappeared mysteriously.

The bitterness of the Brahmin's disappointment now knew no bounds. Till now, he had at least the privilege of seeing the bodies of his children, dead or alive, but now even this pleasure was denied to him. He abused Arjuna, called him an imposter and a braggart, and reviled himself for believing that such a wretch could do things Krishna and Balarama could not. Arjuna, however, left the Brahmin to wail, and proceeded by the power of Samjamani Yoga of which he was a master, to Yamapuri, the abode of the dead. The child was not there. Thence he went to the heaven of Indra and to the kingdoms of Agni, Nirrita, the Moon, Vayu and Varuna. The child was in none of these upper regions. He then searched in vain for the child in the underground regions of serpents and Asuras. Baffled he returned to earth and decided to burn himself to death. But Krishna now asked Arjuna not to immolate himself and said that he would show him the dead child.

Krishna ascended his magic car with Arjuna and drove in the westerly direction. They drove over the seven oceans and the seven islands and reached the kingdom of Night. Krishna pierced the primal gloom with his discus and illuminated the regions of Night. Guided by this light they crossed the kingdom of Night and came upon the kingdom of Waters. Reaching this region the car dived downwards and halted near a celestial mansion where the pilgrims saw the great Vishnu reposing on the snake Ananta with the ten children of the Brahmin on his lap. Krishna and Arjuna worshipped the deity and begged him to give them the children of the Brahmin. Vishnu smiled and blessed them. He told Krishna that he (Krishna) was a portion of himself and that he (Vishnu) had purposely taken the children of the Brahmin to Vaikunta so that he could have the pleasure of this visit. He gave the children to Arjuna, and this hero and Krishna took leave of Vishnu, returned to earth and gave over the children to the Brahmin who prayed for mercy for his past misconduct.

THE STORY OF SATYAVAN AND SAVITRI

Once upon a time there lived a king named Aswapati. The king was virtuous and generous but he had no sons. So, for eighteen years he worshipped Savitri (Sarasvati, wife of Brahma, who is also called Savitri) with incessant devotion and the goddess appeared before him and asked him to name his boon. The king asked for sons. "Thou shalt be blessed with a daughter," said the goddess, "and she shall be greater than a son." Saying this she disappeared.

In due time the queen gave birth to a daughter and she was named Savitri in honour of the goddess whose gift she was. Savitri grew up and when she reached maidenhood she looked like the goddess of beauty herself. The young princess was the object of adoration of the people, but because of her celestial bearing and beauty no man dared to ask for her hand. When Savitri's time for marriage came and no suitor appeared, Aswapati sent his daughter with a royal escort to travel in the neighbouring kingdoms so that she could choose a husband for herself. Savitri travelled far and wide but she fell in love with no one she saw. At last she wandered into a forest hermitage and there saw the man of her choice. He was Satyavan, son of the blind king Dyumatsena who, driven out of his kingdom by an usurper, was living in the forest among the hermits. Satyavan was handsome and brave and, though he lived the life of a hermit, on his person were the auspicious marks of royalty.

Savitri returned to her father and related to him the story of her travels at the end of which she confided to him the name of the person she had chosen for her lord. The sage Narada was present in the court at the time, and the king asked him if he approved of the match. The sage told him that Satyavan was brave, virtuous and handsome and had all the qualities of a great man in abundance, but was a doomed man. "Next year, this day," said Narada, "Satyavan is destined to die." On hearing this the king was alarmed and told his daughter to choose another husband. "Father," said Savitri, "I have but one soul and that is given away to Satyavan. I can't take it back. Hence whether his life be long or short, I will wed Satyavan and no one else."

The sage Narada, observing the constancy of the princess, advised the king to give her in marriage to Satyavan and leave the rest to God. He blessed Savitri, assured the king that everything would turn out for the best, and departed to the celestial regions.

The king then took Savitri to the hermitage of Dyumatsena, gave her in marriage to Satyavan according to the prescribed rites and returned to his kingdom.

Savitri lived with her husband and his father in the hermitage. She was particularly kind and obedient to the old man. Her cheerful disposition and virtuous nature won for her the good opinion of the neighbours and in course of time she became the pet of the hermits who lived in the forest. But gay and smiling as she was to all outward appearances, Savitri's soul was heavy-laden because of the prophecy of Narada. She was counting the days and nights and her anxiety increased as the dreadful day approached. She did not, however, confide the secret to her husband.

At last the fateful day dawned. Savitri got up early, performed all the religious ceremonies of the morning, and prepared the meal for the family. After breakfast, Satyavan took his axe and told Savitri that he was going into the forest to cut wood; upon which she said that she would like to accompany him that day and asked for the old man's permission. At first Dyumatsena was reluctant to let her go out, but she entreated him with great earnestness and he yielded. "Because," he said, "Savitri is about a year here now and has never asked of me any favour."

So Satyavan and Savitri went together into the forest. Satyavan appeared somewhat melancholy and Savitri walked behind him, sad but vigilant, The pair wandered far into the woods and at last Satyavan chose a tree and he made the wood resound with his hatchet. He had been at work for a short while when a thrill of agony shot through his temples and he called out to Savitri. She was watching him and immediately ran to him. Satyavan fainted and fell on the ground and Savitri placed his head on her lap and sat there, determined, with tears rolling down her cheeks.

Suddenly there appeared before her a grisly form, bright yet obscure, dressed in blood-red garments, wearing a crown. He had coppery eyes and bore a noose in his hand. Savitri stood up and with joined hands asked him respectfully who he was. "I am Yama, god of death," said he, And without another word he tore the soul out of Satyavan's body, put the noose round its neck and proceeded with it towards the south. Savitri followed the god of death. After going some distance Yama looked back and saw Savitri. "Woman," said he, "why dost thou follow me?" "God of justice," said Savitri, "your worship knows the sacred laws better than I. It is written in the scriptures that a husband and wife are one and even death has no power to part them. I will follow my lord wherever he goes."

"Thy words," said Yama, "pleaseth me. And thy devotion to thy husband is praiseworthy. Ask thou, therefore, any favour of me except the life of thy husband."

Savitri asked for the restoration of the eyesight of her father-in-law and this was granted. Yama then asked Savitri to return, and himself continued the journey with the soul of Satyavan. He had not gone far when he looked back again and saw the sad, lonely figure of Savitri following him. Pitiless as he is, Yama was moved by the devotion of the lady and he asked her again to name a boon. She asked for the restoration of his kingdom to Dyumatsena. "Be it so," said Yama, and he commanded Savitri to return, and continued his journey. Yama travelled far, far into the regions of twilight and Savitri followed him. As he was passing the regions of twilight Yama looked back again and was astonished to see Savitri. The daring and the devotion of the woman were worthy of another boon. "Savitri," said he, "you are wandering into forbidden regions and your people will be sorrowing for you. Where your husband goes you cannot go. So ask for a final boon except the life of your husband and then you must really depart."

Savitri asked for a hundred sons for herself and Yama granted her the boon. "But my lord," said Savitri, "how can I have sons without my husband? It now becomes incumbent on you to grant me the life of my husband!"

Yama reflected, and remarked that she was a true and brave woman. He loosed the cord that bound Satyavan, gave him back to Savitri, blessed her and sent her back.

Satyavan now woke up as if from sleep and seeing that night had fallen and they were still in the forest was much upset. "Savitri," he said, "I have been sleeping rather long; why did you not wake me up? Besides, I had strange dreams of a grisly form that put a noose round my neck and dragged me towards the south." Savitri smiled and told him all that had happened.

They then returned to the hermitage where Dyumatsena was anxiously waiting for them. He had regained his eyesight. As soon as Savitri and Satyavan reached the hermitage a messenger arrived from Dyumatsena's capital who informed the king that the usurper had been assassinated by the people and they were waiting for Dyumatsena to return to his kingdom and rule over them.

THE LAST JOURNEY OF THE PANDAVAS

After the battle of Kurukshetra, the Pandavas ruled the kingdom for thirty-six years. Then old age came upon the heroes. So they chose a successor, and with Draupadi the queen, set forth on their last journey. The five heroes and the queen travelled towards the North, determined to cross the forests and the great mountains and reach the abode of the gods or perish in the attempt. A lean dirty dog followed them on their journey.

The way was long and the journey perilous, and one by one the heroes collapsed on the road. It was not for all to ascend to heaven in the flesh; this honour was reserved for Yudhishtira, the only one among the Pandavas who was comparatively sinless. Draupadi, Nakula, Sahadeva, Arjuna and Bhima perished on the road and Yudhishtira was left alone

DEATH AND SOUL WANDERINGS

with the dog. The king left the dead to bury the dead and continued his lonesome journey without ever looking back. He travelled over mountains, forests and rivers and reached regions never seen by mortals. Then suddenly there appeared before him Indra with his celestial car. The king of the gods told Yudhishtira that he had come in person to conduct him to the celestial regions because there never lived a man so great and virtuous as Yudhishtira. Indra begged him to enter the car. Yudhishtira now told Indra that without his brothers and Draupadi he would not enter heaven. Their part in the great struggle, he said, had been even greater than his and they deserved to be in heaven before himself. Indra assured the king that, though they could not be taken to heaven in the flesh, their souls had already been transferred to the abode of the blessed. Yudhishtira then saw the dog. It was standing near the car looking expectantly at the king. The great king now stood back and beckoned to the dog to enter the car. The grateful creature wagged its tail and approached the door of the car, when Indra objected. The dog is considered an unclean animal by the Hindus and Indra could not imagine its polluting his car, much less its being taken to heaven. "King of the gods," said Yudhishtira, "this loyal creature has followed me throughout my perilous journey and now I cannot desert it. We either enter the car together or remain outside. This is final." In all his life Yudhishtira had not deserted a companion nor refused sanctuary to the supplicant. He would not now give up his principles for the hope of heaven itself.

The test was over. The dog now transformed itself into Dharmaraja (the god of judgment and father of Yudhishtira) and he blessed his son and asked him to enter the car. The king entered the car and Indra drove him to heaven, where, strangely enough, he saw most of his enemies killed in the battle and none of his allies. He asked Indra where his friends were and was told that they were in hell. Yudhishtira refused to enter heaven and requested Indra to conduct him to hell. He was taken up to the gates of hell and he saw souls in torment and heard familiar voices crying out in agony. "King of the gods," said Yudhishtira, "I cannot understand the justice of this. I am no doubt a mortal and the ways of the gods are not known to me. Anyway, since all my friends who fought on my side are in hell, I prefer to dwell here rather than enjoy the bliss of heaven with my enemies."

The supreme test was over. This vision of heaven and hell was an illusion created by Indra. Yudhishtira was, however, taken up to the gates of hell because he had once spoken an untruth (see page 56); besides no king could ever go to heaven without having a vision of hell as ruling a kingdom is considered practically impossible without committing some sin or other. The brothers and allies of Yudhishtira were really in heaven and the king was finally taken there and given a place of great honour.

Chapter VIII
LOVE AND SEX

LIKE Eros of the Greeks and Cupid of the Latins, Kama is the Hindu god of love. In the *Rig Veda*, Kama (literally, desire) is described as the "first movement that arose in the One, after it had come into life through the power of fervour or abstraction." In one hymn the god is thus addressed: "May Kama, having well-directed the arrow, which is winged with pain, barbed with longing, and has desire for its shaft, pierce thee in the heart." It is in this capacity that he appears in the Puranas and his main function is to create sexual desire in men and women. He wounds his victims by shafts of flowers. The bow of Kama is the sugarcane and the string of the bow is made of humming bees.

His wife is Rati (passion). His friend Vasanta (spring) strings the bow for Kama and selects the shafts:

> "He bends the luscious cane, and twists the string
> With bees, how sweet! but ah! how keen their sting!
> He with five flow'rets tips thy ruthless darts,
> Which through five senses pierce enraptur'd hearts:
> Strong Chumpa, rich in od'rous gold;
> Warm Amer, nurs'd in heavenly mould;
> Dry Nagkeser, in silver smiling;
> Hot Kitticum, our sense beguiling;
> And last, to kindle fierce the scorching flame,
> Love's shaft, which bright Bela name."

Because of his predilection for these five flower-shafts, Kama is also known as Panchabana (he who possesses five shafts).

Kama enjoys everlasting youth and is the most handsome of all the gods. The parrot is his charger and his banner is distinguished by the sign of the Makara— a mythical fish.

Kama is the son of Brahma. As soon as he was born he let loose a shaft on his father and the Creator fell in love with his own daughter. Hindu scriptures describe in detail the mischief done by the god of love among the gods and men. He roams about woodlands, fountains, cities and villages on errands of love, creates desire in ascetics and causes weakness in virtuous women. Spring is the season of his revelry. When the mango tree blossoms and the Koil calls to its mate, when forests and gardens resound with the music of the black bee, the archer begins his depredations. Wounded by the shafts of Kama, faithful wives become adulterous, young ladies yield themselves to betrayers and youthful men commit follies. Lean Rishis practising austerities give up asceticism and run after women. Countless indeed are the frivolities of the god of love.

We have noticed elsewhere how Kama interrupted the asceticism of Shiva and was consumed by the fire that emanated from the third eye of that deity. The *Vamana Purana* observes that the shaft of Kama had its effect and Shiva wandered over the three worlds unable to bear the passion Kama had generated. Shiva first repaired to the cool shades of a forest, but, far from getting relief, his passion was inflamed by the sight of the wives of the hermits living there. He then remained immersed in cold water, but this only boiled the water. Unable to get solace anywhere Shiva at last married Parvati in whose embrace he found relief.

After the death of Kama, the worlds became arid deserts devoid of love, and the gods requested Shiva to bring him back to life. Rati prayed to Parvati in particular and this lady pleaded for the widow, and Shiva agreed to restore Kama to life. Accordingly the god of love was born as Pradyumna, son of Krishna and Rukmini.

As soon as Pradyumna was born Narada went to an Asura named Shambhara and informed him that Pradyumna was destined to kill him. Shambhara, by his magic powers, entered the apartments of Rukmini, stole the child and threw it into the sea. A fish swallowed the child. The fish was caught by a fisherman and sold to Shambhara. Rati had already assumed the form of a mortal woman and had been living in Shambhara's household as cook as previously advised by Narada. The fish was given to Rati for cooking, and when she cut it open Pradyumna came out of its belly. Narada immediately appeared on the scene and told Rati who the child was and granted her a boon by which she could make the child invisible at will. So, Rati nursed Pradyumna and he grew up unperceived by Shambhara. When Pradyumna came of age, Rati one day spoke to him in terms of love and the young man was at first horrified to hear the amorous words of the lady whom he had all along treated as his mother. Rati then told him his origin and their true relationship and the two from then on lived as man and wife.

In course of time Rati became pregnant and Shambhara coming to know of her condition abused her. He was about to lay violent hands on her when Pradyumna appeared on the scene and killed Shambhara in single combat. After this the couple returned to Dwaraka with Narada, and Rukmini and Krishna were delighted to see their long lost son.

The following story is told of Aniruddha, son of Pradyumna and Rati, whose adventures with Usha, daughter of an Asura named Bana, led to a fierce battle in which Shiva and Vishnu fought on opposite sides.

Bana's daughter had a dream of a beautiful youth and she fell in love with him. Her companion Chitralekha drew for her, on a canvas, the pictures of all the kings and their sons who were then living and Usha picked out the picture of Aniruddha, as the one she had seen in the dream. Chitralekha by her magic power descended to Dwaraka and carried off Aniruddha to Usha's palace. Usha hid him inside the palace and spent her days in amorous sport with him. The palace-guards observed a change in the physical appearance of the princess and reported the matter to Bana. Bana had Usha's palace searched, and he found Aniruddha. After a fierce struggle Aniruddha was overpowered and put in prison.

News of Aniruddha's captivity reached Krishna and Pradyumna, and they set out with an army and invaded the kingdom of Bana. Bana was a devotee of Shiva and by virtue of a boon he had received from this deity, was possessed of one thousand arms. Bana fought bravely with his thousand arms; but he found it difficult to stem the tide of Krishna's forces and he prayed to Shiva for help. This deity came in person and fought on the side of Bana. Ultimately the combat resolved itself into one between Shiva's trident and Vishnu's disc. The two weapons fought fiercely but in the end the trident was broken.

Usha was then married to Aniruddha and the couple returned to Dwaraka.

SEX-WORSHIP IN ARCHAIC RELIGIONS

From time immemorial man has traced a mystic connection between human sex-life and all generative phenomena. The connection between sex and life is obvious. Fruitfulness and plenty were mystically traced to sex, and among savages to this day, a good harvest is supposed to be caused by the sex activities of men and women. Hence in the beginning of the harvest season and even at the time of sowing, there were and are, among many savage tribes, festivals in which promiscuous intercourse forms a prominent feature. The forefathers of all nations, now called civilized, were savages, and festivals symbolic of the primitive fertility orgies still exist among them; on these occasions a certain amount of licence, held in horror in normal times, is permitted. The vitality of sex-belief is further illustrated by the theories of modern Freudians who maintain that all human activities are motivated by sex and that the Libido is the primal source of all teleological energy.

In ancient Egypt, the phallus of Osiris was worshipped. Legends say that Osiris was a king who invented agriculture. He appointed his brother Typhon as his regent and travelled among foreign nations and taught them the art of agriculture. When Osiris returned Typhon murdered him, enclosed the dead body in a box and left it to drift down the Nile.

Isis, wife of Osiris, set out in search of the dead body and found it by the seashore in Phoenicia. She hid the body in a secret place and returned to Egypt to see her son Horus. In the meantime Typhon went out hunting and happened to see the body of his brother which he cut into forty pieces and dispersed to the winds. Isis again started on a pilgrimage of discovery and found all the parts of the body except the genitals. In honour of the lost member she ordered a phallus to be made of the wood of the fig-tree for worship.

The genitals of not only humans but even of animals were worshipped by the Mediterranean people. Priapus, a phallic god introduced into Greece probably from Egypt, derives his name from Apis, the bull-god of Egypt. The phalli of goats and asses were particularly worshipped because of the strong sex nature of these animals. "When Juno was invoked to make the Sabian women fruitful the worshippers heard the oracle speak from the sacred forests of Mount Esquilin: 'Let the women of Italy be impregnated by a goat.' "

There were various cults of Venus in Greece, and one of them was that of Venus, the Courtesan. Temples were dedicated to the goddess, and the chief source of income in these temples was the institution of sacred prostitutes who were hired out to visitors. Strabo says that in his day there were about one thousand prostitutes living in the temple of Venus in Corinth.

In ancient Babylon, Mylitta was the goddess of fertility. All the women of the country had to prostitute themselves at least once in honour of the goddess. It is related that once a woman entered the temple for the purpose, she was not allowed to depart till she had found a customer and paid the fee to the goddess. The young and handsome had to live in the temple for a comparatively short time while the ugly had to remain for months before they could get customers. Such usages, it need scarcely be added, were considered highly proper and sacred, and the high and the low had to conform to the priestly code.

The Romans were no less inclined to sex-worship than the other great ancient peoples. Phallus worship and the cults of Venus were introduced into Rome from Egypt, Greece and Syria; and once they were introduced, they found a congenial soil and thrived. The phallus was called Mutinus among the Romans. "The symbol was placed in a small chariot and driven through the towns and villages, the people accompanying it with lascivious songs and dances. Even the most respectable people with families used to crown the figure with flowers."

"In the month of October took place the festival of Bacchus. This festival was celebrated in the sacred wood called Similia, near the river Tiber, and at first only women were admitted. Respectable married women used to take turns in being priestesses, and no scandal attacked the cult till a woman named Pacculla Minia brought in her two sons. Thenceforth other men were introduced and the mysteries took place every month and lasted five days. The men had to be under twenty-eight years of age—older men not being quite so pliable, impressionable or active.

"These Bacchanalian feasts soon became noted for the most shameful indecencies almost impossible to describe. Scenes of all kinds were enacted which would require the pen of a Marquis De Sade to depict in all their bestiality. Crowds of people sought to be initiated into the cult, and Dulare remarks that it was not merely a few but an entire people wished to participate in the abominable orgies. Indeed the orgies became so bad that the senate of Rome had to forbid them under severe penalties."

Judaism and, later, Christianity tried their utmost to separate sex from religion. Although they succeeded to a certain extent, sex-beliefs were so deep-rooted among the people that many concessions had to be made to hoary traditions and certain pagan beliefs, gods and festivals were absorbed into Christianity and given new guises. Sex-cults also thrived in certain monasteries, and orders of knighthood, and only ruthless persecution succeeded in ridding these privileged circles of their sacred orgies.

WORSHIP OF THE LINGAM AND YONI

At what precise date sex-worship received recognition in Hinduism is not known. There is every reason to believe that the worship is not of Aryan origin. The Vedas, far from sanctioning it, speak of it with horror. "May the glorious Indra triumph over hostile beings," says the *Rig Veda;* "let not those whose god is the Sishana (*membrum virile*) approach our sacred ceremony." Again "desiring to bestow strength in the struggle, that warrior (Indra) has besieged inaccessible places at the time when irresistible, slaying those whose god is the Sishana, he, by force conquered the riches of the city with hundred gates."

By the Mahabharata time the worship of the Lingam and Yoni had come to be recognized as orthodox. The superior merit of sex-worship is thus maintained in the *Mahabharata*: "He whose Lingam Brahma, Vishnu and Indra worship is the most eminent. Since children bear not the mark of the lotus (of Brahma) but are marked with the male and the female organs—therefore offspring is derived from Maheswara. All women produced from the nature of Devi as their cause, are marked with the female organ, and all males are manifestly marked with the Lingam of Hara. He who asserts any other cause than Ishwara (Mahadeva) or (affirms) that there is any female not marked by Devi in three worlds including all things movable and immovable, let that fool be thrust out. Know everything which is male to be Ishwara, and all that is female to be Vema, for this whole world movable and immovable is pervaded by these two bodies."

The worship of Shiva, it would appear, was popularized in its present form by Shankara, the Hindu revivalist who, in his crusade against Buddhism, had to make many concessions to popular superstitions so as to counterbalance the influence of Buddhism. With his deep insight into human nature Shankara judged the power of sex-cults correctly and popularized the worship of Mahadeva and Devi and had many temples built all over India where the worship of Shiva in the form of the Lingam was instituted. To placate the lower orders, many stories were also invented of how Shiva assumed the form of a hunter, a Sudra, a fisherman or some other low-caste man.

What was probably unashamed sex-worship among the aborigines had to be symbolized and explained when the belief was incorporated into Hinduism. Hence we find many myths in the Puranas explaining how the worship originated. We have already noticed the story which purports to say that when Brahma and Vishnu started arguing about each other's priority there appeared before them Shiva in the form of the Lingam. In another myth it is related that while Shiva, after the death of Sati, was wandering like a lunatic, he happened to pass through a forest where the wives of some hermits saw him and asked him the cause of his madness. Shiva told them that he had a loving wife whose death he was mourning. A gay young lady did not believe him and expressed astonishment as to how any woman could ever marry such an emaciated ill-looking fellow, and laughed at his story. The infuriated deity caught the woman and ravished her. Her husband came on the scene and imprecated a curse by the power of which Shiva came to be worshipped in the form of the Lingam.

A third story is that when the sage Bhrigu went on a visit to Shiva he was made to wait outside for a long time as Shiva was making love to his wife; and the sage, tired of waiting, cursed Shiva to be worshipped as the Lingam.

Yet another account is that Shiva and Parvati in a romantic adventure strayed into a forest where some Rishis were practising austerities and were seen naked by the pious men who imprecated a curse by which Shiva came to be worshipped as the Phallus.

Lingams are of different shapes and the "uninitiated" would not understand their significance at all. "It is some comparative and negative praise to the Hindus," says Moor,* "that the emblems under which they exhibit the elements and operation of nature are not externally indecorous. Unlike the abominable realities of Egypt and Greece, we see the Phallic emblem in the Hindu Pantheon without offence, and know not until the information be extorted that we are contemplating a symbol whose prototype is indelicate. The external decency of the symbols and the difficulty with which their recondite allusions are discovered both offer evidence favourable to the moral delicacy of the Hindu character."

The cult of the Yoni is said to have originated from the place where that part of Sati fell when her body was cut into pieces by Vishnu (see p. 28). Every place where a part of the body fell became sacred and a temple was built in honour of the relic. The Yoni is said to have fallen in Assam from where the worship spread all over India. Thus the myth of the origin of Phallus-worship in Egypt and that of Yoni-worship in India can be traced to a common source although the sexes have subsequently got mixed up.

The Yonijas (those who worship the Yoni) maintain that the feminine principle is anterior and superior to the male. It is said that Shiva and Parvati had once a dispute between them as to the superiority of the sexes and each one created a race of men. Those who were created by Shiva devoted themselves to the exclusive worship of the male deity; and "their intellects became dull, their bodies feeble, their limbs distorted, and their complexions of different hues." The race created by Parvati, on the other hand, worshipped the female power and they "became powerful, virile and handsome." Mahadeva was enraged at the result and was about to destroy the Yonijas when Parvati interceded on their behalf; the race was, however, exiled from their homeland.

Men who were excommunicated due to pollution such as that supposed to be caused by going overseas, etc., were at one time made to be "reborn" through a metallic Yoni before they were re-admitted into the Hindu fold. In the case of rich people the symbol was made of gold which was, after the ceremony, given to Brahmins.

Clefts and rocks which resemble the Yoni and Lingam are also worshipped. Impotent men hope to gain virility by passing through such a cleft while barren women who wish to become mothers are particularly devoted to the worship of the Lingam.

While the Lingayatas exclusively worship the Lingam and the Saktas Yoni, a popular object of sex-worship is the symbol of coitus "indicated by the Linga inserted in its appropriate receptacle, the Argha (literally, a vessel) or Yoni." A ring at the bottom of a pillar is also indicative of the union of the two principles.

While emblems of the Lingam and Yoni, used in sex-worship, are not indecent, the same cannot be said to be the case with the decorative art of some of the temples in which the artists have left little to the imagination. But then, to the ancients sex was not what it is to modern prudes.

It is also well-known that many temples in India had till recently, their complement of Devadasis — slaves of the gods. While the ostensible functions of these women were to dance before the idols and generally devote themselves to the service of the gods, it cannot be said that they were exclusively devoted to their sacred duties. Abuses were rampant and many temples were no better than sanctuaries of licence. But right-minded Hindus were themselves the first to protest against this institution and at present there are few temples in India where Devadasis are overtly retained.

While sex-worship is generally clothed in decorous forms and most of the devotees worship the principle symbolically, there is a "left-hand" sect of Shaktas who worship sex realistically. The cult remains a jealously guarded secret, and for obvious reasons it is quite impossible to get an authentic account of the true nature of the mysteries. The sacred literature which deals with this branch of Hinduism is known as Tantras. The Tantrics (as the "left-hand" Shaktas are popularly known) hope to obtain salvation by means of Panchatatwas (the five Tatwas). Panchatatwas are vulgarly called the five M's (Makaras). The M's are ('M' is the first letter of each word) Madya (liquor),

---

* Moor, *Hindu Pantheon*.

Mansa (flesh), Matsya (fish), Mudra (corn) and Maithuna (sexual intercourse).

"The principle underlying the Panchatatwa worship appears to be that poison is the antidote of poison, and men must rise by those very things through which they so often lose their manhood. The *Kularnava Tantra* declares; As one falls on the ground one must lift oneself by aid of the ground.' The symbols chosen are very obvious ones: wine, the medicine, dispeller of care and source of merriment; flesh, nourisher of the body; fish, the tasty giver of generative power; corn from the earth and finally sexual intercourse speaking of the love and joy of creation."

Different forms of worship are mentioned in the Tantras. Communal worship is known as Chakrapuja (circle worship). In Chakrapuja an equal number of men and women sit in a circle and partake of "the sacrament." Sexual intercourse is ordinarily permitted only between man and wife. In certain cases, however, a man may have relations with a woman other than his wife, and in this case the couple are temporarily married by a Tantric rite known as Shaiva marriage.

In another form, worshippers select "a woman of low caste or a prostitute and place her on a seat or mat; then bring boiled fish, flesh, fried peas, rice, spirituous liquors, sweetmeats, flowers, etc. These offerings, as well as the female must next be purified by the repeating of incantations. To this should suceed the worship of the guardian deity. The female must be naked during the worship."

After thus seating the woman naked on a pedestal, the priest proceeds with the worship, the details of which we would better leave out.

It is laid down in the texts that "the worshippers must be pure in heart, free from desire and lust, and conscious that they are taking part in a sacrament, the aim of which is to unite participants with Sakti, and to free them from the fetters of the ordinary man." There is, however, difference of opinion among scholars as to whether these injunctions are strictly adhered to or not.

The Tantrics recognize no caste in the Circle. All are equal before the goddess.

In some of the Pujas the devotees have to remain naked throughout the ceremony. Adjoining the Sanctum Sanctorum is an apartment where the congregation strip themselves and keep their clothes. At the end of the worship every one takes the clothes one happens to lay one's hands on, and goes home in them. So complete is the recognition of equality and brotherhood in the sect.

To the credit of the Tantrics it must be mentioned that they made an attempt to abolish Sati before the advent of the British, and encouraged widow-marriages. As a rule the conduct of the generality of the Tantrics, outside the sanctuaries of worship, is considered good. They hold the view that the female is superior to the male and lay down that no female victim should ever be sacrificed before the idol of Devi*.

THE RADHA-KRISHNA CULT

This is a finer form of sex-worship. In this cult, sex-love is held as the symbol of the individual soul's yearning for union with the Universal Soul. The philosophy of the cult is identical with that of the Song of Songs and the mysticism of Sufis.

Except for a casual mention in the *Chhandogya Upanishad*, the name of Krishna is not found in Vedic literature. In the *Mahabharata* however he is a prominent figure. In this epic he appears as a soldier and diplomat, and those accounts in it which are meant to deify him are considered interpolations. It is in the *Vishnu Purana* and the *Bhagbata* that we read the various legends that speak of his divine nature.

Krishna was probably the tribal god of some pastoral Rajput clan who came into prominence after the tenth century. By the eleventh century the worship of Krishna had become well-established on the bank of the Jumna, and from there spread throughout India. Poets and ecstatics did much to popularize the cult by drama, dance and song which gave a mystic and poetic interpretation to the love of the Gopis for Krishna.

The scenes of the activities of the boyhood days of Krishna were the fields of Vrindavan, on the bank of the Jumna, where he played with the cow-boys and danced with the Gopis. The Gopis, maddened by love of Krishna, enchanted by the melody of his flute, left their husbands and parents, and danced and sported with the lord of their hearts in the arcadian fields of Vrindavan. When the full moon shone over the blue waters of the Jumna and the gentle spring breeze blew over the flower-laden trees of Vrindavan, Krishna stole into the groves and played on his flute. Hearing the love call of Krishna, the Braj girls (Gopis) left their sleeping husbands and went in search of him. When the ladies came, the lord of their hearts said: "I called you to show you the beauty of the Jumna and the groves on her banks shining in the silvery beams of the moon. You have seen, O Braj girls, the wonder of the moon playing on the ripples of the blue Jumna and enjoyed the breeze that blew from the cool waters of the river. Now go back to your husbands." The Gopis were heart-broken at these cruel words. "Fie upon you, Krishna." they said in one voice, "you woke us up from sleep and stole our hearts, and now

---

* Tantric worship is dealt with in greater detail in *Kama Kalpa* (Taraporevala).

PLATE LXV

182 HANUMAN
(Copper : S. India)

183 SANI OR THE PLANET SATURN
(*Indian Antiquities*)

PLATE LXVI

THE BANYAN TREE
(From a painting by Solvyns)

PLATE LXVII

185 TREE WORSHIP
(From Fergusson's *Serpent and Tree Worship*)

186 WORSHIPPING THE TULSI PLANT

187 PRAYING PILGRIMS ON THE GANGES
(From *Picturesque India* by Martin Hurlimann)

188 A DYING MAN BROUGHT TO THE GANGES
(From a painting by Mrs. Belons)

PLATE LXVIII

189 BEGGARS HARVEST ON DASARA DAY,
MAHALAKSHMI TEMPLE, BOMBAY
(Photo : Stanley Jepson)

190 HOLI DANCERS
(Photo : Stanley Jepson)

191 THROWING COCOANUTS INTO
THE SEA ON COCOANUT DAY
(Photo : Stanley Jepson)

192 CHOWPATI BEACH ON SHIVRATRI DAY
(Photo : Stanley Jepson)

PLATE LXIX

193 DASARA PROCESSION. MYSORE (Copyright: Archaeological Dept. of India)

194 DASARA CELEBRATION, MYSORE
(Copyright: Archaeological Department of India)

195
LAKSHMI, GODDESS OF WEALTH,
SHE IS WORSHIPPED ON
DIVALI DAY
(From Madeyur)

PLATE LXX

DURGA PUJA
(From a painting by Solvyns)

PLATE LXXI

THE FEAST OF SERPENTS
(From a painting by Solvyns)

PLATE LXXII

HINDU MARRIAGE CEREMONY
(From a painting by Solvyns)

LOVE AND SEX

you leave us in mid-air as it were. You are cold and cruel and have cheated us. We care not for husbands or parents or children and have abandoned everything for your sake. Now grant us our desire."

Then Krishna smiled and danced with the Gopis. He multiplied himself and danced with each one of them, the Rasa-Lila dance, and every lady thought that Krishna loved her most.

The Gopis' desertion of their husbands and parents is said to indicate the liberation of the soul from all earthly attachments.

Of all the Gopis Krishna loved Radha, Ayanagosha's wife, most. Ayanagosha's jealousy was roused and one day while Krishna was making love to Radha he surprised them. But before he came near enough, Krishna transformed himself into the goddess Durga and the man who came intent on murder went back a devotee.

In Jaya Deva's *Gita Govinda* the loves and jealousies of Radha, are graphically described. Radha, jealous and love-lorn, thus laments the absence of the beloved (she is speaking to her companion):

"Though he takes recreation in my absence, and smiles on all around him, yet my soul remembers him whose languishing reed modulates an air, sweetened by the nectar of his quivering lips, while his ear sparkles with gems, and his eye darts amorous glances:—him, whose locks are decked with the plumes of peacocks, resplendent with many coloured moons, and whose mantle gleams like dark-blue cloud illumined with rainbows:—him, whose graceful smile gives new lustre to his lips, brilliant and soft as a dewy leaf—sweet and ruddy as the blossoms of Bandhujiva, while they tremble with eagerness to kiss the daughters of the herdsmen:—him, whose earrings are formed of entire gems in the shape of the fish Makara on the banners of Love—even the yellow-robed god whose attendants are the chief of deities, of holy men and of demons:—him, who reclines under a gay Kadamba tree, who formerly delighted me while he gracefully moved in the dance and all his soul sparkled in his eyes. My weak mind thus enumerates his qualities; and though offended, strives to banish the offence. What else can it do? It cannot part with its affection for Krishna, whose love is excited by other damsels, and who sports in the absence of Radha. Bring, O my sweet friend! that vanquisher of the demon Kesin to sport with me who am repairing to a secret bower; who looks timidly on all sides, who meditates with amorous fancy on his divine transfiguration. Bring him, whose discourse was once composed of the sweetest words, to converse wtih me who am bashful on the first approach, and express thoughts with a smile sweet as honey.

"That god, whose cheeks are beautified by the nectar of his smiles, whose pipe drops in ecstasy from his hands, I first saw in the grove encircled by damsels of Braj; who gazed on him askance from the corner of their eyes. I saw him in the grove with happier damsels; yet the sight of him delighted me. Soft is the gale that blows over yon clear pool, and extends the clustering blossoms of the voluble Asoka; soft, yet grievous to me is the absence of the foe of Madhu. Delightful are the flowers of the Amra, on the mountain top, while the murmuring bees pursue their voluptuous toil; delightful, yet afflicting to me, O friend! is the absence of the youthful Kesava."

Krishna comes to Radha but she, angry because of his prolonged absence, pretends to spurn his amorous advances. Krishna then speaks:

"Grant me but a sight of thee, O lovely Radha! for my passion torments me. I am not the terrible Mahadeva; a garland of water-lilies with subtle threads decks my shoulders—not serpents with twisted folds; the blue petals of the lotus glitter on my neck—not the azure gleam of poison; powdered sandal wood is sprinkled on my limbs—not pale ashes. O, god of love! mistake me not for Mahadeva; wound me not again; approach me not in anger; hold not in thy hand the shaft barbed with an Amra flower. My heart is already pierced by arrows from Radha's eyes, black and keen as those of an antelope; yet mine eyes are not gratified by her presence. Her's are full of shafts; her eyebrows are bows, and the tips of her ears are silken strings: thus armed by Ananga (Kama), the god of desire, she marches herself a goddess, to ensure her triumph over the vanquished universe. I meditate on her delightful embrace; on the ravishing glances darted from the fragrant lotus of her mouth; on her nectar-dropping speech; on her lips, ruddy as the berries of the Vimba."

Radha, half pacified, thus tenderly reproaches him:

Alas! alas!—Go Madhava—depart Kesava; speak not the language of guile; follow her, O lotus-eyed god! follow her who dispels thy care. Look at his eyes, half opened, red with waking through the pleasurable night yet smiling still with affection for my rival. Thy teeth, O cerulean youth! are as azure as thy complexion, from the kisses thou hast imprinted on the beautiful eye of thy darling, graced with dark-blue powder; and thy limbs marked with punctures in love's warfare exhibit a letter of conquest, written in polished saphire with liquid gold."

I close this quotation illustrating the beauty of Indian mystic poetry with the following description of Krishna given in *Gita Govinda*.

"His azure breast glittered with pearls of unblemished lustre, like the full bed of the cerulean Yamuna, interspersed with curls of white foam. From his graceful waist flowed a pale yellow robe, which resembled the golden dust of the water lily, scattered over its blue petals. His passion was inflamed by the glances of her eyes which played like a pair of water birds with azure plumage, that sports near a full blown lotus on a pool, in the season of dew. Bright earrings, like two suns, displayed in full expansion, the flowers of his cheeks and lips, which glistened with the liquid radiance of smiles. His locks interwoven with blossoms, were like a cloud variegated with moonbeams; and on his forehead shone a circle of odorous oils, extracted from the sandal of Malaya—like the moon just appearing on the dusky horizon; while his whole body seemed in a flame, from the blaze of unnumbered gems."*

During the spring, people from all over India go on pilgrimages to Vrindavan. It is believed that pilgrims with sufficient devotion can even now see visions of Krishna dancing with the Gopis in the groves of Vrindavan on moonlight nights.

Although abuses do prevail, the adherents of the Radha-Krishna cult are decent respectable people. Many noble souls of India belonged to this sect and of these Mira demands particular mention. This Rajput princess lived in the days of Akbar and travelled far and wide popularizing the cult, and singing many ballads of mystic love. She was particularly contemptuous of the ascetics of Shiva. "If living on water were to lead to heaven," says Mira, "fishes and turtles would go to heaven before men; if feeding on leaves and nuts were of superior virtue, monkeys and cattle would be liberated first."

The Hindus are well aware that Krishna's midnight adventures with the Gopis are capable of interpretations other than the mystic. In the *Bhagbata* a king asks a sage: "How did the divine lord who became incarnate for the establishment of virtue and the repression of vice, practise its contrary, namely the corruption of other men's wives?"

The sage gives the following reply: "The transgressions of virtue, and the daring acts which are witnessed in superior beings must not be charged as faults in those glorious persons as no blame is imputed to fire which consumes fuel of every description. Let no one other than a superior being ever even in thought practise the same: anyone who, through folly, does so, perishes, like anyone not a Rudra drinking the poison produced from the ocean. The world of superior beings is true and so also is their conduct which is right. These beings, O king, who are beyond the reach of personal feelings have no interest in good deeds done in this world, nor do they incur any detriment from the contrary. How much less can there be any relation of good or evil between the lord of all beings, brute, mortal and divine and the creatures over whom he rules?"

---

* Quoted from Moor's *Hindu Pantheon.*

Chapter IX

THE SUN, MOON, EARTH AND OTHER PLANETS

MYTHS about the heavenly bodies are numerous in Hinduism. While some of the fables are the wild offspring of imagination, others are allegoric of astronomic phenomena.

There is every reason to believe that the real causes of most of the ordinary astronomic phenomena were known to the ancient Hindus. They carefully watched the movements of the heavenly bodies and noted the changes of position of the sun and the consequent difference in the seasons. They could prepare calendars and correctly predict the dates of eclipses. All these speak well of their deductive and inductive abilities. But ancient Hindus had not that spirit of open enquiry that characterizes scientific research in our own times. Knowledge is power and the ancients kept all knowledge secret. The Brahmin never made public the wisdom supposed to be contained in the Vedas, and these could be read only by priests. The physician kept the knowledge of medicine to himself and imparted it only to his son or a favoured pupil. The same was the case with almost all branches of learning, art and craft. Apart from the obvious trade-jealousy involved, knowledge made public was feared to lose its supposed magic powers. Hence it is no wonder that the ancient astronomer kept his mysterious knowledge to himself and gave the people cock-and-bull stories about the phenomena of the heavens. Besides, it was difficult to explain to an ignorant public the true nature and causes of these phenomena. So he spoke in the language the people could understand.

Astrology, some people opine, originated from the observation of the moon's influence on the menstrual seasons of women. In an age when men looked for mystic causes even when obvious physical causes could give satisfactory explantions, the influence of such a distant body as the moon on humans certainly struck thoughtful men as mysterious. Besides such life-giving agents as the sun and moon on which the earth and all the creatures on it depend for sustenance, their mysterious rising and setting, the changes in their course and appearance, the cycle of the seasons and the earth's reaction to them, the glory of the star-studded heavens, the blue expanse of the sky, all these cannot but inspire the thinking mind with a sense of some power in or behind them which is beyond the range of human comprehensibility. And ancient Hindus were a people who looked for mystery in the plainest thing.

THE SUN

The worship of the sun is very ancient and some scholars hold the view that all religions had their origin in sun-worship. Vedic Aryans loved the brighter side of life and hence the sun was an important object of worship. In some hymns of the *Rig Veda* he is mentioned as the only god. The character and greatness of the sun is thus described in the *Rig Veda*:

"Behold the rays of Dawn, like heralds, lead on high
The Sun, that men may see the great all-knowing god.
The stars slink off like thieves, in company with Night,
Before the all-seeing eye, whose beams reveal his presence,
Gleaming like brilliant flames, to nation after nation.

"With speed, beyond the ken of mortals, thou, O Sun!
Dost ever travel on, conspicuous to all.
Thou dost create the light, and with it dost illume
The universe entire; thou risest in the sight
Of all the race of men, and all the host of heaven.

"Light-giving Varuna! thy piercing glance dost scan,
In quick succession all this stirring, active world,
And penetrateth too the broad ethereal space,
Measuring our days and nights, and spying out all creatures.

"Surya with flaming locks, clear-sighted god of day,
Thy seven ruddy mares bear on thy rushing car.
With these thy self-yoked steeds seven daughters of the chariot,
Onward thou dost advance. To thy refulgent orb
Beyond this lower gloom, and upward to the light
Would we ascend, O'Sun! thou god among the gods."

In one place in the *Rig Veda*, Surya (sun) is mentioned as Savitri, wife of the moon. But generally the sun is considered a male deity.

The Hindu Triad is traced to the sun. One of his names is Treyitenu (three-bodied) which signifies his triple capacity for "producing forms by his genial heat, preserving them by his light or destroying them by the concentrated force of his igneous matter."

In the Puranas, the sun is spoken of as an Aditya (son of Kasyapa and Aditi). The Adityas are twelve: Dhartri, Aryamat, Mitra, Varuna, Indra, Vivaswat, Pushan, Parjanya, Anshu, Bhaga, Twashtri and Vishnu. Of these Vishnu is considered the foremost and is, in some accounts, identified with the sun. Others maintain that the Adityas are different names of the sun indicative of his differing appearance in the twelve months.

In the *Vishnu Purana* it is related that Viswakarma deprived the sun of an eighth part of his original brilliance in the manner narrated below.

Surya married Sanjana, daughter of Viswakarma. After bearing him three children Sanjana found her husband's brilliance oppressive, asked her handmaid Chhaya (shadow) to take her place, and went away to a forest. Chhaya did not disclose her identity and Surya did not notice the change for some years. But one day Yama, a son of Sanjana, misbehaved and Chhaya imprecated a curse which immediately took effect. Surya who knew that a mother's curse could not have effect on her child made enquiries and found out who his supposed wife was. The angered luminary drove away Chhaya and went in search of Sanjana whom he found browsing in the forest in the form of a mare. Surya now transformed himself into a horse and the pair lived like this for some time. They, however, grew tired of their animal life, reassumed their proper shapes and returned home. Viswakarma, to avoid a repetition of the incident, ground the sun upon a stone and deprived him of an eighth part of his brilliance with which he forged the discus of Vishnu, the trident of Shiva and the lance of Kartikeya.

The Suryavamsa (solar dynasty of kings) takes its name from the sun.

The sun is represented in art as a dark-red man with three eyes and four arms, riding in a chariot drawn by seven horses (indicative of the seven days of the week). His charioteer is Arun (literally 'the rosy' meaning the dawn). Arun is the brother of Garuda; he has no legs.

There is a sect who worship the sun as the Deity. The numerous sects of orthodox Hindus fall into six main divisions: (1) Vaishnavas (those who worship Vishnu as the principal deity of the pantheon), (2) Shaivas (worshippers of Shiva), (3) Saktas (worshippers of Sakti, see page 75), (4) Ganapatyas (worshippers of Ganapati) (5) Surapats (worshippers of Surya or the sun) and (6) Smarthas who worship all the five with equal impartiality. Of these Vaishnavas and Shaivas are the most numerous and the worshippers of Surya negligibly few. There is, however, no antagonism between the sects; while each of the first five sects worships its own favourite deity as the principal god or goddess of the pantheon, other deities are also worshipped, though given subordinate positions.*

The Gayatri, the most important Mantra of the Vedas, is addressed to the sun. The text is given elsewhere. The nature and power of the Gayatri are thus described: "Nothing in the Vedas is superior to the Gayatri. No invocation is equal to the Gayatri, as no city is equal to Kasi (Benares). The Gayatri is the mother of the Vedas and of Brahmins. By repeating it a man is saved. By the power of the Gayatri the Kshatriya Viswamitra became a Brahmarshi (Brahmin saint, see page 48); and even obtained such power as to be able to create a new world.† What is there indeed that cannot be effected by the Gayatri? For the Gayatri is Vishnu, Brahma and Shiva and the three Vedas."‡

---

* For detailed descriptions of the various sects see authors work, *Hindu Religion, Customs and Manners*.

† When Brahma repeatedly refused to make Viswamitra a Brahmin, Viswamitra in defiance of the creator started creating a new world by the accumulated power of his prolonged austerities. "He made the cocoanut tree from the fruit of which he intended to make men's heads; instead of the Rohita, he made the fish Mrigala; instead of the Kantala tree, he made the Mandara; instead of the goat made by Brahma he made the long-eared goat; instead of the sheep created by Brahma, he made the Dumba; instead of the cold-season rice he made the wet-season rice: instead of the legumes made by Brahma, he made those which grow in the wet season." Brahma became alarmed at the success of Viswamitra's attempt and went to him in the form of a Brahmin and asked for a boon. Viswamitra promised to grant him any boon desired of him and the Brahmin requested him to stop creating.

‡ The Vedas were originally three; the *Atharva Veda* is a later addition.

The mystic monosyllable AUM (this is the correct spelling and not OM) is also traced to the sun. It represents the solar fire as well as the Trinity. "The first letter stands for the creator, the second for the preserver and the third for the destroyer." It is written inside a circle representing the orb of the sun, and its representations are often worn by the Hindus as lockets. In the *Chhandogya Upanishad* AUM is thus described: "The essence of all beings is the earth, the essence of the earth is water, the essence of water the plants, the essence of plants man, the essence of man speech, the essence of speech the *Rig Veda*, the essence of *Rig Veda* the *Sama Veda*, the essence of the *Sama Veda* the Udghita which is AUM."

The Swastika is a solar symbol of Hindu origin. The word is Sanskrit and means "to be and well." It is a sign of munificence and indicates that "the maze of life may bewilder but the path of light runs through it."

The twelve signs of the Hindu zodiac are: Mesha (Aries, the ram), Vrishabha (Taurus, the bull), Mithun (Gemini, the twins), Kirk (Cancer, the crab), Sinha (Leo, the lion), Kanya (Virgo, the virgin), Tula (Libra, the scales), Vrischika (Scorpio, the scorpion), Dhanu (Sagittarius, the archer), Makara (Capricorn, the goat), Kumbha (Aquarius, the water-bearer) and Meena (Pisces, the fish).

USHAS

Some of the most beautiful hymns of the *Rig Veda* are addressed to the goddess Ushas, personification of the Dawn. She is described as the daughter of the sky, sister of Night and wife of Surya. She travels in a shining chariot drawn by seven ruddy cows. One of the hymns addressed to Ushas runs as follows:

> "Hail ruddy Ushas, golden goddess, borne
> Upon thy shining car, thou comest like
> A lovely maiden by her mother decked,
> Disclosing coyly all thy hidden grace
> To our admiring eyes; or like a wife
> Unveiling to her lord with conscious pride,
> Beauties which, as he gazes lovingly,
> Seem fresher, fairer, each succeeding morn.
> Through years and years thou hast lived on and yet
> Thou'rt ever young. Thou art the breath and life
> Of all that breathes and lives, awaking day by day
> Myriads of prostrate sleepers, as from death,
> Causing the birds to flutter in their nests,
> And rousing men to ply with busy feet
> Their daily duties and appointed tasks,
> Toiling for wealth or pleasure or renown."

In the Puranas Ushas is rarely noticed.

THE MOON

In Hindu mythology, the moon is a male deity. One of his names is Soma, and in the Vedas the word is used as the name of a plant from which the drink Soma was extracted. We will notice this character of Soma later.

In the Puranas, the moon is generally called Chandra or Soma. We have already related the legend of his birth from the milk-ocean. In another account he is said to be the son of Surya. A third story is that he is the son of Atri.

In the *Vishnu Purana* the moon is said to receive Amrita (nectar—representing light) from the sun and distribute it among the gods, men, animals and plants. "The radiant sun supplies the moon, when reduced by the draughts of the gods to a single Kala, with a single ray; and in the same proportion as the ruler of the night is exhausted by the celestials, it is replenished by the sun, the plunderer of the waters; for the gods, Maitreya drinks the nectar and ambrosia accumulates in the moon during half of the month, and this being their food, they are immortal. Thirty-six thousand three hundred divinities drink the lunar ambrosia. In this manner the moon with its cooling rays nourishes the gods in the light fortnight, the Pitris in the dark fortnight; vegetables, with the cool nectary aqueous atoms it sheds upon them; and through their development it sustains men, animals and insects, at the same time gratifying them by its radiance."

The Hindus have a lunar zodiac divided into twenty-seven mansions called Nakshatras (asterisms). They are said to be Daksha's daughters whom Chandra married. Of these wives, Chandra was particularly fond of Rohini (Hyades), the fourth daughter of Daksha, and the other wives grew jealous of this pointed partiality and complained to their father. Daksha argued with his son-in-law who proved incorrigible, and in his anger cursed Chandra with a consumption that continued fifteen days at the end of which the ailing god repented, and Daksha restored him to health in as many days. The meaning of the myth is obvious.

The Chandravamsa (lunar dynasty of kings) derives its name from the moon.

Chandra's criminal passion for Tara, wife of Brahaspati, the preceptor of the gods, led him into a good deal of trouble. He performed the Rajasuya sacrifice and, secure from all harm by its power, abducted Tara. In vain did Brahaspati entreat and the seven Rishis preach. The bold sinner refused to return the lady and Brahaspati appealed to Indra who decided to reclaim his preceptor's wife by force. Chandra was informed of Indra's intentions and he entered into an alliance with the Asuras. There was an indecisive action but Brahma made a last appeal to reason and asked Chandra to return the lady to Brahaspati. The moon had by now grown somewhat tired of Tara and he sent her back to Brahaspati. But the lady was found pregnant and Brahaspati would not accept her till the birth of the child. At Brahma's command Tara gave birth to the child immediately, but seeing the beauty and splendour of the babe both Chandra and Brahaspati claimed him. Tara was then asked to name the father of the child and after a good deal of coaxing she admitted that Chandra was his father. The enraged Brahaspati immediately cursed Tara and she was reduced to ashes. Brahma, however, revived her and after a purification ceremony Tara was received back by Brahaspati.

The trouble, however, did not end here. Varuna, father of Chandra (because of his birth from the sea the moon is said to be a son of Varuna, the sea-god) felt ashamed of his son and disinherited him. But Lakshmi, Chandra's sister, requested Parvati to influence her husband to do something for her dishonoured brother. Parvati's suit was successful and Shiva, to exalt Chandra, wore him on his forehead. Thus ornamented, Mahadeva went to a feast of the gods where Brahaspati saw the disgraced sinner thus honoured and objected to his presence among decent gods. There was an argument between Shiva and Brahaspati and the matter was referred to Brahma for settlement. The creator gave his verdict in favour of Brahaspati, and Chandra was consequently forbidden entry into heaven and was asked always to remain in the sky.

Chandra is represented in art as a copper-coloured man. His banner is red. He rides in a car drawn by a pied antelope.

From the circumstance of the lunar month having twenty-eight days (a multiple of seven) the mystic number seven is traced to the moon. One comes across this number very often in the Hindu scriptures. There are seven Rishis, seven Manus, seven oceans and seven sacred rivers. There are seven days in the week. The divine mothers are seven. There are seven island continents in each of which (excepting the first and the seventh) there are seven kingdoms, seven mountains, and seven rivers. The number of hells are seven or a multiple of seven. The Maruts are forty-nine, seven times seven. The Manwantaras are fourteen of which the current one is the seventh. The number is particularly sacred to Agni. He has seven arms, seven tongues, seven abodes and seven sources. Seven sacrificers worship him in seven ways. His fuels are seven and sages seven. Seven books of the *Yajur Veda* are assigned to Agni. He has seven brothers.

The horses of Surya are seven and the cows of Ushas seven. There are seven groups of Apsaras. The height of Kumbhakarna was eighty-four leagues. Mount Meru rises 84,000 leagues above the earth. The circumference of Brahma's heaven, according to one account, is 14,000 leagues.

THE EARTH

In the Vedas and the Puranas, the earth is often referred to as the goddess Prithvi. In the *Rig Veda* Dyau (the sky) is said to be her husband and in the Puranas, Prithu.

Prithu was an Avatar of Vishnu, born of the arm of the dead body of Vena, a wicked king whom the sages murdered on account of his tyranny. But anarchy succeeded Vena and the sages found that a wicked king was better than none. So they opened the thigh of Vena from which sprang forth a black demon. The wickedness of Vena thus leaving him, his arm was opened and Prithu came out of the gaping arm. He married Prithvi but she refused to yield her treasures and there was a famine in the land. Prithu decided to kill Prithvi and chased her. She took the form of a cow and fled to Brahma for protection. The creator refused her asylum but asked her to return to her husband and give him what he wanted. She returned, and Prithu beat and wounded her; in memory of which all the races of men have, ever since, been wounding her with ploughs, spades and other implements of agriculture.

Prithu was obviously the inventor of agriculture among Indo-Aryans, as the myth so clearly indicates.

In course of time Prithvi came to be considered a symbol of patience, bearing all the misdeeds of men without complaint. She is said to be the example of correct behaviour, as she returns good for evil and gives those who tear her bowels the desirable treasures of the earth.

The earth is often represented as a cow.

THE PLANETS

The plantes are said to be nine. They are (1) Ravi (the Sun), (2) Chandra (the Moon), (3) **Mangala** (Mars), (4) Budha (Mercury), (5) Brahaspati (Jupiter), (6) Sukra (Venus), (7) Sani (Saturn), (8) Rahu (Dragon's head: the ascending node), and (9) Ketu (Dragon's tail: the descending node).

The following sacrificial prayer to the planets is recited while performing the rites of the oblations to fire, one of the five daily sacraments of a Brahmin:

"1. The Divine Sun approaches with his golden car, returning alternately with the shades of night, rousing mortal and immortal beings, and surveying worlds. May this oblation to Surya be efficacious. 2. Gods! produce that (moon) which has no foe, which

THE SUN, MOON, EARTH AND OTHER PLANETS

is the son of the solar orb, and became the offering of space for the benefit of this world; produce it for the advancement of knowledge, for protection from danger, for vast supremacy, for empire, and for the sake of Indra's organs of sense. May this oblation to Chandra be efficacious. 3. This gem of the sky whose head resembles fire, is the lord of waters and replenishes the seeds of the earth. May this oblation to Mangala be efficacious. 4. Be roused, O Fire! and thou (O Budha) perfect this sacrificial rite and associate with us; let this votary, and all the gods, sit in this most excellent assembly. May this oblation to the planet Budha be efficacious. 5. O Brahaspati! sprung from eternal truth confer on us abundantly that various wealth which the most venerable of beings may revere; which shines glorious among all people, which serves to defray sacrifices which is preserved by strength. May this oblation to Brahaspati be efficacious. 6. The lord of creatures drank the invigorating essence distilled from food; he drank milk and the juice of the moon plant. By means of the scripture which is truth itself, the beverage thus quaffed became a prolific essence, the eternal organ of universal perception, Indra's organs of sense, the milk of immortality and honey to the manes of ancestors. May this oblation to Sukra be efficacious. 7. May divine waters be auspicious to us for accumulation, for gain, and refreshing draughts; may they listen to us. that we may be associated with good auspices. May this oblation to Sani be efficacious. 8. O Durva! which doth germinate at every knot, at every joint, multiply us through a hundred, through a thousand descents. May this oblation to Rahu be efficacious. 9. Be thou produced by dwellers in this world to give knowledge to ignorant mortals and wealth to the indigent or beauty to the ugly. May this oblation to Ketu be efficacious."

(1) Ravi. Ravivara (Sunday) is named after him. In burnt offerings small pieces of the shrub Arka (*Ascelepias gigantica*) are offered to him. The image of the sun used by astrologers and for planetary worship is a "round piece of mixed metal twelve fingers in diameter."

Ravi is considered a "malefic" or evil planet by Indian astrologers. "A person born under this planet will possess an anxious mind, be subject to diseases and other sufferings, be an exile, a prisoner, and suffer the loss of wife, children and property."

(2) Soma. (Hence Somavara, Monday). The Palasa (*Butea fondosa*) is sacred to him His image is "a piece like the half-moon a cubit from end to end."

The full moon is a "benefic". "If a person is born under him, he will have many friends; will possess elephants, horses and palanquins; be honourable and powerful; will live on excellent food, and rest on superb couches."

(3) Mangala. (Hence Mangalavara, Tuesday). He is identical with Kartikeya. The Khudiru (*Mimosa catechu*) is sacred to him. His image is a "triangular piece six fingers in width."

He is a "malefic" and a person born under his influence "will be full of anxious thoughts, wounded with offensive weapons, imprisoned, oppressed with fear of robbers, fire, etc., and will lose his lands, cattle and good name."

(4) Budha. (Hence Budhavara, Wednesday). Aparamargu (*Achryranthes aspera*) is sacred to him. His image is a "golden bow two fingers in breadth."

Budha is the son of Soma born of Tara, Brahaspati's wife. When the child was born and at Brahma's command Tara hesitated to mention his father's name the child, it is said, threatened to curse her if she would not name his father. Thus intimidated, Tara spoke and Chandra, pleased with the child, said: "Verily, my son, thou art wise." Hence he was named Budha (wise).*

Budha's wife is Ila who becomes a man every other month. The reason for this peculiarity is given in the following legend:

Manu had no children and he performed a sacrifice to Surya so as to beget a son. But due to an irregularity of the ministering priest, the rite was deranged and instead of a son, a daughter, Ila, was born. Manu charged Vasishta, the supervising priest, with negligence of his duties and the sage prayed to Brahma who transformed Ila into a man and named him Sadyumna. One day while Sadyumna was hunting game, he strayed into a sacred forest where he saw Parvati naked in the arms of Shiva. Parvati cursed Sadyumna and he became a woman. Budha now saw her and married her. After the birth of a son, however, Ila wished to become a man and propitiated Vishnu. Caught between the curse of Parvati and the blessing of Vishnu, Sadyamna remains a woman for one month and a man for the next.

Budha by himself is neither a "malefic" nor a "benefic". His influence on persons born under him is dependent upon his association with other planets.

(5) Brahaspati. (Hence Brahaspativara, Thursday). Aswatha (*Ficus religiosa*) is sacred to him. His image is a "piece like the lotus."

Brahaspati is a "benefic". "If a man be born under this planet he will be endowed with an amiable disposition, possess palaces, gardens, lands, and be rich in money and corn. He will possess much religious merit, and have all his wishes gratified. Brahmins,

---
* This Budha is different from Gautama, the Buddha, founder of Buddhism. The similarity of names is accidental.

however, will not be so fortunate as members of other castes, for Brahaspati, being a Brahmin, does not wish to exalt people of his own caste."

6. Sukra. (Hence Sukravara, Friday). He is the son of Bhrigu and is also called Ushanas. He is the preceptor of the Asuras and knows the incantation for bringing the dead back to life. He is blind in one eye. This affliction was caused by Vishnu. When Vishnu assumed the form of a dwarf and went to Bali for three paces of land (see page 18), Sukra understood who the dwarf was and asked Bali to send him away. But regardless of all consequences Bali decided to grant the request of the Brahmin, and as a ratification of the gift, the priest was asked to read the customary formula and pour out the sacred water from a vessel. Sukra, determined to prevent the ruin of his master, entered the water by his magic powers, and the water was held up in the vessel. Vishnu saw through Sukra's trick and dropped a straw into the vessel, which entered the sage's eye. Sukra now came out of the water, blind in one eye.

Sukra is the most auspicious of all the planets. A person born under his influence "will have the faculty of knowing things past, present and future. He will have many wives, a kingly umbrella (an emblem of royalty) and other kings will worship him."

The Urumbasa (a kind of grass) is sacred to Sukra and his image is a "square piece of silver."

7. Sani. (Hence Sanivara, Saturday). The Sami (*Mimosa albida*) is sacred to him and his image is an iron scimitar.

Sani is the son of Surya and Chhaya. He is represented as a lame, uncouth, black man clad in black garments. He rides on a vulture. He is a "malefic among malefics," and Hindus dread his influence above everything else. All misfortunes and calamities are traced to him. A person born under Sani "will be slandered, his riches will be dissipated and his son, wife and friends destroyed; he will live at variance with others and endure many sufferings."

In the reign of king Dasaratha, it is related, Sani threatened a very inauspicious conjunction which, if allowed to take place, would have led to the destruction of the earth. Even the members of the Trinity could not alter the course of the evil planet. In this predicament Vasishta asked Dasaratha to attack the planet and make him change his cursed course. Dasaratha undertook to perform the task and after a violent conflict subdued Sani and averted the catastrophe.

8. Rahu and (9) Ketu. Blades of Durva grass are sacred to Rahu and those of Kusa to Ketu. The image of Rahu is an iron Makara (a mythical fish) and that of Ketu an iron snake.

The myth of the origin of Ketu and Rahu and the story of the latter's enmity with the sun and moon have already been narrated (page 64). Rahu is the son of Brahaspati begotten on an Asura lady.

Rahu and Ketu are "malefics". If a person is born under any one of them, "his wisdom, riches and children will be destroyed; he will be exposed to many afflictions and will be subject to his enemies."

THE STORY OF DHRUVA (THE POLE-STAR)

Once there lived a king. He had a son named Dhruva, born of his chief wife Suniti. But the king had a younger wife on whom he doted. This queen got the king completely under her power, and had Suniti and her son exiled into a forest.

When Dhruva was seven years of age, one day he asked his mother: "Mother dear, who is my father?" Suniti wept and told him that he was a king's son and that his father was still alive. The boy asked for permission to visit his father and the fond mother blessed him and sent him to the king.

On seeing his little son, the king was overcome with joy, and he took Dhruva on his lap and fondled him. While the happy child was thus sitting on his father's lap, his step-mother came on the scene, and seeing the exiled little prince thus honoured, burst into a fit of rage, reviled the king, took the child by force and turned him out of doors.

The child returned to his mother, sad and thoughtful. He was brooding all the way on the impotence of his father. As soon as he reached home he asked his mother: "Mother, is there anyone more powerful in the world than a king?" "Yes," said Suniti, "Narayana is more powerful than kings." "Where does Narayana live?" asked the child again. "He lives," said his mother, "in forests inaccessible to man. But why such queries, my son?" Dhruva did not answer.

That night while his mother was asleep Dhruva got up, prayed to Narayana to take care of her and stole into the forest. He travelled far, far into the depths of the forests. He reached the great forests where the seven Rishis lived and asked them where Narayana was. They told him that the way to Narayana's abode was long and perilous. The child, daring all, continued his journey. He saw the tiger and asked him if he was Narayana. The tiger ran away from him. He saw the bear and the bear ran away from him. Then he met the sage Narada who told him that Narayana was where he stood. He asked the child to sit down and meditate upon him.

The child sat down and meditated, his whole mind fixed on Narayana. Then Narayana translated his child-devotee to Dhruvaloka (the region of the pole-star) where he sits to this day as the pole-star, fixed and steady, his soul in union with Narayana.

PLATE LXXIII

A CAR OF IDOLS TAKEN IN PROCESSION
(From a painting by Solvyns)

PLATE LXXIV

JAGANNATH BEING PUBLICLY WASHED
(From a painting by Solvyns)

PLATE LXXV

DESCENT OF THE GANGES
(From Mamallapuram)

PLATE LXXVI

202 VITHOBA

203 AN ATTENDANT OF JAGANNATH TEMPLE
(From a painting by Solvyns)

204 KRISHNA SUBDUING KALIYA
(Madras Museum)

205 REPEATING THE GAYATRI
(From a painting by Mrs. Belnos)

PLATE LXXVII

206 ANASUYA
(From Madura)

207 WORSHIP OF GANESHA
(From a painting by Mrs. Belnos)

208 DATTATREYA
(From Badami)

209 WORSHIP OF HANUMAN
(From a painting by Mrs. Belnos)

PLATE LXXVIII

KATHA
(From a painting by Solvyns)

PLATE LXXIX

211 IMAGE OF ARDHANARI
(From Raj-Shahi)

212 WORSHIP OF GANGA
(From a painting by Mrs. Belnos)

213 JAGANNATH

214 ANNAPURNA DEVI
(Ivory. From Trivandrum.)

PLATE LXXX

215 BUDDHA, FROM ART GALLERY, TANJORE
(Photo by E. S. Mahalingam)

216 THE BUDDHA
(From Mayurbhanj)

Chapter X

ANIMALS AND BIRDS

IN ancient India there were regular colonies of men who gave up the bustle of city life and retired into the forest to live the contemplative life in the idyllic atmosphere of woods, hills and mountain-streams. These sages wrote most of the Puranas and epics. They lived in intimate contact with animals and birds and for them these were not dumb creatures of blind instinct but intelligent beings, more or less the kith and kin of humans. Hence we find that in most of the Hindu scriptures, animals and birds occupy a place as important as humans. The age the *Ramayana* represents is particularly known as the animal epoch; in this epic of Valmiki, animals and birds are treated not only as humans but are even deified. Pantheism and the doctrine of metempsychosis endorsed these beliefs and gave them a philosophic interpretation.

Nor was the similarity between man and the ape lost upon the ancients. Of all the animal myths in Hinduism those that deal with simians are the most important. In the *Ramayana* the races that aided Rama are called monkeys and bears. This probably indicates the arrogance of the Aryans and their contempt of the aborigines of South India. But the monkeys of the Ramayana period were in no way contemptible beings. They were truthful and loyal allies, and as hard fighters as the gods or Asuras. One of them, Hanuman, was deified and is to this day worshipped together with Rama and Sita or alone.

In the *Ramayana* it is related that the monkey heroes were sons of gods begotten on simian females for the express purpose of helping Rama. When Vishnu decided to incarnate himself as Rama he said to the other gods: "From the bodies of the chief Apsaras, the Gandharvas, the daughters of the Yakshas, and the Hydras; from the bears, the Vidyandharis, the Kinnaries and the female monkeys—procreate sons monkey-formed, in power equal to yourselves. From my mouth, wide gaping, has Jambavan, the mighty bear been produced." The celestials accordingly produced a progeny of sylvan heroes, monkey-formed. "Tapana (the sun) supremely fervid, begot Sugriva; Indra gave birth to Bali, sovereign of the simian tribes, in splendour equalling his illustrious sire; Brahaspati produced the wise, the peerless Tara, the mighty ape, chief in renown amidst the monkey tribe; the son of Kubera was the fortunate Gandhamadana; Viswakarma begot the mighty ape, by name Nala; the son of Pavaka (Agni) was Nila, the fortunate, resplendent as the fire, the hero surpassing in energy, fame, and valour; Varuna was the parent of the monkey Sushena; the son of Marut was Hanuman, the fortunate; destructive as the thunderbolt, as swift as Garuda; excelling in wisdom amidst the chief monkeys .... Thus were produced by millions, monkeys able to assume any form; the great leaders of the simian tribes begot also a race of heroic monkey chiefs; a numerous host, ready to destroy the ten-headed Ravana; heroes of boundless energy in size equal to elephants or mountains; incarnate; in haughtiness and might equalling the tiger and the lion; able to wield in combat rocks and mountains, and tremendously annoy the enemy with their tails and teeth; skilled in every kind of weapon they could remove the greatest mountains, pierce the stoutest trees, and in swiftness put to shame Samudra, the lord of rivers, causing him to overflow his bounds; and mounting in the air seize the very clouds; they could seize inebriated elephants, and with their shout cause the feathered songsters to fall to the ground. For the sake of assisting Rama was the earth covered with these mighty simian chiefs; in appearance resembling the assembled clouds, and in size appalling all with terror."

HANUMAN

He was the most powerful of the monkey chiefs. Hanuman's loyalty to Rama has become proverbial, and he is held up as the symbol of faithfulness and self-surrender. "He is the ideal of the perfect servant, the servant who finds full realisation of manhood, of faithfulness, of obedience; the subordinate whose glory is in his own inferiority."

When Rama on his return to Ayodhya asked Hanuman what boon he desired as a reward for his great service, the faithful monkey only asked for permission to live so long as the story of Rama would be told in this world. The boon was granted and it is believed that Hanuman still lives in some inaccessible mountain.

Hanuman was born of an Apsara who, due to a curse, had been transformed into a monkey. In one account of his birth it is said Hanuman's mother was impregnated by a cake. The story of this cake is that Dasaratha who inadvertently killed a Brahmin performed a sacrifice in expiation, and on the advice of the sage Vasishta made three cakes out of the ghee, sugar and rice used in the sacrifice and gave a cake to each of his wives so as to beget children as, at that time, he had none. Kaikeyi, the favourite wife, was served last as she was the youngest, but this lady took it as a slight and looked at the cake in her hand with disdain. A kite made a swoop and carried off the cake. This kite flew over a mountain where Anjana, the Apsara-monkey, was praying to Shiva for progeny, and dropped it in her hand. Shiva appeared before Anjana and asked her to eat the cake; this she did, and conceived Hanuman.

According to this story, the function of Marut, the wind-god, (whose son Hanuman is reputed to be) was confined to directing the cake in its fall into Anjana's hand.

It may be mentioned here that Kaikeyi repented of her misconduct and the two cakes were shared among the three ladies.

Another account of Hanuman's birth is that while Anjana was wandering in the forest, the wind-god saw the beautiful damsel and ravished her. After everything was over, Anjana protested but Marut pacified her by observing that a son would be born to her and that he would be great.

Wild tales of Hanuman's physical strength are told. He could course through the sky with the swiftness of wind, assume any size he pleased, uproot trees and hills and make himself invisible. He says:

"Sprung from that glorious Father, I
In power and speed with him may vie.
A thousand times, with airy leap,
Can circle loftiest Meru's steep:
With my fierce arms can stir the sea
Till from their beds the waters flee,
And rush at my command to drown
This land with grove and tower and town.
I through the fields of air can spring
Far swifter than the feathered king
And leap before him as he flies
On sounding pinions through the skies.
I can pursue the Lord of Light
Uprising from the eastern height,
And reach him ere his course be sped,
With burning beams engarlanded."

As soon as he was born, Hanuman felt hungry; the mother's breast could not satisfy his fierce hunger and looking about for something edible, the babe saw the rising sun which he mistook for a fruit and leapt into the sky to catch it. The terrified luminary took to flight and Hanuman chased him into Indra's heaven. Indra hurled a thunderbolt on Hanuman which wounded him in the jaw and felled him to the earth. The wind-god, bent upon avenging his son, entered the stomachs of all the gods and they were afflicted with colic. The ailing Indra now apologized to Pavana (a name of the wind-god) and granted Hanuman a boon of immortality; then Pavana left the gods who were relieved of their pain.

In the search of Sita Sugriva, the monkey-king, divided his army into four divisions and sent each division to search one of the four directions. Hanuman was specially selected to take charge of the southern division as, from available evidence, it was surmised that Ravana had carried off Sita southwards. He was also given the signet ring of Rama. The monkeys had but a hazy notion of where Lanka was; nor could they be sure that Ravana had carried off Sita to Lanka and nowhere else. So Hanuman and the monkeys made a vigorous search in the sector under their charge till they came to the ocean. Here was an element the simians dreaded. They sat dejected in the woods near the seashore not knowing what to do. Then they saw Sampati, the vulture, brother of Jatayu, and the bird told them of Lanka, its fortifications, and its distance from the sea. But who would cross the sea? "One monkey said he could bound over twenty leagues, and another fifty, and one eighty; and Angada, son of Bali, could cross over a hundred but his power would not avail for the return." Now an old monkey related to Hanuman the feats of his childhood and observed that he (Hanuman) could jump over to Lanka and back if he would only realize his strength and divine origin. Hanuman meditated, drew strength from his meditation and felt confident of performing the task. He climbed to the top of the mountain Mahendra, shook his powerful body which began to increase in size and, when he felt he was equal to the task, roared like thunder and hurtled through the sky "like a mountain, his flashing eyes like forest fires, his lifted tail like Sakra's banner."

While he was coursing through the sky, a Rakshasi named Saurasa opened her mouth to swallow him. The width of her distended mouth was one hundred leagues. Hanuman suddenly contracted himself to the size of a thumb, entered her mouth, assumed his vast form again and came out of her right ear, leaving her a ponderous carcass that crashed into the sea.

On reaching Lanka, Hanuman reduced his size to that of a cat and wandered over the forts of Lanka. He saw the marvellous palaces of Ravana, built by Viswakarma himself. He even stole into the gaily decorated bed-chamber of Ravana where he saw the king of Lanka sporting with the beautiful Mandodari (his chief wife) and several other ladies.

After many adventures and hair-breadth escapes in the well-guarded palaces and pleasure groves of Ravana, Hanuman at last saw Sita, and delivered his message. He also destroyed the park of Ravana, set fire to Lanka, as mentioned elsewhere, and returned to Rama.

In the battle of Lanka, Rama and Lakshman were mortally wounded by the Rakshasas and nothing but the leaves of a herb that grew on the Himalayas could restore them to health. Hanuman was despatched to bring the herb. But Ravana had promised half his kingdom to anyone who could kill Hanuman, and Kalanemi, an ambitious giant, flew over to the Himalayas in advance of Hanuman and invited this hero, when he reached the mountain, to dinner. An Apsara whom Hanuman had accidentally released from the effect of a curse, told him who his host was, and Hanuman caught Kalanemi by the leg and "whirled him through the air to Lanka where he fell before the throne of Ravana." After thus disposing of Kalanemi, Hanuman began to look for the herb. But due to a machination of Indra he experienced some difficulty in distinguishing the herb and hence he tore down the whole hill and flew with it towards Lanka. While he was passing Ayodhya, the cyclone his course generated was mistaken by Bharata for the work of some evil spirit, and this king let fly an arrow which brought Hanuman down. Grieved at his mistake Bharata told Hanuman that he could rocket him to Lanka by means of another arrow, which offer the hero declined. Hanuman flew on his own strength with the hill, but on nearing Lanka, saw from his elevated position the moon about to rise. As the herb could have effect only before moonrise he swallowed the moon, reached Lanka in time and revived the wounded heroes.

Many more astounding tales of Hanuman's prodigious strength are told which, for wild exaggeration, have few parallels in the whole realm of mythology.

In the *Mahabharata* is an interesting account of a meeting between Hanuman and his half-brother Bhima (Bhima was born of Kunti by the power of Pavana, the wind-god). After Rama's death, Hanuman was living in a mountain fastness spending his days in contemplation of his great master. Bhima, in his search for a mythical flower Draupadi wished to possess, happened to pass this forest and saw an old monkey sleeping across his path. He haughtily asked the monkey to get out of his way. The monkey wished to know who he was. Bhima gave a boastful account of himself and the greatness of the Pandava heroes; upon this, the monkey asked him how such wonderful people happened to wander in the forests without a kingdom and how the beloved wife of such heroes was suffered to be insulted by Duryodhana. Bhima disdained to make answer but asked the monkey to clear the road. The monkey said that he was ailing and requested Bhima to step across him. But Bhima would not do this because, he said, of his respect for his half-brother Hanuman who was a monkey. Nor would he pass him by the head side. After some argument Bhima agreed to pass by the tail-side, but as he started to pass the tail this appendage of the monkey began to lengthen. After walking along the tail for about a league Bhima decided to lift it up with his club, which weapon, however, broke in the attempt. Now the Pandava knew he was dealing with no ordinary ape and he came back to Hanuman and asked him respectfully who he was. Hanuman smiled and disclosed his identity. He entertained Bhima with many tales of ancient days, and described to him the feats performed by the monkeys in the Ramayana battle. Bhima requested Hanuman to show him the form he had assumed for jumping over to Lanka. Hanuman now stood up and began to increase in size; but before he reached his full stature Bhima got frightened of the enormity of the form, fainted and fell down. Hanuman assumed a smaller size, revived his brother, gave him directions as to how to get the flower he was seeking and sent him on his adventurous task.

Hanuman was famous not only for his physical strength but also for his learning. "The chief of the monkeys," says the *Ramayana*, "is perfect: no one equals him in the Shastras, in learning, and in ascertaining the sense of scriptures. In all sciences, in the rules of austerity, he rivals the preceptor of the gods." Rama when he first met Hanuman in Sugriva's residence was much impressed by the learned discourse of Hanuman. He says:

> "One whose words so sweetly flow,
> And in his well-trained memory store,
> The whole *Rig Veda* needs must know.
> The Yajush and the Saman's lore.
> He must have bent his faithful ear
> For his long speech how well he spoke?
> All grammar's varied rules to hear;
> In all its length no rule he broke."

Hanuman is widely worshipped in India especially by the lower classes. In memory of his services to Rama, monkeys are held sacred. In many Indian cities they boldly roam about streets and public parks, molesting passers-by.

SUGRIVA

Sugriva was the son of Surya and king of the monkeys. When Rama was wandering in the forest in search of Sita, he happened to slay a giant named Kabandha who, in grateful return for the liberation

Rama had thus given him, told him of Sugriva, and advised him to form an alliance with the king of the monkeys who was then living in exile. Kabandha thus describes Sugriva:

> "Lord of the Vanars, just and true;
> Strong, very glorious, bright to view,
> Unmatched in counsel, firm, and meek,
> Bound by each word his lips may speak,
> Good, splendid, mighty, bold and brave.
> Wise in each plan to guide and save.
> His brother, fired by lust of sway,
> Drove forth the king in woods to stray;
> In all thy search for Sita, he
> Thy ready friend and help will be."

Rama found Sugriva, Hanuman and some other monkey chiefs dwelling in exile on a hill called Rishyamukha. He made an alliance with Sugriva, killed the usurper Bali and restored the kingdom to its rightful owner.

After regaining his kingdom Sugriva forgot all about Rama and Sita, and spent about a year in sport and merry-making, and Rama had to send Lakshman to him with a peremptory command before Sugriva would dispatch his monkeys to look for Sita. Once he launched the campaign, Sugriva pursued it, as we have seen, with vigour and energy.

In the battle of Lanka he performed feats of valour comparable to those of Hanuman. As soon as Sugriva saw Ravana, the intrepid monkey sprang upon his head, tore his crown and dashed it to the ground. The two had a wrestling bout in which Sugriva got the worst and just escaped with his life. He was all but killed by Kumbhakarna. This monster tore a mountain and hurled it on Sugriva who, struck by it, fell senseless to the ground. Kumbhakarna picked him up to swallow him but in the meantime Sugriva regained consciousness, bit Kumbhakarna on his thigh and made good his escape.

Sugriva killed many Asura generals. Kumbha and Nikumbha met death at his hands. Squint-eye and Big-belly were also killed by Sugriva.

After Rama's victory, Sugriva, his wife, Hanuman and many other monkeys accompanied the hero to Ayodhya from where, after the coronation and a month's feasting, they returned to Kishkindha, their native land.

BALI

This monkey was the son of Indra and half-brother of Sugriva. He usurped the throne and drove Sugriva into exile.

He was obviously more powerful than Sugriva and Hanuman, and it is not clearly explained why Rama decided to seek the aid of Sugriva and not of Bali. Probably Rama did not think it proper to make an alliance with an usurper.

It is said that Ravana lay twelve years in the coils of Bali's tail, unable to extricate himself. This mishap to Ravana was caused by a machination of Narada. This sage one day visited Ravana and the king of Lanka offered him a seat which he kicked into position with his feet. Narada noticed the slight but evinced no anger. On the contrary he smiled delightfully, took his seat, gave his host all the news of the three worlds and began to sing the praise of Ravana. Ravana asked Narada why he had given up singing the praises of the gods and took to the worship of the king of Lanka instead. Narada observed that there was no point in worshipping the gods who were the slaves of Ravana. This king was now mightily pleased, started enumerating his various exploits and asked Narada if in the three worlds there was anyone greater than himself. Narada said there was none, but casually observed that while he was passing Kishkindha he heard the monkey-king Bali boasting that he could lay Ravana low by one blow of his right hand. The infuriated Asura immediately got his car Pushpaka ready and, with Narada, flew to Kishkindha to chastise the impertinent monkey. On reaching Kishkindha, Ravana found that Bali had gone to the Southern Ocean for his morning ablutions and directed his car southwards. He descended on the beach of the Southern Ocean and saw Bali sitting with his face towards the sea. He appeared like a mountain overlooking the sea. The sight of Bali somewhat cooled the ardour of Ravana, but Narada infused courage into him by observing that mere size was nothing compared to agility, and asked him to advance and pull the monkey by the tail. Ravana advanced cautiously and caught hold of Bali's tail. Bali, undisturbed in his ablution, tied Ravana's hands with his tail. The king of Lanka now heaved hard to extricate himself, pressing his heads against Bali's rump. Bali wound his tail round Ravana's heads and legs and, with him, jumped to the Northern, Western and Eastern Oceans and returned to Kishkindha. Twelve long years did Ravana remain in Bali's tail; at the end of this period Bali, in a moment of large-heartedness, liberated Ravana and sent him to Lanka with a warning.

Bali, by his occult powers, could extract half the strength of any person whom he cared to look at. Hence all who fought a face to face battle with Bali lost half their strength which Bali gained, and no one could defeat him in a straight fight. Rama killed him by a strategy which was not considered strictly honourable. He asked Sugriva to challenge Bali and hid himself behind a tree; and while the two were fighting and Sugriva was getting the worst of it, Rama shot

ANIMALS AND BIRDS

the arrow which mortally wounded Bali. Bali resented the cowardly act. He thus reproaches Rama:

> "What fame, from one thou hast not slain
> In front of battle, canst thou gain
> Whose secret hand has laid me low,
> When madly fighting with my foe?
> I held that thou wouldst surely scorn
> To strike me as I fought my foe
> And thought not of a stranger's blow.
> But now thine evil heart is shown,
> A yawning well, with grass overgrown;
> Thou wearest virtue's badge, but guile
> And meanest sin thy soul defile."

Rama gives the weak explanation that Bali was fated to be killed by him. The great monkey reconciles himself to his fate, and dies blessing his slayer.

Bali's son, Angada, fought on the side of Rama and distinguished himself in the battle of Lanka.

JAMBAVAN

This king of the bears was born of Vishnu. The part he played in the battle of Lanka was not so noteworthy as that of Hanuman or Sugriva. After the victory Rama granted him a boon by which he could be killed only by Vishnu. Like Hanuman he outlived the Tretayuga, but was killed by Krishna in the Dwaparayuga. The following is the story of his death:

Satrajit, a Yadava who dwelt in Dwaraka, by a rigorous course of austerities, obtained the solar gem Syamantaka from Surya which yielded him eight stones of gold a day. Krishna happened to see the gem and expressed a desire to possess it. Satrajit, for obvious reasons, did not like to part with it and gave an evasive reply. Soon after this, Prasena, Satrajit's brother went out on a hunting expedition wearing the gem. Prasena strayed away from the main party, and was killed by a lion which took the gem and went about the forest wearing the brilliant booty. Jambavan who was living in a cave in the forest happened to see Syamantaka and he killed the lion and took possession of the gem.

But wild rumours spread in Dwaraka. Satrajit told people that Krishna had once asked him to make a present of the gem to him, and circulated rumours by which Krishna came to be believed as the murderer of Prasena. Krishna decided to find out the real cause of Prasena's death and clear his conduct. With a party of followers he set out on the trail of Prasena and, guided by the hoof-prints of his horse, reached the place where Prasena was killed by the lion. Thence he followed the foot-prints of the lion and came upon the forest in which that animal was killed by the bear. He started on the trail of the bear and reached the mouth of the cave where Jambavan lived. Krishna asked his followers to remain outside, and entered the cave. Jambavan challenged the intruder, and the two fought fiercely in the cave for twenty-one days, at the end of which Jambavan was mortally wounded. Realization now dawned upon the bear and he recognized in Krishna his master Rama. He surrendered the gem, gave his daughter in marriage to Krishna and died singing the praises of Vishnu.

Krishna with his party returned to Dwaraka and gave the gem to Satrajit. This slanderer begged to be pardoned and, by way of expiation, gave his daughter Satyabhama in marriage to Krishna.

In addition to those described, many other simian demigods are mentioned in the *Ramayana*. Nala*, son of Vishwakarma, was the engineer who planned the construction of the bridge. He was as good a craftsman as his renowned father. Sushena, son of Varuna, was a physician, and it was he who told Hanuman of the magic herb that restored Rama and Lakshman to health.

None of these monkeys is, however, worshipped. That honour belongs solely to Hanuman.

THE COW

The cow does not appear to have been particularly sacred in the Vedic times. References in the Vedas and even in the epics indicate that beef was considered by ancient Hindus a desirable item of food. There are passages in the epics which describe how even holy sages entertained their guests with beef and venison. The slaughter of cows was probably prohibited for the advancement of agriculture at a time when this was a difficult occupation and men had to be compelled to take to it and leave off their ancient habit of killing cattle and feeding on their meat.

Whatever the origin of the worship, the cow is at present held to be a sacred animal by the Hindus. She is not only venerated but actually worshipped as a goddess. According to current orthodox beliefs Gohatya (killing a cow) is as great a sin as Brahmahatya (killing a Brahmin). The dung and urine of the cow are also held sacred and are supposed to possess cleansing and magical properties. The ashes of cowdung are often used to put sectarian marks.

The donation of a cow to a Brahmin is an act of great merit. This form of charity is attended by a religious ceremony at the end of which the officiating priest holds the tail of the animal and recites the following prayer:

"1. May the goddess, who is the Lakshmi of all beings, and resides among the gods, assume the shape of a milch cow, and procure me comfort.

---

* This monkey is not to be confused with Nala, hero of the story of Nala and Damayanti.

"2. May the goddess, who is Rudrani in a corporeal form and who is the beloved of Shiva, assume the shape of a milch cow and procure me comfort.

"3. May she, who is Lakshmi reposing on the bosom of Vishnu; she, who is the Lakshmi of the regent of riches; she, who is the Lakshmi of kings, be a boon-granting cow to me.

"4. May she, who is the Lakshmi of Brahma, she who is Swaha, the wife of fire, she who is the exerted power of the sun, moon and stars, assume the shape of a milch cow for my prosperity.

"5. Since thou art Swadha, the food of them who are the chief among the manes of ancestors, and Swaha, the consuming power of them who eat solemn sacrifices, therefore, being the cow that expiates every sin, procure me comfort.

"6. I invoke the goddess, who is endowed with the attributes of all the gods, who confers all happiness, who bestows abodes in all the worlds, for the sake of all people.

"7. I pray to that auspicious goddess of immortality and happiness."

Persons strict in their devotions daily worship the cow early in the morning before going on their daily duties. "First they throw flowers at her feet; then feed her with grass saying: 'O Bhagavati, (goddess), eat!' then walk round her seven times and make obeisance to her."

The cow together with the Brahmin was created by Brahma on the first day of Vaisakh (April-May) and hence this day is sacred to her.

One of the heavens is named after the cow.

The boon-granting cow Saurabhi, as already related, rose from the milk-ocean. There is some confusion as to her nature and identity. Kamadhenu, Nandini and Shabala are said to be her different names in some accounts while others maintain that they are her daughters.

The milch cow with her calf is a favourite subject with Hindu artists and she is symbolic of felicity and plenty. The cow was a favourite of Krishna when he lived as a herdsman in Vrindavan.

Nandi, Shiva's bull, is an object of worship among the Shaivas.

THE HORSE

Although the horse is very frequently mentioned in the *Rig Veda*, this animal has never been an object of worship. But Aswamedha (horse-sacrifice) is the greatest sacrifice a king can perform. Only those monarchs who aspire to universal dominion can perform it. Prior to the performance of the sacrifice a horse with auspicious marks is let loose to wander at will for a year. An army follows the horse and anyone who stops the horse is considered an enemy and his act a challenge to the owner of the horse. He has to be conquered. After a year, the horse is led back, and a grand sacrifice and feasting take place.

Rama in the Tretayuga and Yudhishtira in the Dwaparayuga performed this sacrifice and were acclaimed world-victors.

THE DOG

The connection between death and the dog has already been noticed. Although the dog is now considered by the Hindus as an unclean animal, in a hymn of the *Rig Veda*, Surya himself is identified with the dog. The hymn runs thus:

"He (the sun) flies through the air, looking down upon all beings; we desire to do homage with Havis to thee (who art) the majesty of the heavenly dog.

"In the waters is thy origin, in heaven thy abode, in the midst of the sea and upon the earth thy greatness. That which is the majesty of the heavenly dog, under that form we worship thee with this Havis."

The following popular story is told of how the dog came to be the servant of man.

Brahma created the dog and sent him to the earth with a command to serve the most powerful creature on earth. The dog wandered in the forests of the earth and came upon the elephant. Seeing his ponderous form, the dog very naturally took him for the mightiest creature on earth, and requested him to accept him as his servant. The elephant readily agreed. But when night fell, the wind blew and leaves rustled, the dog barked. "Dog," said the elephant, "do not bark. This is the hour of Night and the lion is abroad; if he hears you he will kill you." "Then," said the dog, "the lion is more powerful than you." And he left the elephant and went to the lion. The lion accepted him as his servant. But when night fell, the wind blew and leaves rustled, the dog barked. "Dog," said the lion, "do not bark. This is the hour of Night and the hunter is abroad. If he hears you, he will kill you." "Then," said the dog, "the hunter is more powerful than you." He left the lion and went to the hunter. At night when the wind blew and leaves rustled, the dog barked and the hunter approved of it. Hence the dog stayed with the hunter.

THE CAT

This animal is the charger of Shashti, a goddess of some local importance in Bengal, and is hence sacred to her. The story is told of a Brahmin girl who stealthily ate food and, when enquiries were made, accused a cat of the theft; on account of which sin she lost her eight children. On performing a propitiatory ceremony in honour of Shashti's cat, the goddess restored the children to her.

A cat crossing one's path is considered an ill-omen, and a devout Hindu would rather return home than continue his journey along the same path.

SERPENTS

The feeling of dread and repugnance venomous reptiles universally inspire, is shared by the Hindus too. It was probably their dreaded powers that led to the deification of serpents. In Hindu scriptures snakes are in some places mentioned as the enemies of mankind and in others as deities. Originally the Indo-Aryans were averse to snake-worship, but later Hinduism absorbed some races who worshipped snakes and with them their beliefs.

The Nagas (snakes), are fabled to live in a magnificent world named Patala, situated in the nether regions. There "dwell the lords of snake-region, Vasuki, Sankha, Kulika, Mahasankha, Sweta, Dhananjaya, Dhritarashtra, Shankhachaurna, Kambala, Aswatara, Devadatta and other large-hearted serpents. Of these some have five hoods, some seven, some ten and some a thousand. The gloom of the nether regions is lighted up by the splendour of the excellent gems gracing their hoods."

The capital of the serpent-world is Bhogawati, a city famed for its wealth. The serpents there are in possession of the best precious stones in the worlds.

The Nagas are said to be the progeny of Kadru (one of the wives of Kasyapa) and mortal enemies of their half-brother Garuda. Because of its habit of sloughing its skin, the serpent is believed to be immortal. It is said that once when Garuda was taking ambrosia from heaven to Patala, he happened to drop some of the nectar on the earth which fell on Kusa grass and snakes greedily licked it up and became immortal. They, however, burnt their tongues and hence they have forked tongues.

The chief of the serpents is said to be Ananta, the thousand-hooded hydra, on whom Vishnu sleeps. The earth is poised on one of his hoods. The word Ananta means "endless." The serpent, particularly one eating its tail, is indicative of eternity.

While Ananta and Vasuki (Shiva wears this serpent as his girdle) are objects of veneration, Kaliya is said to represent sin. This cobra inhabited the river Kalindi (Jumna) and was, as noted elsewhere, a cause of anxiety to the herdsmen among whom Krishna lived. The boy Krishna, one day, entered the river and, after a fierce combat, subdued the monstrous reptile. At the request of the wives of Kaliya, Krishna spared his life but made him depart from Kalindi. The story of this combat is very popular among the Hindus, and Krishna is very often represented as a boy dancing on the hood of Kaliya.

Nagapanchami, the fifth day of the Hindu month of Shravan (July-August) is sacred to snakes and they are particularly worshipped on this day.

GARUDA

This charger of Vishnu is a mythical combination of man and bird. He is an object of great veneration.

Garuda was born of an egg laid by Vinata, one of the wives of Kasyapa. In the *Vishnu Purana* it is related that the egg was laid by Diti and not Vinata.

Once Kadru (mother of serpents) and Vinata (mother of Garuda) had an argument between them respecting the colour of the horse that rose out of the milk-ocean, and they laid a wager by which the loser was to be the other's slave. Garuda's mother lost, and she was imprisoned by the serpents in the nether regions. Garuda prayed for her release but the serpents asked him, by way of ransom, to bring the moon to them so that they could feast on the nectar in the moon. Garuda started for the regions of the moon, but, on the way felt hungry. While passing the regions of the pole-star he met his father Kasyapa (Uranus) and asked him if anything edible could be obtained there. Kasyapa directed his son to a lake where Garuda saw a tortoise and an elephant fighting. "The tortoise was eighty miles long and the elephant one hundred and sixty. Garuda with one claw seized the elephant, with the other the tortoise and perched with them on a tree eight hundred miles high. But the tree was unable to bear his ponderous weight, and, unhappily, thousands of pigmy Brahmins were then worshipping on one of its branches. Trembling, lest he should destroy any of them, he took the bough in his beak, continued to hold the elephant and tortoise in his claws, and flew to a mountain in an uninhabited country where he finished his repast on the tortoise and elephant."

After many more adventures of a like nature, Garuda reached the regions of the moon, seized him, concealed him under the wing and started on his return flight. The gods, determined to regain the moon, attacked Garuda and, after an indecisive action, came to terms with him. Vishnu made him immortal and promised him a higher seat than his own. Garuda, on his part agreed to become the charger of Vishnu. Since then, "Vishnu rides upon Garuda while the latter, in the shape of a flag, sits at the top of Vishnu's car."

Garuda was of immense help to Rama in the battle of Lanka. When Rama, Lakshman and the monkey heroes were struck down by the Nagastras (snake-arrows) of Indrajit, Garuda appeared before Rama and gave him Garudastras (eagle-arrows) which counteracted the effect produced by Nagastras. The coming of Garuda is thus described in the *Ramayana*:

"The rushing wind grew loud,
Red lightings flashed from banks of cloud.

The mountains shook, the wind waves rose,
And smitten by resistless blows,
Uprooted fell each stately tree
That fringed the margin of the sea.
And life within the waters feared:
Then, as the Vanars gazed, appeared
King Garud's self, a wonderous sight,
Disclosed in flames of fiery light.
From his fierce eye in sudden dread
All serpents in a moment fled;
And those transformed to shafts, that bound
The princes, vanished in the ground."

Garuda is said to be the king of birds. One of the Puranas (*Garuda Purana*) is named after him, but in this Garuda does not occupy a place important enough to justify the name. His exploits are chiefly narrated in the epics.

SAMPATI AND JATAYU

These were the sons of Garuda and are mentioned in the *Ramayana* as "mighty vultures of size and strength unparalleled." They lived in the southern forests, and we have elsewhere noticed how Jatayu intercepted the course of Ravana and was mortally wounded by him.

Sampati lived long enough to avenge his brother. The monkeys, who were searching for Sita in the southern quarter, came upon him and he soared high into the sky, had a view of Lanka and discribed it in detail to Hanuman. This hero worked on the instructions given by Sampati and found Sita in the Asoka grove.

THE MYTHICAL ORIGIN OF SPARROWS AND PARTRIDGES

Viswakarma had a son named Viswarupa. He had three heads called the Soma-drinker, the Wine-drinker and the Food-eater. In public, Viswarupa posed as a friend of the gods but secretly he aided the Asuras in many ways. Indra came to know of this double-dealing and he cut off Viswarupa's heads which were turned into birds. "The Soma-drinker became a Kapinjala (Francoline partridge), for Soma was of a brown colour; the Wine-drinker became Kalavinka (sparrow), because when men are intoxicated they make a noise like a sparrow; the Food-eater became Tittiri (partridge) which consequently has a great variety of colour, for its body appears to be sprinkled with ghee and honey.

"Viswakarma, enraged because Indra had slain his son, made a libation to the gods, but did not invite Indra to it. Indra noticing the slight, by force took the vessel containing the Soma juice, and drank it. Viswakarma in anger broke off the sacrifice, and used the few drops of Soma left to give effect to a curse. He employed the right formula for accomplishing the death of Indra, but unfortunately laid stress on the wrong word. So, instead of slaying Indra, he was himself slain by him."*

---

* W. J. Wilkins, *Hindu Mythology*.

PLATE LXXXI

217 QUEEN MAHAMAYA'S DREAM
(From Barhut. Indian Museum, Calcutta)

218 BIRTH AND SEVEN STEPS
(Gandhara. Indian Museum, Calcutta)

219 NATIVITY OF THE BUDDHA
(From Yusufzai : V. and A. Museum)

PLATE LXXXII

220 CASTING THE HOROSCOPE OF THE BUDDHA
(From Sahri Bahlol. Copyright : Archaeological Dept. of India)

221 GAUTAMA APPROACHING THE BODHI TREE
ATTENDED BY DEVAS
(Gandhara. Indian Museum, Calcutta)

222 PRESENTATION OF THE CHILD TO THE SAGE
(Copyright : Archaeological Department of India)

PLATE LXXXIII

223 THE BODHI TREE
(From Barhut. British Museum Photograph)

224 SUBJUGATION OF THE ELEPHANT MALAGIRI
(From Amravati. Copyright: Van Oest, Paris)

225 SIDDHARTHA MEETING AN ASCETIC
THIS SAGE PROBABLY INITIATED GAUTAMA INTO ASCETICISM
(Swat. From Grunwedel's *Buddhist Art in India*)

226 A BUDDHIST MONK
(From *Picturesque India* by Martin Hurlimann)

PLATE LXXXIV

227 CONVERSION OF NANDA
(Copyright : Archaeological Dept. of India)

228 BODHISATVA IN TUSITA HEAVEN
(Amravati. Madras Museum. Photo : India Office)

229 DIPANKARA JATAKA (SUMEDHA FALLING AT THE
FEET OF DIPANKARA)
(Takht-Bahi. Copyright : Archaeological Dept. of India)

230 BODHISATVA UNDER THE PROTECTION
OF MUSALIND
(Bodhgaya. Copyright : Archaeological Dept. of India)

PLATE LXXXV

231 THE ATTACK OF MARA
(Sanchi. Copyright : Archaeological Dept. of India)

232 MAHAKAPI JATAKA (JATAKA OF THE GREAT MONKEY)

233 STATUE OF BODHISATVA
(From Shah-baz Garhi. Louvre Museum)

PLATE LXXXVI

234 DIVISION OF THE RELICS
(Madras Museum)

235 DEVADATTA AND THE ASSASINS
(Gandhara. Indian Museum, Calcutta)

236 THE FIRST SERMON
(Gandhara. Indian Museum, Calcutta)

237 THREE SCENES DEPICTING THE CONVERSION OF NANDA
(From Amravati Photo: India Office)

PLATE LXXXVII

238 CHADANTA JATAKA (BODHISATVA AS A SIX-TUSKED WHITE ELEPHANT)
(Sanchi. Copyright: Archaeological Department of India)

239 THE MIRACLE AT SRIVASTI
(Lahore Museum)

240 FEASTING BY THE MALLAS OF KUSINAGARA
ON RECEIVING THEIR SHARE OF THE RELICS
(Sanchi. Copyright: Archaeological Dept. of India)

PLATE LXXXVIII

241 THE SAGE BEHOLDING
THE CHILD
(From Grunwedel's *Buddhist
Art in India*)

242 THE ELEPHANT CHADANTA
(Ajanta. Beal. *Si-yu-ki*)

243 BUDDHA AND HIS SON
RAHULA
(Amravati. From Fergusson's
Tree and Serpent Worship)

244 SIDDHARTHA ABOUT TO DEPART FROM HIS HOME
(Jamalgarhi. Lahore Museum)

Chapter XI

TREES, PLANTS AND FLOWERS

IN the Vedas, Soma is addressed as the deity representing the liquor-yielding plant Soma.* "Not only are all the hymns of the ninth book of the *Rig Veda*, one hundred and fourteen in number, besides a few in other places, dedicated to his honour, but constant references occur to him in a large proportion of other hymns. In some of these hymns he is extolled as the creator or father of the gods. Evidently at that time he was a most popular deity. Indra was an enthusiastic worshipper of Soma."

In the Vedas, it is said that the plant was originally a native of the mountains where the Gandharvas lived and the goddess Vach (Sarasvati) "went to the Gandharvas" who gave it to her. But when Vach brought it to the gods there arose a dispute among them as to who should have the first draught. "At length this was decided by a race. Vayu first reached the goal, Indra being second. Indra tried hard to win but when near the winning post proposed that they should reach it together, Vayu taking two-thirds of the drink. Vayu said, 'Not so! I will be the winner alone.' Then Indra said, 'Let us come together, and give me one-fourth of the draught divine.' Vayu consented to this and so the juice was shared between them."

The following is one of the hymns addressed to Soma :

"This Soma is a god; he cures
The sharpest ills that man endures
He heals the sick, the sad he cheers,
He nerves the weak, dispels their fears;
The faint with martial ardour fires,
With lofty thoughts the bard inspires
The soul from earth to heaven he lifts;
So great and wondrous are his gifts,

Men feel the god within their veins,
And cry in loud exulting strains :
'We've quaffed the Soma bright
And are immortals grown;
We've entered into light
And all the gods have known.
What mortal now can harm
Or foeman vex us more?
Through thee, beyond alarm
Immortal god, we soar.' "

From this hymn it is clear that Vedic Aryans used to indulge in drink. The use of spirituous liquor was later prohibited and the worship of Soma given up. The reason for this is said to be that Brahma in a state of drunkenness committed incest with his daughter, and cursed intoxicants. In another account it is said Sukra, who happened to drink the ashes of his disciple Kacha in a cup of wine, † cursed liquor and prohibited its use. The real reason was probably a realization of the superiority of sobriety over drunkenness.

Soma later came to be considered identical with the moon. It was probably due to his connection with the Soma drink that the moon came to be known as the receptacle of Amrita, nectar.

THE TULSI PLANT (OCIMUM SANCTUM)

This plant is sacred to Vishnu. Its leaves are supposed to possess medicinal properties. Orthodox Hindus plant it in their gardens and compounds and worship it.

The legend that traces its relationship to Vishnu is curious. It is the story of a ravisher turned lover and husband.

Tulsi was the wife of Jalandhar, an Asura born of the sweat of Mahadeva which fell in the sea.

---

* "The Soma-plant of the *Rig Veda* is the *Asciepias acida* of Roxburgh. It is a creeping plant, almost destitute of leaves. It has small white fragrant flowers collected round the extremities of the branches. Roxburgh says that it yields purer milky juice than any other plant that he knows; and that this juice is mild, and of an acid nature. The tender shoots are often plucked by native travellers. It grows on the hills of the Punjab, in Bolan Pass, in the neighbourhood of Poona, etc. In the Brahmana of *Rig Veda* (Haugh's Translation) is a most interesting account of the Soma sacrifice. This is occasionally made in the present day, but very few priests are acquainted with the ritual of this once celebrated sacrifice" — W. J. Wilkins, *Hindu Mytholo* The correct identity of the plant is, however, a much disputed subject.

† See the story of Kacha and Devayani in Chapter VI.

Jalandhar performed austerities and obtained a boon by which he was to be invincible so long as his wife remained faithful to him. Tulsi or rather Vrinda (this was her name as the wife of Jalandhar) was famous in the three worlds for her conjugal fidelity, and her husband thought himself invincible for all time. He now sent a message to Indra asking him to return the fourteen gems which he and the other gods had churned out of the ocean. Because of his birth from the sea, Jalandhar claimed overlordship of the ocean and held that the churning of the ocean was an act of piracy. Indra, however, thought otherwise, and refused to return the gems. War was declared and Indra, in a panic, ran to Shiva and Vishnu for help. Coming to know from Brahma the secret of Jalandhar's invincibility, Shiva, always proud of his personal attractions, went to Vrinda, asked her to desert her husband and follow him, and was driven out of the place. Vishnu now assumed the form of Jalandhar himself and succeeded in ravishing Vrinda. This lady discovered the fraud, too late though, and cursed Vishnu to become a stone. (Thus the origin of the Salagrama stone, the sacred ammonite found on the bed of the river Gandaki.) Vishnu also cursed her and she became the Tulsi plant.

In course of time the incident was forgotten and Tulsi came to be considered the beloved wife of Vishnu.

A story is told how even Rukmini, the chief wife of Krishna and an incarnation of Lakshmi, gave pride of place to Tulsi. Narada, one day, visited Satyabhama, one of the wives of Krishna, and this lady confided to the sage that she wished to obtain Krishna as her husband in all her future births, and asked him how this could be done. Narada said that the best way of ensuring this was to give her husband to Narada himself, as anything given to a Brahmin could be depended upon to return to the giver in future births in manifold forms. Carried away by Narada's eloquence Satyabhama gave her husband to Narada, and the latter asked Krishna to work as his page, gave him his Vina to carry and proceeded towards the celestial regions. The other wives of Krishna, on coming to know of this, rushed to the sage and implored him to return their husband. They reviled Satyabhama for her presumption, and this lady repented of her rash act and requested Narada to return Krishna to her. Narada now disclosed to them that it was a sin to receive anything in charity from a Brahmin and told them they could buy their husband from him if they cared to. He was asked to name his price and he demanded Krishna's weight in gold. The ladies piled up their ornaments in one pan of the scales, but when Krishna sat in the other this one came down with a thud. Now they sent for Rukmini who was not in the crowd. She came with a leaf of the Tulsi plant, asked the ladies to remove the ornaments from the pan and, when this was done, placed the leaf in the pan when Krishna was lifted upwards in the other.

Rukmini now told all the ladies that Tulsi was more beloved to Krishna than any of them.

On the eleventh day of Kartik (October-November) a ceremony is performed in honour of Tulsi and her marriage with Vishnu. "This ceremony marks the opening of the annual marriage season among high caste Hindus. It is said that he who performs this marriage ceremony assuming that Tulsi is his daughter, gets all the benefits of Kanyadan (giving away a daughter in marriage), a very meritorious act."

Kusa grass (*Poa cynosuroides*) and Durva grass (*Agrostis linearis*) are considered sacred, and form part of the offerings made to the gods in the various forms of worship.

The Banyan tree (the Indian fig tree) is sacred to Vishnu. Because of its longevity and nature of dropping roots from the branches, the tree is considered immortal. Narayana sucking his toe (a symbol of eternity) is represented as lying on a Vat (Banyan) leaf.

The Peepal (*Ficus religiosa*) is sacred to the Trinity. "It is frequented by all the gods and is hence very sacred. No one should touch it. Women should worship it, and go round it a thousand times in one day. In the *Shravan Mahatmya*, it is ordained that this tree should be worshipped on every Saturday of the month of Shravan (July-August). Saint Vaikhilya tells us that Vishnu becomes a Peepal. The thread ceremony of this tree is strongly recommended along with its marriage with Tulsi. Its dry twigs are used in the worship of the sacred fire (to feed it)."

THE PARIJATA TREE

This mythical tree rose out of the milk ocean and Indra planted it in his garden. "Its bark was of gold, and it was embellished with young sprouting leaves of a copper colour, and fruit-stalks bearing numerous clusters of fragrant fruits."

It is related that once Narada brought a flower of this tree to Dwaraka and presented it to his friend Krishna. He waited to see to which of his wives Krishna gave the flower. The flower was given to Rukmini, and Narada went straight to Satyabhama and made a show of sorrow. On her enquiring why he was not in good cheer, the sage told Satyabhama that he had presented Krishna with a flower of the Parijata tree thinking that she (Satyabhama) was his favourite wife and he would present it to her, but was grieved to find that Krishna had given it to Rukmini. Satyabhama's jealousy was roused and she asked Narada what could be done to spite Rukmini. The sage advised her to ask Krishna to bring the Parijata tree itself from heaven and plant it near her house. After giving this advice, he went back to the celestial region and told Indra to guard the Parijata tree carefully as thieves were about.

Satyabhama repaired to the anger-chamber,* and when Krishna came to her she reviled him for cheating her. "You pretend that I am your favourite wife, but treat me as Rukmini's handmaid," she said, and asked him what made him present the Parijata flower to Rukmini. Krishna admitted his guilt and asked her what he could do in expiation. She wanted possession of the Parijata tree. Krishna immediately proceeded to Amaravati, stole into Indra's grove and started uprooting the tree. The king of the gods came upon the scene and caught the thief red-handed; but seeing who his despoiler was, he allowed him, after some show of resentment, to take the tree to Dwaraka.

It is fabled that, after Krishna's death, Dwaraka was submerged in the ocean and the Parijata tree was taken back to heaven.

---

* Ancient Hindu kings who had more than one wife had a room or house, called anger-chamber, set apart for a dissatisfied queen to occupy and demand redress of her grievances.

Chapter XII

PRINCIPAL HINDU HOLIDAYS

TO the Hindus every day is a holy day. Sunday is sacred to the Sun, Monday to the Moon, Tuesday to Mars, Wednesday to Mercury, Thursday to Jupiter, Friday to Venus and Saturday to Saturn. There are particular ceremonies and Pujas to be performed on each day and those who have the time, patience and necessary faith perform them scrupulously. Again, every day is sacred to the moon, and appropriate ceremonies have to be performed in accordance with the varying influence of the waxing or waning moon, which takes into consideration the moon's relationship with other planets and its course through the signs of the lunar zodiac. Nor should the influence of the varying position of the sun be overlooked. Based upon the movements of these heavenly bodies and their supposed influence on mortals is an elaborate system of fasts, feasts and ceremonies which are supported by appropriate legends and fables, explaining their origin and enumerating the benefits obtainable by observing them. In addition to these 'astrological' holidays there are festivals which have a historical significance, and commemorate prehistoric victories, migrations, birthdays of deified heroes and coronations of important kings. But all these are so mixed up that of any particular festival it is well-nigh impossible to say what its real origin and significance are. Again, each province and sect have their favourite holidays which are unimportant to others.

It is quite impossible to enumerate in one chapter all the holidays of the Hindus and describe their folklore in detail. The more important of the holidays and the salient features in their folklore and observance are given below.*

"Vishnu apportioned four chief holidays among the four Varnas or castes." The Brahmins have to observe Rakhi Purnima, the Kshatriyas Dasara, the Vaisyas Divali and the Sudras Holi as the principal holidays.

RAKHI PURNIMA

This festival is celebrated on the full moon day of the Hindu month Shravan (July-August). The presiding deity of this gala day is Varuna, the sea-god. Fairs are held on the seashore or river banks to which people flock in large numbers. There are ceremonial baths, and offerings are made to Varuna. The chief characteristic of the festival is the throwing of cocoanuts into the sea as offerings. Labourers pick up these cocoanuts, hawk them and ply a vigorous trade. Because of the prominent part cocoanuts play in the celebrations, Rakhi Purnima is also known as Narali Purnima (literally, cocoanut-full-moon), or, in popular parlance, Cocoanut Day.

The higher castes renew their sacred threads on this day.

Another interesting feature of the Cocoanut Day is the tying of amulets of 'silk-thread, silver wire, gold wire, corals, pearls, jewels or gold beads according to means' on the wrists of men by their sisters. Women who wish to honour strangers and recognize them as their brothers also tie amulets on the wrists of such persons. Colonel Tod claims, he was once thus honoured by a Rajput princess.

DASARA

This grand festival takes place as the culmination of Navratra (nine nights) celebrations. The Navratra begins on the first night of Aswin (September-October) and lasts for nine nights. Each night (and day too) is sacred to one of the manifestations of Durga, and the goddess is worshipped in the form of an unmarried girl. The girl representing the goddess "should be healthy, beautiful and free from eruptions. She should be of the same caste as the devotee." One girl may be worshipped on nine days or nine girls in one day. In the latter case the worship should take place on the fifth day which is particularly sacred to Durga, and is known as Lalita Panchami.

During the nine days of Navratra, the devotees of Devi either fast or take only one meal a day. Those weak in faith, who find it difficult to observe the fast for nine days, may fast for seven, five or three days. Certain ceremonies are performed and magic formulae repeated by priests. Brahmins are fed and given cash and clothes. As Navratra is sacred to Durga it is also called Durga Puja or Durgotsava.

The fast of Navratra is said to be observed in memory of a similar fast Rama observed to propitiate

---

*For the folklore of most of the holidays I am indebted to Raj Bahadur G. A. Gupta's *Hindu Holidays*.

Durga when he was fighting the battle of Lanka. On the eighth day of Navratra Rama killed Ravana. On the ninth, he performed a sacrifice as thanksgiving, and on the tenth he started on his journey to Ayodhya, in memory of which Dasara is celebrated.

This festival used to be celebrated in right royal fashion by Hindu kings. Early in the morning the gadi (throne) was worshipped with the attendant ceremonies. Then there was a parade of elephants, horses and chariots. The elephants and horses, as they marched past the standard, turned to the Maharajah who occupied for the purpose a prominent place, and saluted him by appropriate gestures. At the end of the "marchpast" ceremony, Brahmins were paid cash or presented with clothes and the morning Durbar was dissolved.

"At about three o'clock in the afternoon the whole army of the state, consisting of artillery, cavalry, infantry, etc., is ready in full dress to take part in the great procession. The elephants, about a hundred in number, are arranged in front of the palace according to the ranks of the Sardars who are privileged to ride them, and the palace officer and his assistants busy themselves calling out the names under which each of the animals has been registered, and despatching them to the residences of the Sardars for whom they are intended. All arrive at the palace in good time, with their mounted orderlies and silver-sticks or Chopdars. The whole army is arranged; some in front of the palace for the procession as orderlies and some on the 'Dasara-maidan' where the sacrifice is scheduled to take place. The route is duly lined with soldiers and guards. When everything is ready, the standard-bearer's elephant is brought forward to the front of the main gate of the palace. He carries, in addition to the standard, the Danka or war-drum. Silence prevails for a few minutes, all standing expectant at the near approach of the Maharajah. As soon as the Maharajah's elephant issues out of the chief gate, the war-drum is sounded by the command of the head of the army who salutes His Highness. On receiving this signal, the few selected Sardars who are privileged to take their elephants inside the gate to wait on the Maharajah, come out one after another, the rest, who had to wait outside the quadrangle, joining the profession in rank and file. For about a mile or two the pageant goes in full swing followed by spectators of all sorts. At the boundary of the city, the Agent to the Governor General, who had previously fixed his camp there, receives the Maharajah."

"The Maharajah alights and sits on a carpet spread under a Shami tree (*Prosopis spicigera*) where arrangements have already been made for the sacrifice. At the end of a Puja, the Maharajah cuts with a sword a calabash fruit (*Cucurbita pepo*), symbolic of the animal sacrifice which used to be a part of the ceremony in ancient days." After the sacrifice, the branches of the Shami tree are "looted" by the Sardars who "call the leaves gold for the time being". "This done, the Maharajah mounts his elephant, and so do the Sardars. A royal salute accosts His Highness and before he turns back a buffalo is sacrificed.* On its return journey the whole procession is greeted with bonfires and fireworks, intermixed with shouts of 'Sriman Maharajah Vijayi Bhava' (may success follow the Maharajah). On arrival of the Maharajah at the palace, another Durbar is held and Khillats distributed according to rank."

With the disappearance of the Princes in India, this ancient festival is losing much of its grandeur.

Dasara is considered an auspicious day for starting military expeditions. Children in some parts of India begin their education on this day. Books are also worshipped on the Dasara day.

DIVALI

This is the New Year Day of the Hindus who follow the Vikram era. The festival falls in October-November. Different legends are narrated to account for its origin. One is obviously that king Vikramaditya was crowned on this day. Another tells us that Bali was deprived of his kingdom by Vishnu on this day. "In Maharashtra women prepare effigies of Bali either in rice-flower or cow-dung, according to grade, worship them and repeat the blessing. 'May all evil disappear, and Rajah Bali's empire be restored.'"

A third story is that Vishnu killed Narakasura (a demon of filth) on Divali day. The most popular belief, however, is that Rama, on his return from Lanka, was crowned on this day.

It is probable that Divali was originally celebrated in honour of Rama's coronation, and Vikramaditya selected this day as the most auspicious for his own coronation; hence the coincidence of the two important events.

The word Divali is a corrupt form of Deepavali (cluster of lights) and the festival is so called because of the illuminations that form the most important feature of the celebrations. In some parts of India effigies of Narakasura or Ravana are made and burnt. "In Bengal it is believed that the night of the Pitris begins at this time and lamps are lighted on long poles to serve as a guide to these benighted souls." Krishna and Govardhana mountain are also worshipped on this day.

Hindu merchants renew their account books, white-wash their offices and houses and generally

---

* In memory of Durga's triumph over Mahisha, the buffalo-demon.

"begin a new life" on the New Year Day. Lakshmi, the goddess of wealth, is particularly worshipped for prosperity in the coming year. Presents are given to relatives, friends and subordinates. There are also the usual pageants of gaily dressed men, women and children who flock to fairs, temples and public parks. Children particularly look forward to this day as the "festival of fireworks and sweet-meats."

On Divali day, it is considered auspicious to gamble. Legends say that Shiva gambled with his wife on this day, lost everything and was driven in penury to the banks of the Ganges. Kartikeya seeing his father's plight, learnt the art of gambling, challenged his mother to a contest, won everything from her and restored his father to his former state of opulence. Ganesha now saw the misery of his mother, learnt the art of gambling and defeated his brother. There were some more reverses and domestic troubles, but subsequently there was reconciliation, on account of which Shiva declared the day as auspicious for gambling.

HOLI

Holi is the Saturnalia of the Hindus, and the most popular holiday among the lower classes. It is a fertility festival which heralds the spring, and occurs in the month of Phalgun (February-March). There are many interesting theories which explain its origin. According to some traditions, the festival is celebrated in honour of Krishna's triumph over the female fiend Putana whom he killed while taking breast. The myth is symbolic of the death of Winter.

Another popular belief is that Kama was burnt to death by Shiva on this day. In South India the songs sung on the occasion of the festival include lamentations of Rati on the death of her husband. The chief features of the Holi celebrations used to be singing of lewd songs, sprinkling of coloured water on one another, rowdy crowds and a general atmosphere of licence. Processions of drunkards singing obscene songs, and dancing, were seen parading the streets, particularly in the Punjab. At present, spraying of coloured water is the main feature of the festival. Women on this day take care to keep indoors. They too, however, celebrate the festival by sprinkling coloured water on one another, or on their brothers and near male relatives.

Even serious old men relax on this day, and meekly suffer themselves to be surprised and painted by women and children. Fools are at times sent on idle errands to friends.

"In some parts of the Madras Presidency a mock-fight takes place between men and women. A woman takes a bundle of sheaves and ascends a tree and the men try to capture the bundle, the women trying to prevent them from doing so. At Indore, the trading classes erect a colossal figure, made of straw and clay, of Nathuram (a divinity of local importance), about forty feet high. Owing to an objectionable feature, this was prohibited, but the Durbar received a numerously signed petition and sanctioned the resumption of the practice on certain conditions.

"On the fifth day after the chief fire ceremonials, presumably representing the cremation of the season, a grand Durbar takes place in the Native States, in which coloured powders and fluids are thrown at the Sardars and Officials. It is called Rangpanchami, and is also observed by people in their houses to mark the conclusion of the festivities."

MAHASHIVARATRA

This festival falls in the month of Magha (January-February). It is preceded by a night of vigil and fasting in honour of Shiva (hence Shivaratra; *Maha* means great) and during the day ample amends are made for the fasting.

It is said that Shivaratra (the festival is also called Shivaratri) originated from a legend of an accidental fast and vigil of a hunter who, on account of this, became a lover of animals and a saint of Shiva. The following is the story of this conversion.

An uncouth hunter named Lubdhaka was arrested by his creditors and confined in a temple of Shiva. There he heard the devotees chanting the name of Shiva and wondered what it meant. In the evening he was released by a devotee who paid off the debt on his behalf. On his regaining freedom the hunter went straight to the forest to seek game and hid himself in the foliage of a Bel tree (*Aegle marmelos*: the leaves of this tree are sacred to Shiva) under which was a hidden Lingam. The hunter while clearing the foliage happened to drop some leaves on the Lingam, an act of great merit. He also repeated, by way of diversion, "Shiva Shiva!" in the manner the devotees did in the temple of Shiva where he had been detained by his creditors. The fellow did not understand what it meant; all the same it added to his merit.

By nightfall there came to the tank near the tree on which he remained hidden, a doe big with young. He drew his bow and took aim, when the doe saw him and prayed him to spare her life. She told him that another doe was following her and he could kill her; if he would not agree to that she would go home deliver her young and give it to her friends and return to be killed. She also told him that she was an Apsara who, on account of her neglect to dance before the idol of Shiva, had been cursed to become a doe and live with an Asura who had been turned into a black buck. The hunter, by virtue of his repeating the name of Shiva, had by now become half a lover of animals,

PRINCIPAL HINDU HOLIDAYS

and he made the doe swear that she would return, and let her go.

Lubdhaka sat on the Bel tree repeating the name of Shiva. He had been starving throughout the day and evening. By midnight when he felt the fiercest pangs of hunger there came another doe. She was restless and apparently seeking her mate. He drew his bow when the doe saw him and begged him to leave her to find her mate after which she promised to return to be killed. In spite of his hunger and a wasted day, Lubdhaka let her go.

Presently came a black buck seeking his mate. The hunter aiming his arrow at him, the buck requested him to be left to find his mate. The hunter let him also go.

The first doe went home and delivered her young. The second doe and the black buck had conjugal happiness; after this, the black buck asked the doe to remain at home, and offered to go himself to the hunter to be killed. The doe would not permit him to be killed alone. So all the three went to the hunter and quarrelled among themselves for precedence in death.

The sins of the hunter, in the meantime, had been expiated by the vigil and the repetition of the name of Shiva, and a realization of the evil of killing game for meat dawned upon him. He preached a sermon to the deer and let them go. At this moment messengers of Shiva came with a celestial car and the hunter was bodily translated to Shivaloka.

Shivaratra is one of the most important festivals of the Hindus. Fairs are held on river beds or seashore, and thousands of people come even from distant places to attend them. In some parts of India singing of obscene songs is indulged in at the fairs.

GANESH CHATURTHI

The fourth day (hence Chaturthi) of Bhadrapad (August-September) is sacred to Ganesha. Clay figures of Ganesha are made, worshipped and then drowned in a river, tank or sea. The images are decorated with flowers and taken in procession to the waterside with music and dancing. When the procession reaches the water-side, the images are placed on dry land, worshipped and then gently drowned.

"After the image is put into the water a handful of clay or sand is brought in the tray or on the stool used for carrying it, and ceremoniously thrown into the barn, the grain barrels, and particularly into the room in which provisions are stored," so as to ensure good crops in the next season.

It is inauspicious to see the moon on Ganesh Chathurthi. If anybody happens to see it on this day he fears to be slandered. It is said Krishna was falsely accused of the murder of Prasena and the theft of Syamantaka due to his looking at the moon on Ganesh Day. This sin can however be expiated by getting oneself abused on the following day. Hence those who see the moon on Ganesh Night provoke their neighbours in the morning and get themselves abused. This is, however, a delicate art and the inexperienced have to practise it with caution.

The cause of the enmity between Ganesha and the moon is said to be this: one day while Ganesha was passing Chandraloka (the region of the moon) he happened to tumble down, and Chandra laughed at him. Now the appearance and gait of Ganesha were matters of much comic comment among the gods but no god had dared to laugh at him as Chandra did. Ganesha, angered at the conduct of the moon, cursed him and declared that whoever would look at him should be falsely accused. Thus, the god who was the pet of the three worlds became inauspicious and all people avoided him like the plague. Chandra, unable to bear the shame of it, hid himself in a lotus flower. The gods missed him but none of them had the power to cancel the effect of Ganesha's curse. So they went to Ganesha himself. Brahma initiated them in Ganesha-puja and on the gods performing this ceremony, Ganesha was propitiated and he asked them what they wanted. On coming to know the object of their suit, he told them that the offender himself should perform the necessary Puja and approach him. Accordingly Brahaspati was sent to Chandra and he instructed him in the Puja; on Chandra performing it, Ganesha appeared before him. Chandra begged to be pardoned. The other gods also pleaded for the repentant sinner. Thus persuaded, Ganesha removed the general effect of the curse but maintained that Chandra's disgrace should be perpetuated and declared that whosoever saw the moon on Ganesh Day should suffer the effect of the curse. He also laid down that those who intentionally or unintentionally looked at the moon on this day should expiate their sins by getting themselves abused on the next day.

DATTA JAYANTI

This is the birthday of Dattatreya (a form of the Trinity) and falls on the fifteenth day of Margashirsha (November-December). Its folklore is more interesting than its observance.

The sage Narada felt unhappy because there were no quarrels anywhere. So he went to Parvati and, while conversing with her, observed that there was no woman in the three worlds to equal Anasuya, wife of Atri, in piety and virtue. Now Parvati had always thought herself the paragon of virtue, and was offended by Narada's speech. She did not, however, say anything but decided to prove the inferiority of Anasuya by demonstration; so as soon as Narada had departed she went to Shiva and asked him to tempt Anasuya and deprive her of her chastity.

From Mount Kailas, Narada went to Brahmaloka, raised jealousy in Sarasvati and, after that, proceeded to Vaikunta where he succeeded in making Lakshmi also ask her husband to tempt Anasuya.

The three gods, Brahma, Vishnu and Shiva started on their journey to Atri's hermitage, met at the junction of the three roads, and, ascertaining the object of each other's journey, decided to act jointly. They transformed themselves into mendicant Brahmins, went to Atri's hermitage and begged for alms. Anasuya came with a handful of grain, but they asked for food. She sent them to bathe in the stream adjoining the hermitage and prepared a meal for them. The mendicants came for the feed, seated themselves and asked Anasuya to strip herself naked and then serve them. Anasuya took a bowl of water, washed her husband's feet with it and, collecting the water again, sprinkled it over the Brahmins who were now turned into babies. She then stripped herself, offered them breast and put them to sleep in a cradle. The gods were also deprived of their power to assume their original forms. Thus trapped, they lived in the hermitage of Anasuya as her children.

Sarasvati, Lakshmi and Parvati, troubled over the prolonged absence of their husbands, set out in search of them. They met at the junction of the three roads, and saw Narada standing there playing on his Vina. The ladies asked the sage if he had seen their husbands, and were told that they were seen going to the hermitage of Atri. They started for the hermitage and, on reaching there, found their husbands in the cradle. Anasuya came to them, and the goddesses, much humiliated, begged her to return their husbands to them. She asked each of the ladies to pick out her husband. But all the babies were alike in appearance, and Lakshmi picked up Shiva to the merriment of Anasuya and the gods. Baffled, the goddesses implored Anasuya to restore their husbands to their original forms. But Anasuya said she had some claim on the babies as she had nursed them for so long, and the gods agreed to remain with her as her offspring in a combined form with three heads and six hands. On getting this assurance she washed the feet of her husband, sprinkled the water on the babies and transformed them to their proper forms. The gods, in their turn, kept their promise and, by combining a part of each of them, produced a three-headed divinity named Dattatreya. The central head represents Vishnu, the right-hand one Shiva and the other Brahma.

RAMANAVAMI

This festival falls on the ninth day of Chaitra (March-April) and is celebrated as the birthday of Rama. During the eight nights preceding it, it is believed to be meritorious to listen to a recital of the *Ramayana*. For this purpose Pundits, well versed in sacred lore, are invited to temples where they entertain the audience with Katha (literally, story-telling).

JANMASHTAMI

This is the birthday of Krishna and falls in the month of Shravan (July-August). It is not celebrated as a very important festival except in places where Krishna-worship is very popular. The feast is also called Gokul Ashtami.

VASANTA PANCHAMI

The fifth day of Magh (January-February) is sacred to Sarasvati. She is worshipped on this day particularly by scribes, scholars and students. While one school holds the view that no writing should be done on this day, and all books, pens, pencils and inkstands should be locked up before an image of Sarasvati, another school maintains that it is auspicious to write important documents on this day.

In addition to these, there are numerous other festivals among the Hindus which have not, however, an all-India importance. Every temple has its tutelary deity and an annual festival is held in honour of this deity on a day fixed by local traditions. These festivals are the most popular in the localities which the temples serve.*

---

* Detailed accounts of these will be found in the author's *Festivals and Holidays of India.*

Chapter XIII

SOME POPULAR STORIES AND LEGENDS

NALA AND DAMAYANTI*

NALA was the prince of Nishadha. He was handsome like Kama and brave like Indra, and in horsemanship there was not his equal in the three worlds.

One day while Nala was walking by the side of a lake in the royal park, he saw some swans gambolling in the water, and caught one of them. The frightened bird prayed to be released and Nala let it go; then, out of gratitude, the swan spoke to him of the marvellous beauty of Damayanti, the princess of Vidarbha. The bird described the lady so minutely and eloquently that Nala saw an image of her before him, and fell in love with her. He requested the swan to go to Damayanti and convey to her a message of love from him. Accordingly, the good bird went to Damayanti, spoke to her of the greatness of Nala, and his love for her, and the princess requited Nala's love.

The time came for Damayanti's Swayamvara (choice of husband) and king Bhimaka, her father, sent invitations to all the kings of the earth, so that she might choose a prince to her liking. Nala also received an invitation, and he eagerly proceeded towards Vidarbha, himself driving the chariot.

In the meantime, Narada, after his travels on earth, returned to heaven and gave news of the Swayamvara to the gods. He extrolled the beauty of Damayanti with all the eloquence he was capable of, and the gods themselves fell in love with her. Indra, Varuna, Agni and Yama decided to attend the Swayamvara and try their luck; so, attired in their finest robes, they proceeded towards Vidarbha.

On their way the gods met Nala. Seeing his noble bearing and skill in horsemanship, they asked him who he was and where he was going. Nala said he was the king of Nishadha and was going for the Swayamvara of Damayanti. The gods saw how handsome Nala was and how well he spoke, and feared that Damayanti might prefer him to them. Moreover, he was a fit messenger for the gods. So they made him promise that he would do their bidding, and then asked him to go to Damayanti as a messenger from them, with a request to choose one of them as her husband. They also gave him a robe by wearing which he could make himself invisible to all except Damayanti. Nala was grieved at the turn affairs had taken, but he was on oath, and hence went to Damayanti as the spokesman of the gods.

Nala saw Damayanti in her garden. She was even more attractive than he had imagined, and Nala thought of the pity of it all. But he subordinated his love to his sense of duty and pleaded ably for the gods, enumerating to her the greatness of each, and the benefits she could get by choosing one of them. Damayanti saw Nala, and from the description the swan had given her, recognized him. She put him on oath, and asked him to reveal his identity and say how he managed to get into the garden unseen by the guards. Nala was thus forced to say who he was, and tell her the circumstances which had led to his extraordinary mission. The princess smiled. "My lord!" she said, "I loved and chose you as my lord on the day the swan described your greatness to me. Pray, go and tell the gods that I care not for all their wealth and splendour. I have given my heart and soul to the king of Nishadha, and him only shall I wed." Nala felt happy, but he still pleaded for the gods and chid her for preferring a mortal to the celetials. He also warned her of the ire of the gods if she displeased them. But neither lure of celestial splendour nor fear of divine wrath could move Damayanti. "The gods know all," she said, " pray, go back and tell them that I cannot wed any one of them."

Nala now went back, happy and miserable at once; happy because he was loved by Damayanti, miserable because of the failure of his mission. The gods were waiting for him. He told them how he had failed. They praised him for his devotion to duty, for they were, they said, in the garden when Nala was pleading for them. They blessed him, wished him the best of luck and allowed him to attend the Swayamvara.

* The story appears in the *Mahabharata*.

For the Swayamvara sat assembled in the great hall of the palace all the mighty kings of the earth. At the appointed time, Damayanti, attired in beautiful robes, entered the assembly like the full-moon in the star-studded sky. Behind her walked her companions and before her went the goddess Sarasvati herself, describing to her the name and style of each of the kings. The suitors looked expectantly at the fateful garland in Damayanti's hand. One by one she passed the kings leaving them in the depth of despair. At last she came to the king of Nishadha. Sarasvati discreetly stood silent; for she saw five kings alike in appearance and attire. Damayanti looked at them and knew who the other four "Nalas" were; they were the four gods who had come to wed her. She uttered a silent prayer to the gods to reveal their identity and the gods heard her prayer. They sat without touching their seats and Damayanti put the garland on Nala.

The four gods praised Damayanti for her constancy, and each of them granted a boon to Nala. After the marriage Nala returned with his bride to Nishadha.

While the gods were going back to the celestial regions they saw Kali* (the evil spirit of Kaliyuga) on his way to Vidarbha to attend the Swayamvara. The gods laughed at him and told him that the Swayamvara was over and Damayanti had chosen Nala for her husband. Kali reviled the gods for permitting a mortal to win Damayanti while they were there, and swore, in sheer spite, that he would bring about the ruin of Nala. He then proceeded to Nishadha and waited for an opportunity to possess Nala. But this king was strict in his observance of all religious ceremonies, and the persevering Kali had to wait years before he could get an opportunity. One day, however, an irregularity in Nala's morning ablutions occurred, and Kali possessed him. Soon after, Pushkara, Nala's brother, whom Kali had already instigated to plot his brother's ruin, challenged Nala to a gambling contest. The king accepted the challenge and the two engaged themselves in gambling.

Nala began to lose heavily. He lost villages, towns and provinces. His counsellors and Damayanti advised the king to give up the contest but the possessed king paid no heed to their entreaties and gambled all the more eagerly. Seeing this, Damayanti feared the worst, and sent her two children to her father's house.

Soon the worst happened. Nala lost everything and was asked by Pushkara to leave his kingdom. The ruined king wept, and told Damayanti that he was no more worthy of her and that she should go to her father's house. Moreover, he added, he was condemned to wander in the forests, and Damayanti,

* He is not to be confused with Kali, wife of Shiva.

who all along had been brought up in the lap of luxury, could not bear the horrors of forest-life. But the loyal lady maintained that her place was beside her husband and with him she could bear any hardship. If he wanted her to go to her father, well, she said, they would both go to him. This the pride of Nala would not allow him to do. So the royal couple left their kingdom on a dark night and went into the wilderness.

In the jungle, Nala felt hungry, and, seeing some wild birds, spread his clothes for a net to catch them; but the birds were in reality a contrivance of Kali, and they flew away with his clothes laughing at the naked king. After this, Nala and Damayanti satisfied their hunger with what berries and roots they could find in the woods.

At night the two lay down under a tree, and the travel-worn lady soon fell asleep. Nala could not get sleep, but lay thinking of his fate and that of Damayanti. Suddenly an idea struck him. The possessed man, his reason perverted by Kali, thought that if he were to desert Damayanti she would find her way to her father's kingdom and be happy! No sooner had he conceived the idea than he got up, gently tore half the clothes of Damayanti, wore the same and ran away from her!

In the morning when Damayanti woke up, she saw not Nala. She could never imagine that he was capable of deserting her in the thick of the forest, and at first thought that he was hiding himself in play somewhere. She called his name aloud. But no one answered her. By and by the horrible truth dawned upon her. Nala had deserted her! She wept and went about the forest like a mad woman, calling out the name of her lord.

By nightfall she came upon a caravan on its way to a neighbouring city. She was hospitably received by the traders, and they promised to take her to the city. But at night a herd of wild elephants attacked the caravan and caused much loss of life and property. The merchants put down their misfortune to the presence of Damayanti among them and, suspecting her to be a witch, drove her away from the camp. Thus Damayanti was again left alone in the wilderness. After many more adventures in the forest with wild beasts and wilder men, she at last came to the city of Chedi, her scanty clothes all torn, her body bruised, her hair dishevelled, looking more or less, like a mad beggar woman. Children followed her through the streets and pelted her with stones. She happened to pass by the side of the palace, and the queen, seeing her from the balcony of her apartment took pity on the harassed woman and sent a messenger to conduct her to her presence. Accordingly Damayanti was taken to the queen. The royal lady asked her who she was, and Damayanti told her that she was a merchant's daughter, that their caravan, while passing through the forest, was attacked by wild elephants, that all her people were killed, and that she alone escaped with her life. The queen seeing her good manners and noble bearing, and hearing her sweet speech, asked her to remain in the palace as a companion to her daughter. Damayanti agreed and stayed at the court of Chedi.

As soon as news of the exile of Nala and Damayanti reached Bhimaka, this king sent messengers throughout all the kingdoms of the earth to look for them. One of these messengers came to the court of Chedi, saw Damayanti and told the queen who she was. The delighted queen, who was a relative of Bhimaka, chid Damayanti for hiding the truth from her, and sent her with a royal escort to Vidarbha.

Now for Nala. After deserting Damayanti, he wandered in the forest and saw a serpent surrounded by a forest fire. The reptile prayed to Nala to rescue it, and the chivalrous king, at great personal danger to himself, saved it from the flames. But as soon as it was out of danger the serpent bit Nala, and he became transformed into a swarthy ugly fellow. On Nala's asking the serpent what kind of reward this was, the serpent told him that it was a blessing in disguise. It would help him to remain unrecognized in his exile, it said. The serpent also taught him an incantation, by repeating which he could assume his original form at will.

Thus changed in person, Nala wandered over many lands till he reached Ayodhya where he took up a situation as charioteer to king Rituparna, and gave his name as Bahuka. He had lived there for some time when a messenger sent by Damayanti to look for Nala arrived at the court. Bahuka showed interest in the man and fell into conversation with him. Now, the messenger had instructions from Damayanti to ask anyone suspected of being Nala the following question: "Where art thou fled, O gambler, leaving me alone in the forest with half my clothes?" Seeing Bahuka's interest in Damayanti the messenger put him the question. Bahuka, visibly agitated, made answer: "The gambler is unworthy of you, noble lady, who ardently seeks the wretch who so shamefully deserted you. Still he asks for your forgiveness for he was beside himself when he deserted you."

The messenger returned to Vidarbha and narrated to Damayanti the reply Bahuka had given him. But the description he gave her of the person was that of one who, in no way, could be Nala. At any rate she decided to see him for herself, and sent a trusted Brahmin with a message to Rituparna informing him that Nala's whereabouts were unknown and inviting him to a second Swayamvara of Damayanti. The message was contrived to reach Ayodhya on the day previous to the supposed wedding. Damayanti knew that only Nala could drive the chariot from Ayodhya to Vidarbha in one day.

Rituparna was one of those lovers of Damayanti who had attended her first Swayamvara but had to come away disappointed. He was still in love with the lady and was eager to attend her second Swayamvara. But time was short, and he asked his charioteer if he could reach Vidarbha next day. Bahuka said he could. The charioteer selected the fleetest horses from the stable and yoked them to the lightest chariot; and when he took the reins and goaded the horses, the carriage sped with the swiftness of wind. So great indeed was the speed of the chariot that when Rituparna accidentally dropped his scarf and would have stayed to pick it up, Bahuka said that it lay five miles behind, and drove faster! Marvelling at the horsemanship of Bahuka, Rituparna decided to spring a surprise on his charioteer and said, while passing a tree, that it had so many branches, so many leaves and so many flowers. The amazed charioteer pulled up reins, got down from the chariot and counted the branches, leaves, and flowers of the tree, and found them correct. Bahuka begged Rituparna to teach him this science of numbers, and Rituparna demanded that he should be taught the art of horsemanship in return. Bahuka agreed and they taught the sciences to each other; and as soon as Nala learnt the science of numbers, by its power, Kali was ejected out of his person and he came to himself. He, however, retained the ugly form the serpent had transformed him into.

Damayanti was anxiously waiting for the arrival of Rituparna, and when she saw, from the terrace of the palace, the chariot coming whirling through the sky, as it were, she felt almost certain that the charioteer was Nala and no one else. But when she saw him she felt much depressed because he looked so very unlike Nala. She, however, sent a Brahmin to enquire of him if he knew aught of Nala and observe if he showed any emotion. The Brahmin went to Bahuka and asked him if he had heard anything about Nala. Bahuka answered with much emotion: "Only Nala's self of Nala knows, and Nala will, of himself, no sign betray." Damayanti ordered that no food should be served to him. He was to be given only uncooked rice and vegetables, neither fire nor water to cook them, and spies were ordered to watch what he did with the rice and vegetables. Nala produced fire and water by the power of the boons Agni and Varuna had once given him and cooked his food. The spies saw the miracle and reported it to Damayanti. She asked them to bring a morsel of the food Bahuka cooked. When this was brought she tasted it and was convinced that it was of Nala's cooking. And lastly Damayanti sent her children to the charioteer who embraced them and wept. Now she went to him herself and Nala, unable to contain himself, proclaimed his identity and embraced her. "But how could you, Damayanti," said he, "forgetting your Nala seek another husband?"

She swore that the second Swayamvara was a ruse, asked him if he saw there any preparations for it, and called upon the gods to declare that, throughout the prolonged absence of her lord, she had been faithful to him. The gods heard her prayer and a voice spoke from the void: "Nala! Damayanti has always been true to you." A shower of flowers fell from the sky and celestial music was heard.

Rituparna, who had been at first much intrigued to find there were no preparations for the Swayamvara, now came to know who his charioteer was. He blessed Nala and Damayanti and took his leave.

Nala now challenged his brother to a gambling contest, and, by the power of the science of numbers he had learnt, easily defeated Pushkara and won the kingdom from him. He generously forgave his wicked brother and allowed him to remain in the kingdom in opulence. And Nala reigned in Nishadha for many years.

Those who read the story of Nala or listen to it will be free from all the evil effects of Kaliyuga.

SHAKUNTALA

Once upon a time there lived a king named Dushyanta. He went on a hunting expedition and, chasing a fawn, strayed away from the main party and came to a forest where some Rishis had their hermitage. He entered a flower-garden by a river-bank and, in it, beheld a damsel beautiful as a nymph. She was in the full bloom of her youth, and scantily clad as a hermit's daughter. The contours of her youthful body were marvellous to behold and the king was wounded by the shafts of Kama; but he feared to acknowledge even to himself his desire for the lovely maiden, as he took her for the daughter of a Brahmin hermit, marriage between a Kshatriya and a Brahmin girl being forbidden. But on speaking to her and her companion who was beside her, Dushyanta came to know that the maiden was the daughter of King Viswamitra.* Emboldened by this knowledge Dushyanta asked for Shakuntala's hand and the maiden, already burning with love of him, eagerly consented to become his wife. Kanva, Shakuntala's foster-father, was not in the hermitage at that time, and Shakuntala and Dushyanta got married according to the Gandharva rite.† Dushyanta spent some time in sport with his bride and, on his departure to his kingdom promised her that he would come back shortly and conduct her to his court.

Months passed and Dushyanta did not return. Shakuntala showed signs of pregnancy and it became difficult for her to conceal her condition any longer. So her companion spoke to Kanva, with becoming modesty, of what had taken place, and the sage decided that Shakuntala should now be with her husband, and sent her to Dushyanta with two trusted disciples and a lady companion.

The party reached the court of Dushyanta, and the king received them in an open assembly. But when Kanva's disciples presented Dushyanta with his wife, the king, strangely enough, denied all knowledge of having ever seen Shakuntala. The hermits told the king that Shakuntala was incapable of telling a lie and accused him of betraying an innocent girl. Shakuntala also spoke at length of the sin of betrayal and the greatness of the virtue of truthfulness. "You speak very well," said the king, "but how can I accept as my wife a woman big with child whom I know not?"

Then there was a voice from heaven: "O King! Shakuntala is thy lawful wife and the child in her womb is thine!"

Now Dushyanta embraced his wife, and told her that he had been waiting for this divine proof so that the whole assembly might be convinced of the legality of their marriage.

The son of Dushyanta and Shakuntala was Bharata from whom India (Bharatam) takes its name.

The above is a summary of the original story of Shakuntala, narrated in the *Mahabharata*. In the well-known play of Kalidasa, the poet, for dramatic effect, introduces some characters and incidents outside the theme of the original story. According to Kalidasa,

---

* "When the sanctified ascetic Viswamitra, who had for thousands of years been engaged in the most rigid mortification, beheld Menaka, the Apsara sent by Indra to debauch him, 'bathing, of surpassing form, unparalleled in beauty, in appearance resembling Sri, her clothes wetted by the stream, exhibiting her fascinating symmetry of frame; he, subdued by the arrows of Kandarpa, approached her; and five times five years, spent in dalliance with this seducing female, passed away like a moment.' 'What!' exclaimed at length the reflecting sage, 'my wisdom, my austerities, my firm resolution, all destroyed at once by a woman! Seduced by the crime in which Indra delights, am I stripped of the advantages arising from all my austerities'" — The *Ramayana*.

Shakuntala was born of this amour, Menaka, unable to seduce Viswamitra again, left the new-born babe beside him and went to the celestial regions. The babe was found by the hermit Kanva who brought her up as his daughter.

† Because of the free love supposed to exist among Gandharvas and Apsaras, love-marriages are known among the Hindus as Gandharva marriages.

Dushyanta, as a token of the marriage, gives his signet ring to Shakuntala and departs. Shakuntala sits in the hermitage dreaming of her lover when the sage Durvasa comes and knocks at the door. She does not hear him, and he imprecates a curse which deprives Dushyanta of his memory of Shakuntala. The door is subsequently opened, and the sage tempers the curse with a blessing and declares that the sight of the signet ring would restore his lost memory to Dushyanta. But, while Shakuntala with her companions proceeds to the court of her husband, she goes to a lake to wash her hands and loses the ring without noticing the loss. On Shakuntala reaching the court, Dushyanta naturally enough, denies ever having met her. Her companions, determined not to take her back, leave her at the court, and the king drives her out. Outside the palace, Menaka, Shakuntala's mother, descends from heaven and carries her off to the celestial regions where she lives and gives birth to her son.

The lost ring is swallowed by a fish and the fish caught by a fisherman. He sees the ring in its belly and takes it to the king. On seeing the ring his lost memory is restored to Dushyanta, and he institutes a vain search for his wife throughout the earth. When the king thus lives in despair, a messenger with a celestial car comes from Indra, seeking his assistance in a battle with the Asuras. The king proceeds to heaven, defeats the Asuras and returns to earth with the blessings of the gods. On his way down he happens to pass the house where Shakuntala lives and there sees his son, falls into conversation with him, ultimately finds Shakuntala, and, with his wife and child, returns to his kingdom.

VIKRAMADITYA

Vikramaditya is a legendary king who is said to have ruled in Ujjain in the 4th century A.D. But the era that goes by his name indicates that he lived in the first century B.C. (Vikram era starts from 56 B.C.). There is a collection of popular stories known as *Tales of Vikramaditya* which speak of his adventures. It is said that he propitiated the goddess Kali, and obtained a boon from her by which he was allowed to reign for a hundred years. On his speaking of this boon to his minister Bhatti, the latter observed that he could give him a further lease of hundred year's life. Vikramaditya felt surprised and asked Bhatti how this could be done, upon which the minister told him that since Kali's boon was for a hundred years' reign, Vikramaditya could reign for six months in a year and go into voluntary exile for the remaining six, appointing his minister as regent, and thus double his span of life. The king acted upon the advice of his minister and lived six months every year in self-imposed exile. Most of the Vikramaditya tales narrate his adventures during the period of his exile.

Of the legends of Vikramaditya, the most interesting are the *Tales of a Vetala* (possessed corpse). These tales (twenty-five in number) are in the form of riddles told by Shiva in a temple, for the entertainment of Parvati. The Brahmin attendant of the temple overheard the stories, and Shiva, who caught him eavesdropping, cursed him to become a Vetala and hang head downwards on the branch of a Murucca tree. The Brahmin prayed for mercy, and Shiva declared that he would be released from the effect of the curse by Vikramaditya to whom the Vetala was recommended to narrate the stories, and ask for a solution of the riddles.

Vikramaditya, in the course of his wanderings in the forest, sees the Vetala and at the request of a sage, undertakes to transfer the repugnant being to another forest. The Vetala agrees to migrate but imposes a condition on the king that he carries him and remains silent during the journey. Vikramaditya now takes the Vetala on his shoulders and proceeds towards the outskirts of the forest when the Vetala narrates a story, asks the king to solve the riddle it contains, and pronounces a curse if he would not. Thus fallen between two stools, the king breaks silence to solve the riddle and the Vetala goes back to the Murucca tree. Vikramaditya makes twenty-five attempts to transfer the Vetala at the end of which all the riddles are solved and the Vetala becomes once again the Brahmin he was.

The following is one of the stories told by the Vetala:

In the district called Brahmasthala, on the bank of the Jumna, there lived a Brahmin named Agniswamin. He had a daughter named Mandaravati who, in loveliness, excelled the Apsaras. When the maiden came of age to be married, there arrived from Kanyakubja, three young accomplished Brahmins seeking her hand. Each one of these suitors demanded the maiden for himself and threatened to commit suicide if she was given to another. So her father, afraid to cause the death of any, declared that Mandaravati could not be given in marriage to any of them. But the young Brahmins remained in the house day and night, their eyes feasting on the beauty of Mandaravati's countenance.

Then the maiden suddenly fell ill and died. The three lovers distracted with grief carried the dead body of Mandaravati to the cremation ground and burnt it. After the cremation, one of the Brahmins dwelt in the burial ground sleeping on the ashes of Mandaravati and living on the alms he could get by begging. The second took her bones to the Ganges and lived on the banks of the river meditating on Mandaravati. The third became a wandering mendicant.

The Wanderer, in the course of his travels, reached a village named Vajraloka where he was hospitably received in the house of a Brahmin. This Brahmin was very learned and pious, and was in possession of a book which contained an incantation for bringing the dead back to life. The Wanderer came to know of this and, at night, while his host was sleeping, he stole the book and, with the intention of bringing Mandaravati back to life, proceeded towards Brahmasthala. Travelling day and night, he at last reached the cremation ground and saw the first lover sleeping on the ashes of his beloved. The second lover who had gone to the Ganges also returned to the spot, and thus the three lovers again met. Collecting the ashes of Mandaravati the lover who had the Book of Life with him opened the book, recited the incantation and Mandaravati came back to life. But the lovers started quarrelling among themselves. "She is mine," said the one who recited the charm, "because I brought her back to life by the power of the charm I repeated." "She is mine," said the one who had slept on her ashes, "because I preserved her ashes." "She belongs to me," said the third, "for the merit of my pilgrimage and the sanctity of the waters of the Ganges restored her to life."

"Now, king Vikramaditya," says the Vetala, "give judgment to decide their dispute. Whose wife ought the maiden to be? If you know and do not say it, your head shall fly to pieces."

Vikramaditya reflected and said: "The one who restored her to life by a charm, though he endured hardships, must be considered her father, because he performed that office for her; and he who carried her bones to the Ganges is considered her son; but he who out of love lay on her ashes and so remained in the cemetery embracing her and practising asceticism, is to be called her husband, for he acted like one in his deep affection."

The king having thus broken silence, the Vetala went back to the Murucca tree.

THE LEGEND OF JAGANNATH

The celebrated temple of Jagannath (Lord of the Universe) at Puri is, as is well known, an important centre of pilgrimage. "Tradition declares Jagannath to be, and common belief accepts him as, an appearance of Vishnu himself, and not the incarnation of a portion of his essence. There is, however, considerable reason for doubting whether originally Jagannath had any connection with Vishnu. It is possible that he was the local divinity of some unknown tribe whose worship was engrafted into Hinduism; and the new god, when admitted into the pantheon, was regarded as another manifestation of Vishnu; or what is more probable, as

* W. J. Wilkins, *Hindu Mythology*.

Puri was a head centre of Buddhism, when that system was placed under a ban and its followers persecuted, the temple was utilized for Hinduism, and Jagannath, nominally a Hindu deity, was really Buddhistic, the strange, unfinished image being nothing else than a disguised form of the symbols of the central doctrine of the Buddhist faith. Possibly, in order to be free from persecution, it was taught that this was a form of Vishnu. There are several legends professing to account for the form in which he is worshiped, and for the peculiar sanctity of Puri, the chief place of his worship. There is a peculiarity in the phraseology employed by the people who visit his shrine; they speak of going to see Jagannath, not to worship him as is the case with other gods; and it is the sight of the image in the temple, or as it is being bathed, or drawn in its ponderous car that is so eagerly desired as a means by which sin in the worshipper is destroyed."*

"The strange unfinished" idol is believed to be the work of Viswakarma himself. It is fabled that a relic of Krishna was found by a king named Indradhumna who, desirous of placing it in an image of Vishnu, prayed to Viswakarma to make the image. "The architect of the gods consented to this, but was most careful in explaining to the king that if anyone looked at him, or in any way disturbed him while he was at work, he would immediately desist, and leave the image in an unfinished state. The king promised to observe this condition and Viswakarma commenced his work. In one night he raised a grand temple in the blue mountains of Orissa, and then began to make the image. For fifteen days the king managed, with difficulty, to restrain his impatience, but then foolishly tried to see the god at work. The angry deity at once ceased, as he had threatened, and the image was left with a most ugly face, and without hands and feet. The king, exceedingly grieved as he saw the result of his curiosity, went in distress to Brahma who comforted him with the promise that he would render the image famous in its present form. The king invited the gods to be present at its inauguration. Several accepted the invitation and Brahma himself officiated as priest, and gave eyes and a soul to the god. Thus the fame of Jagannath was completely established. The original image of this deity is closely copied in other places besides Puri; and by his side there is generally an image of Krishna's favourite brother, Balarama, and his sister Subhadra."

KHANDEHRAO

Khandehrao (popularly known as Khandoba) is a manifestation of Shiva and is the tutelary deity of the Maharathas. Tradition has it that Shiva assumed this form to kill two demon-brothers named Mani and Mall.

The seven Rishis, so runs the story, had their hermitages on Manichurna mountain. Mani and Mall, finding the hermitages to be obstacles in their hunting expeditions, destroyed them. The sages complained to Shiva, and this deity assumed the form of Bhairava (Khandehrao), and at the head of an army of seven crore legions of fierce creatures, descended on Manichurna mountain and engaged the forces of Mani. After a fierce battle Mani was killed when Mall appeared with his armies. Bhairava vanquished Mall also.

"The Rishis requested Shiva to remain on the mountain in their midst, and he did so in the form of a double-Lingam of the Swayambhuva or self-evolved type, that is, not shaped by human hands. A large city soon grew on the spot. It was named Prema-puri or the town of love... Behind the image of Khandehrao is that of his consort 'Mhalsabai' riding and attended by a dog. Khandehrao is supposed to be riding on a yellow horse, his flag is yellow, and the demons he killed were also yellow."

At Jejury there is a famous temple dedicated to Khandehrao. The deity is particularly beloved of the Dhangar or shepherd caste from whom he is fabled to have abducted a maiden named Banai.

VITHAL OR VITHOBA

Vithoba is a very popular deity of Maharashtra, and his shrine at Pandharpur is a famous centre of pilgrimage. Many legends are current about the origin of Vithoba. According to one story, he is a manifestation of Vishnu himself, and according to another, of Krishna, the eighth incarnation of Vishnu. Both are, however, agreed that it was the filial devotion of a Brahmin named Pundalik that was responsible for the Vithoba manifestation.

Pundalik, we are told, was going on a pilgrimage to Benares with his wife and aged parents. He made his parents walk while his wife and himself rode on a mule. When the pilgrims reached Pandharpur they halted for rest and took up their abode in the house of a hospitable Brahmin. Early next morning when Pundalik got up he saw three elegant ladies, richly ornamented, doing menial duties in the household. His curiosity was roused and he asked them who they were. At first they did not disclose their identity because he was a wicked man, they said, who ill-treated his parents. They then informed him that they were the river goddesses Ganga, Yamuna and Sarasvati and had, because of the ideal conduct of the Brahmin towards his parents, voluntarily undertaken to perform menial duties in his household. Struck with remorse, Pundalik gave up his pilgrimage, remained in Pandharpur and acted for the rest of his life in the most exemplary manner towards his parents.

Vishnu (or Krishna) hearing of his fame for filial devotion came to see him. The visitor arrived when Pundalik was attending on his parents and, annoyed at the disturbance, heaved a brick at him; a more charitable version says that he only threw the brick for the god to sit on as he was too busy to find a better seat. Anyway, the god remained at Pandharpur and his image stands on a brick.

THE MYTHICAL ORIGIN OF THE GANGES

Ganga is a goddess worshipped by the Hindus as the personification of the sacred river Ganga (Ganges), a dip in whose waters is believed to wash away sins. In the Vedas, Ganga does not occupy an important place. In the Vedic times the Aryans had not penetrated into the land watered by the Ganges but were mostly inhabiting the Punjab, and hence Sindhu (the Indus) and Sarasvati were the sacred streams of the Vedic period. In the Puranas, however, no stream is said to be so sacred as Ganga.

Ganga, the goddess, was the daughter of Himavan and sister of Parvati. Her father gave her in marriage to the gods and hence the river Ganga flowed only in the celestial regions. Bhagiratha, a scion of the Solar race, by labours comparable to those of Hercules, is said to have brought the river to the earth. The following is the story of the descent of Ganga.

Sagara, king of Ayodhya, had no children. He propitiated the sage Bhrigu, who granted him a boon by which Kesini, one of his two wives, gave birth to a son and the other, Sumati to a gourd. The rind of the gourd burst open and produced sixty thousand sons.

When his children grew up, Sagara felt himself powerful enough to perform the Aswamedha sacrifice and dethrone Indra. Accordingly he made preparations for the sacrifice and let loose the horse to wander at will. Indra, coming to know the intentions of Sagara, assumed the form of an Asura, drove away the horse to the nether regions, and let it browse near the place where the mighty sage Kapila was sitting in meditation.

On the disappearance of the horse, the officiating priest went in a panic to Sagara, and predicted ruin for the kingdom on account of the deranged sacrifice. Sagara now asked his sixty thousand sons to dig their way to the nether regions and regain the horse. The mighty sons of Sagara began to dig the earth, and each one digging a league, burrowed sixty thousand leagues into the bowels of the earth. The earth herself complained of the deeds of Sagara's sons to Brahma, and Brahma pacified her by saying that the princes were courting their own death, and asked her to wait a little longer. When the sons of Sagara could not find the horse, even in those deep regions which they searched, they returned to their father; he asked them to go back to their work and not to return to Ayodhya without finding the horse. So the princes again started burrowing. They bored their way right through the earth and came upon the mighty elephants supporting the earth, but still could not find the horse. They looked for the horse in all directions and, at last, saw it browsing near the hermitage of the sage Kapila. They thought that the sage had stolen the horse and rushed to him with the intention of laying violent hands on him. The meditating sage opened his eyes in anger, and the sons of Sagara were reduced to ashes by the flames that emanated from his eyes. Not one of them escaped to carry the news to Sagara.

Sagara, apprehending the worst, sent his grandson Ansuman (by his first-born who had, subsequent to the birth of the son, taken to asceticism) in search of his uncles. This prince, in his quest, reached the hermitage of Kapila and saw the horse. He saluted the sage reverently and asked him if he knew aught of his uncles. The sage, pleased with his humility, told him what had happened to the sons of Sagara. He also observed that they could be brought back to life if the sacred waters of the celestial Ganga could be made to flow over their ashes. Ansuman thanked the sage and, with his permission, drove back the horse to Ayodhya and completed the sacrifice.

Now Sagara began to make plans to bring Ganga down to the nether regions where the ashes of his sons lay, but during his thirty thousand years' reign Sagara could not succeed in his attempt. He died bequeathing the task as a legacy to his grandson. But neither Ansuman nor his son Dilipa could succeed where Sagara had failed, and it was given to Bhagiratha, son of Dilipa, to accomplish this work. Bhagiratha performed austerities of a very severe nature and propitiated Brahma who agreed to order Ganga to descend to the earth. But he warned Bhagiratha that the earth could not sustain the shock of her fall, and asked him to propitiate Shiva and request him to receive the goddess in his locks. Bhagiratha accordingly underwent a further course of penances, at the end of which Shiva was propitiated, and he consented to sustain the shock of Ganga's fall. Brahma then commanded Ganga to descend to earth and the goddess, none too pleased with the prospect of an earthly course, decided to engulf the whole earth in her fall and carry Shiva himself with her to the nether regions. She came in terrible torrents, roaring and foaming, uprooting trees and tearing hillocks, but on her descent to Kailas she found in Mahadeva more than a match for her. For he caught her in his locks and the goddess, unable to extricate herself from the maze of his hair, wandered aimlessly in his head, her spirit broken, her strength dissipated. Bhagiratha had again to perform austerities before Shiva would release her. On her issuing out of Shiva's head she fell to the earth, dividing herself into several branches, and gave birth to the sacred streams of India. One branch followed Bhagiratha who rode in a car, swift as wind, guiding the goddess to the ashes of his ancestors. But in her course Ganga happened to flood the sacrificial ground of Jahnu and the puissant sage drank up the whole river. Bhagiratha had now to propitiate the sage who, at his request, allowed the river to come out of his ear. After this, the course of Ganga was smooth and uneventful. Bhagiratha led her to the sea and thence to the nether regions where the ashes of his ancestors lay. On the sacred waters flowing over the ashes, the sons of Sagara came to life.

Because of these labours of Bhagiratha which caused the descent of the goddess, Ganga is also known as Bhagirathi (daughter of Bhagiratha). The name of Bhagiratha became proverbial for persistence and perseverance, and the achievement of any object difficult of attainment is referred to as the result of Bhagiratha-prayatnam (labours of Bhagiratha).

ANNAPURNA DEVI (GODDESS OF DAILY BREAD)

This is a widely worshipped manifestation of Parvati and was occasioned by a domestic quarrel between Shiva and Parvati.

Shiva, as a mendicant, supported the family by begging; but one day, due to excessive smoking he could not go on his daily rounds. The previous day's provision was consumed by the hungry children, the rat of Ganesha and the peacock of Kartikeya. So the elder members of the family had to starve. While Shiva was wondering why he was fated to starve like this when all other gods lived in opulence, Narada appeared before him. On enquiring of the sage if he knew the cause of his misery, Narada told Shiva that it was all on account of Parvati. "An auspicious wife," said the learned sage, "brings good fortune to her husband, and an inauspicious one misfortunes. Look at Vishnu! He married Sri and has ever since been living in plenty." After imparting this information to Shiva the sage repaired to the kitchen where he saw the starving Parvati sitting in a melancholy mood. She asked the sage if he knew why she was condemned to such penury, and Narada told her that it was all on account of her husband. "A capable husband," said he, "supports his family and keeps them in opulence. Look at Sarasvati! She married the creator and lives in a heaven the like of which does not exist in the three worlds. It pains me to say so, noble lady, but there is no getting away from the fact that the genius of your husband is essentially destructive, and he cares not for his wife and children."

PLATE LXXXIX

245 **THE GREAT DECEASE**
(Gandhara. Indian Museum, Calcutta)

246 **SIDDHARTHA DRIVING THROUGH THE CITY**
(Sanchi. Copyright: Archaeological Dept. of India)

PLATE XC

247 A PILGRIM BEFORE
A STATUE OF BUDDHA AT BODHGAYA
(From *Picturesque India* by Martin Hurlimann)

248 ADORATION OF THE BUDDHA AS SYMBOLIZED
BY A STUPA
(From Barhut, Indian Museum, Calcutta. Photo : India Office)

249   TWO SCULPTURES OF THE BUDDHA PREACHING   250
(Gandhara. Indian Museum, Calcutta)

PLATE XCI

251 ADORATION OF THE BUDDHA AS SYMBOLIZED BY THE WHEEL OF THE LAW
(Barhut. Indian Museum, Calcutta, Photo: India Office)

252 KUBERA AND HARITI
(Sahri Bahlol, Peshawar Museum. Photo: Dr. J. Ph. Vogel)

253 THE BUDDHA ATTENDED BY DEVAS TEACHING THE NAGAS
(Calcutta Museum)

254 WORSHIP OF THE ALMSBOWL OF THE BUDDHA
(Amravati. Madras Museum: Photo: India Office)

PLATE XCII

255

Top:—WORSHIP OF THE HAIRLOCK OF BUDDHA IN TUSITA HEAVEN

Middle:—A GOD ANNOUNCING THE CONCEPTION OF MAYA

Bottom—AJASAT VISITING THE BUDDHA

(Indian Museum, Calcutta, Photo: Johnston and Hoffmann)

256

Top:—ADORATION OF THE BUDDHA BY SUDDHODANA
Middle:—DREAM OF MAYA AND THE RETURN TO KAPILAVASTU
Bottom:—FIGURE OF A WATCHMAN

(Sanchi. From *Early Indian Sculpture* by L Bachhofer)

257

Top:—ENLIGHTENMENT

Middle:—REPRESENTATION OF THE EASTERN QUARTER OF HEAVEN

Bottom:—APSARAS DANCING IN HEAVEN

(From Barhut. Indian Museum, Calcutta.
Photo: Johnston and Hoffmann)

PLATE XCIII

258 ASOKA AND QUEEN WORSHIPPING THE BODHI TREE
(Sanchi. Copyright: Archaeological Deptartment of India)

259 **REPRESENTATION OF A STUPA**
(Amravati. British Museum. Photo: D. A. A. S. I.)

PLATE XCIV

260 THE GREAT RENUNCIATION
(Indian Museum, Calcutta)

261 THE BUDDHA'S COFFIN
(Gandhara. Indian Museum, Calcutta)

262 GAUTAMA MEETING HIS FUTURE WIFE
(Amravati. Madras Museum. Photo: Musee Guimet)

263 THE MUSICAL ENTERTAINMENT IN THE PALACE
(Amravati. Madras Museum. Photo: India Office)

PLATE XCV

264 THE JAIN SAINT GAUTAMESHWARA
(Sharavana Belgola, Mysore;
Photograph, India Office, London)

265 A JAIN GODDESS
(Bronze, Mysore : From *Art of India and Pakistan*, Sir Leigh Ashton)

266 THE JAIN SCHOLAR HEMACHANDRA SURI
(From *Jain Miniatures* by Dr. Moti Chandra)

PLATE XCVI

267 **TRISALA IN HER PALACE**
(From *La Peinture Indienne* I. Stchoukine)

268 **TRISALA REJOICING AT THE MOVEMENT OF THE FOETUS**
(From *Jain Miniatures* by Dr. Moti Chandra)

269 **PLUCKING OF THE HAIR**
(From *Jain Miniatures* by Dr. Moti Chandra)

270 **CONSECRATION OF TRISALA**
(From *La Peinture Indienne* by I. Stchoukine)

Parvati brooded over the words of Narada and decided to desert her husband. So the next day, while Shiva was out begging, she collected her children and proceeded towards her father's house. Narada, however, did not want things to go so far and appeared before her. He told her that though Shiva had many faults he had redeeming features as well which the other gods envied. He advised her to go to the houses where Shiva used to go for begging, in advance of her husband; and collect all the food from them. She did so with the result that her husband returned home hungry with his begging bowl empty. Parvati now fed him with the food she had collected, and Mahadeva was so pleased with her that he embraced her violently and became one with her.

Parvati feeding her husband is known as Annapurna Devi while the combined form in which Shiva became one with his wife is called Ardhanari (half-woman).

THE STORY OF HARISCHANDRA

Once a discussion arose in the court of Indra as to who, in the three worlds, was the most truthful and righteous person. The sage Vasishta maintained that none could excel Harischandra, the then Emperor of Aryavarta, in virtue and righteousness. "Harischandra," said Vasishta, "is never known to have broken a promise or to have withheld any gift a Brahmin had asked for. He rules his kingdom so wisely and justly that there is no sorrow or premature death in the land. The rains never fail in the seasons and plenty rules the land. No widow mourns the death of her lord and no mother, of her child. The king does nothing to gain selfish ends and rules the land for the people and the Brahmins. In the three worlds, I assure you, there is not so great a person as Harischandra."

The sage Viswamitra, ever jealous of the fame of Vasishta, thought otherwise. He had a high opinion of himself and considered Vasishta's contention an insult to himself and all the celestials. He wondered how Vasishta could exalt a mortal above celestials and sages. "What do you know about kings, Vasishta?" he thundered addressing his rival, "you have never been a king, and a Brahmin is easily duped by the hypocrisy of rulers. I was a king myself, and well acquainted with the ways of kings. Most of them pose as saints but are sinners at heart. Hence I ask you, on behalf of the gods and the sages, to withdraw your remarks about king Harischandra."

Vasishta was not prepared to accede to the request of Viswamitra and the argument between the sages became violent and hot. At last Viswamitra said: "Harischandra is a king and can very well afford to practise the various virtues. He has wealth and fame, health, a beautiful woman as his wife and a robust boy as his son. Give me leave to test him under adversity, and I will very soon show what sort of a man he is."

The gods agreed that this was the only way of ending the quarrel, and gave Viswamitra permission to test Harischandra under adversity. He was allowed to deprive Harischandra of his kingdom, wife and son, and health and happiness. On receiving this permission Viswamitra requisitioned the service of the malevolent Sani (planet Saturn), ever ready to perform any mission of cruelty.

While king Harischandra was, one day, holding Durbar, Viswamitra entered the assembly dressed as a poor Brahmin. Seeing the Brahmin, the king immediately rose from his throne and paid him respect. But the Brahmin stood aloof with a frown on his face and a curse on his trembling lips. Harischandra became apprehensive and asked the Brahmin the cause of his displeasure. "I am probably the only starving person in this land of plenty," said the Brahmin, miserable but haughty, "and I have come here to beg a boon of you." The wily Brahmin made Harischandra promise that he would be given anything and everything asked for. After extracting this promise, Viswamitra asked for the kingdom of Harischandra. The king, without showing any hesitation or displeasure, immediately abdicated in favour of Viswamitra and publicly announced it in the assembly.*

Now, no gift to a Brahmin could be properly ratified without a minor gift known as Dakshina. Viswamitra, on receiving the kingdom, promptly demanded Harischandra's weight in gold as the ratification of the gift. The king ordered the treasury to be opened for getting the necessary gold, when Viswamitra objected as, in giving away the kingdom. Harischandra had also given away the treasury of the kingdom. The king saw the force of the Brahmin's argument, but did not know how to get the required amount for Dakshina. "There is one thing you can do," said Viswamitra, "you have only your son, wife and your own person as your private property; sell these and pay me my Dakshina. If you are unwilling to do this, say so, and I shall give you your kingdom back and go my way." Harischandra refused to go back on his word. He would rather keep his promise and die a slave, than break it and live a king. So he decided to sell his son and wife and himself and pay all that he could to ratify the gift.

Viswamitra would not allow the sale of Haris-

---

* In a different version of the story it is related that Viswamitra made Harischandra dream, one night, that he had given away his kingdom to a Brahmin, and Viswamitra came in the morning to claim it.

chandra and his family in his own kingdom. So the king with his wife and son travelled on foot to the free city of Benares where he put his wife and son and himself to public auction. Sani had, by now, assumed the form of a trader and was waiting in Benares for Harischandra's arrival. He bought queen Taramati and her son Rohidas, as he specialized in the persecution of women and children. An accomplice of Viswamitra who had assumed the form of a Dom (keeper of cremation grounds) for the purpose, bought Harischandra. Viswamitra collected the proceeds of the sale as his Dakshina, and went back to his kingdom. But in a subtle form he was ever present near Harischandra to take advantage of any opportunity that might lead to the fall of the king.

In Sani, Taramati found a hard taskmaster. She had to drudge day and night and was hardly allowed to have any sleep. The dreadful old man always found fault with her, scolded her whenever she came in his way and even abused and beat her. Her little son was treated even worse.

The lot of Harischandra was no better. The Dom was a hard man to please. He gave Harischandra certain tasks and created numerous obstacles which prevented his performing them properly. For instance, he would ask him to work as a water carrier but cause holes to be made in the pots used for carrying water. He put Harischandra in many other jobs and always found some excuse to kick him. At last Harischandra was appointed the doorkeeper of the cremation ground and his chief duty was to see that nobody entered the place to cremate the dead without first paying the prescribed fee.

Taramati and Rohidas were living a miserable life in the house of the impossible Sani, but they could snatch a few moments, when the evil planet was not looking, to indulge in mutual affection. Sani came to know of it and with the help of Viswamitra decided to put an end to this. They caused the child, while he was cutting grass in his master's pastures, to be bitten by a poisonous snake. The child died instantly and the dead body was brought to Taramati. The fond mother gave herself up to wailing and lamentation. But Sani came on the spot and complained bitterly of her lack of sense of proportion. The death of the child had involved him in a dead loss, he said, and instead of trying to make good the loss by working harder, the foolish woman was wasting all her time in weeping over the dead child as if by so doing she could bring him back to life. He threatened to drive home the point by a handy cudgel he was holding, when Taramati fell at his feet and implored him to grant her a few hours' leave of absence to take her dead child to the cremation ground and burn it according to the prescribed rites. Even Sani could not refuse this request; besides he did not want the dead body to remain in his premises for long. But when Taramati reminded him that she had not a pie in the world to pay the Dom's fee, Sani told her that it was her business and not his. Nor was there anyone to help her carry the corpse to the burning ground; and so, the body of the son of King Harischandra had to be carried to the cremation ground by his own mother!

Alone, her heart laden with sorrow and her eyes full of tears, queen Taramati carried her son's body to the cremation ground in pouring rain. At the gate of the burning ground she was stopped by the watchman for the fee. Harischandra recognized his wife; so did Taramati her husband. They fell into each other's arms and the queen related to him all that had happened to her and of the death of their beloved son. Harischandra wept with her on hearing her sad story. He also told her of his misfortunes and of his present wretched job.

The fee of the Dom had, however, to be paid, and Harischandra demanded it of his wife, as he was duty bound. Neither her entreaties nor his affection for his wife and son would permit the king to do an obviously wrong thing. "Darling," said he to Taramati, "it is not right for me to let you enter the cremation ground with the dead child without levying the fee due to my master. I would rather see my wife die of sorrow and the dead body of my son decay under my very nose than virtually rob the Dom of his legitimate fee." Taramati became desperate. In her mother's affection for a lost child she failed to recognize the force of Harischandra's argument. In a mad moment, with the strength of a tigress she pushed aside the watchman, rushed to the cremation ground with the dead body of her son, placed it on a pile and set fire to it. Harischandra watched the burning pyre helplessly from the gate. At the moment, the Dom, instructed by Viswamitra, appeared on the spot, and demanded of Harischandra the fee he was supposed to have collected for burning the dead body; Harischandra explained to him all that had happened but the Dom pretended not to believe him. He reviled Harischandra and laid violent hands on him for neglecting his duty. He then proceeded to the burning pyre, scattered it about, put out the fire, made Taramati pick up the charred body of Rohidas and drove her out of the cremation ground.

Nor was this the end of Taramati's humiliation. The pitiless Viswamitra spread a report in the city that a witch had been found near the cremation ground burning her son alive, and had been caught in the act by the Dom. People now rushed towards the cremation ground and saw Taramati with the charred body of her son, and they very naturally took her for a witch.

SOME POPULAR STORIES AND LEGENDS

Besides, the ordeal in the cremation ground had driven the poor woman mad and she had the wild look of a witch. She was seized by the minions of law and taken to the magistrate of the city.

At that moment Viswamitra appeared before Harischandra and confided to him that he would not only give Harischandra his kingdom back but would also restore Taramati to freedom if he, Harischandra, would only tell him that in giving away his kingdom to Viswamitra he had acted foolishly, and would now demand it back by word of mouth. But Harischandra would not go back on his given word and was willing to let things take their own course regardless of consequences.

Taramati could not defend herself, and on the false evidence given by the Dom, she was declared guilty by the magistrate and sentenced to death. The death sentence, in those days, was carried out by the owner of the cremation ground, and the Dom told off Harischandra to do the executioner's work.

The queen was brought to the cremation ground for being beheaded. Her hands were tied behind her back, and a howling crowd stood by to watch the execution. Harischandra looked with pity on Taramati's alabaster neck on which, in happier days, he had lavished all his love; and now it had to be cut into two by a sword wielded by his own hand. He knew Taramati was guiltless. But as a hangman his duty was not to probe into the conscience of the doomed but to do the job. He could not now shirk his duty. No, not Harischandra. He would strike the fatal blow.

The gods looked on from above. The air resounded with the curses of celestials on Viswamitra. Harischandra lifted his sword for the mortal blow. But lo! the lifted hand stood paralysed. There was heard a voice from heaven proclaiming the innocence of Taramati and the greatness of Harischandra. The three great gods manifested themselves on the spot and declared Viswamitra beaten. He was asked to give back his kingdom to Harischandra. Brahma gave back life to the body of Rohidas, and the happy boy stood up between his parents, more handsome than ever. The gods showered celestial flowers from above on Harischandra and his family. There was rejoicing in the three worlds, and Viswamitra and his evil accomplices slunk away in shame.

Chapter XIV

THE BUDDHA

UNLIKE most of the subjects dealt with in the preceding chapters, the Buddha (Buddha is an appellation meaning the "enlightened") is more or less a historical figure. It is true that popular imagination has made him as mythical a figure as any that can be found in Hinduism; yet it is possible to trace a nucleus of definite historical value from which the myths and legends concerning the Buddha have developed.

THE HISTORICAL ELEMENT IN BUDDHA MYTHS

Reliable accounts of his life indicate that the Buddha lived in the sixth century B.C. East India was at that time divided into a number of independent principalities, some of which were monarchies and others oligarchies in which the elective principle was followed in choosing a ruler. The Sakyas belonged to the latter, and Suddhodana was their ruler. Siddhartha, the Buddha, was born of Suddhodana by his first wife Mahamaya, also called Maya or Mayadevi. The surname of Siddhartha was Gautama.

From his very boyhood the prince showed a meditative turn of mind. He studied the scriptures with care, but did not take much interest in the military exercises beloved of his caste. Much of his time was spent in contemplation and lonely wanderings. What puzzled the young man was the existence of poverty, sickness, senility and death. "Is there no remedy for these?" was the burden of his thoughts. Another thing that oppressed his sensitive mind was the arrogance of the priestly caste. His intuition of human equality revolted at the exclusive pretensions of the sacerdotal caste who "placed themselve even above the gods in the heavens, who were said to live by their sufferance." Under their intellectual tyranny the religious life of the community became stagnant. Among the Brahmins themselves there was, to be sure, ample scope for discussion, suggestion and even heresies. But popular religion had lost all spontaneity and consisted chiefly in feeding the priests and paying them cash, and animal sacrifices for gods. The last-named way of salvation was particularly repugnant to Siddhartha. His compassionate nature could not tolerate the shedding of blood in the name of religion. He had no use for gods who thirsted for blood.

Suddhodana watched his contemplative son with apprehension. He wanted the prince to be a soldier and statesman and not a recluse. So he thought marriage would tie him to the realities of life, and accordingly made arrangements for his marriage with Yasodhara, daughter of Dandapani. But Dandapani was a soldier and would not give his daughter in marriage to a weakling and demanded that Siddhartha should prove his proficiency in arms. Hence a tournament was held in which Siddhartha acquitted himself well, and he married Yasodhara.

But marriage did not bring happiness to Siddhartha. In sexual pleasure he found, on the contrary, a further incentive to renunciation. He pitied mankind for pursuing phantom joys, mistaking them for realities. The desire to find a solution to human suffering became an obsession with Siddhartha, and he thought of it day and night. He despised the pleasures of the court and envied the life of the ascetic. So determined was he on renunciation that when the news of the birth of a son was brought to him he said to himself: "Alas! one more fetter to be broken." At last he felt he could bear a worldly life no longer, and against all the persuasions and entreaties of his parents, wife and relatives, Siddhartha forsook the world for the wilderness.

For some years Siddhartha lived as the disciple of certain Brahmin teachers. He weighed his masters' doctrines and found them wanting. Hence he repaired to the forest and decided to seek the goal alone. Following the method of the Hindu ascetics, he underwent privations and practised austerities. But this only reduced his flesh without elevating the spirit, and he gave up asceticism and took regular meals. After some more years of wanderings and contemplation, he, at last, felt that he had discovered a solution of the mystery of life. He returned to the cities and preached a way of salvation for all humanity. He converted many noblemen, princes and learned Brahmins, and collected a good many disciples.

On the metaphysical side, Buddhism is not fundamentally different from Hinduism. It stands in the same relation to Hinduism as Christianity to Judaism. The central doctrine of metempsychosis is common to Hinduism and Buddhism. The Philosophy of Buddhism is traceable to the Upanishads. The word "Nirvana" is borrowed from Hinduism. While the Buddhistic conception of salvation is said to be negative and that of Hinduism positive, both admit the loss of individuality as a necessary condition for liberation and the difference between annihilation and a merging with the infinite is difficult to comprehend though easy to put in writing. As regards the ethical precepts of Buddhism, there was, to be sure, enough in the Hindu sacred books of the time to enable a seeker after liberation to find sound rules of conduct. Even the pessimism, so characteristic of Buddhism, is but an emphasis on certain Hindu trends of thought.

Buddhism was not then so much a religious revolt against Hinduism as a challenge to Hindu social conceptions. Had the Buddha propounded his doctrines without challenging the sanctions of caste (not difficult for a believer in the doctrine of metempsychosis), the Brahmins would have accepted his teachings as an orthodox form of thought. But in declaring that a Brahmin and a Chandala had equal chances of attaining Nirvana, the Buddha shook the very foundations of Hindu society, and antagonized the Brahmins for ever. For a time it looked as though Buddhism had suceeded in overcoming the age-old resistance of Hinduism and establishing itself throughout India. Under the leadership of Asoka (third century B.C.), a prince who, after a number of brilliant military conquests, became a convert to the new faith, Buddhism reached the zenith of its glory in India. But gradually the insistence on too high an ideal of perfection began to bring its own retribution. Married life came to be looked upon as an inferior sort of existence, and the monasteries, under the patronage of princes, became fabulously rich and attracted a good number of idlers, charlatans and disappointed voluptuaries. Some of them degenerated into dens of vice. Tantric cults found favour with some sects and there was not the guiding hand of a Buddha or Asoka to put things right. In the misfortunes of Buddhism, Brahminism found its opportunity and made a vigorous attempt at a revival. The success of Brahminism was almost phenomenal. In a comparatively short time it succeeded in completely driving out Buddhism from the land of its birth, absorbing, no doubt, a good many of its beliefs and practices.

Now for the mythology of the Buddhists. Although in the Buddha's scheme of salvation there is no place for God, popular Buddhism accepts the Hindu pantheon in its broad outlines. Indra, referred to by Buddhism as Sakra, a name borrowed from Hinduism, is recognized as the king of the gods. Dharmaraja occupies the position of Yama. Mahakala and Mahakali (Shiva and Parvati) are the gate-keepers of the Buddha, and Kubera his body-guard. Kubera's wife, Hariti, is an important deity in the Buddhistic pantheon. Tara is another goddess, even more important than Hariti. The gods and goddesses are gnerally subordinate to the Buddha.

In building up their pantheon, the Buddhists appear to have freely copied from Hinduism. Or it may be, Puranic Hinduism borrowed much from Buddhism. Anyway, the most interesting and characteristically Buddhistic myths are those connected with the life of Gautama.

THE LEGENDARY BUDDHA: NATIVITY

In the forty-fifth year of her age, Mahamaya, the first wife of Suddhodana, king of Kapilavastu, had a strange dream. While she lay sound asleep, after the festivities of Asari Purnima,* the queen dreamt that she saw a spotless white elephant with a white lotus in his trunk entering her womb.

In the morning, Mahamaya narrated her dream to Suddhodana. The king invited sixty-four learned Brahmins to a feast, entertained them and requested them to interpret the queen's dream. The wise men pondered over the meaning of the strange dream, and unanimously opined that the dream indicated the queen's conception, and predicted that she would give birth to a male child. On hearing this, Suddhodana rejoiced, for he had no son and was daily praying for one.

As it was predicted so it happened. The queen showed signs of pregnancy and the court physicians were ordered to attend her daily. The gods, too, guarded Mahamaya, and the precious embryo that was to be the Buddha. As the pregnancy of Mahamaya advanced, her body became transparent and the child could distinctly be seen in her womb "like an image in a crystal casket."

While the last month of her pregnancy was drawing to a close, Mahamaya desired to visit her father's house in Devadaha. So Suddhodana ordered the road from Kapilavastu to Devadaha to be made even and decorated. When everything was ready, Mahamaya travelled to Devadaha in a golden palanquin. On the way was a grove of Sal trees called Lumbini Grove, and the queen, seeing the beautiful trees in full bloom, desired to spend some time in the grove, and asked the palanquin-bearers to take her there. In the grove, while she was enjoying the fragrance of flowers and the music of birds and bees, she felt attracted by the beauty of a flower-laden bough. The bough bent down by itself and while Mahamaya stretched forth her hand to hold it, she gave birth to her child without pain or pollution.

---
* A Bacchanalian festival of the Sakyas.

"Mahabrahma received the child in a golden net; from him the guardian deities received it on a tiger's skin and gave it to the care of the nobles who wrapped it in folds of the finest and softest cloth. But the Buddha was independent of their aid and leapt on the ground and when he touched it, a lotus bloomed. He looked to the four points and the four half points, above and below, and saw all deities and men acknowledge his supremacy. He stepped seven steps northward and a lotus marked each footfall. He exclaimed: 'I am the most exalted in the world; I am chief in the world; I am the most excellent in the world, hereafter there is to me no other birth.'"

News of the birth of a son was brought to Suddhodana and it was announced to the people by beat of drum.

It is said that the Buddha, his wife Yasodhara, his charioteer Channa, his favourite horse Kantaka, his most earnest disciple Ananda and the Bo-tree under which he attained Buddha-hood were all born on the same day.

On the day the Buddha was born, a sage who lived in the Himalayas had a vision of gods rejoicing on the birth of the child. The sage, leaving his wild home, came to the palace of Suddhodana. The king welcomed him and enquired of him what noble deed he had done to deserve a visit from so holy a man. "I have come, great king," said the sage, "to see thy babe." The child was shown to the sage.

> The babe beholding, passing bright,
> More glorious than the race divine,
> And marked with every noble sign,
> The saint was whelmed with deep delight;
> And crying, 'Lo! an infant graced
> With every charm of form I greet!'
> He fell before the Buddha's feet,
> With fingers joined, and round him paced.
> Next round the babe his arms he wound
> And 'One,' he said, 'of two careers
> Of fame awaits in coming years
> The child in whom these signs are found;
> If such an one at home abide,
> He shall become a king, whose sway
> Supreme a mighty armed array
> On earth shall 'stablish far and wide.
> If, spurning worldly pomp as vain,
> He choose to lead a tranquil life,
> And wander forth from home and wife,
> He then a Buddha's rank shall gain.'

The sage, after much lamentation, because of his senility which would not let him live long enough to witness the greatness of the child, took leave of the king and departed towards his Himalayan home.

Astrologers who cast the child's horoscope also gave a double interpretation of the influence of the planets. "Either the child will become a great emperor or, on beholding four signs (representing senility, sickness, death and renunciation), give up the world and become a Buddha," they predicted. Suddhodana chose the former career for his son and decided to plan his life accordingly.

On the fifth day after the birth of the child, the naming ceremony was performed. "Eighty thousand relatives were present on the occasion and one hundred and eight Brahmins attended to foretell his fate and fix his name. 'This prince,' said they, 'will, hereafter, be a blessing to the world; to himself also will be great prosperity.' In consequence of which he was called Siddhartha. A hundred princesses of perfect form became foster mothers to the child."

Two days after the naming ceremony Siddhartha's mother died. The child was then nursed by Prajapati, second wife of Suddhodana who was also a sister of Mahamaya.

BOYHOOD AND EDUCATION

The child grew up into a beautiful boy and was educated by the best teachers in the kingdom. He eagerly learnt what his teachers taught him, and indeed knew more than they. He did not, however, show much interest in military exercises but loved to wander alone in the groves.

Siddhartha had few companions in his boyhood. Devadatta, a cousin, and Nanda (better known as Ananda), a half-brother, are mentioned; of these, the former was a rival and the latter a friend. The story of a quarrel between Siddhartha and Devadatta is also narrated. One beautiful evening, Siddartha was walking in the royal park when he saw a group of royal swans flying towards the Himalayan regions. The calmness of the evening, the gentle breeze, the clear sky and the golden rays of the setting sun filled the prince with a sense of tranquillity and happiness, when suddenly one of the flying birds, wounded by an arrow, fell in front of him. Siddhartha took the bird, washed and dressed its wounds and nursed it. But Devadatta who had shot the arrow came to know of it, went to Siddhartha, and claimed the bird. Siddhartha refused to surrender the bird and maintained that his cousin had no business to injure a harmless being for sport. Devadatta reviled him, and departed in wrath saying that he would get the bird through the proper channel. He then went and complained to the Assembly of Elders who sent for Siddhartha and asked for an explanation. Siddhartha maintained that the bird belonged to the one who nursed it, and not to the one who disabled it. The Elders upheld this view and ga judgment in favour of Siddhartha.

Devadatta never forgave his cousin and remained, as we shall see later, his life-long enemy.

Suddhodana, because of the prediction of the astrologers, took every care to guard his son from any unseemly sights that might put into his mind thoughts of senility, sickness, death or renunciation. He had three palaces built for the residence of the prince and in these "every delight abounded and sorrow and death might not even be mentioned." Able soldiers guarded the palaces day and night.

MARRIAGE

When Siddhartha was sixteen years of age, arrangements were made for his marriage. The maiden Suddhodana selected for his son was Yasodhara, daughter of a chief named Dandapani. But Dandapani, as mentioned elsewhere, would not give his daughter in marriage to one who was not a soldier, and Siddhartha was asked to give proof of his skill in arms; accordingly a tournament was held.

"On the appointed day, the first person to appear on the scene was Devadatta.... He was beside himself with jealousy, and seeing a white elephant of great size brought into the city, he laid hold of it by the trunk with his left hand and killed it with one blow of the right. After Devadatta, came prince Sundarnand who asked the multitude who had killed the elephant. They named Devadatta. 'It is an evil deed of Devadatta,' he exclaimed, and seizing the carcass of the animal by the tail threw it outside the city gate. Gautama came next and he asked the crowd: 'Who has killed the elephant?' 'Devadatta,' they said. 'This is an evil deed of Devadatta'; said Siddhartha. 'By whom,' he asked again, 'was it thrown outside the city gate?' 'By Sundarnand'; they replied. 'That,' said the prince 'is a good deed. Yet this beast has such a great carcass that when it rots it will fill the whole city with stench.' Then standing on the carriage he put one foot to the ground; and with his great toe lifted the elephant by the tail and hurled it over the seven walls and seven moats of the city, and it fell in a place two miles distant from the city."

In the tournament the intellectual and military skill of the combatants was tested. In practically every item, Siddhartha beat his opponents. He stood first in horse race, chariot race, music, recitation, mathematics and elocution. In archery and wrestling, Devadatta and Siddhartha were acclaimed equals. In fencing Siddhartha did not take part, and Devadatta stood first.

On the last day of the tournament, Yasodhara entered the lists with a garland in her hand to choose her husband and, as Devadatta stood up expectantly to receive the garland, she bestowed it upon the neck of Siddhartha.

A different version of Siddhartha's marriage is also told. According to this, Suddhodana, so as to enable his son to choose the most beautiful damsel in the kingdom for a bride, caused a number of jewels to be made, and had it proclaimed that the prince would present them one by one to the maidens of the noble families of the realm. Five hundred maidens came to receive the gifts, and when all the jewels had been given away, Yasodhara arrived. She smiled at the prince and asked him playfully if he had nothing to give her. Siddhartha took his signet ring and bestowed it upon her, and thus accepted her as his bride.

For some time after marriage Siddhartha lived happily with his wife. He found delight in the company of the beautiful Yasodhara. The palaces and parks resounded with melodious music, and dancers skilled in their art amused the royal couple. There was no talk of sorrow or death. Siddhartha ate the choicest food, drank cool perfumed drinks, made love to his young wife and was as happy as man could be.

"THE FOUR SIGNS"

"Meanwhile the Devas reflected that time was passing and the Great One ought no longer to linger amid the pleasures of the palace, but must go forth on his mission. They therefore filled all space with this thought, 'It is time to go forth,' so that it reached the mind of the prince; and at the same time the music of the singers and the gestures of the dancers assumed a new meaning, and seemed to tell no more of sensuous delights but of the impermanence and vanity of every object of desire."

Now the prince felt tired of the pleasures of the palace and wished to visit the city. Suddhodana gave orders to clean and decorate the roads, and special instructions were given to see that no old or sick men came near the roads. But in spite of all the precautions of the king, the Devas defeated his purpose. One of them assumed the shape of an old man and, when Siddhartha drove out into the city, appeared before his chariot. He was "aged, worn out, with swollen veins on his body and broken teeth, wrinkled and grey-haired, bent, crooked as a root, broken, leaning on a stick, feeble, without youth, his throat uttering inarticulate sounds, his body bent and supported by a staff, trembling in all his limbs and parts of limbs."

Seeing this strange figure Siddhartha asked his charioteer: "What human form is this, so miserable and so distressing, the like of which I have never seen before?" The charioteer replied: "This is what is called an old man." The prince again asked the charioteer what he meant by the word "old". "Old age implies," said the charioteer, "the loss of bodily power, decay of the vital functions, and failure of mind and memory. This poor man before you is old and approaching his end."

The prince asked again: "Is this law universal?" "Yes," replied the charioteer, "this is the common lot of all living creatures: All that is born must die."

The prince became melancholy, and ordered his charioteer to drive him back to the palace.

Next day, when the prince went out, he saw a sick man. "He was overcome by hot fever, his body exhausted, soiled by his own excreta, without any one to help him, without shelter and breathing with difficulty." Siddhartha enquired of his charioteer: "Who is this unhappy being?" "This is a sick man," said the charioteer. "Is sickness common to all men?" asked the prince again. "Yes, sickness comes to all," was the reply. Siddhartha became thoughtful and asked his charioteer to drive him home.

On the third day the prince saw a dead body carried on a bier. "Who is this, borne onwards on his bed, covered with strangely coloured garments, surrounded by people weeping and lamenting?" asked the prince. "This," said the charioteer, "is the dead body of a man; he has ended his life; he has no further beauty of form and no desires of any kind; he is one with the stones and the felled tree; he is like a ruined wall or fallen leaf; no more shall he see his father or mother, brother or sister, or relatives either; his body is dead, and your body also must come to this." The last words of the charioteer went home. "Siddhartha, thou too shalt die"; the prince heard someone say.

On the fourth day the prince saw a monk standing on the road, "quiet, tranquil, full of discretion and self-control, not allowing his glance to wander, nor looking farther than the length of a yoke, having attained the path that brings peace of mind and honour, showing that peace of mind in his forward and his backward steps, peace of mind in the looking and the turning away of his eyes, peace of mind in his bending and his stretching, peace of mind in the wearing of his coat, begging-bowl and monk's frock."

" 'Who is this?' the prince enquired. 'This man,' said the charioteer, 'devotes himself to charity, and restrains his appetites and his bodily desires. He hurts nobody, but does good to all and is full of sympathy for all.' "

"Then the prince asked the ascetic to give an account of himself. The latter replied: 'I am called a homeless ascetic; I have forsaken the world, relatives and friends; I seek deliverance for myself and desire the salvation of all creatures, and I do harm to none.' "

The words of the monk and his appearance fired the imagination of the troubled prince. At last he had found a man whose thoughts were similar to his own. An irresistible longing to follow the monk seized him. But at that moment news of the birth of a son was brought to him, and he returned home.

RENUNCIATION

On seeing the "four signs" Siddhartha made up his mind to retire from the world. He felt there was no meaning in living in the midst of pleasures if the end of life be senility, decay and death. He pitied man who, blind to the gaping chasm beneath, lived as though momentary pleasures were realities.

Siddhartha told his father of his resolution to lead a religious life. Suddhodana was dismayed. He tried to persuade his son to give up the idea and, not succeeding in this, decided to prevent his son's escape. He doubled the strength of the guards of the palace, reinforced the women's apartments and asked the dancing girls to divert the prince's attention to mundane matters by their seductive art.

On the night Siddhartha had decided to depart, there was revelry as on no other occasion. The revellers sang, drank deep and fell asleep where they sat. "Siddhartha beheld the sight of his women lying dead in sleep, some with their garments torn away, others with dishevelled hair, some with their ornaments fallen off, others with broken diadems, some whose shoulders were bruised and others with naked limbs and mouths awry and eyes squinting... And meditating on the idea of purity and penetrating the idea of impurity, he saw that from the sole of the foot to the crown of the head, the body originates in impurity, is compounded of impurity, and exhales impurity without end. Then he spoke: 'O hell of living beings, with many entrances; dwelling-place of death and age, what wise man, having looked thereon, would not consider his own body to be his enemy?' "

He went away from the place and asked his charioteer to get his favourite horse ready for a journey. Siddhartha then entered Yasodhara's apartments. She lay asleep with her babe Rahula, who was then seven days old. The father desired to fondle his child. But one of the hands of Yasodhara lay resting on the child and Siddhartha, afraid of awaking her, restrained his parental impulse and left the room.

The Devas aided the departure of Siddhartha. The gates of the palace were held open by them and they lulled the guards to sleep. Siddhartha rode on his horse Kantaka, and Channa followed him. The charioteer, with tears in his eyes, entreated the prince to give up the idea of flight, but Siddhartha pacified him by saying that he was going for the good of all. They travelled throughout the night and by morning reached a river. Siddhartha crossed the river and asked Channa: "What is the name of this river?" "Anoma" (illustrious), said Channa. "From here," said the prince, "I retire from the world." He then asked Channa to return home with the horse. But the faithful charioteer wanted to accompany his master. "No, Channa," said

Siddhartha, "your time is not yet come. Besides, my father will grieve for my absence without knowing what came of me, and so you go back and tell him not to grieve for me." Channa now kissed his master's feet and Kantaka licked them with his tongue. Then the two returned. But the horse after walking a few paces fell down and died, and Channa came back alone to Kapilavastu and narrated to Suddhodana all that had happened. Yasodhara, on hearing the sad story, cut off her hair and lived the life of a nun.

THE SEARCH AFTER TRUTH

While Siddhartha was proceeding on his journey, he saw a hunter with whom he exchanged clothes. Presently he saw a barber who shaved his head. The hunter and the barber were Devas who had assumed these forms for the purpose.

After a few days' wandering, Siddhartha became the disciple of a Brahmin teacher of Vaisali named Arara Kalama who had three hundred disciples. He learnt everything that Kalama had to teach but Kalama's system did not satisfy Siddhartha. He declined an offer of Kalama to remain as his assistant and again started on his quest.

From Vaisali Siddhartha proceeded to the kingdom of Magadha and took up his abode in Rajagriha, where king Bimbisara visited him and requested him, in vain, to give up his religious life and return to Kapilavastu. Bimbisara was much impressed by the earnestness of Siddhartha and asked to remember him if, at any time, he found a solution to the riddle of life.

Near Rajagriha was a famous college of philosophy conducted by the sophist Rudraka. Siddhartha attended the lectures but found that mere acquisition of knowledge could bring no enlightenment and so he left the college. Five students of Rudraka, seeing Gautama's earnestness and spirit of enquiry, became his disciples and followed him. Siddhartha now decided to practise austerities in the manner of Hindu sages. He fasted or ate only a modicum of millet seed, exposed himself to wind and rain and took Yogic exercises. His health suffered and his body was reduced to a skeleton. One day, while he was practising an exercise in breathing, he fainted and was on the point of death. He, however, recovered but felt that asceticism would bring him no enlightenment. He went out again begging for food and received a dainty meal as an offering from Sujata, daughter of a rich villager. She offered it in a golden dish, and to Siddhartha it seemed a good omen. "He took the food and went out of the village and bathed in a river, and would have crossed to the other side, but the current carried him away, and had it not been that a Deva dwelling in a certain great tree on the farther bank stretched out his jewelled arm to draw him to land, he would have been drowned. He reached the shore, however, and sat down to take his meal; after which he cast the golden dish into the river where it was caught by a Naga, who took it to his palace. But Sakra, in the form of a Garuda, snatched it from the Naga's hand and carried it to the Tusita heavens."

In the meantime messengers were daily coming to Siddhartha from Suddhodana requesting him to return to his father. He sent them away with a final message that the resolution he had taken was irrevocable and Suddhodana ought to rejoice rather than grieve.

When Siddhartha's five disciples saw that he had given up asceticism, they took him for a failure and deserted him. Thus Siddhartha was again left alone to tread the difficult path.

ENLIGHTENMENT

Well over seven years did Siddhartha spend in the search. But the end seemed still far off. Neither learning nor self-mortification brought him enlightenment. Was there, after all, no solution to the riddle of life? Had he deserted his wife and parents and undergone privations, all in vain? Anyway there was no going back. He would pursue the path till he got what he wanted or perish in the attempt. With this grim determination, he proceeded to the Bo-tree born on the same day as himself. The gods rejoiced because the great event was near at hand. Thousands of them accompanied him as he proceeded towards the sacred tree. Birds soared in joy over his head.

Reaching the Bo-tree Siddhartha sat down under it determined not to get up till he found a solution to the riddle of life. Now there was joy in heaven, but evil spirits lamented. The chief of the latter, Mara,* marched towards the Bo-tree with an army of demons to distract Siddhartha and prevent his attaining Buddhahood. First Mara went to Siddhartha disguised as a messenger from Suddhodana and informed him that Devadatta had usurped the throne and was oppressing his subjects. But Siddhartha observed that if the Sakya chiefs were cowardly enough to tolerate an oppressive tyrant, they deserved no better ruler, and took to his meditation undisturbed by the news. Then Mara raised a violent storm and rain, and his army assailed Siddhartha with javelins, swords, arrows, rocks, hillocks and burning charcoal, but none of them had any effect on Siddhartha, for the gods protected him. Threats proving of no avail, Mara sent his two daughters to seduce him. But Siddhartha preached a sermon to them and the ladies went away blessing him.

---

* Mara is the Hindu god of love elaborated by the Buddhists into an embodiment of evil. Sexual desire being considered by Buddhists as the greatest enemy of man, the god of desire was given the role of The Enemy.

The fight started at eventide and went on throughout the night. By morning the two temptresses departed and enlightenment dawned upon Siddhartha, and he became the Buddha. He understood the mystery and meaning of existence. "I have attained the Buddhaship," he exclaimed; "I have overcome Mara; all evil desire is destroyed, I am lord of the three worlds."

THE TEACHER

The Buddha had now solved the mystery of life. But he found that the path to enlightenment and Nirvana was difficult to tread. He feared that the ordinary run of mankind, caught in the maze of the unreal pleasures of the world, were not likely to understand him and pay heed to his teaching. Then what was he to do? Was he to keep the newly acquired secret to himself and tread the path alone, or turn the Wheel of Law for the benefit of a world without understanding? The Blessed One thought thus: "I have penetrated this doctrine which is profound, difficult to perceive and to understand, which brings quietude of heart, which is exalted, which is unattainable by reasoning, abstruse, intelligible (only) to the wise. These people, on the other hand, are given to desire, intent upon desire, delighting in desire. To these people, therefore, the law of causality and the chain of causation will be a matter difficult to understand; most difficult to understand will be also the extinction of all Samskars, the getting rid of all the sub-strata of existence, the destruction of desire, the absence of passion, quietude of heart, Nirvana. Now if I proclaim the doctrine and other men are not able to understand my preaching, there would result but weariness and annoyance to me."

Now Brahma appeared before the Buddha and prayed to him with joined hands to teach the Dharma to mankind. But Mara put unholy thoughts into the mind of the Blessed One and told him that he should attain Nirvana alone. Good, however, triumphed over evil, and the Buddha decided to preach and convert mankind to the newly found way of liberation.

Shortly after making this resolve, two merchants came that way and offered food to the Buddha. He ate with them and preached to them. They were converted and became his first lay followers. The Buddha now decided to preach his doctrine to Kalama and Rudraka, the two Brahmin teachers under whom he had lived as a disciple. On his way he had to cross the Ganges, but he had no money to pay the ferryman. So, when the ferryman demanded the toll, the Buddha said to him: "Row me across the river, and I shall row you across the ocean of life." The ferryman, however, did not agree to this, and the Buddha soared over the stream.

* Oldenberg.

On reaching the other side of the Ganges, the Buddha learnt that Kalama and Rudraka were no more. But the five disciples who had deserted him were still alive, and he preached to them and converted them. They were his first disciples and together with himself formed the first order of Buddhist monks.

The number of disciples and lay followers increased, and the Buddha selected men to preach the new doctrine far and wide, he himself remaining in a particular area.

The gist of the Buddha's teaching is that life is misery, and all people should strive to obtain liberation from the chain of existence by means of good deeds. Says the Buddha: "Birth is painful, decay is painful, death is painful, union with the unpleasant is painful, painful is the separation from the pleasant, and any craving that is unsatisfied, that too is painful." Again, "what think ye, disciples," he asks, "whether is more the water which is in the great oceans or the tears which have flowed from you and have been shed by you, while ye strayed and wandered on this long pilgrimage and sorrowed and wept, because that was your portion, and that which ye loved was not your portion? A mother's death, a brother's death, the loss of relatives, the loss of property, all this you have experienced through long ages, and while ye experienced it through long ages, more tears have flowed from you and have been shed by you, while ye strayed and wandered on this pilgrimage and sorrowed and wept, because that was your portion which ye abhorred and that which ye loved was not your portion, than all the waters in the four great oceans."*

"Buddha's four 'Sublime Verities' containing the germ of his system are as floows: The first is that pain exists; the second, that desire is the cause of pain; the third that pain can be ended by Nirvana or exemption from existence, practical annihilation; the fourth shows the way that leads to Nirvana. The great thing is to get rid of desire, and when this is accomplished, the soul is ready for complete Nirvana, and a man dying in this state will not be born again."

About caste, the Buddha said it was a matter of common consent and not of birth. "Birth cannot make a Brahmin any more than a non-Brahmin. It is by work and merit, by his wisdom, piety and self-sacrifice that one becomes a Brahmin."

The success of the Buddha's mission was mainly due to his extraordinary personality and the glamour of a prince turned saint. The Buddha's fame spread far and wide and he went from city to city preaching and making converts. "In one of his wanderings he came upon a nest of five hundred robbers to whom he preached and at whose hands he ate. They were all reclaimed and exchanged the tools of burglary for the bowls and staves of piety."

At Srivasti, the Buddha converted thousands of people by working miracles. He walked on air emitting waves of light from his body; then he preached to the people multiplying himself manifold.

Among the Buddha's converts were princes, scholars, sophists, philosophers and men of all occupations and castes. When he stayed in the city of Rajagriha, king Bimbisara himself came to do him honour with a retinue of "twelve myriads of men." The king and most of his retinue were converted. Bimbisara remained a friend of the Buddha to the end of his life and was an able patron of Buddhism.

The Buddha now thought of his home. His son Rahula had also grown up into a young man and persuaded Suddhodana to send for the Buddha. When the invitation came, the Buddha was much touched by the message and decided to visit the home of his childhood. Accordingly he started for Kapilavastu at the head of a procession of monks and disciples. On reaching the city, he went on his usual begging round and the news of this reaching Prajapati, she went in panic to Suddhodana and said to him: "My son is walking from house to house begging for alms." Suddhodana, deeply agitated, went to his son and asked him why he was thus bringing disgrace on the royal house. "Do you not belong to the race of kings?" he said. "The race to which I belong," replied the Buddha meaning the race of Buddhas, "beg for their food." The Buddha then preached to his father. "O Father," said he, "I have now found the Law; and when one finds a treasure, to whom can he offer it more fittingly than to his own father? So do I offer it to you. Do not delay; let me share with you the treasure I have found."

Suddhodana spake no more. He took hold of his son's begging bowl and led him home. There he was welcomed by all the household; but one of them was missing. It was his wife Yasodhara. She was not there. She had studiously kept herself away as she wanted to test his love and see if her husband would miss her and ask for her. Gautama understood why she was not present. He exclaimed: "The princess is not free from desires as I am. She is sorrowing alone because she has not seen me for long. Let her embrace me lest her heart should break." So saying the Buddha entered her apartments. Yasodhara was overcome with emotion and she fell down at his feet to kiss them, and wept. Suddhodana then narrated to him how she had been sorrowing for his absence, and living the life of a nun. "When my daughter heard, O Master," said he, "that you had put on the yellow robes, from that time forth she dressed only in yellow; when she heard of your taking but one meal a day, she adopted the same custom; when she heard that you renounced the use of elevated couches, she slept on a mat spread on the floor; when she heard you had given up the use of garlands and unguents, she also used them no more. And when her relations sent a message saying 'Let us take care of you,' she paid no attention to them. Such are my daughter's virtues, O Blessed One."

The next touching scene was the meeting between Nanda (called Ananda in the scriptures) and the Buddha. The marriage of Ananda had been arranged to take place the next day. "Gautama went up to the pavilion where Nanda was lodged and told him that the greatest festival of all is the life of a monk who has vanquished all evil desires and acquired the knowledge of truth, and Nirvana. He then gave him his own alms-bowl and took him to the grove where he had been staying." There Nanda was converted and remained his most devoted disciple to the end of his life. Some accounts relate that Nanda was converted on being shown a vision of heaven and goddesses.

The story of the conversion of Rahula is also told. Yasodhara sent her son to his father to demand of him his patrimony. Rahula went to his father and said: "Father, I am the prince! when I am crowned a king over all the earth, I have need of treasure; for son is heir to his father's property." On hearing this the Blessed One turned to his disciple Sariputra and said: "Beloved disciple, Rahula has come to ask me for his inheritance. He asks for a worldly inheritance which cannot last. I will give him a spiritual inheritance which would be everlasting. Let him be admitted to our Order."

Suddhodana made a last effort to reclaim his son and make him a king. But the Buddha refused, and said that Sauvana, Rahula's son, should be considered Suddhodana's heir, as Nanda and Rahula had become monks.

Yasodhara and Prajapati became his disciples, and, later, with the reluctant permission of the Buddha, founded the order of nuns.

The Buddha also visited the Lumbini grove where he was born, and then departed from Kapilavastu amidst the lamentations of Suddhodana and his people.

Nor was preaching all that the Buddha did. A story is told of how he prevented a battle which was about to be fought between the Sakyas and the Kolis. The river Rohini flowed between Kapilavastu and Koli and in a year of drought people of both the cities claimed sole right for the use of the water. A battle seemed imminent when the Buddha came upon the scene. He asked the people: "Which do you price more, the waters of Rohini or the life of men?"

They replied that the life of men is more precious than the waters of Rohini. Then he exposed to them the folly of wasting life for the waters of Rohini and settled the dispute to the satisfaction of both the parties.

DEVADATTA

The proselytizing zeal of the Buddha created many enemies for him. The Brahmins were particularly alarmed, because their privileged position was successfully challenged for the first time. There had been, of course, many thinkers like the materialist Brahaspati, who, even before the Buddha, had taught doctrines contrary to Brahminism. But they and a few disciples held these impious views and these views mostly died with them. But here, in the Buddha's method, was a new technique unprecedented in the history of the development of Indian religious thought. Preaching to the masses and conversion of hundreds of people were unknown before. And the Brahmins feared, with good reason, that if the Buddha were allowed to have his own way, they would be deprived of their privileged position and even daily bread; hence they and certain leaders of other sects decided to combat him by fair means or foul.

Three attempts on the life of the Buddha are recorded. All were instigated by Devadatta. Indeed, the evil deeds attributed to this person are so many that he appears to be more a conception than an individual. He is said to have attained much power, occult and material, by austerities and intrigues. He had many disciples and had managed to worm his way into the confidence of Ajasat (Ajatasatru), Bimbisara's son, who under the instigation of Devadatta, murdered his own father and seized the throne.

As soon as Ajasat became king, Devadatta asked for and got from him thirty-one able men to carry out the foul deed he was contemplating. He deputed, one of them to murder the Buddha, two to murder the murderer, four to murder the two, eight to murder the four and the remaining sixteen to murder the eight. The last sixteen Devadatta decided to murder himself so that the matter might be kept secret. But all the would-be murderers, on seeing the Buddha and hearing his sermons, became his disciples and lived with him.

On another occasion, while the Buddha was walking by the foot of a cliff, Devadatta had a rock propelled at him. The Blessed One had a narrow escape, the rock having broken into two and slightly hurt his foot.

Devadatta made yet another attempt on the life of the Buddha. Nalagiri, a fierce elephant, was given an extra dose of beer, and let loose on the path of the Buddha while he was begging for alms. The friars who were accompanying the Buddha were frightened and entreated him to escape. The Buddha paying no heed to their entreaties, they decided to protect him and formed a ring round him. But he peremptorily ordered them back to their proper places. In spite of this, Ananda decided to walk in front of him and face the beast, but a temporary paralysis came upon him and he found himself unable to move.

The elephant, while approaching the Buddha, saw a child which he was about to seize when the Blessed One ordered the beast to leave the child alone. Obedient to this command, the elephant left the child and ran towards the Buddha. But when it came near the Blessed One "its fury abated and it approached in the gentlest way and knelt before him." The Buddha now preached to the elephant and it "repeated the five commandments to all the people."

After the conversion of the elephant, the Buddha sent his disciples to preach to the followers of Devadatta. This mission was successful, and the disciples of Devadatta deserted him while he lay asleep, and went over to the Buddha. Shortly after, Devadatta fell ill and lay ailing for nine months. This misfortune seemed to have brought him repentance. For, as soon as he recovered, he decided to visit the Buddha, and proceeded towards the monastery in which he lived. But as he approached the gate of the monastery the earth gaped and shot up flames of fire which began to consume him. Devadatta cried out to the Buddha for help, "repeated a verse of a hymn by which he accepted the three gems, the Buddha, the Law and the Church; and this will help him eventually, though he none-the-less went to hell and received a body of fire sixteen hundred miles in height."

THE BUDDHA VISITS TAVATIMSA (TRAYATIMSA) HEAVEN

Now the Devas beheld the wonders wrought upon the earth by the Blessed One and desired to see him in their midst. Accordingly the Buddha visited Tavatimsa heaven and remained there for three months. Indra decorated his own throne for the Blessed One to sit on. But the throne of Indra was fifteen leagues in height whereas the height of the Blessed One was only twelve cubits. Indra did not know how to adjust the throne to the proportion of the distinguished visitor, but when the Buddha approached the throne it reduced itself to convenient dimensions and looked as though it was specially made for the Buddha. The Blessed One preached to the Devas and myriads of them entered the path.

"When the time came for the Buddha to return to earth, Indra caused three ladders to extend from Heaven to earth, two of gold and one of silver. On one of the golden ladders which had steps alternately of gold, silver, coral, ruby, emerald and other gems, the Buddha descended, preceded by Indra blowing his conch. On the other golden ladder proceeded the Devas with instruments of music; and on the silver ladder the Brahmas, carrying umbrellas. Thus the Buddha returned to his own hermitage."

ATTAINMENT OF NIRVANA

The Buddha lived to a ripe old age and was eighty-four when he died. The end was, however, hastened by a regrettable incident. While he was staying in a mango grove in Pava, a smith named Chunda desired to entertain him. He prepared a dish of pork and offered it to the Buddha. The Buddha ate it, but it gave him a colic which took a serious turn. The old man's body was already feeble and he felt the end was nigh. Lest Chunda should be blamed, he spoke to his disciples: "Inform the smith Chunda that his offering will bring great reward, for it will be the immediate cause of my attaining Nirvana. There are indeed two offerings which will bring great reward. One was given by the lady Sujata before I reached supreme wisdom, the other has just now been made by Chunda. These are the two foremost gifts."

The Buddha was removed from the main camp to a grove of Sal trees owned by the Mallas of Kusinagara. The news of his illness spread throughout the neighbouring kingdoms, and princes, nobles, queens, priests, enquirers and all manner of people came to see him. Although he was on the point of death, he gave strict instructions to the attendants to allow everyone to come to him, particularly those who had any doubts to clear.

When the end was approaching, the Buddha spoke to Ananda: "Now I depart to Nirvana; I leave with you my ordinances; the elements of the all-knowing one will indeed pass away, but the three gems will remain." "But Ananda broke down and wept bitterly. Then the Buddha continued: 'O Ananda, do not let yourself be troubled; do not weep. Have I not taught you that we must part from all that we hold most dear and pleasant? No being soever born or created can overcome the tendency to dissolution inherent in life itself; a condition of permanence is impossible. For a long time, Ananda, your kindness in act and thought and speech has brought you very near to me. You have always done well; persevere, and you too, shall win perfect freedom from this thirst of life, this chain of ignorance.' Then he turned to the other mourners and commended Ananda to them. He said also that the least of those present who had entered the path to release should never entirely fail, but should at last prevail and reach Nirvana. After a pause he said again: 'Mendicants, I now impress it upon you that the parts and powers of man must be dissolved; work out your salvation with diligence.'

Shortly afterward the Buddha became unconscious and passed away."*

The body lay in state for six days. On the seventh, it was burnt. It is said that attempts at setting fire to the pile failed but when the appointed time came, it ignited itself. After the body was consumed, the relics of the Blessed One remained like a "heap of pearls."

Eight princes claimed the relics and they disputed so violently for possession of them that it looked as though there would be a war for the remains of the man who, throughout his life, had striven for peace and goodwill among men. Reason, however, prevailed and the relics were divided into eight parts and each one was given to a prince. The princes took them to their respective kingdoms and enshrined them in beautiful Stupas. Worship of the relics and the Stupas is a distinguishing feature of Buddhism.

SOME DISTINCTIVE BUDDHIST MYTHS

The Hinayana or primitive Buddhism generally followed the teachings of the Buddha and his immediate disciples, and as such laid greater stress on the simple moral life than on learning, speculation or ritual; but the rise of the Mahayana (Greater Vehicle), gave Buddhism a pantheon and mythology, as varied and fantastic as those of Hinduism. The rise of the Mahayana is connected with the conversion to Buddhism of the Kushans and other Central Asian tribes who invaded India and settled in the country. Many of their beliefs and practices, which were absorbed by Buddhism, enriched its mythology.

THE BUDDHAS

Gautama Buddha had declared that he was not the only Buddha, but several Buddhas or enlightened beings had made known the Law to the worlds before him and many would, after his Parinirvana. He did not mention the exact number of the Buddhas, but by the time of the Third Council of Buddhism held in 243 B.C. in Pataliputra under the auspices of the Emperor Asoka, the Buddhist Church had declared that the Buddhas who preceded Gautama were twenty-four. A good many details about their birth place, stature, the trees under which they obtained enlightenment, etc., are given in the Pali scriptures. Their names are: (1) Dipankara, (2) Kaundinya, (3) Mangala, (4) Sumanas, (5) Raivata, (6) Sobhita, (7) Anavamadarsin, (8) Padma, (9) Narada, (10) Padmottara, (11) Sumedha, (12) Sujata, (13) Priyadarsin, (14) Arthadarsin, (15) Dharmadarsin, (16) Siddhartha, (17) Tishya, (18) Pushya, (19) Vipasyin, (20) Sikhin, (21) Visvabhu, (22) Krakucchanda, (23) Kanakamuni or Konagamana, and (24) Kasyapa.

The last five of these are believed to have

---

* Sr. Niveditta and Coomaraswamy, *Myths of the Hindus and Buddhists.*

appeared in the present Kalpa or world cycle. They, together with Gautama Buddha and Maitreya (more of whom presently), constitute the Seven Buddhas of the current Kalpa. The idea has a close resemblance to the Seven Manus of the Hindu Manwantaras, already noticed.

While the Hinayana conception stops here, the Mahayana carries the idea further. According to Mahayana conceptions Buddhas are not twenty-four or twenty-six but innumerable; but five out of these, known as Dhyani Buddhas, are the most important. They are in effect the Dhyani (meditative) forms of the last human Buddhas of the current Kalpa and are known as Vairochana (of Krakucchanda), Akshobhya (of Kanakamuni), Ratna Sambhava (of Kasyapa), Amitabha (of Gautama) and Amogha Siddha (of Maitreya). Above all these Dhyani Buddhas is the Adi Buddha or Primordial Buddha, who is more or less identical with the Supreme Being of the Brahmins.

Tantric influences invested each Dhyani Buddha with a Sakti or female companion. Nor is the Adi Buddha without a Sakti. His Sakti is known as Prajna (transcendent wisdom) and creation is believed to have emanated from a union of the two.

BODHISATVAS

One of the distinctive features of Mahayana Buddhism, as compared with the Hinayana, is the worship of Bodhisatvas. These are, more or less, gods of mercy and compassion with Paradises of their own where they admit their devotees for the enjoyment of the pleasures of the senses before they are dissolved into Nirvana.

The older school relied more on individual efforts for the attainment of Nirvana than on any help from above. But popular Buddhism found the ideal too elevating for the weakness of generality of men, and Mahayana came to humanity's aid by supplying a pantheon of Bodhisatvas, ever ready to help suffering creatures and willing to hear their supplications, and amenable to their prayers.

In the next chapter it will be seen that Gautama Buddha, before he was born in the womb of Mahamaya, was considered a Buddha Elect or Bodhisatva. He attained this position by virtue of a vow he had taken to obtain enlightenment and become a Buddha, and from then on went through various rebirths in each of which he did his utmost to help suffering creatures. By the accumulated merit of these virtuous deeds he was translated to the Tusita heaven where he presided as the reigning Bodhisatva till his time came to appear on earth in his last birth as Gautama. And when he descended to the earth, he appointed Maitreya as his successor in Tusita heaven; Maitreya will, in his turn, descend to earth when the law taught by Gautama Buddha will be forgotten, which will be exactly five thousand years after the death of Gautama Buddha.

Maitreya (Pali, Metteya) is the only Bodhisatva the Hinayana recognizes. But in Mahayana, Bodhisatvas, like the Buddhas, are innumerable. In fact every creature is a potential Bodhisatva in as much as he or she is consciously or unconsciously striving after Nirvana; the recognized Bodhisatva is, however, one who has dedicated his life for the alleviation of suffering in the world. The more important of the Bodhisatvas are however beings who have even refused Buddhahood and the inaction or annihilation it implies, in order to help and save suffering creatures, even those condemned to hells.

Though Bodhisatvas are innumerable, five are the most important. These are the sons or emanations of the five Dhyani Buddhas and the main function of these Bodhisatvas is to superintend religion in the world during the intervals between one human Buddha and another. The names of these Bodhisatvas are: (1) Samanta Bhadra, (2) Vajrapani, (3) Ratnapani, (4) Padmapani* and (5) Visvapani, emanations of Vairochana, Akshobhya, Ratna Sambhava, Amitabha and Amogha Siddha respectively. Buddhism thus has five triads, each consisting of a Dhyani Buddha, Dhyani Bodhisatva and a human Buddha; of the five the most important is the triad consisting of Amitabha, Padmapani and Gautama; Padmapani holds a unique position in the theistic Buddhism of all Mahayana countries, and in China he underwent a complete transformation and is worshipped as Kuan Yin, the goddess of mercy. There are many other Bodhisatvas worshipped in the Mahayana countries, too numerous in fact to be mentioned here.

BUDDHIST COSMOLOGY

The Buddhists speak of the universe as a system called Chakravala, divided into three main planes: (1) Hells, (2) Worlds of animals, ghosts, demons and men, and (3) Heavens. These planes are built below, around and above the mythical mountain Meru. The hells, 136 in number, are situated under the base of Meru. Each hell is reserved for a particular type of sinner; the lowest, known as Avici, is the most horrible to which are condemned the revilers of the Buddha and the Law. The Buddhist hells are, however, purgatories where the wicked are purified in fire and torture, after which they are reborn in some other plane. The shortest duration of hell life is five hundred hell years, each day of which equalling fifty years according to human reckoning.

---

* Also known as Avalokitesvara.

Above the hells, built around Meru, are four worlds of animals, ghosts, demons and men. Over these four worlds rise the first heaven, called the Heaven of the Four Great Kings or Maharajahs. The Four Kings are (1) Dhritarashtra, guardian of the East, (2) Virudhaka, guardian of the South, (3) Virupaksha, guardian of the West, and (4) Kubera or Vaisravana, guardian of the North. Above the Heaven of Four Kings rises the Trayatimsa (Tavatimsa) Heaven of Saka (Sakra, Indra): this is a Heaven of Thirty-three Divinities, hence its name Trayatimsa.

The first two heavens are built round the top of Meru; above these two, rise twenty-four heavens which have nothing for support but float in space above Meru. These are self-luminous regions, not requiring the light of the sun. The famous Tusita heaven where Gautama Buddha resided as the Bodhisatva and Maitreya now waits, is the second of these self-luminous regions. The lowest six heavens are known as Deva Lokas inhabited by beings who are capable of enjoying the pleasures of the senses. The remaining twenty heavens are Dhyana Lokas (regions of abstract meditation) and Arupa Lokas (formless worlds), reserved for men of a high order like the Buddhas, Arhats (saints), Pratyeka Buddhas (individual Buddhas as distinguished from universal Buddhas who are world teachers), etc.

The Buddhists too like the Hindus believe in world cycles called Kalpas. But the Buddhist Kalpa appears to be much longer than the Hindu. "Suppose," the Buddha is said to have observed, "there is a solid rock, sixteen miles high, sixteen miles broad and sixteen miles long and it is gently touched by a fine piece of cloth once in a hundred years; the time taken to wear away the rock is nothing when compared to the ages that constitute a Kalpa."

THE SIX GATIS

There are only six possible Gatis or courses of life through which beings have to pass. These are: (1) Hell dwellers; (2) Pretas (Ghosts) "ever consumed with hunger and thirst"; (3) Asuras or demons; (4) Animals, birds, insects, etc., (5) Humans, and (6) Celestials. Of these, men and celestials constitute the desirable forms of Gatis and the others are considered undesirable.

For the purposes of rebirth, the Buddhists consider trees and plants, in fact the whole vegetable kingdom, as lifeless.

PLATE XCVII

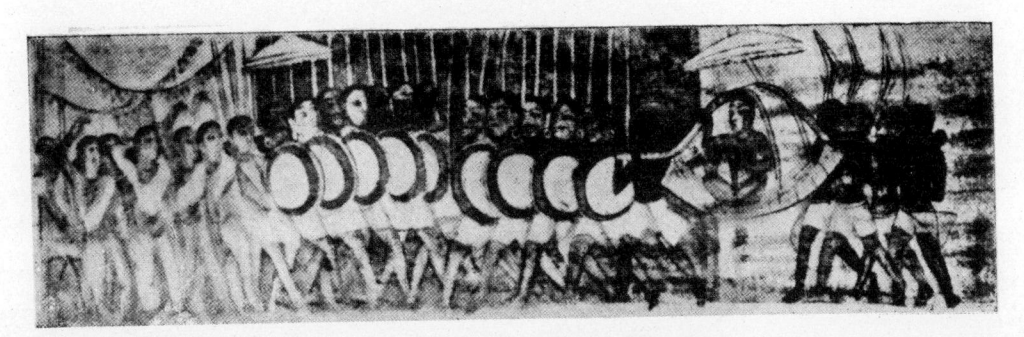

271 A DIGAMBAR MONK IN PROCESSION
(From *Jain Miniature Paintings from W. India* by Dr. Moti Chandra)

272 A JAIN DEPUTATION
(From *Studies in Indian Painting* by N. C. Mehta)

273 SCENE FROM A JAIN TEMPLE
(From *Studies in Indian Painting* by N. C. Mehta)

PLATE XCVIII

274 SIDDHARTHA AND TRISALA

275 NIRVANA OF PARASVANATHA
(From *Jain Miniatures* by Dr. Moti Chandra)

276 TRISALA RECOUNTING
HER DREAM TO SIDDHARTHA
(From *Jain Miniatures* by Dr. Moti Chandra)

277 BIRTH OF MAHAVIRA
(From *Jain Miniatures* by Dr. Moti Chandra)

PLATE XCIX

278 TRISALA WITH ATTENDANTS
(From *Jain Miniatures* by Dr. Moti Chandra)

279 MAHAVIRA
(From *Jain Miniatures* by Dr. Moti Chandra)

PLATE C

280 A JAIN MARRIAGE PROCESSION
(From *Jain Miniatures* by Dr. Moti Chandra)

281 A JAIN LAYMAN
(From *Jain Miniatures* by Dr. Moti Chandra)

282 JAIN SCULPTURE AND ORNAMENT, JINANATHPUR BASTI, SHRAVANA BELGOLA, MYSORE
(From *History of Fine Art in India & Ceylon* by V. Smith)

Chapter XV

JATAKA TALES

According to the belief of the Buddhists, the Buddha did not attain Buddhahood in one life. He became perfectly enlightened as the result of good deeds done in numerous births reaching back to countless ages. In the rebirths, after he became conscious of his mission, he is spoken of a Bodhisatva (Buddha-elect) and the story of Bodhisatva's birth is narrated in the Jataka tales.

In the beginning we are introduced to a person named Sumedha who, on meeting Dipankara (the Buddha of the age) and hearing his sermons decides to become a Buddha himself. He then scrupulously follows the Law and, after death, undergoes a series of births in various forms and places, and at last becomes Santusita, by which name he is known during his stay in Tusita heaven prior to his last descent to earth as Siddhartha. In the Jataka tales, some five hundred and fifty births of the Bodhisatva are mentioned. Of these, "eighty-three times he was an ascetic; a monarch fifty-eight; the Deva of a tree forty-three; a religious-teacher twenty-six; a courtier twenty-four; a Purohita Brahmin twenty-four; a prince twenty-four; a nobleman twenty-three; a learned man twenty-two; the Deva Sakra twenty; an ape eighteen; a merchant thirteen; a man of wealth twelve; a deer ten; a lion ten; a swan eight; a snipe six; an elephant six; a fowl five; a slave five; a golden eagle five; a horse four; a bull four; Mahabrahama four; a peacock four; a serpent four; a potter three; an outcaste three; a guana three; twice each a fish, an elephant-driver, a jackal, a crow, a woodpecker, a thief, and a pig; and once each a dog, a curer of snake bites, a gambler, a mason, a smith, devil-dancer, a scholar, a silversmith, a carpenter, a water fowl, a frog, a hare, a cock, a kite, a jungle fowl, and a Kindura. It is evident, however, that this list is imperfect."

In most of these births Yasodhara was his mate. The following are some of the Jataka tales.

BODHISATVA AS A HARE

Once upon a time, the Bodhisatva came to life as a hare, and he lived in a wood. He had three friends — a monkey, a jackal and an otter. The hare was elected leader of the group because of his wisdom and holiness. He taught his followers the greatness of charity, contentment and self-sacrifice, and need for fasting on prescribed days.

One morning, the otter went out in search of prey, and found some fish buried underground. The otter dug up the fish, cried three times enquiring if there was anyone to claim the fish, and, finding no one, brought it home. Then he remembered that it was a day of fast, and hence he refrained from eating it, and thought himself very virtuous on that account.

The jackal who had sallied forth in quest of prey on the same day, came to a hut in a field and saw two spits of roasted flesh. He also cried three times enquiring if it had any owner, and, finding none, brought it home. But remembering that it was a day of fast he kept the fare for the next day.

The monkey too went out, found some mangoes, brought them home and kept the fast.

On this day, the hare, while he was sitting on the Kusa grass, on which he used to feed, thought of people who might be hungry and starving. "If any person comes to beg food of me," thought he, "what will I offer him? I cannot offer him grass. Well," said he, "I will give him my own flesh to eat."

As soon as the Bodhisatva thought in this manner, the throne of Sakra grew hot. This was what always happened when some great event was planned or done on earth. Sakra desiring to know why his throne grew hot, looked down and saw the hare. He knew of the thought of the hare and desired to test his sincerity. So he assumed the form of a beggar and descended to the earth.

First Sakra went to the otter and begged for food. The otter offered him fish which he politely refused. He then went to the jackal and the monkey in turn, but refused the meat and mangoes they offered. Finally he went to the hare and begged for food. The hare asked him to lay a fire and, when this was done, the Bodhisatva shook his body thrice, in order that the lice and vermin living in his coat might escape unhurt, and then jumped right into the burning fire so that the mendicant could have roasted meat for his dinner. But as soon as the Bodhisatva jumped into the fire the burning embers froze and became snow.

Sakra smiled and revealed his identity. "I wanted to test your sincerity," he said to the Bodhisatva

Sakra now desired to perpetuate this great deed of the hare; so, he squeezed a nearby mountain and with the juice thus obtained daubed the figure of a hare on the moon so that all the world might know of the hare's self-sacrifice, and remember it till the end of time.

Thus the origin of the hare-mark on the moon.

BODHISATVA AS A JUDGE

Once upon a time when Brahmadatta was king of Benares the Bodhisatva was his Chief Justice. He judged cases rightly and people all over the kingdom praised his wisdom.

At that time there lived in the city of Benares two traders. One of them, when he went on a journey, gave the other five hundred ploughshares to keep till his return. But no sooner had the owner of the ploughshares departed on his travels than the other sold away the ploughshares, kept the money for himself and scattered mouse-dung in the store-house where the ploughshares had been kept. When the trader who had gone on a journey returned and asked for the ploughshares, the one who had sold them told him that they had been eaten by mice, and showed the mouse-dung in the storehouse as proof thereof.

Now, the owner of the ploughshares knew that he was cheated but there was no use of protesting. So he pretended to believe the story, remarking: "Alas! very unfortunate!" and went to his house. Next day, however, he came back and invited his friend's young son for a walk. The boy accepted the invitation and, as the man and the boy were walking together, the man fell upon the boy, seized him and locked him up in a room in his house.

The father of the boy, not finding his son, asked the trader who had taken the boy for a walk where his son was. "Alas, friend!" said the trader who had confined the boy in his house, "while your son and I were walking on the road, a kite made a swoop and carried away the boy." The father of the boy did not believe the story, and asked the trader since when kites were known to carry away young men. "If things that ought not to happen do happen," said the trader, "what can I do, my friend?"

The father of the boy waxed wroth on hearing these words of the trader, went to the court of law and addressed his complaint to the Chief Justice. The Chief Justice sent for the accused and asked him for an explanation; and finding that the man persisted in saying that a kite had carried away the boy, he wanted to know of him since when kites were known to carry away young men. "My lord," said the accused, "since the days mice have started eating iron ploughshares."

Now the Bodhisatva thought there was something deeper in the matter and asked for an explanation from the accused. The accused narrated to him the story of the ploughshares, upon which, the Bodhisatva understood on whom the guilt lay, and asked the father of the boy to return the price of the ploughshares to their owner. This was done, and the boy was released and sent back to his father.

The Bodhisatva thus gave fair judgment in all cases and people praised his wisdom.

BODHISATVA AS A LION

Once, the Bodhisatva was born as a lion, and when he grew into a strong, beautiful animal, he made his home in a forest near the Western Ocean.

Now, in a palmgrove on the shores of the Western Ocean there lived a hare. One day, the hare, after feeding, laid himself down to sleep under a young palm tree which stood under a vilva tree. He could not get sleep but lay awake thinking. "If the earth should be destroyed," thought the hare, "what would become of me?" Just as this thought came to the mind of the hare, a large fruit of the vilva tree fell on a palm leaf and made a noise like thunder. The hare mistook the noise for the collapse of the earth and took fright. "Just as I feared," said he to himself, and took to flight to escape from the impending doom. On his way, another hare saw him scampering and asked where he was running. "Don't ask me, friend," said the fleeing hare; "the earth is collapsing and I am trying to escape while there is yet time." The second hare on hearing the dreadful news also took to flight. Other hares saw these two fleeing, and hearing from them that the earth was collapsing joined them without enquiring about details. Thus all the hares of the forest started running, no one knew where, to get away from the end of the world.

A herd of deer saw the hares and, hearing from them that the earth was collapsing joined them. Soon buffaloes, rhinoceroses, tigers, elephants, in short all the animals of the forest were in full flight, all crying that the earth was collapsing.

Now they came near the home of the lion that was the Bodhisatva and, when he heard them crying aloud that the earth was collapsing, he looked about him and saw there was nothing wrong with the earth. "Surely," thought he, "it must be some noise which was misunderstood by them. If I don't make an effort and stop them, all these foolish animals will perish."

So he went to the middle of the forest and roared three times. This frightened the beasts all the more but they stopped running and took cover. Then the lion went to them and asked them why they were running. The elephants answered him: "The earth is collapsing." "Who saw the collapse of the earth?" he asked again. "The tigers," said the elephants. The

Bodhisatva asked the tigers, and they said that the rhinoceroses knew all about it. The rhinoceroses, however, did not happen to know, and referred him to the wild oxen. The wild oxen were no wiser. Nor did the buffaloes, elks, boars and deer see the collapse of the earth. At last the Bodhisatva came to the hares and on enquiry, found out the hare that had started the flight. "Did you see the earth collapsing?" he asked the hare. "Yes, my lord," said the hare still trembling with fear. "I saw it myself in the palmgrove and heard the sound of its collapse."

The Bodhisatva now asked the animals to remain where they were and took the hare to the palmgrove. There he inspected the place pointed out by the hare, saw the palm tree and the fruit of the vilva tree and guessed the cause of the noise aright. Then he came back to the beasts and told them the whole story.

The animals went away to their homes much relieved, and praised the wisdom of the Bodhisatva.

BODHISATVA AS A WHITE ELEPHANT

In a valley in the Himalayas there was a beautiful lake. Around the lake were seven thickets of flowers and plants, and beyond the thickets seven mountains, of which Golden Mountain was the last and the highest. In Golden Mountain was a large cave called Golden Cave in which lived a herd of eight thousand elephants with the Bodhisatva as the leader. He was pure white in colour, stood eighty-eight hands high and was a hundred and twenty hands in length. He had a silvery trunk and six tusks of different hues. His name was Chadanta.

Chadanta had two wives, Chullasubhadha and Mahasubhadha, of whom the former was jealous of the latter. One day while the white elephant, with his two wives standing on either side, was browsing in a grove of Sal trees he shook a flower-laden bough with his trunk and it happened that the flowers fell on Mahasubhadha and the twigs and red ants on Chullasubhadha. The latter took it to heart and said to herself: "He throws dead leaves, twigs and red ants over me and fragrant flowers over the wife who is dear to him."

On another occasion, when the elephants were disporting themselves under a Banyan tree that stood by the lake, one of the elephants found a beautiful lotus and gave it to the Bodhisatva, who presented it to Mahasubhadha. Chullasubhadha could not bear this slight and decided to avenge herself. So one day when the Bodhisatva entertained some holy men, Chullasubhadha also gave them food and secretly prayed that she should be born as the daughter of King Madha. Shortly after this she died and was born as the daughter of Madha. She grew into a beautiful maiden and was given in marriage to the king of Benares. This king was very fond of his bride and one day she told him that she had a boon to beg of him. The king said he would do anything for her, and the queen asked him to send for all the hunters in the kingdom. This was done, and when the hunters came, the queen selected a man named Sonuttara of great size and fierce look for the work she had in view. She called him privately and told him: "There is a white elephant with six tusks inhabiting the woods near a lake in the Himalayas and you should go and bring me his tusks. Great will be your reward if you do this."

The hunter agreed to do her bidding, and the queen equipped him with all the tools, provisions and followers necessary for crossing the seven mountains and capturing the elephant. Sonuttara set forth with an army of hunters towards the forests of the Himalayas. But all his men perished on the way, and he alone reached the seven mountains. The mountains were high and the forests were thick, and it took Sonuttara seven years, seven months and seven days to reach the lake. At last he reached the lake, saw the elephant herd and noted the place where the white elephant browsed. As the elephant went back in the evening, Sonuttara dug a pit at the place where he had browsed, covered the mouth of the pit with grass and leaves and hid himself in a tree. Next day, the white elephant came and fell in the pit and Sonuttara wounded him with arrows. Chadanta trumpeted in agony and the herd ran away in fear.

When the elephants ran away from the place, Sonuttara came down from the tree, and the Bodhisatva asked him why he wanted to kill him. "Because," said the hunter, "the queen of Benares wants your tusks." Now the Bodhisatva understood who the queen of Benares was and why she wanted to kill him. But he did not resent it; on the contrary, he asked the hunter to cut his tusks as soon as he could. Sonuttara however, found it difficult to reach his tusks because of the great height of the Bodhisatva. So the Bodhisatva allowed him to climb up his trunk and cut his tusks. But the tusks of the Bodhisatva were hard as iron and Sonuttara could not cut them. So the Bodhisatva, suffering immense pain, took the saw from the hunter's hand and sawed his tusks with his own trunk, and gave them to him. After this, he collapsed in a pool of blood and died.

Sonuttara took the tusks to the queen of Benares and narrated to her the story of Bodhisatva's death. When the queen beheld the tusks and heard the hunter's story, the memory of the happy days she had spent with her lord came to her mind. It broke her heart, and she died on the same day.

BODHISATVA AS A PRIEST

Long long ago, when Yasapani was king of

Benares, the Bodhisatva was his family priest. The king had a minister named Kalaka who took bribes and gave the king evil counsel.

One day, as the Bodhisatva was going to the palace to pay homage to the king, he saw, on his way, a man wailing and beating his breast. The Bodhisatva asked why he was in such a state of despair, and was told by the man that he had been ruined on account of Kalaka's giving unfair judgment against him. He heard the man's case and, finding that he had been unfairly dealt with, took him to the court of law. Here the Bodhisatva set aside the judgment of Kalaka, heard the case again and gave fair verdict. There were many people in the court and they applauded the Bodhisatva. The sound of their applause was so loud that the king in his palace heard it and he enquired of his attendants about the cause of the commotion. They told him that the Bodhisatva had judged a case fairly which had been wrongly judged by Kalaka. On hearing this, the king sent for the Bodhisatva and made him a judge.

Kalaka now became jealous of the Bodhisatva and plotted his ruin. He told the king that the Bodhisatva was more popular than the sovereign and hence a danger to the throne, and in proof thereof he showed to the king how a large number of people followed him wherever he went. The king saw the multitude that followed the Bodhisatva wherever he went and became alarmed. Hence he asked the minister how he could get rid of the Bodhisatva. "I want an excuse to put him to death," said the king. Then Kalaka told the king to ask the Bodhisatva to do some impossible task and kill him for not doing it. The king saw that this was a good plan and sent for the Bodhisatva. When he came the king told him: "Wise sir, we are tired of our old garden; now we crave for a new one and wish to walk in it to-morrow. If you cannot make it you must die."

Now, as is well known, it takes years to make a garden with trees, flower-lawns and water courses, and the Bodhisatva reflected, and understood that Kalaka had instigated the king to speak to him in this manner. But he knew it was no use resenting a royal order and hence he said: "If I can, my lord, I shall make it." Saying this he went his way.

That night while the Bodhisatva lay in his bed thinking, Sakra appeared before him and asked him why he lay thinking in his bed. The Bodhisatva told him of the king's command. "Wise sir," said Sakra, "you may sleep in comfort. I will make the garden for you." Sakra accordingly made the garden and when the king woke up in the morning, lo! the garden was ready for him to walk in, complete with trees, flower-lawns and fountains.

The king now sent for Kalaka, and told him, when he came, that the Bodhisatva had done the impossible. "Did I not tell Your Majesty," said the cunning Minister, "that he is dangerous? If he can make a garden in one night, he can surely dethrone a monarch in a day!" The king was now all the more alarmed, and on the advice of Kalaka again sent for the Bodhisatva. When the latter came, the king asked him to make a lake possessed of the seven precious stones. The Bodhisatva replied that he could if he could and then went his way. That night Sakra appeared before him, and made the lake; it was even more beautiful than the king desired.

Yasapani next asked the Bodhisatva to build a palace to go with the lake and the park. This was also done by Sakra, when the king asked his priest to make a jewel fit to go with the palace.

Sakra made the jewel for the Bodhisatva and the latter presented it to the king. The king, as usual, sent for Kalaka. But when he came this time Yasapani did not consult him about the next step to be taken, but asked his attendants to put him to death. This was speedily done by the attendants and the people.

After this, the king reigned peacefully and trusted the Bodhisatva for a loyal servant and true friend.

BODHISATVA AS A MONKEY

Once upon a time, a herd of eight thousand monkeys lived on a huge mango tree that stood on a bank of the Ganges in a forest of the Himalayas. The Bodhisatva was the leader of the monkeys, and he protected the herd from all harm.

Now the fruits of the mango tree on which the monkeys lived were sweeter than all other fruits in the world. But one branch of the tree overhung the stream, and the Bodhisatva thought that if some of the mangoes should fall in the river, they might drift down and be seen by some one who might come in search of the tree and do the monkeys harm. So he ordered the monkeys to strip that branch bare and pluck all the fruits on it. The monkeys did as they were told, but unfortunately one fruit remained unseen and it fell in the stream and drifted down.

The king of Benares, while he was taking a bath in the river, happened to see the fruit drifting down and he took it and ate it. Seeing that it was sweeter than any mango he had ever tasted, the king asked his courtiers to find out where the tree stood. They had a search made for the tree but could not find it anywhere in the kingdom; thereupon, the king set out with a big army along the banks of the Ganges and found the tree in the forest. The king saw that the monkeys were eating the fruits of the tree, and desiring to have all the mangoes for himself, he asked his archers to shoot the monkeys.

When the monkeys saw the archers they were

alarmed, because the nearest tree on to which they could escape stood on the other bank of the stream, and no monkey was strong enough to bound over the stream. Then the Bodhisatva comforted them by saying that he would save them all. After giving them this assurance, he jumped into the stream and, quick as thought, swam over to the other bank before any archer could shoot him. He then made a calculation as to the width of the stream, cut a long bamboo pole, tied one end of it to his waist, and, fastening the other end to a tree jumped towards the mango tree. But alas! the bamboo was short by the length of the body of the Bodhisatva and he could just catch a branch of the mango tree but not alight on it. He, however, asked the monkeys to escape as fast as they could over his own body and the bamboo pole, and all the monkeys escaped. But the last monkey was a wicked one who was jealous of Bodhisatva's leadership, and as he escaped over the body of his leader smote him and broke his spine. The Bodhisatva, already exhausted by the weight of the stream of monkeys that had passed over his body, could hardly sustain this blow and remained suspended between the trees, on the point of death.

The king of Benares saw all that had happened and took pity on the Bodhisatva. He ordered his men to climb the tree, and bring the monkey to him. When the monkey was brought to him, the king spoke kindly to him and had his body cleaned, washed and dressed. But with all the efforts of the king to restore him to health, the Bodhisatva died on the same day.

RESULT OF NOT HEEDING BODHISATVA'S WARNING

A Brahmin who lived in a village, knew the charm called Vedabha, and the Bodhisatva was his pupil. Now, a person who knew this charm could, by repeating it on a certain auspicious conjunction of the planets, receive from the sky a shower of the Seven Things of Price—gold, silver, pearl, coral, catseye, ruby and diamond.

One day, the Brahmin started on a journey to the city of Chedi, and took the Bodhisatva with him as his companion. While they were travelling through a jungle they fell among a gang of five hundred robbers who bound the Brahmin by ropes and asked the Bodhisatva to go home and bring their ransom.

Now, it happened that on this day there was the auspicious conjunction of the planets, favourable for repeating the charm Vedabha, and the Bodhisatva knew this. But he warned his master against repeating the charm. "For," said the Bodhisatva, "if you do this, evil will come upon the robbers and you." The Bodhisatva, although he was only the pupil of the Brahmin, knew much more than his master.

After giving the above advice to his master, Bodhisatva went away to the village to bring the ransom. But as soon as he had departed, the Brahmin thought to himself: "Why should I wait for my liberty till the arrival of my pupil when I can get all the money I want from the sky? No, I will repeat the charm, receive the shower of wealth, and pay up the ransom." Then he repeated the charm and a shower of the Seven Things of Price fell from the sky. The robbers who beheld this wonder were much delighted. They collected in baskets all the wealth they cared to have, and proceeded on their way home. The Brahmin, not knowing what else to do, followed them. They had not gone far when a second gang of five hundred robbers fell upon them and demanded booty. "If you want booty," said the leader of the first gang, "please get hold of the Brahmin who is following us. He can call forth a shower of wealth from the sky. In fact all the wealth we have got was given to us by the Brahmin." Hearing this, the second gang allowed the first to go with their booty, and caught hold of the Brahmin. "Give us booty," said they to him. But the Brahmin told them that the shower of precious things could be obtained only on an auspicious conjunction of stars and that this would next happen after a year.

"Rogue," said the robbers, "you enriched those robbers within an hour and want us to wait for a year." So saying they laid violent hands on him and did him to death. They then pursued and overtook the first gang, killed all of them and took possession of the booty. But now a violent quarrel broke out among the second gang of robbers for the spoils, and all of them, except two, were killed. The two survivors decided to divide the treasure equally between them. But by now they were hungry, and one of them went to a village to buy food while the other guarded the treasure. As soon as the former had departed, the other robber thought that it would be better for him to have all the treasure, and decided to kill his partner on his return. But the one who went for food also thought in a similar manner and decided to kill the one who stood guard over the treasure; so, after purchasing food for two he ate his own share, mixed poison in the remainder and brought it to his partner. But as soon he came near the treasure, he was killed by the robber who guarded the treasure, who, on eating the poisoned food, himself died on the spot.

When the Bodhisatva returned with the ransom, he did not find his master or the robbers at the appointed place. He saw, instead, treasure lying strewn about the place and understood that his teacher, heedless of his warning, had repeated the charm and received the shower of wealth from the sky. He then started on the trail of the robbers and came upon the dead body of his master. He cremated it, and again went in search of the robbers. Presently, he came to the place where the robbers had killed themselves; but not finding the treasure there, he looked for survivors, and following the footprints of the two who had carried away the treasure, he finally reached the place where the two robbers had met with death, and saw the treasure.

"Thus," mused the Bodhisatva, "did all the robbers and my master perish due to not paying heed to my advice." He then removed the treasure to his house and lived happily till the end of his life.

Chapter XVI

JAINISM

JAINISM, like Buddhism, was inspired by the prevailing discontent against Brahminism. The ritual and sacrifices enjoined by the Brahmanas gave the Brahmins a position of superiority which the Kshatriyas were not inclined to tolerate. As the martial and ruling classes, they found the claims of the Brahmins difficult to understand, but as long as the infallibility of the Vedas was recognized, the Brahmins, as the sole custodians, interpreters and students of the Vedas had to be accepted as the better caste. Hence the Kshatriya rebels of East India rejected the authority of the Vedas which, naturally, placed them outside the pale of Hinduism.

HISTORY

Vardhamana, called Mahavira, the founder of Jainism was of royal birth. He was the second son of Siddhartha, a Kshatriya chieftain of the Republic of Vaisali in Videha (Bihar). He was born in the township of Besarh, identified as the village of the same name situated near Patna. The exact date of his birth is a disputed point, the Swetambaras (one of the major sects among the Jains) believing that he was born in 599 B.C. and the Digambaras (the rival sect) that he was born 60 years earlier.

Vardhamana, from a very early age, showed ascetic leanings, and was attracted to a religious order founded by Parsvanatha who did not approve of Brahminical practices and is revered by the Jains as a Tirthankara (Ford Finder of whom more presently) and the forerunner of Mahavira. According to the Swetambara tradition Vardhamana, not wishing to offend the susceptibilities of his parents, married and settled down as a house-holder and did not renounce the world till the death of his parents; the Digambaras, however, maintain that from the very start he followed the higher call and remained a celibate.

Anyway, both are agreed that he gave up the world at the age of thirty and joined the order of Parsvanatha's mendicants. But a monastic life did not hold him long. He found the discipline of the monks too lax, and left them, after a year, to wander alone. In his twelve years of wandering life he never stayed in a village for more than one night.

In the thirteenth year, Vardhamana took up his abode in a place called Jrimbhakagrama near Parsvanatha hills. Here he attained Kevala Jnana or omniscience and came to be known as Jina or the Conqueror (of Karma), and the Jains take their name from this title of Mahavira. He now assumed the role of the teacher. The gist of Mahavira's teaching is that birth counts for little, and caste for less; that the object of life is liberation from the fetters of Karma through right living and the practice of asceticism; that the greatest sin is causing injury to living beings.

Although these principles did not appeal greatly to the warlike Kshatriyas, Mahavira's rejection of the authority of the Vedas and the superiority of the Brahmins did find favour with them. He himself, as a Kshatriya, had extensive social connections among the ruling classes, and these naturally were attracted by the teachings of their kinsman. Within a short period Mahavira collected a large number of disciples, both men and women, and counted as his followers the kings of Magadha, Prayaga, Videha, Kausambi, Champapuri, and many nobles and petty chiefs.

Thirty years Mahavira spent in teaching the Jain religion. In his seventy-second year, while staying in Pavapuri (Patna) as the guest of king Hastipala, the great ascetic of India passed away "all alone, and cut asunder the ties of birth, old age and death."

Mahavira had two important disciples, Gosala and Gautama Indrabhuti. The former lived with him for six years, but struck out an independent line of his own, rejected the doctrines of his master, and founded a sect of absolute fatalists who did not long survive him. Gautama, on the other hand, was a staunch and trusted disciple, and on him fell the leadership of the community after Mahavira's Nirvana. His only shortcoming that delayed his attainment of omniscience was his attachment to his master. He got over it on the night of Mahavira's decease, the Master having sent him away on the fateful night. After Mahavira's death he became a Kevalin (omniscient being) and is revered by the Jains as an Arhat, next in rank to a Tirthankara.

Suddharma was also an important disciple of Mahavira but he obtained omniscience after Gautama. He was a Brahmin converted by Mahavira and he was the head of the community after Gautama's death. All the present Jain monks consider themselves the spiritual descendents of Suddharma. During Mahavira's ministry he had divided the order under different leaders, and only the community of five hundred monks under Suddharma kept up the continuity, the others having perished by the lapse of time.

Mahavira divided the whole Jain community into four Tirthas or orders: monks, nuns, laymen and laywomen. The discipline for the last two was, for obvious reasons, less strict and they supported the monks and nuns to whom all occupations were prohibited. These lived on the charity of laymen and laywomen, studiously working out their salvation through a wandering or monastic life. Monks who attained the higher knowledge were permitted to commit religious suicide by starvation, but indiscriminate suicide was disallowed.

Jainism obtained a very strong foothold in East India and the great Mauryan Emperor Chandragupta was converted to the faith. During the closing years of this monarch's life a devastating famine overtook his kingdom and the large body of Jain monks proved too great a burden for the starving population to support. Hence under the leadership of Chandragupta, an exodus of Jain monks to South India took place, and these monks spread the faith in the South, and Shravana Belgola in Mysore became a famous centre of Jainism.

By the conversion of Samprati, grandson of Asoka, Jainism obtained a powerful ally. Samprati, like his illustrious grandfather, was a missionary at heart, and did for Jainism what Asoka did for Buddhism. Under his able guidance Jainism spread all over India and got a foothold even in Afghanistan. Central and Western India became strongholds of Jainism, and under Samprati this religion obtained even greater popularity than Buddhism. Samprati's indiscriminate charity also brought in corruption in the monasteries, and some of the monks, far from pursuing an ascetic course of life, started enjoying the good things of life. The old monk Hahagiri, brought up in the sterner, earlier school remonstrated with the easy going monks; but they turned a deaf ear and the old puritan committed suicide.

Jainism became the state religion of Gujarat under king Kumarapala who was converted to the faith by the celebrated Jain scholar Hemachandra. Kumarapala prohibited the killing of animals in his kingdom, and built several Jain temples.

During the Hindu revival that drove Buddhism out of India, Jainism too fell on evil days. But by making several concessions to Brahminism it escaped the fate of Buddhism; for though driven out of Eastern India, its home, Jainism still flourished in Western India where the majority of Jains are found at present. The classes that follow this persuasion now are not kings and nobles, but the trading castes. Though their numerical strength, compared to the Hindu population, is negligible, their influence, because of their wealth and commercial acumen, is quite considerable. A peculiarity of present-day Jains is that they allow paid Brahmins to officiate as priests in domestic worship although Brahmins are excluded from temple worship. It was probably by making this important concession that Jains managed to escape annihilation. Jainism did not, however, make any headway in countries other than India, though we have some record of Jain missionary activities outside India under Samprati.

JAIN BELIEFS

The Jains, like the Buddhists, believe that life is essentially evil and the object of life is deliverance. But while the Buddhists maintain that the path to deliverance is through right action, the Jains believe that liberation is best brought about by asceticism and inaction.

Jains do not believe in a Creator of the Universe. Creation implies a desire to create and a desire denotes something wanting and implies imperfection. The perfect being is without desire or activity, and as such a God who creates or demands obedience or praise from man has no place in Jain theology. The universe is self-existent and is indestructible. There are gods, no doubt, but they are little better than humans; we will have to notice them presently.

The philosophy of Jainism draws its inspiration mainly from the atheistic Sankhya system.* According to this ancient philosophic system of the Hindus, Jivas (souls) and Ajiva (non-soul) are the only reals in the universe. The Jains believe in Jivas as the quiescent finer reals, and in Ajiva as the grosser real. Jivas are numberless, each with an entity of its own. When a Jiva gets fettered by matter, a division of Ajiva, it is led to Karma or activity (or in common parlance, life).

How the Jiva gets fettered by Ajiva without the intervention of a third cause is not clearly explained. Jains are aware of this flaw in their system, but are not perturbed by it. For the great thing is not to find out why the Jiva gets fettered, but to liberate it. The fact of the bondage is taken as self-evident and as such the main thing is to cut the bond. The man whose house is on fire does not waste his time enquiring how the house caught fire but proceeds straight away to put out the fire.

The Jains are masters of detail and have studied, analysed, divided and classified Jivas and the numerous components of Ajiva; a detailed account of the metaphysics of the Jains, which is an exact science, cannot possibly be given in this work.

---

* For a detailed account of this system refer to the author's book *Hindu Religion, Customs and Manners*.

Like the Buddhists and Hindus, the Jains attach great importance to Karma, the law that rules all life. Transmigration of souls is believed in as a corollary of Karma. Man though, in one sense, its slave, is also master of Karma in as much as he can completely liberate himself from its shackles by following the Jain way of life.

About the nature of ultimate release, the Jains differ substantially from the Buddhists. While the Buddhist Nirvana is complete annihilation or something very near it, the liberated Jiva, according to the Jains, retains its entity. It is above desire and activity, serene, and never more to be lured by Ajiva into Karma.

There are several sects among the Jains but the most important division is as Swetambaras (white clad) and Digambaras (sky clad). The division appears to have persisted from the time of Parsvantha himself, but the personality and prestige of the earlier leaders prevented it from developing into a serious schism. Towards the close of the first century of the Christian era, the dissenting Digambaras, however, were separated from the main body.

The differences in belief between the two sects, though many, are not fundamental. The main dispute is about clothes. The Digambaras believe that complete emancipation is possible only in a state of absolute nudity; that as long as even a piece of white cloth hangs from the loins of a saint, he cannot obtain liberation since his attachment to that piece of cloth pulls his Jiva down to the meshes of Karma; besides, wearing of clothes implies consciousness of shame, and a sinner alone has the need to be ashamed of himself. The Swetambaras, on the other hand, believe that white robes do not hinder liberation, and may be worn even by the strictest ascetic.

From these differing standpoints the two sects have written the history of the community and the biography of their leaders agreeable to their own pet notions, each account differing from the other. The Digambaras, for instance, maintain that Mahavira gave up clothes on his initiation, the Swetambaras that he did not: similarly, the Digambaras maintain that the Tirthankaras should be represented in art without clothes whereas the Swetambaras think it proper that they should be provided with loin cloths. The dispute about Mahavira's marriage has already been noticed.

An important feature of Jainism is its extreme view on Ahimsa or non-killing. Injury to living beings (according to Jains, the vegetable kingdom and dead matter are not without life) is to be avoided at all costs; it is not intentional killing alone that leads to sin but even inadvertent destruction of life. The Jain view of metempsychosis includes a possibility of edified mortals and even gods assuming forms in the animal or vegetable kingdom, and as such destruction of animals, insects, garlic and pests might lead to injury to one's own superiors and is to be avoided. It is difficult to understand how a religion that rose among the warlike Kshatriyas came to attach so much importance to non-killing. It was probably due to the exaggerated importance attached to Ahimsa that Jainism fell out of favour among the Kshatriyas.

The absolute prohibition of killing prevented the generality of the population of the country, engaged in various occupations, from becoming Jains. Agriculture needs ploughing which destroys earthworms; fishermen could not very well become Jains, nor could butchers. Hence it was among the business communities that Jainism found favour, and at present it remains mainly a religion of bankers, jewellers, clerks and money lenders.

The fear of destroying life is so deep rooted among Jains that they would not eat after nightfall lest in the dark they should swallow insects with the meal. A Jain monk covers his mouth with a mask lest flies be inadvertently trapped in an open mouth. The less a man walks about, the better for his soul, since he is likely to tread upon a smaller number of insects. Hence the greatest virtue is to sit and fast.

LEGENDS OF MAHAVIRA

As in the case of the Buddha, many legends have collected round the personality of Mahavira. His mother Trisala, also called Priyakarini, had prior to his birth, sixteen (the Swetambaras say fourteen) auspicious dreams foretelling the greatness of the coming child.

In the first dream Trisala saw a white elephant, in the second a white bull, in the third a white lion leaping. In the fourth dream she had a vision of Sri, the goddess of wealth, in the fifth she smelt the fragrance of Mandara flowers, and in the sixth saw the full moon shedding its silvery beams all over the universe. In the seventh dream Trisala saw the sun, radiant and red.

There is some dispute between the Swetambaras and the Digambaras about the eighth dream. The latter believe, she saw a pair of sporting fish indicating, of course, happiness, while the former contend that it was Indra's banner on a golden pole that the queen saw.

In the ninth dream she saw a golden pitcher according to the Swetambaras and two pitchers according to the Digambaras. In the tenth dream Trisala had the vision of a lotus lake filled with flowers and resounding with the hum of bees and beetles. In the eleventh she saw the celestial milk ocean and in the twelfth a celestial palace inhabited by musical gods.

The thirteenth dream was about a huge vase piled with precious stones; the vase was as high as Mount Meru. The fourteenth dream was about a clear, beautiful conflagration fed by clarified butter.

The Digambaras hold that Trisala also dreamt of a throne of rubies and diamonds, and of a celestial king who deigned to rule on the terrestrial plane. Each sect has its own pet interpretations of these dreams.

Trisala revealed these dreams to her husband, and the wise men whom the latter consulted foretold the birth of either a great emperor or a Tirthankara. It will be remembered that a similar prophecy foretold the birth of the Buddha, and his father took elaborate precautions to ensure that his son should become an emperor. Vardhamana's father did not, however, wish to interrupt his son's calling and allowed him to find his own vocation.

A legend tells us that Vardhamana was not actually conceived by Trisala but by Devananda, wife of of a Brahmin named Rishabhadeva, and the gods, to prevent the child's birth in "the miserable Brahmin household," transferred the embryo to the womb of the Kshatriya lady Trisala. The legend shows the feeling that existed between the Brahmins and the Kshatriyas at the time, and indicates that Trisala was probably Vardhamana's stepmother.

On the twelfth day of the birth the naming ceremony took place and the child was named Vardhamana (increasing), for "from the day the embryo was placed in Trisala's womb, the wealth of the family in gold, silver, corn, jewels, pearls and precious stones increased."

The child grew up into a handsome lad of great strength of body and mind. He performed prodigious feats of strength. One day, for instance, when Vardhamana with some boys was playing in his father's garden, a mad elephant charged on the lads. The frightened young men ran for life, but Vardhamana caught the beast by its trunk, gave it a vigorous shake up, ran up its head, and rode on its back. On another occasion when he was again playing in the garden, a god, to test the boy's strength of mind, lifted Vardhamana high up in the air, but the young man, far from getting frightened, tore the hair of the god and beat him so mercilessly that he was glad to be rid of his obstreperous burden. On this, the other gods who were watching the scene called the boy Mahavira or great hero because he conquered the god.

Jains vividly describe the scene of Mahavira's enlightenment. As the Bodhi tree is associated with the Buddha's enlightenment, the Asoka tree is associated with Mahavira's attainment of omniscience. His initiation took place under this tree and the gods themselves attended the ceremony. Contemptuous of bodily pain Mahavira tore off his hair instead of shaving it, a penance Jain nuns and monks even now imitate on initiation. Indra, king of the gods, presented him a robe but the Digambaras who believe that Mahavira was unclad, doubt the authenticity of this legend.

Anyway, both the sects are agreed that most of the gods of the Jain pantheon attended the supreme moment of his enlightenment. Mahavira fasted for two and half days under an Asoka tree, not even taking water, and at the end of the fast, adoring gods and men carried him in a beautiful palanquin to a park where a five-tiered throne had been constructed for him. Here he stripped himself of all clothes and the gods Vaisravana caught them as he flung them to the ground from the lofty throne.

Many stories are told of Mahavira's absolute indifference to worldly possessions and his insensibility to physical pain. At the time of his enlightenment he had given up all his possessions in charity but a Brahmin named Somadatta reminded him that he had received nothing from him. Mahavira then had only the robe Indra had given left with him, and he cut the robe into two and gave one portion to the Brahmin. The Brahmin took the robe to a tailor who said that it would be necessary to get the other half to make a decent garment of it. Somadatta did not wish to ask, for shame, for the last bit of Mahavira's worldly possession, so he decided to steal it. While the ascetic was practising penances on a thorny shrub, Somadatta sneaked in, and as the robe slipped off Mahavira's loins by accident, he stole the robe and made off with it. But the Brahmin, during the course of thieving, hurt his hand on the thorns. Mahavira did not notice the theft immediately because of his absorption in meditation, but came to know of it later when all that he did was to make a parable out of it, telling his disciples how thorny the road to worldly life was but how great the deliverance from the thorny path.

On one occasion when Mahavira was meditating in a field, some mocking herdsmen, in rough sport, drove nails into his ears and scorched his feet, but the saint continued his meditations without in the least being disturbed by the cruel activities of the herdsmen.

Again, once while the ascetic was sitting in meditation on the outskirts of a village called Kumaragrama, a farmer who passed by, saw the idler and wished to give him some work. His bullocks were grazing nearby and the farmer asked Mahavira to tend the flock till his return. The farmer received no reply but took it for granted that his orders would be carried out. He went away but on return after some time did not find his bullocks. He asked his newly employed assistant what had happened to them but could only hear his deep breath as a reply. Thinking it useless to ask the man anything more about it, he set out in search of his cattle but a day and night long search yielded no results. Next morning he returned again to Mahavira and found the bullocks lying down happily near the meditating saint. The farmer could only attribute this to a motive of Mahavira to steal the bullocks. He started screwing Mahavira's neck, but fortunately god Indra who had been watching the scene from the very start intervened and saved the saint. From this time onwards Indra assumed the role of Mahavira's bodyguard and constantly protected him and thus saved mankind from similar sacrilege.

Legends have also collected round the death scene of Mahavira. All the rulers of the world were present at the death-bed. The dying man preached to them continuously for six days. On the seventh he ascended a diamond throne constructed in a magnificent hall for the purpose. The hall and the throne were illuminated by supernatural light. All night he preached the last sermon, and towards dawn all his hearers fell asleep when he died alone and unseen by any one. Even his own disciples, though present, did not see him die. When the sleeping audience woke up at dawn they saw what had happened. Since the light of the world was gone, they decided to illuminate all the buildings and parks of the city with torch and wick lights; thus the Jain account of the origin of the well-known Indian Festival of Lights (Divali).

The Digambaras, as the followers of the more austere tradition, believe that there was no king, no hall, no diamond throne, no supernatural light, not even a humble audience at the time of Mahavira's Nirvana, but he died all alone, unseen by any one, undisturbed by anything.

Mahavira's previous births have also been enumerated. He was, among other things, a carpenter, a monk, a king for several rebirths, a lion and a god. His birth as Mahavira was the twenty-seventh and last. These birth stories, however, lack the charm of the Jataka tales, and need not be given in detail here.

The reader will not have failed to notice the similarity between the legends connected with the Buddha and Mahavira. Both Buddhism and Jainism have many things in common and the founders lived in the same century in the same province; hence Mahavira was, for long, confused as the Buddha by Western scholars, and it was but lately that they recognized the fact that Mahavira was a historical personage, quite separate from the Buddha.

TIRTHANKARAS

We have seen that Jains do not believe in God, but they do believe in gods and demons. The greatest beings are not, however, gods but Tirthankaras (literally, Ford Finders) or liberated souls who, while living, had also been world teachers.

Free souls are of two kinds: The omniscient Siddhas, disembodied and in supreme bliss, free from Karma and the whirl of life; and the Arhats who have obtained omniscience but have not yet shed the mortal coil. Below the Arhats come Acharyas or heads of orders, Upadhyayas or teachers, and Sadhus or simple ascetics. These three, together with the Arhats and Siddhas, are known as the Panchaparameshtins or five supreme ones.

The Siddhas, then, are the greatest of souls. But all Siddhas are not Tirthankaras. This rare distinction belongs only to those who have attained the five kinds of knowledge* and have, in addition, preached and taught the Jain religion in its pure and original form. To have an adequate idea of the nature and stature of Tirthankaras, it is necessary for the reader to know something about the mythical chronology of the Jains.

The Jains conceive time as a moving point on the circumference of an eternally revolving wheel. The point, obviously, has its downward and upward movements. The downward movement, known as Avasarpini (under the influence of a bad serpent, hence Sarpini) denotes a period of steady degeneration till the lowest point is reached, when the upward trend known as Utsarpini (under the influence of a good serpent) starts with its ultimate end in a blissful age.

We are now living in the Avasarpini. The Avasarpini has six ages of progressive degeneration: (1) Susama Susama, (2) Susama, (3) Susama Dusama, (4) Dusama Susama, (5) Dusama, and (6) Dusama Dusama.

The first age, as the name indicates, was a period of "great happiness." This age lasted for four crores of Sagaropama.† Men born in this age were six miles in height and each one had two hundred and fifty-six ribs. All mothers gave birth to twins, a boy and a girl, and the population of the sexes always remained equal. The twins were able to look after themselves from the fourth day onwards, and the parents died

---

* The five kinds of knowledge are: Mati Jnana or simple knowledge, gained through the senses; (2) Sruta Jnana or speculative knowledge, mainly obtained through study and contemplation; (3) Avadhi Jnana or intuition of past events; this knowledge is common among celestials and devils but rare among humans; (4) Manahparyaya Jnana or knowlege of the thoughts and feelings of others: only gifted men can attain this high knowledge; and (5) Kevala Jnana or omniscience; only Arhats and Siddhas can attain this supreme knowledge.

† Sagaropama, Sagara, Palya and Purva are mythical time divisions the exact length of which is known only to the omniscient. The number of years these represent are so fantastically astronomic that ordinary men and women can have no conception of their length or duration.

invariably on the 49th day of the birth of the twins. Ten Kalpa Virkshas (boon granting trees) supplied all the needs of men and women in this age. There was no need for work or for cooking, and there was no killing. The men of this age ate only one meal in four days. All men and women lived without religion, for there was no sin and no misery, and all passed on to the regions of bliss on death.

Susama was the age of mere happiness. The height of man was reduced to four miles and his ribs to one hundred and twenty-eight. The twins started eating from the third day and their parents died on the sixty-fourth day of their birth.

In Susama Dusama (the age of happiness and misery, the former predominating), sin and sorrow appeared for the first time. Degeneration set in. The height of man was reduced to two miles and his ribs to sixty-four. Hunger increased and a man ate one meal in two days. The Kalpa Vrikshas started withering, and the need for agriculture, cooking and other occupations arose with their accompaniment of destruction of life. In this age appeared the first Tirthankara, Rishabhadeva or Adinatha (First Lord) who preached the Jain religion, and taught men seventy useful arts, and women sixty-four. He introduced politics and statecraft, and established a kingdom. His daughter Brahmi invented the eighteen alphabets.

The next age Dusama Susama (the age of misery and happiness, misery predominating) is interesting as it was in this period that the remaining twenty-three Tirthankaras lived. This age lasted one crore of crores of Sagaropama minus forty-two thousand years. The height of man was reduced to five hundred spans and his ribs to thirty-two. Every one ate one meal a day. The need for religion became urgent, and Tirthankara after Tirthankara preached and taught. People of this age did not all obtain liberation but some were reborn in the various regions of the universe. The practice of religion was fully established.

Dusama (the age of evil), in which we live, is predominantly evil. The stature of man is reduced to seven cubits and his ribs to sixteen. The length of this age is twenty-one thousand years, and it started three years after Mahavira, the twenty-fourth Tirthankara obtained liberation. There will be no Tirthankara in this age and Jainism itself is doomed to die out towards the end.

But the worst is yet to come. For in Dusama Dusama (the age of greater evil) which will last for twenty-one thousand years, men, devoid of the saving knowledge of religion, will be ruled entirely by their base instincts. The height of man will be reduced to one cubit and his ribs to eight. Virtue will entirely disappear and no one will live for more than sixteen years. Famines and pestilence will ravage the world. Sexual morality will completely disappear. Howling winds will sweep over a deserted earth, and the little weak men will seek refuge in caves, ravines and in the Ganges and in the sea. When degeneration reaches its lowest point, Utsarpini, the upward trend will start. We are told that Utsarpini will start in the month of Shravana (July-August). There will be continuous rain for seven days, and the scorched earth will again clothe herself in green.

The ages of the Utsarpini are the same as those of Avasarpini but in reverse order. There will be twenty-four Tirthankaras in Utsarpini too. The first of these will appear in Dusama Susama and the remaining twenty-three in Susama. When the zenith of the upward course is reached in Susama Susama, Avasarpini will start again, and thus the mystic wheel rotates endlessly and aeons roll on aeons.

The Tirthankaras, as we have seen, are the greatest of beings and their worship is recommended. But the Jains worship the Tirthankaras not because they are able to grant boons or favours but on the broad principle that worship of sacred persons is good for the soul of the worshipper. Tirthankaras are all above desires, even the desire of saving souls, and as such no Tirthankara can convert a sinner into a saint and send him to heaven. In Jainism there is no short cut to salvation. Every one must patiently and diligently work out one's own liberation by penance and right living.

The twenty-four Tirthankaras of the Avasarpini were:

(1) Rishabhadeva: As we have seen, this sage appeared in Susama Dusama. His father was Nabhiraja and mother Maru Devi. Rishabha means bull and he was so called because his mother, when he was conceived, had a dream of a white bull coming towards her. He was born in Ayodhya and had a golden yellow complexion. His height was 500 bowshots and he lived 8,400,000 Purva of time. He had one daughter and one hundred sons. He attained Nirvana on Mount Kailas in the Himalayas. His sign is the bull.

(2) Ajitanatha: This Tirthankara appeared in Dusama Susama, fifty lakhs of crores of Sagara after Rishabhadeva. He was like his predecessor, born in Ayodhya. His father was king Jitasatru and mother Vijaya Devi. His height was 450 bowshots and complexion yellow. He attained liberation on Mount Parsvanatha at the age of seventy-two lakhs of Purva of time. His

emblem is the elephant.

(3) Sambhavanatha: Born of Jitari and Sena in Srivasti, he was 400 bowshots in height. The interval between Ajitanatha and Sambhavanatha was 30 lakhs of crores of Sagara. Of golden yellow complexion, he lived for sixty lakhs of Purva of time and attained Nirvana on Mount Parsvanatha together with one thousand ascetics. His sign is the horse.

(4) Abhinandana: Born in Ayodhya of king Samvara and queen Siddartha, ten lakhs of crores of Sagara after Sambhavanatha, he lived for fifty lakhs of Purva and attained Nirvana on Mount Parsvanatha. His complexion was golden yellow and height 350 bowshots. His sign is the monkey.

(5) Sumatinatha: Nine lakhs of crores of Sagara after Abhinandana, was born the fifth Tirthankara in Ayodhya. His father was king Megharatha. A story is told of his mother Sumangala similar to that of Solomon's judgement between the two mothers who claimed the same baby. Sumatinatha was 300 bowshots in height and lived for 40 lakhs of Purva. His complexion was golden yellow. His sign is the curlew.

(6) Suparsvanatha: Born in Kasi nine thousand crores of Sagara after his predecessor, his height was 200 bowshots and complexion green. His father Supratishta was king of Benares. His mother Prithvi suffered from leprosy but was cured of the fell disease prior to her illustrious son's birth. He lived for 20 lakhs of Purva and obtained Nirvana on Mount Parsvanatha. His sign is the Swastika.

(7) Chandraprabha: The name indicates moonbeams. The Tirthankara's mother Lakshmana in pregnancy wished to drink the moon, and for her satisfaction a silver plate of water in which was a reflection of the moon was brought to her, and she drank of it. Hence her son was named Chandraprabha. His father Mahasena was king of Chandrapuri. He was born 900 crores of Sagara after his predecessor. He was of white complexion, of 150 bowshots in height, and lived for 10 lakhs of Purva. He attained Nirvana on Mount Parsvanatha. His sign is the crescent.

(8) & (9). As in the case of sex of the nineteenth Tirthankara, there is some dispute about the order, stature, longevity and parentage of the eighth and ninth Tirthankaras, Suvidhinatha and Pushpadanta. The former was so named because on his birth his clan gave up internecine warfare and took to the practice of the arts of peace (Suvidhi); Pushpadanta had teeth (Danta) like flowers (Pushpa). The emblem of Suvidhinatha is the crocodile and that of Pushpadanta, the crab, though there is no complete agreement on this point. Each was shorter than the seventh Tirthankara but taller than the tenth. Both died on Mount Parasvanatha.

(10) Sitalanatha: As soon as he was conceived, his mother Sunanda was blessed with a miraculous cooling power (Sitalata) and she could cure anyone who suffered from a fever by laying her hand on the patient. His father was Dridharatha, king of Bhadrikapuri, in which city the Tirthankara was born nine crores of Sagara after his predecessor. He was ninety bowshots in height and lived for one lakh of Purva, at the end of which he obtained Nirvana on Mount Parsvanatha. His complexion, was golden yellow. His sign is the Srivatsa Swastika according to the Swetambaras, and the sacred fig tree according to the Digambaras.

(11) Sreyamsanatha: He was born in Simhapuri, one crore of Sagara after his predecessor, of king Vishnu and queen Vishnu. His height was eighty bowshots. He lived for eighty-four lakhs of years and obtained Nirvana on Mount Kailas. His complexion was golden yellow. His sign is the rhinoceros according to one account and the eagle according to another.

(12) Vasupujya: He was born in Champapuri fifty-four Sagara after his predecessor. He attained Nirvana in the same place. His height was seventy bowshots and colour red, and he lived for 72 lakhs of years. His father's name was Vasupuja and mother's Vijaya. His sign is the buffalo.

(13) Vimalanatha: On his conception his mother Suramya was endowed with clearness of vision, hence his name Vimalanatha (lord of clearness). A legend says that she showed her clear vision in the following manner: A pilgrim and his

wife stayed in a temple which was inhabited by a female demon. She fell in love with the pilgrim and assumed the shape of his wife, and the confused man could not tell which of the two was his real wife. In this predicament he went to king Kritavarman, Vimalanatha's father, and begged him to solve the difficulty. The king was as confused as the pilgrim himself but the queen came to his aid. She asked the two women to stand far away from the pilgrim and reach out their hands to touch him. The human wife could not touch her husband because of the distance, but the demoness elongated her hand by her magic powers and touched the pilgrim, and thus betrayed herself. Vimalanatha was born thirty Sagaras after his predecessor. He was sixty bowshots in height and lived for sixty lakhs of years. He was of golden yellow complexion. Born in Kampilya, he attained Nirvana on Mount Parsvanatha. His sign is the boar.

(14) Anantanatha: He appeared in Ayodhya nine Sagara after Vimalanatha. His father's name was Simhasena and mother's Sarvayasa. He was fifty bowshots in height and lived for thirty lakhs of years. His complexion was golden yellow and he attained Nirvana on Mount Parsvanatha. His sign, according to the Swetambaras, is the falcon, and according to the Digambaras; the bear.

(15) Dharmanatha: He was born in Ratnapuri of king Bhanu and queen Suvrata. The interval of time between Anantanatha and Dharmanatha was four Sagara. His height was forty-five bowshots and he lived for ten lakh of years. He was of golden yellow complexion and attained Nirvana on Mount Kailas. His sign is the thunderbolt.

(16) Santinatha: He was so called because his mother Achira, on conceiving him, brought peace (Santi) to the people of the country which was, till then, being ravaged by a terrible plague. Santinatha's father Visvasena was king of Hastinapura and the Tirthankara was born in this city three Sagara minus 3/4th Palya after Dharmanatha's demise. He lived one lakh of years and his height was forty bowshots. He attained Nirvana on Mount Parsvanatha. His complexion was golden yellow, and his sign, is the deer.

(17) Kuntanatha: Half a Palya separates this Tirthankara from his predecessor. He was born of king Surya and queen Sridevi in the city of Hastinapura. He was thirty-five bowshots in height and lived for 95,000 years. He was golden yellow in complexion and attained Nirvana on Mount Parsvanatha. His sign is the goat.

(18) Aranatha: After half a Palya since Kuntanatha, appeared this Tirthankara in Hastinapura. His father was king Sudarsana and mother queen Mitra. He was thirty bowshots in height, lived for 84,000 years and died on Mount Parsvanatha. He was of golden yellow complexion and his sign is the fish.

(19) Mallinatha: The sex of this personage is a disputed point. The Swetambaras maintain that the Tirthankara was a woman, whereas the Digambaras, who believe that no woman can obtain liberation, that he was a man. According to the Swetambara tradition, Mallinatha, in a previous birth, used to perform penances in the company of five monks. They never hid anything from one another and always performed the same type of penances and fasted on the same days. Mallinatha was, however, overcome by an unholy desire to excel his companions in virtue and fasted, on the quiet, for an extra day. For this sin he was reborn as a woman, but his Karma had been worn off and nothing could prevent his becoming a Tirthankara. Digambaras, of course, reject the story and stoutly maintain that he was born a man. Mallinatha was born in Mithila of king Kumbha and queen Prabhavati, and attained Nirvana on Mount Parsvanatha, having lived for 55,000 years. One thousand crores of years separate Mallinatha and Aranatha. Mallinatha was of a golden blue hue, and was twenty-five bowshots in height. The emblem of the Tirthankara is the Kumbha or water jar.

(20) Munisuvrata: He was born 54 lakhs of years after Mallinatha in Rajagriha. His father's name was Sumitra and mother's Padmavati. He was twenty bowshots in height, lived for 30,000 years and attained Nirvana on Mount Parsvanatha. He was dark, and his sign is the tortoise.

(21) Naminatha: Six lakhs of years after Munisuvrata, appeared Naminatha. He was born in Mithila of king Vijaya and queen Vipra. A legend says that while Vipra was pregnant the city was besieged by an enemy and all hope of saving it was lost; but on the advice of the astrologers, the queen appeared on the city wall and the effulgent light the embryo shed filled the enemy with fear and awe, and the besieging army bowed down before the queen and hence her son was named Naminatha (the lord of those who bowed down). Naminatha was fifteen bowshots in height and he lived for 10,000 years. His complexion was golden yellow and he attained Nirvana on Mount Parsvanatha. His emblem is the blue lotus.

(22) Neminatha: He was born in Dwaraka of king Samudravijaya and queen Sivadevi. He was ten bowshots in height and lived for 1,000 years. He attained Nirvana on Mount Girnar. Krishna and Baldeva lived in his time and were his cousins. Neminatha appeared five lakhs of years after Naminatha. He was of a dark hue with an inner tinge of red. His sign is the conch.

(23) Parsvanatha: He was born in Kasi of king Asvasena and queen Vama, 84,000 years after Neminatha. He was nine cubits in height and lived 100 years. He was dark blue in colour and attained Nirvana on Mount Parsvanatha. His sign is the serpent. Unlike his predecessors, Parsvanatha is a historical personage, and we have already had occasion to notice him as the forerunner of Mahavira.

(24) Mahavira: He appeared 250 years after Parsvanatha. He was seven cubits in height, and his complexion was golden yellow. The lion is his emblem. We have already dealt with this Tirthankara in some details as the real founder of Jainism.*

It is interesting to note that all the 24 Tirthankaras were of royal birth, and had nothing to do with Brahmins and Brahminism. Besides the Tirthankaras, there are thirty-nine other personages who are worthy of great honour. These are the 12 Chakravartins, 9 Narayanas or Vasudevas, 9 Pratinarayanas or Prativasudevas, and 9 Balabhadras. These together with the 24 Tirthankaras form the sixty-three sacred persons of Jain hagiology. Lesser than these but still important are 9 Naradas, 11 Rudras, 24 Kamadevas, 48 parents of Tirthankaras and 14 Kulakaras. These 106 form the second group of sacred personages. A detailed description of all these great souls, pre-eminently holy as they were, is likely to bore any reader who is not a Jain ascetic.

The Jains also know the names and the present habitat of the twenty-four Tirthankaras who will appear in the Utsarpini. These will be:

(1) Padmanabha: He will appear in Dusama Susama of the Utsarpini. He is at present in the first hell working out his Karma.

(2) Suradeva: He and his twenty-two successors will appear in Susama. At present he is in the second Devaloka (heaven).

(3) Suparsva: He is now in the third Devaloka.

(4) Swayamprabhu: He is now in the fourth Devaloka.

(5) Sarvanubhuti: He is now in the second Devaloka. In a previous birth he was Dritaketu, uncle of Mallinatha, the lady Tirthankara of the Avasarpini.

(6) Devasruta: He is now in the first Devaloka.

(7) Udayaprabhu: He is now in the twelfth Devaloka.

(8) Pedhala: Now in the first Devaloka.

(9) Potila: Now in the first Devaloka.

(10) Satakirti: Now expiating his Karma in the third hell.

(11) Munisuvrata: He is now in the eighth Devaloka. In a previous birth this would-be Tirthankara was the well-known Devaki, mother of Krishna, of Hindu mythology.

(12) Amama: He is now in the third hell. He is no other than the famous Krishna of the Hindus who, the Jains believe, has not yet liberated himself but will in the Susama of the coming Utsarpini.

(13) Nikasaya: He is now in the fifth Devaloka. In a previous birth he was the spiritual preceptor of Ravana, of Hindu mythology.

(14) Nisupalaka: He is now in the sixth Devaloka. He was, in a previous birth, Balarama, Krishna's half brother.

(15) Nirmama: He is now in the fifth Devaloka.

(16) Chitragupta: He is now in the second Devaloka and was once Rohini, the stepmother of Krishna and mother of Balarama.

(17) Sumadhi: Now in the twelfth Devaloka, living as a woman.

---

* The lists of Tirthankaras differ in names, details, etc. in various Jain texts; there is, however, agreement on 1st, 23rd and 24th Tirthankaras, and in the total number twenty-four.

(18) Samavarnatha: Now living as a woman in the eighth Devaloka.
(19) Yasodhara: He was once the famous Hindu ascetic Dwaipayana Vyasa, and is at present a celestial.
(20) Vijaya: Now in the twelfth Devaloka. He was a relative of Krishna in a previous birth.
(21) Malyadeva: Now in the fifth Devaloka.
(22) Devajina: Now in the twelfth Devaloka.
(23) Anantavirya: He is now in Graiveyika (upper region situated above Devalokas).
(24) Bhadrajina: This last of the Tirthankara of the Utsarpini is now living in the highest Devaloka.

After Bhadrajina there will be no more Tirthankara in the Utsarpini. The world will progress towards Susama Susama and when this age is completed, Avasarpini will start again and thus the wheel whirls on endlessly.

GODS AND DEMONS

Though the Jains do not believe in a Supreme Being, in a Trinity, or even in a Real as the mainstay of the rolling universe, yet they believe in most of the gods, sages, demi-gods and demons of Hindu mythology. The gods are different from humans, but they are not almighty or all-virtuous. They have their divine failings. Though they enjoy certain occult powers, and as such may be considered superior to humans, in some respects they are definitely inferior. No god, for instance, can attain liberation unless he be born as man. Liberation is possible only to humans. Yet some gods are worthy of honour and a few are actually worshipped due, no doubt, to Hindu influence.

If there is no short cut to salvation in Jainism, there is also no need for utter despair. For no demon is eternally damned. They are also working out their Karma, and in crores and crores of Sagaras of Purva of Palya of Sagaropama are capable of attaining liberation. The hells are, like the hells of Buddhism and Hinduism, but purgatories.

To get some idea of the nature, occupations and habitats of demons and gods, it is necessary for the reader to be acquainted with the Jain conception of the universe. Spatially the universe is divided into three: The upper, middle and lower regions. The Jains represent the conception by the headless figure of a man. The waist of the figure represents the middle region, the leg the lower region and the trunk the upper region.

The nether region is subdivided into seven hells, the lowest and darkest being the seventh hell, at the right foot of the mystic figure. The first hell is called Ratna Prabha or jewel; the second, Sarkara Prabha or sugar; the third, Valuka Prabha or sand; fourth Pankha Prabha or mud; fifth, Dhuma Prabha or smoke; sixth, Tama Prabha or darkness; and seventh, Maha Tama Prabha or greater darkness. These hells are torture chambers, and the lesser gods are engaged in torturing souls here.

The gods that live in hells and torture their victims are of fifteen kinds: The Amba wreck the nerves of the victims; the Ambarasa hew flesh from bones; the Sama bastinado their victims; the Sabala tear out the flesh; the Rudra torture with spears; the Maharudra mince the flesh; the Kala roast the victims; the Mahakala tear them with pincers; the Asipala are swordsmen and cut with the swords; the Dhanu are archers and shoot their victims; the Kumbha torture with chillie powder; the Valu steep their victims in hot sand; the Vetarani dash sinners against stones; the Kharasvara force souls to sit on thorns; and the Mahaghosha shut them up in dark holes.

On a level with the hells but on the other side, represented by the left leg of the figure, is Patala. Patala has a mixed population of godlings and demons. The godlings are called Bhavanapati and are classified into ten. The demons are divided into two major groups called Vyantaras and Vana Vyantaras, and each group has several sub-divisions. Of the better known demons of the Vyantara group are: the Pisacha who haunt the Kadamba Tree; the Bhuta who haunt the Sulasa tree; the Yaksha who haunt the Banyan tree; the Gandharva who haunt the Timbara tree; and the Mahoraga who haunt the Naga tree. All these are black demons. The Rakshasas who haunt the Khatamba tree and the Kimpurushas who haunt the Champaka tree are white Vyantaras.

More fearsome than the Vyantaras are the Vana Vyantaras. They are of eight classes: Anapanni, Panapanni, Isivayi, Bhutavayi, Kandiye, Mahakandiye, Kohanda and Pahanga.

The middle region is the terrestial plane in which we live. It has eight ring shaped continents, each separated from the other by a ring shaped ocean. In the centre of this region rises the mighty mountain Meru. Moksha or liberation can only be obtained from this region.

The upper region is subdivided into two: Kalpa and Kalpathitha. The dimensions of Kalpa has been ascertained but not of Kalpathitha. The former region is situated immediately above the middle region, and is again subdivided into sixteen Devalokas or heavens: They are numbered from bottom upwards as: (1) Saudharma, (2) Aisana, (3) Sanatkumara, (4) Mahendra, (5) Brahma, (6) Brahmottara, (7) Lautaka, (8) Kapisht, (9) Sukra, (10) Mahasukra, (11) Satara, (12) Sahasrara, (13) Ananta, (14) Pranata, (15) Arana and (16) Achyata.

The Kalpathitha portion is subdivided into nine Graiveyikas and five Pancha Anuttaras.

The better class of gods live in the upper regions. All gods of the upper region are not, however, of the same importance. They are broadly divided into Jyotishi and Vimanavasi or gods of the brighter regions and gods of the sky. Each of these divisions is subdivided into many. While this classification is based on the regions they live in, there is another grouping based on occupations, very much like the caste system of the middle region. There are noble and servile castes among the gods. Of the latter, the scavengers who keep the streets of celestial cities clean are the lowest. They are untouchables and live outside city walls.

There is yet another division based on their spiritual condition. Some gods are indifferent to religion, and turn a deaf ear to the sermons of the great; others are of a religious bent of mind and attentive to the sermons of the sages. All gods are happy. They eat and drink and sing. As in Hindu mythology, Indra is the king of gods according to Jain conceptions too.

Above Kalpathitha itself is the zenith of the universe called Siddha Sila where the Siddhas (liberated souls) live in bliss unending. The twenty-four Thirthankaras of the Avasarpini are there.

BIBLIOGRAPHY

COLEMAN, CHARLES. *Hindu Mythology*
COOMARASWAMY, DR. A AND SR. NIVEDITTA. *Myths of the Hindus and Buddhists*
CUTNER, H. *A Short History of Sex-Worship*
DANIELOU, ALAIN. *Hindu Polytheism*
DELEURY. G. A. *The Cult of Vithoba*
ELLIOT, SIR CHARLES. *Hinduism and Buddhism*
ELLIS, E. S. *1,000 Mythological Characters Briefly Described*
GOUR, SIR H. S. *The Spirit of Buddhism*
GUPTE, RAI BAHADUR G. A. *Hindu Holidays and Ceremonials*
IONS, VERONICA. *Indian Mythology*
JONES, SIR WILLIAM. *Complete Works*
KEITH, A. B. *Indian Mythology* ('Mythology of All Races' Series, Vol. VI)
MACKENZIE, D. A. *Indian Myth and Legend*
MARGUERITE, ASPINWALL. *Jataka Tales Retold*

MAX MULLER. *Contribution to the Science of Mythology*
MCDONNEL, A. A. *Vedic Mythology*
MEHTA, R. J. *Masterpieces of Indian Sculpture*
MOOR, E. *Hindu Pantheon* (Edited by W. O. Simpson)
NIVEDITTA, SR. See Coomaraswamy
PAYNE, E. A. *The Saktas*
RADHAKRISHNAN, S. *Indian Philosophy*
ROGRIGUES, E. A. *Hindu Pantheon*
ROY, P. C. (Tr.) *Mahabharata*
SANYAL, J. M. (Tr.) *Bhagbata*
SIMPSON, REV. W. O. See Moor
TAWNEY, C. H. *Ocean of Story* (Translation of *Katha Sarit Sagara* of Somadeva)
THOMAS, P. *Hindu Religion, Customs and Manners*
WILKINS, REV. W. J. *Hindu Mythology*
WILLIAMS, SIR M. *Buddhism*
WILSON, H. H. *Vishnu Purana*

GLOSSARY AND INDEX

Abhinandana, a Tirthankara, 137
Acharyas, Jain, 135
Achyuta, a name of Vishnu, 16
Adam, 10
Adi Buddha, Primal Buddha, 123
Adi Kavi, a name of Brahma, 15
Adinatha, a Tirthankara, 135
Aditi, wife of Kasyapa, 33, 47, 80
Aditya, son of Aditi, 16, 41, 47, 80
Advaita philosophy, 13, 64
Afghanistan, 132
Agastya, a sage, 21, 34, 48
Agni, god of fire, 6, 22, 31, 32, 33, 34, 47, 58, 69, 101
Agni Purana, 46
Agniswamin, name of a Brahmin, 105, 106
Ahalya, wife of Gautama, 33
Ahar, a Vasu, 48
Ahimsa, non-injury, 133
Airavatam, Indra's elephant, 33, 58, 63
Aja, a name of Brahma, 14
Ajamila, a Brahmin, 67
Ajasat, Ajatasatru, a king, 121
Ajitanatha, a Tirthankara, 136
Ajiva, lifeless matter; 132
Ajmer, 15
Akbar, emperor, 5, 68, 78
Akrura, a messenger, 23
Akshobhya, a Buddha, 123
Alaka, heaven of Kubera, 35
Alexander, 4
Amama, a Tirthankara, 139
Amaravati, heaven of Indra, 33, 63, 94, 95
Amba, a kind of demons, 140
Ambadi, an ancient country, 22
Ambalika, a princess, 49, 50, 60
Ambasara, a kind of demon, 140
Ambika, a princess, 49, 50, 60
Amer, a flower, 72
Amitabha, a Buddha, 123
Amogha Siddha, a Buddha, 123
Amra, a flower, 77
Amrita, nectar, 81
Anala, a Vasu, 48
Ananda, Buddha's disciple, 115, 120, 121
Ananda, felicity, 46
Ananga, a name of Kama, 77
Ananta, a mythical serpent, 41, 91
Ananta, heaven, 140
Anantanatha, a Tirthankara, 138
Anantavirya, a Tirthankara, 140
Anasuya, wife of Atri, 47, 99, 100
Anavamadarshin, a Buddha, 122
Andhakupa, a hell, 66
Andhatamisra, a hell, 66
Anga, an ancient kingdom, 51
Angada, a monkey chief, 86
Angiras, a sage, 33, 45 46

Anila, a Vasu, 48
Aniruddha, son of Pradyumna, 73
Anjana, mother of Hanuman, 86
Annapurna Devi, goddess, 40, 108
Anoma, a river, 117
Anshu, an Aditya, 80
Ansuman, a king, 108
Aparamargu, a kind of grass, 83
Apis, the bull god of Egypt, 3, 73
Apsara, celestial dancer, 49, 63, 85
Aquarius, sign of the Zodiac, 81
Arabian Nights, 5
Arana, heaven, 140
Aranatha, a Tirthankara, 138
Arara Kalama, a sophist, 118, 119
Ardhanari, a deity, 108, 109
Argha, a vessel, 75
Arhat, holy man, 124, 131, 135
Aries, sign of the Zodiac, 81
Arjuna, Pandava hero, 16, 24, 29, 50-56, 68-72
Arka, a shrub, 83
Arthadarsin, a Buddha, 122
Arun, charioteer of Surya, 80
Arundhati, wife of Vasishta, 47
Arupa Loka, formless world, 124
Aryamat, an Aditya, 80
Aryans, 3, 5, 36, 57, 66, 67, 85, 93
Arya Samaj, a sect, 3, 4, 13
Aryavarta, India, 109
Asari Purnima, a festival, 114
Asia Minor, 2, 4
Asipala, a kind of demon, 140
Asipatravana, a hell, 66
Asoka, emperor, 114, 122, 132
Asoka tree, 92, 134
Assyrian, 57
Asura, enemy of gods, 7, 9, 16, 28, 29, 31, 40, 57-64, 82, 84, 124
Asvapathi, a king, 69-70
Aswamedha, horse sacrifice, 90, 107
Aswatara, a mythical serpent, 91
Aswatha, *Ficus Religiosa*, 83
Aswathaman, an elephant, 56
Aswathaman, son of Drona, 55, 56
Aswin, a Hindu month, 96, 107
Aswins, divine twins, 3, 36, 50
Atharva Veda, 4, 65, 80
Atmabhu, a name of Brahma, 15
Atmalingam, real Lingam, 58, 59
Atri, a sage, 45, 47, 81, 99, 100
Aum, mystic monosyllable, 14, 81
Aurora, 3
Avadhi Jnana, mystic knowledge, 135
Avalokiteswara, Bodhisatva, 123
Avasarpini, Jain mythical age, 135-140
Avatar, incarnation, 16
Avici or Avichimat, a hell, 66, 123
Ayanaghosha, a herdsman, 77

Ayodhya, an ancient kingdom, 19, 20, 22, 41, 48, 85, 97, 103, 104, 107, 136, 138

Babylon, 4, 10, 73
Bacchanalian festival, 4, 74
Bacchus, Greek god, 3, 74
Bahuka, Nala's assumed name, 103, 104
Baka, an Asura, 61, 62
Balabhadras, Jain holy men, 139
Balarama, brother of Krishna, 3, 16, 21-24, 68, 106
Bali, a monkey chief, 21, 57, 85, 88, 89
Bali, an Asura king, 17, 63, 64, 84, 97
Bana, a Asura king, 73
Banai, a demi-goddess, 107
Banyan tree, 94, 127
Behula, a lady, 43, 44
Bel, tree, 98
Bela, flower, 105
Benares, 26, 52, 53, 67, 80, 110, 126, 127
Bengal, 41, 97
Bentinck, Lord William, 68
Berkley, 6
Besar, a town, 131
Bhadrajina, a Tirthankara, 140
Bhadrapad, a Hindu month, 99
Bhaga, an Aditya, 41, 80
Bhagbata, 7, 10, 11, 15, 24, 61, 66
Bhagiratha, a king, 107, 108
Bhagirathi, Ganges, 107
Bhagvadgita, 16, 22, 55
Bhairava, a form of Shiva, 107
Bhairavi, a goddess, 39
Bharadwaja, a sage, 45, 48, 50
Bharata, half brother of Rama, 19-22, 87
Bharata, son of Dushyanta, 104
Bharatam, India, 104
Bharatavarsha, India, 12
Bhatti, a minister, 105
Bhavanapati, a godling, 140
Bhavani, a goddess, 39
Bhavishya Purana, 35
Bhima, a prince, 50, 51, 61, 62, 70, 71, 87
Bhimaka, a king, 24, 101, 102
Bhishma, incarnation of a Vasu, 49-56, 60
Bhogavati, a mythical city, 58, 91
Bhuta, demon, 140
Bhrigu, a sage, 16, 33, 40, 45, 46, 75, 84, 107
Bihar, 131
Bimbisara, king, 118, 120
Birbal, a court wit, 5
Bodhisatva, Buddha elect, 123-130
Bo tree, 115, 118, 134
Brahaspati, preceptor of gods, 18, 81-84, 99
Brahm, the Supreme Being, 8, 13-14
Brahma, the creator god, 3, 6, 7, 8, 9, 11-16, 40, 41, 47, 48, 58, 59, 99, 100
Brahmadatta, a king, 126
Brahmahatya, Brahminicide, 66
Brahmaloka, heaven of Brahma, 100
Brahmana, a branch of Hindu sacred literature, 4, 66
Brahmani, a goddess, 15
Brahmarshi, Brahmin saint, 48, 80
Brahmastra, a magic weapon, 48
Brahmi, a goddess, 42, 136
Brahmin, priestly caste, 4, 9, 10, 18, 26, 47, 48, 53, 96, 114, 131

Brahmo Samaj, a sect, 13
Brahmottara, a heaven, 140
Braj, an ancient country 76
British, 76
Buddha, 1, 16, 24, 113-132
Buddhi, wife of Ganesha, 31
Buddhism, 5, 8, 13, 74, 106, 113-131
Budha, a planet, 82, 83
Budhavara, Wednesday, 83

Calabash fruit, 97
Cambyses, 4
Cancer, sign of Zodiac, 81
Capricorn, sign of Zodiac, 81
Castor & Pollux, 3
Central Asia, 122
Ceylon, 17, 58
Chadanta, an elephant, 127
Chaitra, a Hindu month, 108
Chakra, discus of Vishnu, 9, 16
Chakrapuja, circle worship, 76
Chakravala, world system, 123
Chakravartins, Jain holy men, 139
Chakshusha, a Manu, 45
Champaka Nagar, a legendary town, 42-44
Champapuri, a city, 131
Chamundi, a goddess, 42
Chand Sadagar, a merchant, 42-44
Chandala, outcaste, 66, 114
Chandika, a goddess, 39
Chandra, moon, 3, 58, 64, 81, 82, 99
Chandragupta Maurya, emperor, 132
Chandraloka, region of moon, 99
Chandraprabha, a Tirthankara, 137
Chandravamsa, lunar dynasty, 81
Channa, charioteer of Buddha, 115, 117, 118
Chaos Egg, 3
Charybdis, 37
Chaturdasa Ratnam, fourteen gems, 63, 64
Chedi, a city, 60, 102, 103, 129
Chhandogva Khandogva, Upanishad, 76, 81
Chhaya, handmaid of Sanjana, 80, 84
Chinnamastaka, a goddess, 40
Chitragupta, a Tirthankara, 139
Chitragupta, record keeper of Yama, 35, 66, 67
Chitrakuta, a forest, 31
Chitralekha, a handmaid, 73
Chitraratha, a king, 58
Christian, 2, 4, 6, 13, 64, 65, 68, 74, 113
Chullasubbadha, a cow elephant, 127
Chumpa flower, 72
Chunda, an Asura, 38
Chunda, a smith, 122
Coconut Day, see Rakhi Purnima
Columbus, 1
Copernicus, 1
Corinth, 73
Cow worship, 89
Cupid, 3, 72
Cyclops, 2

Daityas, Asuras, 12, 47, 57
Daksha, a semi-divine being, 26, 27, 31, 36, 45, 46, 81
Dakshina, minor gift, 109
Damayanti, a princess, 101-104

GLOSSARY AND INDEX

Danava, Asura, 9, 48, 57
Dandaka, a forest, 19-22, 33, 48
Dandapani, a chief, 113, 116
Darius, Persian emperor, 4
Darwinism, 6
Dasara, festival, 96-97
Dasaratha, king, 19, 20 84, 85, 86
Dasyus, enemies of Aryans, 5
Datta Jayanti, a festival, 99-100
Dattatreya, a form of Trinity, 99-100
Dawn, personification of, 81
Dayanand, Swami, 13
Deepavali, see Dipavali
Delhi, 49, 55
Deva, a god, 9, 48, 124
Devadaha, an ancient town, 114
Devadasis, temple dancers, 75
Devadatta, a serpent, 91
Devadatta, the arch-enemy of the Buddha, 115, 116-118, 121, 122
Devajina, a Tirthankara, 140
Devaki, mother of Krishna, 22, 23
Devaloka, heaven, 138, 139, 140
Devanagiri script, 41
Devananda, a lady, 134
Devarshi, divine sage, 48
Devasena, wife of Kartikeya, 31, 32,
Devasruta, a Tirthankara, 139
Devayani, daughter of Sukra, 62, 63, 93
Devi, a name of Durga, 38-40, 74, 75, 96, 97
Dhananjaya, a mythical serpent, 91
Dhangar caste, 107
Dhanu, a demon, 140
Dhanu, sign of the Zodiac, 81
Dhanu, a Vasu, 48
Dhanwantari, physician of gods, 64
Dharma, moral law, 9, 10
Dharmadarsin, a Buddha, 122
Dharmanatha, a Tirthankara, 138
Dharmaputra, Yudhishtira, 50
Dharmaraja, Yama, 50, 66, 67, 114
Dhatri, an Aditya, 80
Dhrishtadyumna, son of Drupada, 52-56
Dhritarashtra, a Buddhist deity, 124
Dhritarashtra, a mythical serpent, 91
Dhritarashtra, father of Kauravas, 50-60
Dhruva, pole star, 48, 84
Dhruvaloka, region of the pole star, 84
Dhuma Prabha, a hell, 140
Dhumralochana, an Asura, 38
Dhyanalokas, heavens, 124
Dhyani Buddhas, 123
Digambaras, Jain sect, 131-140
Dilipa, a king, 108
Dipankara, a Buddha, 122, 125
Diti, wife of Kasyapa, 36, 47, 57, 91
Divali or Deepavali, festival, 97, 98, 135
Divine Mothers, 42
Dom, keeper of cremation ground, 110, 111
Draupadi, a princess, 51-56, 70, 71, 87
Dravidian, 5
Drona, a teacher, 48, 50, 60
Drupada, a king, 51-56
Dulare, 74

Durga, an Asura, 38, 39
Durga, goddess, 3, 38-40, 96, 97
Durga Puja, festival, 96-97
Durva grass, 84
Durvasa, a sage, 48, 63
Duryodhana, a prince, 50-56, 57
Dusama, mythical time division, 135-140
Dushyanta, a king, 104, 105
Dussasana, a prince, 50
Dwaipayana Vyasa; See Vyasa
Dwaparayuga, a mythical age, 9, 10
Dwaraka, a city, 23, 24, 60, 61, 68, 72, 89, 95
Dyaus, the sky, 33, 82
Dyumatsena, a king, 69, 70

Eden, 10
Egypt, 2, 4, 10, 37, 73-75
Ekachakra, an ancient town, 53-56, 61, 62
Emusha, a boar, 17
Eros, 3
Esquiline, Mt, 73
Europe, 2, 4, 68

Finnish myths, 3
Fire god, see Agni
Four Kings, Buddhist deities, 124
Freudians, 73
Furies, 37

Gadha, mace, 16
Gana, a group of deities, 30, 48
Ganapatya, a sect, 80
Gandhamadana, a monkey chief, 85
Gandhari, queen, 24, 50
Gandharva, celestial musician, 9, 12, 49, 64, 85, 93, 140
Gandharva marriage, 104, 105
Gandiva, a bow, 68
Ganesha, elephant headed deity, 3, 4, 29, 30, 31, 48, 58, 59, 98, 99
Ganesha Chaturthi, festival, 99
Ganga, Ganges, 4, 5, 11, 12, 16, 31, 49, 68, 98, 105, 107, 108, 128, 136
Garuda, mythical bird, 16, 20, 30, 41, 47, 80, 91, 92
Garuda Purana, 92
Garudastra, a weapon, 91
Gatis, courses of life, 124
Gautama, Buddha, 113-119
Gautama, Indrabhuti, Jain saint, 131
Gautama, Indra's Guru, 33, 45, 46, 48
Gayatri, a Mantra, 48, 80
Gayatri, a name of Sarasvati, 15, 42
Gemini, sign of Zodiac, 81
Genesis, 6
Germans, 3
Gibralter, 1
Girivrija, a city, 20
Girnar, Mount, 139
Gita see Bhagvadgita
Gita Govinda, 77-78
Godavari, river, 20
Gohatya, sin of killing cow, 89
Gokarna, a place, 59
Gokula, a country, 23, 100
Golden Mountain, 127
Gopis, milk maids, 23, 76-78
Gosala, Jain saint, 131

Govardhana, a mountain, 23, 97
Govinda, a name of Vishnu, 41
Graiveyika a mythical space division, 141
Great Bear, constellation of, 45, 47
Greece, 1-5, 13, 37, 55, 72-75
Gujaras, 5
Gujarat, 5, 132

Hades, 10
Hahagiri, Jain monk, 132
Hanuman, monkey god, 4, 9, 21, 85-87
Hara, a name of Shiva, 67
Hari, a name of Vishnu, 16, 40
Harischandra, a king, 109-111
Hariti, a Buddhist deity, 114
Hastinapur, a city, 49-56, 138
Hastipala, king, 131
Hebrew, 4, 11
Hemachandra, Jain scholar, 132
Hercules, 2
Herodotus, 1, 2
Hesiod, 10
Himalayas, 12, 21, 87, 115, 127, 128
Himavan, Himalayas, 11, 37
Hinayana, a Buddhist sect, 122, 123
Hinduism, 4, 5, 8, 64, 65, 106, 113-144, 131
Hindus, 3, 4, 5, 6, 13, 64, 65, 89
Hiranyagarbha, name of Brahma, 15
Hiranyakasipu, an Asura, 17, 58
Hiranyaksha, an Asura, 17, 57, 58
Holi, festival, 4, 98
Homer, 2
Horus, Egyptian deity, 3, 73
Huns, 5

Ikshvaku, a race, 61
Ila, wife of Budha, 83
India, 2, 4, 5, 80, 85, 104
Indo Aryans, 4, 5, 26, 68, 82
Indore, 98
Indra, a god, 3-6, 12, 17, 23, 31-33, 48, 50, 58, 61, 63, 71, 74, 80, 86, 93-95, 101, 105, 109, 121, 134
Indradhumna, a king, 106
Indrajit, son of Ravana, 33, 91
Indrani, a goddess, 33, 42
Indraprastha, a city, 54, 55
Indus, river, 26, 107
Isani, a form of Shiva, 36
Isis, Egyptian goddess, 2, 37
Isivayi, a kind of demon, 140
Islam, 5, 68
Iswara, name of Shiva, 36
Italy, 73

Jack, the Giant Killer, 57
Jagannath, legend of, 106
Jahnu, a sage, 108
Jain, 5, 8, 13, 131-141
Jajati, king, 63
Jalandhar, an Asura, 93, 94
Jamadagni, a sage, 18, 45, 48
Jambavan, bear, 85-89
Jambudwipa, mythical island, 12
Jambu tree, 12
Janaka, a king, 19
Janmashtami, festival, 100

Janus, 3
Jara, a hunter, 24
Jarasandha, an Asura, 61
Jason, 2
Jataka Tales, 125-130
Jatayu, a vulture, 22, 92
Jaya, gate keeper of Vishnu, 58, 61
Jayadeva, a poet, 77-78
Jeans, Sir James, 6
Jehovah, 1, 6
Jejury, a shrine, 107
Jesus, 57
Jina, victorious, 131
Jitasatru, king, 136
Jiva, living forms, 132
Jrimbhakagrama, a village, 131
Judaism, 74, 113
Jumna, river, 5, 77, 78, 105
Juno, 3, 73
Jupiter, 3, 82, 96
Jyotish, group of gods, 141

Kabandha, an Asura, 87, 88
Kacha, son of Brahaspati, 62, 63, 93
Kadru, wife of Kasyapa, 91
Kaikeyi, wife of Dasaratha, 19-22, 86
Kailas, Mount 6, 28, 30, 31, 37, 59, 99, 100, 136
Kal or Kala, Time, 7, 39
Kala, demon, 140
Kalaka, a minister, 128
Kalanemi, an Asura, 87
Kalaratree, goddess, 39
Kalaratriya Mantra, 39
Kalasutra, a hell, 66
Kalavinka, a bird, 92
Kala Yavana, an Asura, 61
Kali, a goddess, 4, 13, 39-40, 105
Kali, evil spirit of Kaliyuga, 102-104
Kalidasa, poet, 104, 105
Kalika Purana, 39
Kalindi, a river, 23, 91
Kaliya, a serpent, 23, 91
Kaliyuga, the age of Kali, 9, 10, 11, 24, 25, 104
Kalki, an incarnation of Vishnu, 10, 16, 25
Kalpa, a Day of Brahma, 9, 10, 45, 122
Kalpa, a mythical space division, 140
Kalpatita, a mythical space division, 141
Kalpa Vriksha, boon granting tree, 135
Kama, love god, 3, 31, 32, 72, 77, 98
Kamadevas, Jain holy men, 139
Kamadhenu, boon granting cow, 18, 31, 63, 90
Kamakshi, a goddess, 39
Kamal, a name of Lakshmi, 8
Kamala, Lakshmi, 40
Kamalasana, Brahma, 15
Kambala, a serpent, 91
Kanakamuni, a Buddha, 122, 123
Kandiye, kind of demons, 140
Kansa, a demon king, 22, 23, 57
Kantaka, Buddha's horse, 115, 117, 118
Kanva, a sage, 104, 105
Kanya, sign of the Zodiac, 81
Kanyakubja, a city, 105
Kapila, a sage, 107, 108
Kapilavasthu, a city, 114, 118, 120, 121

GLOSSARY AND INDEX

Kapinjala, a bird, 92
Kapisht, a heaven, 140
Karma, law of, 9, 40, 131, 132, 133
Karna, a demi-god, 49-56
Karthavirya, a king, 18, 48
Kartik, a Hindu month, 94
Kartikeya, god of war, 3, 31, 32
Kasi, Benares, 80
Kasyapa, a Buddha, 122, 123
Kasyapa, a sage, 18, 33, 36, 45, 46, 47, 57, 80, 91
Kasyapa, tortoise, 16
Katha, story telling, 4, 100
Kaumari, a goddess, 42
Kaundinya, a Buddha, 122
Kauravas, sons of Dhritarashtra, 22, 24, 48, 50-57
Kausalya, a queen, 19-21
Kausambi, a city, 131
Kausitak Brahmana, 65
Kausitaka Upanishad, 65
Kausthubha, a jewel, 64
Kesava, a name of Vishnu, 77
Kesin, an Asura, 23, 31, 77
Kesini, a queen, 107
Ketu, the descending note, 64, 82, 84
Kevala Jnana, omniscience, 131
Kevalin, liberated being, 131
Khandehrao, Khandoba, legend of, 106, 107
Khandogya Upanishad, 2
Khara, an Asura, 20-22, 140
Khillats, presents, 97
Khudiru, a plant, 84
Kimpurusha, a kind of demon, 140
Kinnara, celestial musician, 12, 49, 85
Kirk, sign of the Zodiac, 81
Kishkindha, an ancient kingdom, 88, 89
Kitticum, a flower, 72
Kohanda, demon, 140
Kolis, a people, 120
Konagamana, a Buddha, 122
Krakucchanda, a Buddha, 122, 123
Krimibhojana, a hell, 66
Krishna, incarnation of Vishnu, 4, 13, 16, 22-24, 41, 46, 47, 54, 57, 60, 68, 72, 73, 76-78, 89, 91, 94, 95, 100, 106, 107, 139
Kritayuga, a mythical age, 9
Kritu, a Prajapati, 45, 46
Kronos, 10
Kshatriya, warrior caste, 10, 18, 47, 48, 96, 131-133
Kuan Yin, Chinese Bodhisatva, 123
Kubera, god of wealth, 31, 35, 36, 58, 114, 124
Kulakaras, Jain holy men, 139
Kularnava Tantra, 76
Kulika, a mythical serpent, 91
Kumara, Kartikeya, 31, 32
Kumarapala, a king, 132
Kumbha, demon, 140
Kumbha, sign of the Zodiac, 81
Kumbhakarna, a demon, 21, 58, 59, 60, 87
Kumbhipaka, a hell, 66
Kuntanatha, a Tirthankara, 138
Kunti, a queen, 50-56
Kurma, tortoise, 16, 63
Kurukshetra, an ancient battle field, 55, 70
Kusa grass, 68, 84, 94
Kushans, 122

Kusinagra, an ancient city, 122
Kytabh, an Asura, 9
Lakshman, half brother of Rama, 16, 19-22, 87, 91
Lakshmi, a goddess, 15, 16, 19, 40, 41, 64, 89, 90, 94, 100
Lakshmindra, a merchant prince, 43, 44
Lalita Panchami, festival, 96-97
Lanka, Ceylon, 19-22, 33, 35, 36, 58, 59, 60, 86, 87, 97
Lautaka, a heaven, 140
Leo, sign of Zodiac, 81
Libra, sign of Zodiac, 81
Lingam, phallus, 14, 29, 58, 59, 67, 74-76, 98
Lingayat, a sect, 75
Lubdhaka, a hunter, 98, 99
Lucifer, 57
Lumbini, grove, 114, 120
Lunus, Roman deity, 3

Madar, a mountain, 40
Madha, a king, 127
Madhava, a name of Vishnu, 77
Madonna, 2
Madras, 18, 98
Madri, a queen, 50
Madya, liquor, 75, 76
Magadha, an ancient kingdom, 61, 118, 131
Magh or Magha, a Hindu month, 98, 100
Mahabalipuram, an ancient city, 18
Mahabharata, 4, 9, 11, 15, 28, 49-56, 74, 76, 87, 104
Mahabrahma, a Buddhist deity, 115, 125
Mahadeva, a name of Shiva, 3, 28, 59, 74, 75, 93
Mahaghosha, demon, 140
Mahakala, a deity, 114
Mahakali, a deity, 114
Mahakandiye, brood of demons, 140
Mahamaya, mother of the Buddha, 113, 114, 116
Mahapralaya, great cataclysm, 9
Maharajahs, Buddhist deities, 123, 124
Maharashtra, 32, 97, 107
Maharshi, great sage, 48
Mahasankha, a mythical serpent, 91
Mahashivaratra, festival, 98
Mahasubhadha, a cow elephant, 127
Mahasukra, a heaven, 140
Maha Tama Prabha, a hell, 140
Mahatatwa, the great reality, 7
Mahavira, see Vardhamana
Mahayana sect, 122, 123
Mahayuga, the great age, 9, 10
Mahendra, heaven, 140
Mahendra mountain, 86
Mahesa, Shiva, 40, 74
Maheswari, a goddess, 42
Mahisha, buffalo demon, 38, 96, 97
Mahoraga, brood of demon, 140
Maithuna, coitus, 76
Maitreya, Metteya, Bodhisatva, 122, 123, 124
Makara, mythical fish, 33, 72, 77
Makara, sign of Zodiac, 81
Makaras, five M's, 75-76
Malabar, 18
Malaya, 78
Mall, an Asura, 107
Mallas, a clan, 122
Mallinatha, a Tirthankara, 138

Malyadeva, a Tirthankara, 140
Manaparyaya Jnana, mystic knowledge, 135
Manasa, a goddess, 42-44
Mandara, a mountain, 16, 21, 63
Mandaravati, story of, 105, 108
Mandhata, a king, 61
Mandodari, wife of Ravana, 86
Mangala, a Buddha, 122
Mangala, a planet, 82, 83
Mani, an Asura, 107
Manichees, 4
Manichurna mountain, 107
Mansa, flesh, 76
Manthara, the hunchback, 19
Mantra, incantation, 9, 21
Manu, code of, 7, 8, 11, 45, 48
Manu, world teacher, 11, 16, 45, 68, 83
Manwantara, reign of Manu, 11, 45, 123
Mara, love god, 118, 119
Margashirsha, a Hindu month, 99
Mariammen, a minor goddess, 42
Maricha, a demon, 20
Marichi, a sage, 45
Markandeya, a sage, 11, 67
Markandeya Purana, 40
Marquis de sade, 74
Mars, 3, 82, 96
Maru Devi, queen, 136
Marut, wind god, 6, 36, 86
Mati Jnana, mystic knowledge, 135
Matsya, fish, 16, 76
Matsya Purana, 15, 29
Maya, illusion, 5, 8, 14, 15
Maya, Mayadevi, Buddha's mother; see Mahamaya
Mayasura, architect, 53
Media, 2
Mediterranean, 1, 2, 4, 73
Meena, sign of Zodiac, 81
Mena, wife of Himavan, 37
Menaka, an Apsara, 48, 104, 105
Men of Bronze, 10
Men of Gold, 10
Men of Iron, 10
Men of Silver, 10
Mercury, 82, 96
Meru, a mythical mountain, 12, 21, 123, 124, 140
Mesha, sign of Zodiac, 81
Methu, an Asura, 9
Metteya; see Maitreya
Mhalsabai, a goddess, 107
Minerva, 3
Mira, a saint, 78
Mithila, an ancient kingdom, 19, 138
Mitharaists, 4
Mithun, sign of Zodiac, 81
Mitra, an Aditya, 41, 80
Mitra, Rajendralala, 67
Mleccha, barbarian, 61
Mohini, female form of Vishnu, 64
Mithraists, 4
Muchukunda, a warrior, 61
Mudra, corn, 76
Munda, an Asura, 38
Mundane Egg, 7

Muni, sage, 7
Munisuvrata, a Tirthankara, 138, 139
Murucca tree, 105, 106
Muslim, 5, 64
Muthra, Mathura, a city, 22, 23, 24, 61
Mutinus, phallus, 74
Mylitta, Babylonian goddess, 73
Mysore, 132

Nabhiraja, a king, 136
Nagapanchami, festival, 91
Nagas, serpent race, 5, 42, 43, 44, 91, 92
Nagastra, magic arrow, 91
Nagkeser, a flower, 72
Nakshatra, asterism, 81
Nakula, a prince, 50, 70, 71
Nala, a king, 101-104
Nala, a monkey, 85
Nalagiri, elephant, 121
Naminatha, a Tirthankara, 139
Nanda, a herdsman, 23
Nanda, Ananda, Buddha's disciple, 115
Nandi, Shiva's bull, 3, 29, 38, 90
Nandini, a mythical cow, 90
Nara, waters, 78
Narada, a Buddha, 122
Narada, sage, 24, 45, 46, 47, 59, 61, 69, 72, 84, 85, 94, 95, 99-101, 108, 109
Naradas, Jain holy men, 139
Narakaloka, hell, 65
Narakasura, a demon, 97
Narali Purnima, festival, 96
Narasimha, incarnation of Vishnu, 16, 17
Narasimhi, wife of Narasimha, 42
Narayana, Vishnu, 1, 7, 8, 41, 67, 84
Narayanas, Jain holy men, 139
Nathuram, saint, 98
Navaratra, festival, 96, 97
Neminatha, a Tirthankara, 139
Neptunus, 3
Nikasaya, a Tirthankara, 139
Nila, a monkey chief, 85
Nile, 4, 73
Nirmama, a Tirthankara, 139
Nirrita, a Vedic deity, 36, 69
Nirvana, liberation, 113, 114, 119, 120, 122, 123, 133, 135
Nishadha, a kingdom, 101-104
Nisumbha, an Asura, 35
Nisupalaka, a Tirthankara, 139
Niyoga, levirate, 49
Noah's Ark, 11
North Pole, 46, 47

Olympian, 10
Om, see Aum
Onam, festival, 17
Orissa, 106
Osiris, 3, 73
Oudh, 19

Paccula Minia, Roman lady, 74
Padma, a Buddha, 122
Padma, a goddess, 8
Padma or Padmam, lotus, 8, 16, 40
Padmala, a name of Lakshmi, 60
Padmanabha, a Tirthankara, 139

GLOSSARY AND INDEX

Padmanatha, a name of the Deity, 9
Padmapani, a Bodhisatva, 123
Padmottara, a Buddha, 122
Pahanga, kind of demons, 140
Palasa, shrub, 83
Pali language, 122
Pallas, 37
Palya, a mythical time division, 135, 139
Panapanni, kind of demons, 140
Pancha Anuttara, heaven, 141
Panchabana, name of Kama, 72
Panchala, a princess, 51-56
Panchali, a princess, 51-56
Pancha Parameshtin, Jain holy men, 135
Panchatatwas, five fundamentals, 75, 76
Pandavas, five princes, 22, 24, 29, 48, 50-56, 57, 60, 70, 71
Pandharpur shrine, 107
Pandu, a king, 50, 51
Pankha Prabha, a hell, 140
Pannagas, mythical serpents, 9
Parameshti, a name of Brahma, 15
Parasu, axe, 18
Parasurama, incarnation of Vishnu, 16, 18, 30, 48, 51, 56
Parasvanatha, a Tirthankara, 131, 132, 133, 139
Parasvanatha hill, 131, 136-140
Parijata tree, 63, 94, 95
Parinirvana, decease, 122
Parjanya, an Aditya, 80
Parthians, 5
Parvati, a goddess, 27-29, 37-40, 72, 75, 99, 100, 105, 108, 114
Patala, nether world, 10, 58, 91
Pataliputra, an ancient city, 122
Pava, Patna, 122, 131
Pavan or Pavana, wind god, 36, 86
Pedhala, a Tirthankara, 139
Peepal tree, 94
Persia, 4
Phalgun, a Hindu month, 98
Phallus, 4, 74
Phoenicia, 73
Pillars of Hercules, Gibralter, 2
Pisacha, demon, 140
Pisces, 81
Pitamaha, a name of Brahma, 14, 15
Pitamber, a name of Vishnu, 9
Pitris, manes, 33, 48, 81, 97
Pleiades, 32, 45, 47
Pluto, 35
Pollux, 3
Potila, a Tirthankara, 139
Prabhasa, a place, 24
Prachetas, Daksha, a Prajapati, 45, 46
Pradymna, incarnation of Kama, 72, 73
Prahlad or Prahlada, a devotee of Vishnu, 17, 18, 57
Prajapati, a name of Brahma, 3, 8
Prajapati, foster mother of Buddha, 115, 120
Prajapatis, semi-divine beings, 45-47
Prajna, transcendental wisdom, 123
Prakriti, nature, 7
Pralaya, cataclysm, 11
Pralihasa, a Vasu, 48
Pranata, a heaven, 140
Prasena, a Yadava, 89
Pratinarayanas, Jain holy men, 139
Prativasudevas, Jain holy men, 139
Pratyekabuddhas, individual Buddhas, 124
Pratyush, a Vasu, 48
Prayaga, a city, 131
Premapuri, a city, 107
Preta, ghost, 124
Priapus, 73
Prithu, an incarnation of Vishnu, 82
Prithvi, earth, 33, 82
Priyadarsin, a Buddha, 122
Priyakarini, a queen, 135
Pulaha, a sage, 45, 46, 68
Pulastya, a sage, 45, 46, 58
Pundalik, a Brahmin, 107
Punjab, 93, 98
Puranas, Hindu scriptures, 4, 5, 7, 12-14, 26, 32, 64, 80
Purandara, name of reigning Indra, 33
Puri, a city, 106
Purochana, an accomplice, 52
Purusha, male principle, 6
Purusha Sukta hymn, 6
Purva, mythical time division, 135, 139
Pushan, a god, 36, 41, 48, 65, 80
Pushkar, lake, 15
Pushkara, a prince, 102, 103, 104
Pushpadanta, a Tirthankara, 137
Pushpaka, a celestial car, 35, 36, 58, 88
Pushya, a Buddha, 122
Putana, a fiend, 23, 98

Ra, Egyptian deity, 3
Radha, beloved of Krishna, 76-78
Radha-Krishna cult, 76-78
Rahu, ascending node, 64, 82
Rahula, son of the Buddha, 117, 120
Raivata, a Buddha, 122
Raivata, a Manu, 45
Rajagriha, an ancient city, 118, 120, 138
Rajanya, Kshatriya, 6
Rajarshi, royal sage, 48
Rajas, a quality, 7
Rajasuya sacrifice, 81
Rajeswari, a goddess, 39
Rajput, 76, 78
Rakhi Purnima, festival, 96
Rakshasa, demon, 7, 9, 19, 20-22, 36, 57-64, 140
Raktavira, an Asura, 40
Rama, Ramachandra, 4, 16, 19, 20, 48, 57, 59, 60, 85-89, 96, 100
Ramanavami, festival, 100
Ramayana, 4, 17-22, 33, 85-89, 100
Rambha, an Apsara, 49, 57
Rangapanchami, festival, 98
Rasa Lila, dance, 12, 77, 78
Rati, goddess of love, 31, 72, 73, 98
Ratnapani, a Bodhisatva, 123
Ratnaprabha, a hell, 140
Ratnasambhava, a Buddha, 123
Raurava, a hell, 66
Ravana, demon king of Lanka, 19, 36, 41, 57, 58-60, 85-88
Ravi, sun, 82, 83
Ravivara, Sunday, 83
Renuka, wife of Jamadagni, 48
Rig Veda, 4, 6, 7, 26, 32, 41, 57, 65, 72, 74, 79, 81
Rishabhadeva, a Brahmin, 134

Rishabhadeva, a Tirthankara, 135
Rishi, sage, 4, 9, 11, 28, 31, 45, 48
Rishyamukha, a mountain, 88
Rituparna, a king, 103, 104
Rohidas, a prince, 110-111
Rohini, a river, 120, 121
Rohini, favourite wife of Chandra, 81
Rohini, wife of Vasudeva, 22
Roman, 3, 4, 5, 74
Roxburg, 93
Roy, Raja Ram Mohan, 13
Rudra, a deity, 7, 26, 41, 48, 90
Rudra, kind of demons, 140
Rudraka, a sophist, 118, 119
Rudras, Jain holy men, 139
Rukmini, wife of Krishna, 24, 41, 60, 72, 73, 94
Ruru, a mythical animal, 66

Sabala, demon, 140
Sabian women, 73
Sadhu, ascetic, 135
Sadyumna, a bisexual character, 83
Sagara, a king, 107, 108
Sagara, a mythical time division, 135, 139
Sagaropama, a mythical time division, 135, 139
Sagittarius, 81
Sahadeva, a prince, 50, 70, 71
Sahasrara, heaven, 140
Saka, Sakra, Indra, 118, 124, 125, 128
Sakti, see Shakta
Sakuni, a master gambler, 53, 54
Sakya clan, 113, 114, 120
Salagrama, Shaligrama, stone, 94
Sal tree, 114, 122
Sama, kind of demons, 140
Samantabhadra, a Bodhisatva, 124
Samavarnatha, a Tirthankara, 140
Sama Veda, 4, 81
Samba, son of Krishna, 24
Sambhavanatha, a Tirthankara, 137
Samhita, collection of hymns, 4
Samjamani Yoga, 69
Sampati, a mythical vulture, 86, 92
Samprati, a king, 132
Sanaka, a sage, 7
Sananda, a sage, 7
Sanatanists, orthodox Hindus, 13
Sanatkumara, a sage, 7
Sanatkumara, heaven, 140
Sani, Saturn, 30, 82, 84, 109-111
Sanjana, wife of Surya, 80
Sankara, Shankara, philosopher, 74
Sankha, a mythical serpent, 91
Sankhya system of philosophy, 13, 132
Sanskrit, 3, 41
Santana, a sage, 7
Santinatha, a Tirthankara, 138
Santusita, Bodhisatva, 125
Saptamatrikas, Seven Mothers, 42
Saptarshis, Seven Sages, 45, 47, 48
Sarameya, Surameya, Yama's dog, 67
Sarasvati, a goddess, 3, 15, 41, 42, 59, 69, 93, 99, 100, 107
Sarasvati Pooja, festival, 42
Sarasvati, river, 107
Sariputra, disciple of Buddha, 120

Sarkara Prabha, hell, 140
Sarpini, an age, 135
Sarvanubhuti, a Tirthankara, 139
Satakirti, a Tirthankara, 139
Satapatha Brahmana, 16, 17, 65
Satara, heaven, 140
Satarupa, goddess, 15
Sati, Shiva's spouse, 27, 28, 31, 37, 74
Sati, widow burning, 68, 76
Satrajit, a Yadava, 89
Satrughna, half brother of Rama, 19
Saturn, 82, 84, 96, 109-111
Saturnalia, 98
Satwa, a quality, 7
Satyabhama, wife of Krishna, 89, 94, 95
Satyavan, a prince, 69, 70
Satyavati, a queen, 49, 50
Satyavrata, a Manu, 45
Satyuga, an age, 9
Saudharma, heaven, 140
Saurabhi, a mythical cow, 63
Saurapati, a sect, 80
Saurasa, demoness, 86
Sauvana, grandson of Budha, 120
Savitri, a name of Sarasvati, 15, 27, 48, 69
Savitri, a princess, 69, 70
Savitripathi, a name of Brahma, 15
Scandinavian myths, 3
Scorpio, 81
Scylla, 37
Scythians, 5
Semitic, 3, 6, 10, 13
Shaiva sect, 5, 26, 80
Shakta, Sakta, Shakti, goddess, 5, 37, 75, 80, 123
Shakta, Sakta, sect, 75, 80
Shakuntala, 104, 105
Shambhara, an Asura, 72, 73
Shami tree, 96
Shankh, conch, 16
Shankhachaurna, a mythical serpent, 91
Shantanu, king, 49, 50
Shashti, a goddess, 90
Shashtimatriya, name of Kartikeya, 32
Shastra, science, 57, 87
Shesha, a mythical serpent, 11, 16, 24, 28, 36, 41
Shikhandin, eunuch, 55
Shishupala, a king, 24, 57, 58, 60, 61
Shitala, a goddess, 41
Shiva, a god, 3, 5, 13-15, 26-29, 37, 58, 59, 64, 67, 72, 98-100, 106, 107, 108, 114
Shiva Purana, 31
Shivaratra, Shivaratri, festival, 99
Shoshunu, a weapon, 39
Shraddha, a ceremony, 67, 68
Shravan, a Hindu month, 91, 94, 100
Shravana Belgola, Jain centre, 132
Shravan Mahatmya, 94
Siddha, semi-divine being, 12, 48, 135
Siddhartha, a Buddha, 122
Siddhartha, father of Mahavira, 131
Siddhartha, prince, 113, 114-119, 125
Siddhasila, a mythical space division, 141
Siddhi, wife of Ganesha, 31
Sikhin, a Buddha, 122

GLOSSARY AND INDEX

Similia, 74
Sindhu, Indus, 107
Sinha, sign of Zodiac, 81
Sishana, phallus, 74
Sita, heroine of *Ramayana*, 4, 19-22, 41, 85-89
Sitalanatha, a Tirthankara, 137
Skanda, name of Kartikeya, 32
Skanda Purana, 24, 30
Smartha, a sect, 80
Smriti, branch of sacred literature, 4
Sobhita, a Buddha, 122
Sol, 3
Solomon, king, 137
Soma, a drink, 4, 5, 32, 92, 93
Soma, moon, 81-83
Soma, plant, 93
Somadatta, a Brahmin, 134
Somavansa, lunar dynasty, 49
Somavara, Monday, 83
Somnath, a shrine, 30
Sonuttara, a hunter, 127
South India, 32, 85, 132
Soviet Russia, 2
Sreyamsanatha, a Tirthankara, 137
Sri, Lakshmi, 3, 41
Srivasti, a place, 120
Sruta Jnana, mystic knowledge, 135
Strabo, 73
Stupa, 122
Subhadra, a princess, 52, 106
Subrahmanya, Kartikeya, 32
Suchimukha, a hell, 66
Sudharma, Jain saint, 131
Suddhodana, king, 113, 114, 116, 117, 118, 120
Sudra caste, 6, 10, 96
Sufi, 5, 76
Sugriva, a monkey chief, 21, 57, 85, 87, 88
Sujata, a Buddha, 122
Sujata, a lady, 122
Suka, a sage, 48
Sukra, a heaven, 140
Sukra, preceptor of Asuras, 62, 82-84, 93
Sukramukha, a hell, 66
Sumadhi, a Tirthankara, 139
Sumala, a demon, 36
Sumanas, a Buddha, 122
Sumati, a queen, 107
Sumatinatha, a Tirthankara, 137
Sumbha, an Asura, 38
Sumedha, a Buddha, 122
Sumedha, Bodhisatva, 125
Sumitra, queen, 29
Sundarnand, a prince, 116
Suniti, a queen, 84
Suparsva, a Tirthankara, 139
Suparsvanatha, a Tirthankara, 137
Supreme Being, 5, 13, 57, 64
Sura, liquor, 57, 58, 63
Surabhi; see Saurabhi
Suradeva, a Tirthankara, 139
Surapat, a sect, see Saurapat
Surpanakha, a demoness, 20
Surya, sun god, 3, 35, 36, 50, 58, 64, 79-81
Survyavansa, solar dynasty, 80

Susama, a mythical time division, 135-140
Sushena, a monkey, 89
Suvidhinatha, a Tirthankara, 137
Swadha, a goddess, 90
Swaha, a goddess, 31, 47, 90
Swarochisha, a Manu, 45
Swastika, 81, 137
Swayambhu, name of Brahma, 14
Swayambhuva, a Manu, 45
Swayamprabhu, a Tirthankara, 139
Swayamvara, form of marriage, 27, 101, 102, 103, 104
Sweta, a mythical serpent, 91
Swetambara, Jain sect, 131-140
Syamantaka, a jewel, 89, 99
Syria, 74

Thittareya Brahmana, 17
Takshaka, a mythical serpent, 58
Tama Prabha, a hell, 140
Tamas, a quality, 7
Tamasa, a Manu, 45
Tamisra, a hell, 66
Tanmatras, a principle, 7
Tantras, scriptures, 76
Tantrics, a sect, 75, 76
Taptasurmi, a hell, 66
Tara, a goddess, 114
Tara, a monkey chief, 85
Tara, wife of Brahaspati, 81
Taragam, a forest, 28
Taraka, a demon, 31, 32
Taramati, a queen, 109-111
Taurus, 81
Tavatimsa heaven, 121, 124
Thebes, 10
Thilothama, an Apsara, 49
Threta, an age, 9, 10
Thugs, 39
Tiber, 74
Tirtha, order, 132
Tirthankara, world teacher, 131-141
Tishya, a Buddha, 122
Titans, 2
Tod, Col. 96
Trayatimsa, see Tavatimsa heaven
Treyitenu, sun, 80
Triad, Hindu, 6, 14
Trikadruka, festival, 32
Trinity, Hindu, 13, 80, 81, 99, 100
Trisala, a queen, 133, 134
Trojan war, 55
Troy, 10
Tula, sign of Zodiac, 81
Tulsi plant, 93, 94
Tusita heaven, 123, 124
Twashtr, Twashtri, a god, 36, 41, 80
Typhon, Egyptian god, 3, 73

Ucchaisravas, a mythical horse, 31, 63
Udayaprabhu, a Tirthankara, 139
Udghita, mystic monosyllable, 81
Ugrasena, a king, 22, 24
Ujjain, a city, 105
Ulysses, 2
Uma, a goddess, 28, 30, 31, 37, 58

Upaddhyayas, Jain holy men, 135
Upanishad, 4, 6, 66
Urumbasa grass, 84
Urvasi, an Apsara, 34, 49
Usha, a princess, 73
Ushanas, Sukra, 62, 84
Ushas, dawn, 3, 26, 81
Utsarpini, a mythical time division, 135-140
Uttami, a Manu, 45

Vach, a goddess, 41, 93
Vahan, charger, 16
Vaikhalya, a sage, 94
Vaikunta, heaven of Vishnu, 16, 30, 41
Vairochana, a Buddha, 123
Vaisakh, a Hindu month, 90
Vaisali, an ancient city, 118, 131
Vaishnava, a sect, 5, 14-20, 80
Vaishnavi, a goddess, 42
Vaisravana, a name of Kubera, 35, 124
Vaisya caste, 6, 10, 96
Vaitarani, a hell, 66
Vajra, Indra's weapon, 33
Vajrakantaka, a hell, 66
Vajrapani, a Bodhisatva, 123
Valmiki, author of *Ramayana*, 58, 85
Valu, a kind of demon, 140
Valuka Prabha, a hell, 140
Vamana, dwarf incarnation of Vishnu, 16, 17
Vamana Purana, 72
Vanaras, monkeys, 88
Varaha, boar incarnation of Vishnu, 16, 17
Varaha Purana, 30
Varahi, a goddess, 42
Vardhamana Mahavira, founder of Jainism, 131, 132, 134
Varna, caste, 96
Varuna, sea god, 3, 6, 34, 35, 41, 46, 58, 80, 101, 103
Varuni, a goddess, 63
Vasanta, spring, 31, 72
Vasantapanchami, festival, 100
Vasishta, a sage, 45, 46, 47, 48, 83, 109-111
Vasudeva, a name of Vishnu, 7
Vasudeva, father of Krishna, 22, 23, 60
Vasudevas, Jain holy men, 139
Vasuki, a mythical serpent, 58, 63
Vasupujya, a Tirthankara, 137
Vasus, a group of deities, 41, 48
Vat, banyan tree, 94
Vayu, a god, 36, 50, 58, 93
Vayu Purana, 17
Veda, 4, 7, 9-11, 13, 26, 32, 74, 131
Vedabha, a charm, 129
Vema, a goddess, 74
Vena, a wicked king, 82
Venamala, a name of Vishnu, 9
Venus, 3, 40, 73, 74, 82, 96
Vetala, possessed corpse, 105, 106
Vetarini, a kind of demon, 140
Vibhishana, brother of Ravana, 21, 22
Vichitravirya, a prince, 49, 61
Vidarbha, a city, 60, 101-104

Videha, a kingdom, 131
Vidura, a sage, 52
Vijaya, an attendant on Vishnu, 58, 61
Vijaya, a Tirthankara, 140
Vijaya, wife of Yama, 35
Vijayadevi, a queen, 136
Vikramaditya, a legendary king, 97, 105, 106
Vikram era, 97, 98, 105
Vimalanatha, a Tirthankara, 137
Vimanavasi, gods, 141
Vimba tree, 77
Vina, a musical instrument, 42, 46, 94
Vinata, wife of Kasyapa, 47, 91
Vinayakas, group of deities, 30
Vindhya mountains, 38
Vipasyin, a Buddha, 122
Viraj, mythical progenitor of mankind, 8, 45
Virgo, 81
Viruddhaka, a Buddhist deity, 124
Virupaksha, a godling, 124
Vishnu, a god, 3, 5, 10, 13-25, 42, 57, 61, 63, 64, 67, 69, 80, 85, 93, 94, 99, 100, 107
Vishnu Purana, 4, 16, 17, 25, 48, 76, 80
Visvabhu, a Buddha, 122
Visvapani, a Bodhisatva, 123
Viswadevas, a group of deities, 41
Viswakarma, a god, 3, 35, 36, 80, 85, 92, 106
Viswamitra, a sage, 19, 45, 46-48, 80, 104, 109-111
Viswarupa, son of Viswakarma, 92
Vithal, Vithoba, a god, 107
Vivaswat, an Aditya, 80
Vrikodara, a name of Bhima, 62
Vrinda, wife of Jalandhar, 94
Vrindavan, a sacred site, 22, 76-78
Vrischika, sign of Zodiac, 81
Vrishabha, sign of Zodiac, 81
Vulcan, 3, 36
Vyantara, a kind of demon, 140
Vyasa, a sage, 31, 46, 48, 50, 140

Western India, 131
Western Ocean, 126

Yadavas, a race, 24, 61
Yajur Veda, 4, 14
Yakshas, semi-mythical beings, 7, 9, 57, 85, 140
Yama, god of death, 16, 35, 42, 50, 58, 65, 66, 67, 69, 80, 101
Yamapuri, abode of Yama, 35, 67
Yami, a goddess, 42, 65
Yamuna, river Jumna, 4, 23, 77, 78, 101
Yasapani, a king, 127
Yasoda, foster mother of Krishna, 23
Yasodhara, a Tirthankara, 140
Yasodhara, wife of the Buddha, 113-117, 120, 121, 125
Yoganidra, a goddess, 23
Yoni, symbol of Sakti, 40, 74
Yonijas, worshippers of Yoni, 75
Yudhishtira, a king, 29, 50-57, 60, 70, 71
Yuga, an age, 9

Zeus, 10
Zodiac, signs of, 81